George Catlin

Illustrations of the Manners, Customs and Condition of the North

American Indians

Vol. II

George Catlin

Illustrations of the Manners, Customs and Condition of the North American Indians
Vol. II

ISBN/EAN: 9783337177546

Printed in Europe, USA, Canada, Australia, Japan

Cover: Foto ©ninafisch / pixelio.de

More available books at **www.hansebooks.com**

ILLUSTRATIONS

OF THE

MANNERS, CUSTOMS, AND CONDITION

OF THE

NORTH AMERICAN INDIANS

WITH

LETTERS AND NOTES

WRITTEN DURING EIGHT YEARS OF TRAVEL AND ADVENTURE AMONG THE
WILDEST AND MOST REMARKABLE TRIBES NOW EXISTING.

WITH THREE HUNDRED AND SIXTY ENGRAVINGS,

FROM THE

Author's Original Paintings.

BY GEO. CATLIN.

IN TWO VOLUMES.

VOL. II.

TENTH EDITION.

LONDON:
HENRY G. BOHN, YORK STREET, COVENT GARDEN.
1866.

CONTENTS

· OF

THE SECOND VOLUME.

A 4

APPENDIX A.

APPENDIX B.

APPENDIX C.

LETTERS AND NOTES

NORTH AMERICAN INDIANS.

LETTER—No. 32.

FORT LEAVENWORTH, *LOWER MISSOURI.*

THE readers, I presume, will have felt some anxiety for me and the fate my little craft, after the close of my last Letter ; and I have the very great satisfaction of announcing to them that we escaped *snags* and *sawyers*, and every other danger, and arrived here safe from the Upper Missouri, where my last letters were dated. We, (that is, Ba'tiste, Bogard and I,) are comfortably quartered for awhile, in the barracks of this hospitable Cantonment, which is now the extreme Western military post on the frontier, and under the command of Colonel Davenport, a gentleman of great urbanity of manners, with a Roman head and a Grecian heart, restrained and tempered by the charms of an American lady, who has elegantly pioneered the graces of civilized refinements into these uncivilized regions.

This Cantonment, which is beautifully situated on the west bank of the Missouri River, and six hundred miles above its mouth, was constructed some years since by General Leavenworth, from whom it has taken its name. Its location is very beautiful, and so is the country around it. It is the concentration point of a number of hostile tribes in the vicinity, and has its influence in restraining their warlike propensities.

There is generally a regiment of men stationed here, for the purpose of holding the Indians in check, and of preserving the peace amongst the hostile tribes. I shall visit several tribes in this vicinity, and most assuredly give you some further account of them, as fast as I get it.

Since the date of my last epistles, I succeeded in descending the river to this place, in my little canoe, with my two men at the oars, and myself at the helm, steering its course the whole way amongst snags and sand-bars.

Before I give further account of this downward voyage, however, I must recur back for a few moments, to the Teton River, from whence I started, and from whence my last epistles were written, to record a few more incidents which I then overlooked in my note-book. Whilst painting my portraits amongst the Sioux, as I have described, I got the portrait of a noble Shienne chief, by the name of Nee-hee-o-ee-woo-tis, the wolf on the hill (PLATE 115). The chief of a party of that tribe, on a friendly visit to the Sioux, and the portrait also of a woman, Tis-see-woo-na-tis (she who bathes her knees, PLATE 116). The Shiennes are a small tribe of about 3000 in numbers, living neighbours to the Sioux, on the west of them, and between the Black Hills and the Rocky Mountains. There is no finer race of men than these in North America, and none superior in stature, excepting the Osages; scarcely a man in the tribe, full grown, who is less than six feet in height. The Shiennes are undoubtedly the richest in horses of any tribe on the Continent, living in a country as they do, where the greatest herds of wild horses are grazing on the prairies, which they catch in great numbers and vend to the Sioux, Mandans and other tribes, as well as to the Fur Traders.

These people are the most desperate set of horsemen, and warriors also, having carried on almost unceasing wars with the Pawnees and Blackfeet, "time out of mind." The chief represented in the picture was clothed in a handsome dress of deer skins, very neatly garnished with broad bands of porcupine quill-work down the sleeves of his shirt and his leggings, and all the way fringed with scalp-locks. His hair was very profuse, and flowing over his shoulders; and in his hand he held a beautiful Sioux pipe, which had just been presented to him by Mr. M'Kenzie, the Trader. This was one of the finest looking and most dignified men that I have met in the Indian country; and from the account given of him by the Traders a man of honour and strictest integrity. The woman was comely, and beautifully dressed; her dress of the mountain-sheep skins, tastefully ornamented with quills and beads, and her hair plaited in large braids, that hung down on her breast.

After I had painted these and many more, whom I have not time at present to name, I painted the portrait of a celebrated warrior of the Sioux, by the name of Mah-to-chee-ga (the little bear), who was unfortunately slain in a few moments after the picture was done, by one of his own tribe; and which was very near costing me my life for having painted a side view of his face, leaving one-half of it out of the picture, which had been the cause of the affray; and supposed by the whole tribe to have been intentionally left out by me, as "good for nothing." This was the last picture that I painted amongst the Sioux, and the last, undoubtedly, that I ever shall paint in that place. So tremendous and so alarming was the excitement about it, that my brushes were instantly put away, and I embarked the next day on the steamer for the sources of the Missouri, and was glad to get underweigh.

The man who slew this noble warrior was a troublesome fellow of the same tribe, by the name of Shon-ka (the dog). A "hue and cry" has been on his track for several months; and my life having been repeatedly

116

115

threatened during my absence up the river, I shall defer telling the whole of this most extraordinary affair, until I see that my own scalp is safe, and I am successfully out of the country. A few weeks or months will decide how many are to fall victims to the vengeance of the relatives of this murdered brave; and if I outlive the affair, I shall certainly give some further account of it.*

My voyage from the mouth of the Teton River to this place has been the most rugged, yet the most delightful, of my whole Tour. Our canoe was generally landed at night on the point of some projecting barren sand-bar, where we straightened our limbs on our buffalo robes, secure from the annoyance of mosquitos, and out of the walks of Indians and grizzly bears. In addition to the opportunity which this descending Tour has afforded me, of visiting all the tribes of Indians on the river, and leisurely filling my portfolio with the beautiful scenery which its shores present—the sportsman's fever was roused and satisfied; the swan, ducks, geese, and pelicans—the deer, antelope, elk, and buffaloes, were "*stretched*" by our rifles; and some times—" pull boys! pull!!! a war party! for your lives pull! or we are gone!"

I often landed my skiff, and mounted the green carpeted bluffs, whose soft grassy tops, invited me to recline, where I was at once lost in contemplation. Soul melting scenery that was about me! A place where the mind could think volumes; but the tongue must be silent that would *speak*, and the hand palsied that would *write*. A place where a Divine would confess that he never had fancied Paradise—where the painter's palette would lose its beautiful tints—the blood-stirring notes of eloquence would die in their utterance—and even the soft tones of sweet music would scarcely preserve a spark to light the soul again that had passed this sweet delirium. I mean the prairie, whose enamelled plains that lie beneath me, in distance soften into sweetness, like an essence; whose thousand thousand velvet-covered hills, (surely never formed by chance, but grouped in one of Nature's sportive moods)—tossing and leaping down with steep or graceful declivities to the river's edge, as if to grace its pictured shores, and make it " a thing to look upon." I mean the prairie at *sun-set*; when the green hill-tops are turned into gold—and their long shadows of melancholy are thrown over the valleys—when all the breathings of day are hushed, and nought but the soft notes of the retiring dove can be heard; or the still softer and more plaintive notes of the wolf, who sneaks through these scenes of enchantment, and mournfully how—l——s, as if lonesome, and lost in the too beautiful quiet and stillness about him. I mean *this* prairie; where Heaven sheds its purest light, and lends its richest tints—*this round-topp'd bluff,*

---

* Some months after writing the above, and after I had arrived safe in St. Louis, the news reached there that the Dog had been overtaken and killed, and a brother of his also, and the affair thus settled. The portraits are in Vol. II. (PLATES 273, 274, and 275), and the story there told.

where the foot treads soft and light—whose steep sides, and lofty head, rear me to the skies, overlooking yonder pictured vale of beauty—this solitary *cedar-post*, which tells a tale of grief—grief that was keenly felt, and tenderly, but long since softened in the march of time and lost. Oh, sad and tear-starting contemplation ! sole tenant of this stately mound, how solitary thy habitation ! here Heaven wrested from thee thy ambition, and made thee sleeping monarch of this land of silence.

Stranger ! oh, how the mystic web of sympathy links my soul to thee and thy afflictions ! I knew thee not, but it was enough ; thy tale was told, and I a solitary wanderer through thy land, have stopped to drop familiar tears upon thy grave. Pardon this gush from a stranger's eyes, for they are all that thou canst have in this strange land, where friends and dear relations are not allowed to pluck a flower, and drop a tear to freshen recollections of endearments past.

Stranger ! adieu. With streaming eyes I leave thee again, and thy fairy land, to peaceful solitude. My pencil has faithfully traced thy beautiful habitation ; and long shall live in the world, and familiar, the name of " *Floyd's Grave.*"

Readers, pardon this digression. I have seated myself down, not on a prairie, but at my table, by a warm and cheering fire, with my journal before me to cull from it a few pages, for your entertainment ; and if there are spots of loveliness and beauty, over which I have passed, and whose images are occasionally beckoning me into digressions, you must forgive me.

Such is the spot I have just named, and some others, on to which I am instantly transferred when I cast my eyes back upon the enamelled and beautiful shores of the Upper Missouri ; and I am constrained to step aside and give ear to their breathings, when their soft images, and cherished associations, so earnestly prompt me. " Floyd's Grave" is a name given to one of the most lovely and imposing mounds or bluffs on the Missouri River, about twelve hundred miles above St. Louis, from the melancholy fate of Serjeant Floyd, who was of Lewis and Clark's expedition, in 1806 ; who died on the way, and whose body was taken to this beautiful hill, and buried in its top, where now stands a cedar post, bearing the initials of his name (PLATE 118).

I landed my canoe in front of this grass-covered mound, and all hands being fatigued, we encamped a couple of days at its base. I several times ascended it and sat upon his grave, overgrown with grass and the most delicate wild flowers, where I sat and contemplated the solitude and stillness of this tenanted mound ; and beheld from its top, the windings infinite of the Missouri, and its thousand hills and domes of green, vanishing into blue in distance, when nought but the soft-breathing winds were heard, to break the stillness and quietude of the scene. Where not the chirping of bird or sound of cricket, nor soaring eagle's scream, were inter-nosed 'tween God and man ; nor aught to check man's whole surrender of

117

118

G. Catlin

his soul to his Creator. I could not *hunt* upon this ground, but I roamed from hill-top to hill-top, and culled wild flowers, and looked into the valley below me, both up the river and down, and contemplated the thousand hills and dales that are now carpeted with green, streaked as they *will* be, with the plough, and yellow with the harvest sheaf; spotted with lowing kine— with houses and fences, and groups of hamlets and villas—and these lovely hill-tops ringing with the giddy din and maze, or secret earnest whispers of lovesick swains—of pristine simplicity and virtue—wholesome and well-earned contentment and abundance—and again, of wealth and refinements —of idleness and luxury—of vice and its deformities—of fire and sword, and the vengeance of offended Heaven, wreaked in retributive destruction !— and peace, and quiet, and loveliness, and silence, dwelling *again*, over and through these scenes, and blending them into futurity !

Many such scenes there are, and thousands, on the Missouri shores. My canoe has been stopped, and I have clambered up their grassy and flower-decked sides ; and sighed all alone, as I have carefully traced and fastened them in colours on my canvass.

This voyage in my little canoe, amid the thousand islands and grass-covered bluffs that stud the shores of this mighty river, afforded me infinite pleasure, mingled with pains and privations which I never shall wish to forget. Gliding along from day to day, and tiring our eyes on the varying landscapes that were continually opening to our view, my merry *voyageurs* were continually chaunting their cheerful boat songs, and " every now and then," taking up their unerring rifles to bring down the stately elks or antelopes, which were often gazing at us from the shores of the river.

But a few miles from " Floyd's Bluff" we landed our canoe, and spent a day in the vicinity of the *" Black Bird's Grave."* This is a celebrated point on the Missouri, and a sort of telegraphic place, which all the travellers in these realms, both white and red, are in the habit of visiting : the one to pay respect to the bones of one of their distinguished leaders ; and the others, to indulge their eyes on the lovely landscape that spreads out to an almost illimitable extent in every direction about it. This elevated bluff, which may be distinguished for several leagues in distance (PLATE 117), has received

e name of the " Black Bird's Grave," from the fact, that a famous chief of the O-ma-haws, by the name of the Black Bird, was buried on its top, at his own peculiar request ; over whose grave a cedar post was erected by his tribe some thirty years ago, which is still standing. The O-ma-haw village was about sixty miles above this place ; and this very noted chief, who had been on a visit to Washington City, in company with the Indian agent, died of the small-pox, near this spot, on his return home. And, whilst dying, enjoined on his warriors who were about him, this singular request, which was literally complied with. He requested them to take his body down the river to this his favourite haunt, and on the pinnacle of this towering bluff, to bury him on the back of his favourite war-horse, which was to be buried alive, under him, from whence he could see, as he said, " the Frenchmen passing up and down the river in their boats." He owned, amongst many horses, a noble white steed that was led to the top of the grass-covered hill ; and, with great pomp and ceremony, in presence of the whole nation, and several of the Fur Traders and the Indian agent, he was placed astride of his horse's back, with his bow in his hand, and his shield and quiver slung— with his pipe and his *medicine-bag*—with his supply of dried meat, and his tobacco-pouch replenished to last him through his journey to the " beautiful hunting grounds of the shades of his fathers"—with his flint and steel, and his tinder, to light his pipes by the way. The scalps that he had taken from his enemies' heads, could be trophies for nobody else, and were hung to the bridle of his horse—he was in full dress and fully equipped ; and on his head waved, to the last moment, his beautiful head-dress of the war-eagle's plumes. In this plight, and the last funeral honours having been performed by the *medicine-men*, every warrior of his band painted the palm and fingers of his right hand with vermilion ; which was stamped, and perfectly impressed on the milk-white sides of his devoted horse.

This all done, turfs were brought and placed around the feet and legs of the horse, and gradually laid up to its sides ; and at last, over the back and head of the unsuspecting animal, and last of all, over the head and even the eagle plumes of its valiant rider, where altogether have smouldered and remained undisturbed to the present day.

This mound which is covered with a green turf, and spotted with wild flowers, with its cedar post in its centre, can easily be seen at the distance of fifteen miles, by the *voyageur*, and forms for him a familiar and useful land-mark.

Whilst visiting this mound in company with Major Sanford, on our way up the river, I discovered in a hole made in the mound, by a " ground hog" or other animal, the skull of the horse ; and by a little pains, also came at the skull of the chief, which I carried to the river side, and secreted till my return in my canoe, when I took it in, and brought with me to this place, where I now have it, with others which I have collected on my route.

There have been some very surprising tales told of this man, which will render him famous in history, whether they be truth or matters of fiction. Of the many, one of the most current is, that he gained his celebrity and authority by the most diabolical series of murders in his own tribe ; by administering arsenic (with which he had been supplied by the Fur Traders) to such of his enemies as he wished to get rid of—and even to others in his tribe whom he was willing to sacrifice, merely to establish his superhuman powers, and the most servile dread of the tribe, from the certainty with which his victims fell around him, precisely at the times he saw fit to predict their death ! It has been said that he administered this potent drug, and to them unknown *medicine*, to many of his friends as well as to foes ; and by such an inhuman and unparalleled depravity, succeeded in exercising the most despotic and absolute authority in his tribe, until the time of his death !

This story may be true, and it may not. I cannot contradict it ; and I am sure the world will forgive me, if I say, I cannot believe it. If it be true, two things are also true ; the one, not much to the credit of the Indian character ; and the other, to the everlasting infamy of the Fur Traders. If it be true, it furnishes an instance of Indian depravity that I never have elsewhere heard of in my travels ; and carries the most conclusive proof of the incredible enormity of white men's dealings in this country ; who, for some sinister purpose must have introduced the poisonous drug into the country, and taught the poor chief how to use it ; whilst they were silent accessories to the murders he was committing. This story is said to have been told by the Fur Traders ; and although I have not always the highest confidence in their justice to the Indian, yet, I cannot for the honour of my own species, believe them to be so depraved and so wicked, nor so weak, as to reveal such iniquities of this chief, if they were true, which must directly implicate themselves as accessories to his most wilful and unprovoked murders.

Such he has been heralded, however, to future ages, as a murderer—like hundreds and thousands of others, as " horse thieves"—as " drunkards"— as " rogues of the first order," &c. &c.—by the historian who catches but a glaring story, (and perhaps fabrication) of their lives, and has no time nor disposition to enquire into and record their long and brilliant list of virtues, which must be lost in the shade of infamy, for want of an historian.

I have learned much of this noble chieftain, and at a proper time shall recount the modes of his civil and military life—how he exposed his life, and shed his blood in rescuing the victims to horrid torture, and abolished that savage custom in his tribe—how he led on and headed his brave warriors, against the Sacs and Foxes ; and saved the butchery of his women and children—how he received the Indian agent, and entertained him in his hospitable wigwam, in his village—and how he conducted and acquitted himself on his embassy to the civilized world.

So much I will take pains to say, of a man whom I never saw, because other historians have taken equal pains just to mention his name, and a solitary (and doubtful) act of his life, as they have said of hundreds of others, for the purpose of consigning him to infamy.

How much more kind would it have been for the historian, who never saw him, to have enumerated with this, other characteristic actions of his life (for the verdict of the world) ; or to have allowed, in charity, his bones and his name to have slept in silence, instead of calling them up from the grave, to thrust a dagger through them, and throw them back again.

Book-making now-a-days, is done for money-making ; and he who takes the Indian for his theme, and cannot go and see him, finds a poverty in his matter that naturally begets error, by grasping at every little tale that is brought or fabricated by their enemies. Such books are standards, because they are made for white man's reading only ; and herald the character of a people who never can disprove them. They answer the purpose for which they are written; and the poor Indian who has no redress, stands stigmatized and branded, as a murderous wretch and beast.

If the system of book-making and newspaper printing were in operation in the Indian country awhile, to herald the iniquities and horrible barbarities of white men in these Western regions, which now are sure to be overlooked; I venture to say, that chapters would soon be printed, which would sicken the reader to his heart, and set up the Indian, a fair and tolerable man.

There is no more beautiful prairie country in the world, than that which is to be seen in this vicinity. In looking back from this bluff, towards the West, there is, to an almost boundless extent, one of the most beautiful scenes imaginable. The surface of the country is gracefully and slightly undulating, like the swells of the retiring ocean after a heavy storm. And everywhere covered with a beautiful green turf, and with occasional patches and clusters of trees. The soil in this region is also rich, and capable of making one of the most beautiful and productive countries in the world.

Ba'tiste and Bogard used their rifles to some effect during the day that we loitered here, and gathered great quantities of delicious grapes. From this lovely spot we embarked the next morning, and glided through constantly changing scenes of beauty, until we landed our canoe at the base of a beautiful series of grass-covered bluffs, which, like thousands and thousands of others on the banks of this river, are designated by no name, that I know of; and I therefore introduce them as fair specimens of the *grassy bluffs* of the Missouri.

My canoe was landed at noon, at the base of these picturesque hills—and there rested till the next morning. As soon as we were ashore, I scrambled to their summits, and beheld, even to a line, what the reader has before him in PLATES 119 and 120. I took my easel, and canvass and brushes, to the top of the bluff, and painted the two views from the same spot; the one looking up, and the other down the river. The reader, by imagining these hills to be five or six hundred feet high, and every foot of them, as far as they can be discovered in distance, covered with a vivid green turf, whilst the sun is gilding one side, and throwing a cool shadow on the other, will be enabled to form something like an adequate idea of the shores of the Missouri. From this enchanting spot there was nothing to arrest the eye from ranging over its waters for the distance of twenty or thirty miles, where it quietly glides between its barriers, formed of thousands of green and gracefully sloping hills, with its rich and alluvial meadows, and woodlands—and its hundred islands, covered with stately cotton-wood.

In these two views, the reader has a fair account of the general character of the Upper Missouri; and by turning back to PLATE 39, VOL. I., which I have already described, he will at once see the process by which this wonderful formation has been produced. In that plate will be seen the manner in which the rains are wearing down the clay-bluffs, cutting gullies or sluices behind them, and leaving them at last to stand out in relief, in

119

120

G. Catlin

these rounded and graceful forms, until in time they get seeded over, and nourish a growth of green grass on their sides, which forms a turf, and protects their surface, preserving them for centuries, in the forms that are here seen. The tops of the highest of these bluffs rise nearly up to the summit level of the prairies, which is found as soon as one travels a mile or so from the river, amongst these picturesque groups, and comes out at their top; from whence the country goes off to the East and the West, with an almost perfectly level surface.

These two views were taken about thirty miles above the village of the Puncahs, and five miles above "the Tower;" the name given by the travellers through the country, to a high and remarkable clay bluff, rising to the height of some hundreds of feet from the water, and having in distance, the castellated appearance of a fortification.

My canoe was not unmoored from the shores of this lovely spot for two days, except for the purpose of crossing the river; which I several times did, to ascend and examine the hills on the opposite side. I had Ba'tiste and Bogard with me on the tops of these green carpeted bluffs, and tried in vain to make them see the beauty of scenes that were about us. They dropped asleep, and I strolled and contemplated alone; clambering *"up one hill"* and sliding or running *"down another,"* with no other living being in sight, save now and then a bristling wolf, which, from my approach, was reluctantly retreating from his shady lair—or sneaking behind me and smelling on my track.

Whilst strolling about on the western bank of the river at this place, I found the ancient site of an Indian village, which from the character of the marks, I am sure was once the residence of the Mandans. I said in a former Letter, when speaking of the Mandans, that within the recollection of some of their oldest men, they lived some sixty or eighty miles down the river from the place of their present residence; and that they then lived in nine villages. On my way down, I became fully convinced of the fact; having landed my canoe, and examined the ground where the foundation of every wigwam can yet be distinctly seen. At that time, they must have been much more numerous than at present, from the many marks they have left, as well as from their own representations.

The Mandans have a peculiar way of building their wigwams, by digging down a couple of feet in the earth, and there fixing the ends of the poles which form the walls of their houses. There are other marks, such as their caches—and also their mode of depositing their dead on scaffolds—and of preserving the skulls in circles on the prairies; which peculiar customs I have before described, and most of which are distinctly to be recognized in each of these places, as well as in several similar remains which I have met with on the banks of the river, between here and the Mandans; which fully convince me, that they have formerly occupied the lower parts of the Missouri, and have gradually made their way quite through the heart of the great Sioux country; and having been well fortified in all their locations, as in

c

their present one, by a regular stockade and ditch; they have been able successfully to resist the continual assaults of the Sioux, that numerous tribe, who have been, and still are, endeavouring to effect their entire destruction. I have examined, at least fifteen or twenty of their ancient locations on the banks of this river, and can easily discover the regular differences in the ages of these antiquities; and around them all I have found numerous bits of their broken pottery, corresponding with that which they are now manufacturing in great abundance; and which is certainly made by no other tribe in these regions. These evidences, and others which I shall not take the time to mention in this place, go a great way in my mind towards strengthening the possibility of their having moved from the Ohio river, and of their being a remnant of the followers of Madoc. I have much further to trace them yet, however, and shall certainly have more to say on so interesting a subject in future.

Almost every mile I have advanced on the banks of this river, I have met evidences and marks of Indians in some form or other; and they have generally been those of the Sioux, who occupy and own the greater part of this immense region of country. In the latter part of my voyage, however, and of which I have been speaking in the former part of this Letter, I met the ancient sites of the O-ma-ha and Ot-to towns, which are easily detected when they are met. In PLATE 121 (letter A), is seen the usual mode of the Omahas, of depositing their dead in the crotches and on the branches of trees, enveloped in skins, and never without a wooden dish hanging by the head of the corpse; probably for the purpose of enabling it to dip up water to quench its thirst on the long and tedious journey, which they generally expect to enter on after death. These corpses are so frequent along the banks of the river, that in some places a dozen or more of them may be seen at one view.

Letter B in the same plate, shews the customs of the Sioux, which are found in endless numbers on the river; and in fact, through every part of this country. The wigwams of these people are only moveable tents, and leave but a temporary mark to be discovered. Their burials, however, are peculiar and lasting remains, which can be long detected. They often deposit their dead on trees, and on scaffolds; but more generally bury in the tops of bluffs, or near their villages; when they often split out staves and drive in the ground around the grave, to protect it from the trespass of dogs or wild animals.

Letter C (same plate), shews the character of Mandan remains, that are met with in numerous places on the river. Their mode of resting their dead upon scaffolds is not so peculiar to them as positively to distinguish them from Sioux, who sometimes bury in the same way; but the excavations for their earth-covered wigwams, which I have said are two feet deep in the ground, with the ends of the decayed timbers remaining in them, are peculiar and conclusive evidence of their being of Mandan construction;

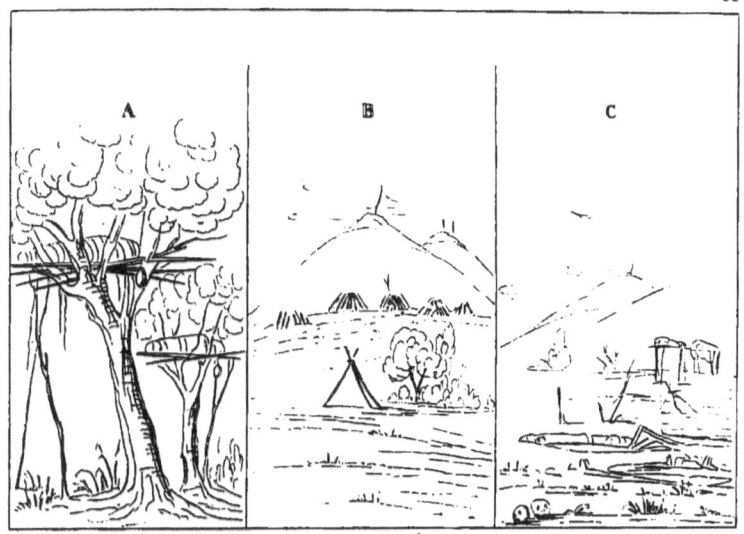

A   B   C

121

G. Catlin.

122

and the custom of leaving the skulls bleached upon the ground in circles (as I have formerly described in PLATE 48, VOL. I.), instead of burying them as the other tribes do, forms also a strong evidence of the fact that they are Mandan remains.

In most of these sites of their ancient towns, however, I have been unable to find about their burial places, these characteristic deposits of the skulls; from which I conclude, that whenever they deliberately moved to a different region, they buried the skulls out of respect to the dead. I found, just back of one of these sites of their ancient towns, however, and at least 500 miles below where they now live, the same arrangement of skulls as that I described in PLATE 48. They had laid so long, however, exposed to the weather, that they were reduced almost to a powder, except the teeth, which mostly seemed polished and sound as ever. It seems that no human hands had dared to meddle with the dead; and that even their enemies had respected them; for every one, and there were at least two hundred in one circle, had mouldered to chalk, in its exact relative position, as they had been placed in a circle. In this case, I am of opinion that the village was besieged by the Sioux, and entirely destroyed; or that the Mandans were driven off without the power to stop and bury the bones of their dead.

Belle Vue (PLATE 122) is a lovely scene on the West bank of the river, about nine miles above the mouth of the Platte, and is the agency of Major Dougherty, one of the oldest and most effective agents on our frontiers. This spot is, as I said, lovely in itself; but doubly so to the eye of the weather-beaten *voyageur* from the sources of the Missouri, who steers his canoe in, to the shore, as I did, and soon finds himself a welcome guest at the comfortable board of the Major, with a *table* again to eat from—and that (not " *groaning*," but) *standing* under the comfortable weight of meat and vegetable luxuries, products of the labour of cultivating man. It was a pleasure to see again, in this great wilderness, a civilized habitation; and still more pleasant to find it surrounded with corn-fields, and potatoes, with numerous fruit-trees, bending under the weight of their fruit—with pigs and poultry, and kine; and what was best of all, to see the kind and benevolent face, that never looked anything but welcome to the half-starved guests, who throw themselves upon him from the North, from the South, the East, or the West.

At this place I was in the country of the Pawnees, a numerous tribe, whose villages are on the Platte river, and of whom I shall say more anon. Major Dougherty has been for many years the agent for this hostile tribe; and by his familiar knowledge of the Indian character, and his strict honesty and integrity, he has been able to effect a friendly intercourse with them, and also to attract the applause and highest confidence of the world, as well as of the authorities who sent him there.

An hundred miles above this, I passed a curious feature, called the "Square Hills" (PLATE 123). I landed my canoe, and went ashore, and to their tops, to examine them. Though they appeared to be near the river, I found it half a day's journey to travel to and from them; they being several miles from the river. On ascending them I found them to be two or three hundred feet high, and rising on their sides at an angle of 45 degrees; and on their tops, in some places, for half a mile in length, perfectly level, with a green turf, and corresponding exactly with the tabular hills spoken of above the Mandans, in PLATE 39, VOL. I. I therein said, that I should visit these hills on my way down the river; and I am fully convinced, from close examination, that they are a part of the same original superstratum, which I therein described, though seven or eight hundred miles separated from them. They agree exactly in character, and also in the materials of which they are composed; and I believe, that some unaccountable gorge of waters has swept away the intervening earth, leaving these solitary and isolated, though incontrovertible evidences, that the summit level of all this great valley has at one time been where the level surface of these hills now is, two or three hundred feet above what is now generally denominated the summit level.

The mouth of the Platte (PLATE 124), is a beautiful scene, and no doubt will be the site of a large and flourishing town, soon after Indian titles shall have been extinguished to the lands in these regions, which will be done within a very few years. The Platte is a long and powerful stream, pouring in from the Rocky Mountains and joining with the Missouri at this place.

In this voyage, as in all others that I have performed, I kept my journal, but I have not room, it will be seen, to insert more than an occasional extract from it for my present purpose. In this voyage, Ba'tiste and Bogard were my constant companions; and we all had our rifles, and used them often. We often went ashore amongst the herds of buffaloes, and were obliged to do so for our daily food. We lived the whole way on buffaloes' flesh and venison—we had no bread; but laid in a good stock of coffee and sugar. These, however, from an unforeseen accident availed us but little; as on the second or third day of our voyage, after we had taken our coffee on the shore, and Ba'tiste and Bogard had gone in pursuit of a herd of buffaloes, I took it in my head to have an extra very fine dish of coffee to myself, as the fire was fine. For this purpose, I added more coffee-grounds to the pot, and placed it on the fire, which I sat watching, when I saw a fine buffalo cow wending her way leisurely over the hills, but a little distance from me, for whom I started at once, with my rifle trailed in my hand; and after creeping, and running, and heading, and all that, for half an hour, without getting a shot at her; I came back to the encampment, where I found my two men with meat enough, but in the most uncontroulable rage, for my coffee had all boiled out, and the coffee-pot was melted to pieces!

This was truly a deplorable accident, and one that could in no effectual way be remedied. We afterwards botched up a mess or two of it in our frying-pan, but to little purpose, and then abandoned it to Bogard alone, who thank-

123

124

fully received the dry coffee-grounds and sugar, at his meals, which he soon entirely demolished.

We met immense numbers of buffaloes in the early part of our voyage and used to land our canoe almost every hour in the day; and oftentimes all together approach the unsuspecting herds, through some deep and hidden ravine within a few rods of them, and at the word, "pull trigger," each of us bring down our victim (PLATE 125).

In one instance, near the mouth of White River, we met the most immense herd crossing the Missouri River—and from an imprudence got our boat into imminent danger amongst them, from which we were highly delighted to make our escape. It was in the midst of the "running season," and we had heard the "roaring" (as it is called) of the herd, when we were several miles from them. When we came in sight, we were actually terrified at the immense numbers that were streaming down the green hills on one side of the river, and galloping up and over the bluffs on the other. The river was filled, and in parts blackened, with their heads and horns, as they were swimming about, following up their objects, and making desperate battle whilst they were swimming.

I deemed it imprudent for our canoe to be dodging amongst them, and ran it ashore for a few hours, where we laid, waiting for the opportunity of seeing the river clear; but we waited in vain. Their numbers, however, got somewhat diminished at last, and we pushed off, and successfully made our way amongst them. From the immense numbers that had passed the river at that place, they had torn down the prairie bank of fifteen feet in height, so as to form a sort of road or landing-place, where they all in succession clambered up. Many in their turmoil had been wafted below this landing, and unable to regain it against the swiftness of the current, had fastened themselves along in crowds, hugging close to the high bank under which they were standing. As we were drifting by these, and supposing ourselves out of danger, I drew up my rifle and shot one of them in the head, which tumbled into the water, and brought with him a hundred others, which plunged in, and in a moment were swimming about our canoe, and placing it in great danger (PLATE 126). No attack was made upon us, and in the confusion the poor beasts knew not, perhaps, the enemy that was amongst them; but we were liable to be sunk by them, as they were furiously hooking and climbing on to each other. I rose in my canoe, and by my gestures and hallooing, kept them from coming in contact with us, until we were out of their reach.

This was one of the instances that I formerly spoke of, where thousands and tens of thousands of these animals congregate in the *running season*, and move about from East and West, or wherever accident or circumstances may lead them. In this grand crusade, no one can know the numbers that may have made the ford within a few days; nor in their blinded fury in such scenes, would feeble man be much respected.

During the remainder of that day we paddled onward, and passed many of their carcasess floating on the current, or lodged on the heads of islands and sand-bars. And, in the vicinity of, and not far below the grand turmoil, we passed several that were mired in the quicksand near the shores; some were standing fast and half immersed; whilst others were nearly out of sight, and gasping for the last breath; others were standing with all legs fast, and one half of their bodies above the water, and their heads sunk under it, where they had evidently remained several days; and flocks of ravens and crows were covering their backs, and picking the flesh from their dead bodies.

So much of the Upper Missouri and its modes, at present; though I have much more in store for some future occasion.

Fort Leavenworth, which is on the Lower Missouri, being below the mouth of the Platte, is the nucleus of another neighbourhood of Indians, amongst whom I am to commence my labours, and of whom I shall soon be enabled to give some account. So, for the present, Adieu.

125

G Callin

126

LETTER—No. 33.

FORT LEAVENWORTH, *LOWER MISSOURI*.

I MENTIONED in a former epistle, that this is the extreme outpost on the Western Frontier, and built, like several others, in the heart of the Indian country. There is no finer tract of lands in North America, or, perhaps, in the world, than that vast space of prairie country, which lies in the vicinity of this post, embracing it on all sides. This garrison, like many others on the frontiers, is avowedly placed here for the purpose of protecting our frontier inhabitants from the incursions of Indians; and also for the purpose of preserving the peace amongst the different hostile tribes, who seem continually to wage, and glory in, their deadly wars. How far these feeble garrisons, which are generally but half manned, have been, or will be, able to intimidate and controul the warlike ardour of these restless and revengeful spirits; or how far they will be able in desperate necessity, to protect the lives and property of the honest pioneer, is yet to be tested.

They have doubtless been designed with the best views, to effect the most humane objects, though I very much doubt the benefits that are anticipated to flow from them, unless a more efficient number of men are stationed in them than I have generally found; enough to promise protection to the Indian, and then to *ensure* it; instead of promising, and leaving them to seek it in their own way at last, and when they are least prepared to do it.

When I speak of this post as being on the *Lower Missouri*, I do not wish to convey the idea that I am down near the sea-coast, at the mouth of the river, or near it; I only mean that I am on the lower part of the Missouri, yet 600 miles above its junction with the Mississippi, and near 2000 from the Gulf of Mexico, into which the Mississippi discharges its waters.

In this delightful Cantonment there are generally stationed six or seven companies of infantry, and ten or fifteen officers; several of whom have their wives and daughters with them, forming a very pleasant little community, who are almost continually together in social enjoyment of the peculiar amusements and pleasures of this wild country. Of these pastimes they have many, such as riding on horseback or in carriages over the beautiful green fields of the prairies, picking strawberries and wild plums— deer chasing—grouse shooting—horse-racing, and other amusements of the garrison, in which they are almost constantly engaged; enjoying life to a very nigh degree.

In these delightful amusements, and with these pleasing companions, I have been for a while participating with great satisfaction ; I have joine.l several times in the deer-hunts, and more frequently in grouse shooting, which constitutes the principal amusement of this place

This delicious bird, which is found in great abundance in nearly all the North American prairies, and most generally called the Prairie Hen, is, from what I can learn, very much like the English grouse, or heath hen, both in size, in colour, and in habits. They make their appearance in these parts in the months of August and September, from the higher latitudes, where they go in the early part of the summer, to raise their broods. This is the season for the best sport amongst them ; and the whole garrison, in fact are almost subsisted on them at this time, owing to the facility with which they are killed.

I was lucky enough the other day, with one of the officers of the garrison, to gain the enviable distinction of having brought in together seventy-five of these fine birds, which we killed in one afternoon ; and although I am quite ashamed to confess the manner in which we killed the greater pa t of them, I am not so professed a sportsman as to induce me to conceal the fact. We had a fine pointer, and had legitimately followed the sportsman's style for a part of the afternoon ; but seeing the prairies on fire several miles ahead of us, and the wind driving the fire gradually towards us, we found these poor birds driven before its long line, which seemed to extend from horizon to horizon, and they were flying in swarms or flocks that would at times almost fill the air. They generally flew half a mile or so, and lit down again in the grass, where they would sit until the fire was close upon them, and then they would rise again. We observed by watching their motions, that they lit in great numbers in every solitary tree ; and we placed ourselves near each of these trees in turn, and shot them down as they settled in them; sometimes killing five or six at a shot, by getting a range upon them.

In this way we retreated for miles before the flames, in the midst of the flocks, and keeping company with them where they were carried along in advance of the fire, in accumulating numbers ; many of which had been driven along for many miles. We murdered the poor birds in this way, until we had as many as we could well carry, and laid our course back to the Fort, where we got much credit for our great shooting, and where we were mutually pledged to keep the secret.

The prairies burning form some of the most beautiful scenes that are to be witnessed in this country, and also some of the most sublime. Every acre of these vast prairies (being covered for hundreds and hundreds of miles, with a crop of grass, which dies and dries in the fall) burns over during the fall or early in the spring, leaving the ground of a black and doleful colour.

There are many modes by which the fire is communicated to. them, both by white men and by Indians—*par accident*; and yet many more where it is voluntarily done for the purpose of getting a fresh crop of grass, for the grazing of their horses, and also for easier travelling during the next summer, when there will be no old grass to lie upon the prairies, entangling the feet of man and horse, as they are passing over them.

Over the elevated lands and prairie bluffs, where the grass is thin and short, the fire slowly creeps with a feeble flame, which one can easily step over (PLATE 127); where the wild animals often rest in their lairs until the flames almost burn their noses, when they will reluctantly rise, and leap over it, and trot off amongst the cinders, where the fire has past and left the ground as black as jet. These scenes at night become indescribably beautiful, when their flames are seen at many miles distance, creeping over the sides and tops of the bluffs, appearing to be sparkling and brilliant chains of liquid fire (the hills being lost to the view), hanging suspended in graceful festoons from the skies.

But there is yet another character of burning prairies (PLATE 128), that requires another Letter, and a different pen to describe—the war, or hell of fires! where the grass is seven or eight feet high, as is often the case for many miles together, on the Missouri bottoms; and the flames are driven forward by the hurricanes, which often sweep over the vast prairies of this denuded country. There are many of these meadows on the Missouri, the Platte, and the Arkansas, of many miles in breadth, which are perfectly level, with a waving grass, so high, that we are obliged to stand erect in our stirrups, in order to look over its waving tops, as we are riding through it. The fire in these, before such a wind, travels at an immense and frightful rate, and often destroys, on their fleetest horses, parties of Indians, who are so unlucky as to be overtaken by it; not that it travels as fast as a horse at full speed, but that the high grass is filled with wild pea-vines and other impediments, which render it necessary for the rider to guide his horse in the zig-zag paths of the deers and buffaloes, retarding his progress, until he is overtaken by the dense column of smoke that is swept before the fire—alarming the horse, which stops and stands terrified and immutable, till the burning grass which is wafted in the wind, falls about him, kindling up in a moment a thousand new fires, which are instantly wrapped in the swelling flood of smoke that is moving on like a black thunder-cloud, rolling on the earth, with its lightning's glare, and its thunder rumbling as it goes.

* * * * *

When Ba'tiste, and Bogard, and I, and Patrick Raymond (who like Bogard had been a free trapper in the Rocky Mountains), and Pah-me-o-ne-qua (the red thunder), our guide back from a neighbouring village, were jogging along on the summit of an elevated bluff, overlooking an immense valley of high grass, through which we were about to lay our course.—— * *

* * * * * * *

' Well, then, you say you have seen the prairies on fire?" Yes. " You have seen the fire on the mountains, and beheld it feebly creeping over th grassy hills of the North, where the toad and the timid snail were pacing from its approach—all this you have seen, and who has not? But who has seen the vivid lightnings, and heard the roaring thunder of the rolling conflagration which sweeps over the *deep-clad* prairies of the West? Who has dashed, on his wild horse, through an ocean of grass, with the raging tempest at his back, rolling over the land its swelling waves of liquid fire?" What! " Aye, even so. Ask the red savage of the wilds what is awful and sublime—Ask him where the Great Spirit has mixed up all the elements o death, and if he does not blow them over the land in a storm of fire? Ask him what foe he has met, that regarded not his frightening yells, or his sinewy bow? Ask these lords of the land, who vauntingly challenge the thunder and lightning of Heaven—whether there is not one foe that travels over their land, too swift for their feet, and too mighty for their strength—at whose approach their stout hearts sicken, and their strong-armed courage withers to nothing? Ask him *again* (if he is sullen, and his eyes set in their sockets) —' Hush !———sh !———sh !'—(he will tell you, with a soul too proud to confess—his head sunk on his breast, and his hand over his mouth)— ' that's *medicine!'*   *   *   *   *   *

　　*   *   *   *   *   *   *

I said to my comrades, as we were about to descend from the towering bluffs into the prairie—" We will take that buffalo trail, where the travelling herds have slashed down the high grass, and making for that blue point, rising, as you can just discern, above this ocean of grass; a good day's work will bring us over this vast meadow before sunset." We entered the trail, and slowly progressed on our way, being obliged to follow the winding paths of the buffaloes, for the grass was higher than the backs of our horses. Soon after we entered, my Indian guide dismounted slowly from his horse, and lying prostrate on the ground, with his face in the dirt, he *cried*, and was talking to the Spirits of the brave—" For," said he, " over this beautiful plain dwells the Spirit of fire! he rides in yonder cloud—his face blackens with rage at the sound of the trampling hoofs—the *fire-bow* is in his hand— he draws it across the path of the Indian, and quicker than lightning, a thousand flames rise to destroy him; such is the talk of my fathers, and the ground is whitened with their bones. It was here," said he, " that the brave son of Wah-chee-ton, and the strong-armed warriors of his band, just twelve moons since, licked the fire from the blazing wand of that great magician. Their pointed spears were drawn upon the backs of the treacherous Sioux, whose swifter-flying horses led them, in vain, to the midst of this valley of death. A circular cloud sprang up from the prairie around them! it was raised, and their doom was fixed by the Spirit of fire! It was on this vast plain of *fire-grass* that waves over our heads, that the swift foot of Mah-to-ga was laid. It is here, also, that the fleet-bounding wild horse mingles his bones with the red man; and the eagle's wing is melted

128

127

G. Catlin.

as he darts over its surface. Friends! it is the season of fire; and I fear, from the smell of the wind, that the Spirit is awake!"

Pah-:ne-o-ne-qua said no more, but mounted his wild horse, and waving his hand, his red shoulders were seen rapidly vanishing as he glided through the thick mazes of waving grass. We were on his trail, and busily traced him until the midday-sun had brought us to the ground, with our refreshments spread before us. He partook of them not, but stood like a statue, while his black eyes, in sullen silence, swept the horizon round; and then, with a deep-drawn sigh, he gracefully sunk to the earth, and laid with his face to the ground. Our buffalo *tongues* and pemican, and marrow-fat, were spread before us; and we were in the full enjoyment of these dainties of the Western world, when, quicker than the frightened elk, our Indian friend sprang upon his feet! His eyes skimmed again slowly over the prairies' surface, and he laid himself as before on the ground.

"Red Thunder seems sullen to-day," said Bogard—"he startles at every rush of the wind, and scowls at the whole world that is about him."

"There's a rare chap for you—a fellow who would shake his fist at Heaven, when he is at home; and here, in a *grass-patch*, must make his *fire-medicine* for a *circumstance* that he could easily leave at a shake of his horse's heels."

"Not sae sure o' that, my hooney, though we'll not be making too lightly of the matter, nor either be frightened at the mon's strange octions. But, Bogard, I'll tell ye in a 'ord (and thot's enough), there's something more than odds in all this 'medicine.' If this mon's a fool, he was born out of his own country, that's all—and if the divil iver gits him, he must take him cowld, for he is too swift and too wide-awake to be taken alive—you understond thot, I suppose? But, to come to the plain matter—supposin that the Fire Spirit (and I go for somewhat of witchcraft), I say supposin that this *Fire Spirit* should jist impty his pipe on tother side of this prairie, and strike up a bit of a blaze in this high grass, and send it packing across in this direction, before sich a death of a wind as this is! By the *bull barley*, I'll bet you'd be after 'making medicine,' and *taking* a bit of it, too, to get rid of the racket."

"Yes, but you see, Patrick——"

"Neever mind thot (not wishin to distarb you); and suppose the blowin wind was coming fast ahead, jist blowin about our ears a warld of smoke and chokin us to dith, and we were dancin about a *Varginny reel* among these little paths, where the divil would we be by the time we got to that bluff, for it's now fool of a distance? Givin you time to spake, I would say a word more (askin your pardon), I know by the expression of your face, mon, you neever have seen the world on fire yet, and therefore you know nothin at all of a *hurly burly* of this kind—did ye?—did ye iver see (and I jist want to know), did ye iver see the fire in high-grass, runnin with a strong wind, about five mile and the half, and thin hear it strike into a *slash* of *dry* cane brake! ! I would jist ax you that? By thuneder you niver have—for your eyes would jist stick out of your head at the thought of it! Did ye iver look way into the backside of Mr. Maelzel's Moscow, and see the flashin flames a runnin up; and then hear the poppin of the *militia fire* jist afterwards? then you have jist a touch of it! ye're jist beginnin—ye may talk about fires—but this is sich a *baste of a fire!* Ask *Juck Sanford*, he's a chop that can tall you all aboot it. Not wishin to distarb you, I would say a word more—and that is this—If I were advisin, I would say that we are gettin too far into this imbustible meadow; for the grass is dry, and the wind is too strong to make a light matter of, at this sason of the year; an now I'll jist tell ye how M'Kenzie and I were sarved in this very place about two years ago; and he's a worldly chop, and niver aslape, my word for that——hollo, what's that!"

Red Thunder was on his feet!—his long arm was stretched over the grass, and his blazing eye-balls starting from their sockets! "White man (said he), see ye that small cloud lifting itself from the prairie? he rises! the hoofs of our horses have waked him! The *Fire Spirit* is awake—this wind is from his nostrils, and his face is this way!" No more—but his swift horse darted under him, and he gracefully slid over the waving grass as it was bent by the wind. Our viands were left, and we were swift on his trail. The extraordinary leaps of his wild horse, occasionally raised his red shoulders to view, and he sank again in the waving billows of grass. The tremulous wind was hurrying by us fast, and on it was borne the agitated wing of the soaring eagle. His neck was stretched for the towering bluff, and the thrilling screams of his voice told the secret that was behind him. Our horses were swift, and we struggled hard, yet hope was feeble, for the bluff was yet *blue*, and nature nearly exhausted! The sunshine was *dying*, and a cool shadow advancing over the plain. Not daring to look back, we strained every nerve. The roar of a distant cataract seemed gradually advancing on us—the winds increased, the howling tempest was maddening behind us—and the swift-winged *beetle* and *heath hens*, instinctively drew their straight lines over our heads. The fleet-bounding antelope passed us also; and the *still swifter* long-legged hare, who leaves but a shadow as he flies! Here was no time for thought—but I recollect the heavens were overcast—the distant thunder was heard—the lightning's glare was reddening the scene—and the smell that came on the winds struck terror to my soul! *   *   *   *   The piercing yell of my savage guide at this moment came back upon the winds—his robe was seen waving in the air, and his foaming horse leaping up the towering bluff.

Our breath and our sinews, in this last struggle for life, were just enough to bring us to its summit. We had risen from a *sea of fire!* "Great God! (I exclaimed) how sublime to gaze into that valley, where the elements of nature are so strangely convulsed!" Ask not the poet or painter how it looked, for they can tell you not ; but ask the *naked savage*, and watch the electric twinge of his manly nerves and muscles, as he pronounces the lengthened "hush——sh———" his hand on his mouth, and his glaring eye-balls looking you to the very soul !

I beheld beneath me an immense cloud of black smoke, which extended from one extremity of this vast plain to the other, and seemed majestically to roll over its surface in a bed of liquid fire ; and above this mighty desolation, as it rolled along, the whitened smoke, pale with terror, was streaming and rising up in magnificent cliffs to heaven !

I stood *secure*, but tremblingly, and heard the maddening wind, which hurled this *monster* o'er the land—I heard the roaring thunder, and saw its thousand lightnings flash ; and then I saw *behind*, the black and smoking desolation of this *storm* of *fire !*

LETTER No. 34.

FORT LEAVENWORTH, *LOWER MISSOURI.*

SINCE writing the last epistle, some considerable time has elapsed, which has, nevertheless, been filled up and used to advantage, as I have been moving about and using my brush amongst different tribes in this vicinity. The Indians that may be said to belong to this vicinity, and who constantly visit this post, are the Ioways—Konzas—Pawnees—Omahas—Ottoes, and Missouries (primitive), and Delawares—Kickapoos—Potawatomies—Weahs—Peorias—Shawanos, Kaskaskias (semi-civilized remnants of tribes that have been removed to this neighbourhood by the Government, within the few years past). These latter-named tribes are, to a considerable degree, agriculturalists; getting their living principally by ploughing, and raising corn, and cattle and horses. They have been left on the frontier, surrounded by civilized neighbours, where they have at length been induced to sell out their lands, or exchange them for a much larger tract of wild lands in these regions, which the Government has purchased from the wilder tribes.

Of the first named, the Ioways may be said to be the farthest departed from primitive modes, as they are depending chiefly on their corn-fields for subsistence; though their appearance, both in their dwellings and personal looks, dress, modes, &c., is that of the primitive Indian.

The Ioways are a small tribe, of about fourteen hundred persons, living in a snug little village within a few miles of the eastern bank of the Missouri River, a few miles above this place.

The present chief of this tribe is Notch-ee-ning-a (the white cloud, PLATE 129), the son of a very distinguished chief of the same name, who died recently, after gaining the love of his tribe, and the respect of all the civilized world who knew him. If my time and space will admit it, and I should not forget it, I shall take another occasion to detail some of the famous transactions of his signal life.

The son of White Cloud, who is now chief, and whose portrait I have just named, was tastefully dressed with a buffalo robe, wrapped around him, with a necklace of grizzly bear's claws on his neck; with shield, bow, and quiver on, and a profusion of wampum strings on his neck.

Wy-ee-yogh (the man of sense, PLATE 130), is another of this tribe, much istinguished for his bravery and early warlike achievements. His head was dressed with a broad silver band passing around it, and decked out with the crest of horsehair.

129   130

131   132

G.Catlin.

Pah-ta-coo-che (the shooting cedar, PLATE 131), and Was-com-mun (the busy man, PLATE 132), are also distinguished warriors of the tribe; tastefully dressed and equipped, the one with his war-club on his arm, the other with bow and arrows in his hand; both wore around their waists beautiful buffalo robes, and both had turbans made of vari-coloured cotton shawls, purchased of the Fur Traders. Around their necks were necklaces of the bears' claws, and a profusion of beads and wampum. Their ears were profusely strung with beads; and their naked shoulders curiously streaked and daubed with red paint.

Others of this tribe will be found amongst the paintings in my Indian Museum; and more of them and their customs given at a future time.

The Konzas, of 1560 souls, reside at the distance of sixty or eighty miles from this place, on the Konzas River, fifty miles above its union with the Missouri, from the West.

This tribe has undoubtedly sprung from the Osages, as their personal appearance, language and traditions clearly prove. They are living adjoining to the Osages at this time, and although a kindred people, have sometimes deadly warfare with them. The present chief of this tribe is known by the name of the "White Plume;" a very urbane and hospitable man, of good portly size, speaking some English, and making himself good company for all white persons who travel through his country and have the good luck to shake his liberal and hospitable hand.

It has been to me a source of much regret, that I did not get the portrait of this celebrated chief; but I have painted several others distinguished in the tribe, which are fair specimens of these people. Sho-me-cos-se (the wolf, PLATE 133), a chief of some distinction, with a bold and manly outline of head; exhibiting, like most of this tribe, an European outline of features, signally worthy the notice of the enquiring world. The head of this chief was most curiously ornamented, and his neck bore a profusion of wampum strings.

Meach-o-shin-gaw (the little white bear, PLATE 134). Chesh-oo-hong-ha (the man of good sense, PLATE 135), and Wa-hon-ga-shee (no fool, PLATE 136), are portraits of distinguished Konzas, and all furnish striking instances of the bold and Roman outline that I have just spoken of.

The custom of shaving the head, and ornamenting it with the crest of deer's hair, belongs to this tribe; and also to the Osages, the Pawnees, the Sacs, and Foxes, and Ioways, and to no other tribe that I know of; unless it be in some few instances, where individuals have introduced it into their tribes, merely by way of imitation.

With these tribes, the custom is one uniformly adhered to by every man in the nation; excepting some few instances along the frontier, where efforts are made to imitate white men, by allowing the hair to grow out.

In PLATE 135, is a fair exhibition of this very curious custom—the hair being cut as close to the head as possible, except a tuft the size of the palm of the hand, on the crown of the head, which is left of two inches in length : and in the centre of which is fastened a beautiful crest made of the hair of the deer's tail (dyed red) and horsehair, and oftentimes surmounted with the war-eagle's quill. In the centre of the patch of hair, which I said was left of a couple of inches in length, is preserved a small lock, which is never cut, but cultivated to the greatest length possible, and uniformly kept in braid, and passed through a piece of curiously carved bone ; which lies in the centre of the crest, and spreads it out to its uniform shape, which they study with great care to preserve. Through this little braid, and outside of the bone, passes a small wooden or bone key, which holds the crest to the head. This little braid is called in these tribes, the " *scalp-lock*," and is scrupulously preserved in this way, and offered to their enemy if they can get it, as a trophy ; which it seems in all tribes they are anxious to yield to their conquerors, in case they are killed in battle ; and which it would be considered cowardly and disgraceful for a warrior to shave off, leaving nothing for his enemy to grasp for, when he falls into his hands in the events of battle.

Amongst those tribes who thus shave and ornament their heads, the crest is uniformly blood-red ; and the upper part of the head, and generally a considerable part of the face, as red as they can possibly make it with vermilion. I found these people cutting off the hair with small scissors, which they purchase of the Fur Traders ; and they told me that previous to getting scissors, they cut it away with their knives ; and before they got knives, they were in the habit of burning it off with red hot stones, which was a very slow and painful operation.

With the exception of these few, all the other tribes in North America cultivate the hair to the greatest length they possibly can ; preserving it to flow over their shoulders and backs in great profusion, and quite unwilling to spare the smallest lock of it for any consideration.

The Pawnees are a very powerful and warlike nation, living on the river Platte, about one hundred miles from its junction with the Missouri ; laying claim to, and exercising sway over, the whole country, from its mouth to the base of the Rocky Mountains.

The present number of this tribe is ten or twelve thousand ; about one half the number they had in 1832, when that most appalling disease, the small-pox, was accidentally introduced amongst them by the Fur Traders, and whiskey sellers ; when ten thousand (or more) of them perished in the course of a few months.

The Omahas, of fifteen hundred ; the Ottoes of six hundred ; and Missouries of four hundred, who are now living under the protection and surveillance of the Pawnees, and in the immediate vicinity of them, were all powerful tribes, but so reduced by this frightful disease, and at the same time, that they were unable longer to stand against so formidable enemies as they had around them, in the Sioux, Pawnees, Sacs, and Foxes, and at last

133 134

135 136

G. Catlin

last merged into the Pawnee tribe, under whose wing and protection they now live.

The period of this awful calamity in these regions, was one that will be long felt, and long preserved in the traditions of these people. The great tribe of the Sioux, of whom I have heretofore spoken, suffered severely with the same disease; as well as the Osages and Konzas; and particularly the unfortunate Puncahs, who were almost extinguished by it.

The destructive ravages of this most fatal disease amongst these poor people, who know of no specific for it, is beyond the knowledge, and almost beyond the belief, of the civilized world. Terror and dismay are carried with it; and awful despair, in the midst of which they plunge into the river, when in the highest state of fever, and die in a moment; or dash themselves from precipices; or plunge their knives to their hearts, to rid themselves from the pangs of slow and disgusting death.

Amongst the formidable tribe of Pawnees, the Fur Traders are yet doing some business; but, from what I can learn, the Indians are dealing with some considerable distrust, with a people who introduced so fatal a calamity amongst them, to which one half of their tribe have fallen victims. The Traders made their richest harvest amongst these people, before this disease broke out; and since it subsided, quite a number of their lives have paid the forfeit, according to the Indian laws of retribution.*

The Pawnees have ever been looked upon, as a very warlike and hostile tribe; and unusually so, since the calamity which I have mentioned.

Major Dougherty, of whom I have heretofore spoken, has been for several

* Since the above was written, I have had the very great pleasure of reading the notes of the Honourable Charles A. Murray, (who was for several months a guest amongst the Pawnees), and also of being several times a fellow-traveller with him in America; and at last a debtor to him for his signal kindness and friendship in London. Mr. Murray's account of the Pawnees, as far as he saw them, is without doubt drawn with great fidelity, and he makes them out a pretty bad set of fellows. As I have before mentioned, there is probably not another tribe on the Continent, that has been more abused and incensed by the system of trade, and money-making, than the Pawnees; and the Honourable Mr. Murray, with his companion, made his way boldly into the heart of their country. without guide or interpreter, and I consider at great hazard to his life: and, from all the circumstances, I have been ready to congratulate him on getting out of their country as well as he did.

I mentioned in a former page, the awful destruction of this tribe by the small-pox; a few years previous to which, some one of the Fur Traders visited a threat upon these people, that if they did not comply with some condition, " he would let the small-pox out of a bottle and destroy the whole of them." The pestilence has since been introduced accidentally amongst them by the Traders; and the standing tradition of the tribe now is, that " the Traders opened a bottle and let it out to destroy them." Under such circumstances, from amongst a people who have been impoverished by the system of trade, without any body to protect him, I cannot but congratulate my Honourable friend for his peaceable retreat, where others before him have been less fortunate; and regret at the same time, that he could not have been my companion to some others of the remote tribes.

years their agent; and by his unremitted endeavours, with an unequalled familiarity with the Indian character, and unyielding integrity of purpose, has successfully restored and established, a system of good feeling and respect between them and the "pale faces," upon whom they looked, naturally and experimentally, as their destructive enemies.

Of this stern and uncompromising friend of the red man, and of justice, who has taken them close to his heart, and familiarized himself with their faults and their griefs, I take great pleasure in recording here for the perusal of the world, the following extract from one of his true and independent Reports, to the Secretary at War; which sheds honour on his name, and deserves a more public place than the mere official archives of a Government record.

" In comparing this Report with those of the years preceding, you will find there has been little improvement on the part of the Indians, either in literary acquirements or in agricultural knowledge.

" It is my decided opinion, that, so long as the Fur Traders and trappers are permitted to reside among the Indians, all the efforts of the Government to better their condition will be fruitless ; or, in a great measure checked by the strong influence of those men over the various tribes.

" Every exertion of the agents, (and other persons, intended to carry into effect the views of the Government, and humane societies,) are in such direct opposition to the Trader and his interest, that the agent finds himself continually contending with, and placed in direct and immediate contrariety of interest to the Fur Traders or grossly neglecting his duty by overlooking acts of impropriety ; and it is a curious and melancholy fact, that while the General Government is using every means and expense to promote the advancement of those aboriginal people, it is at the same time suffering the Traders to oppose and defeat the very objects of its intentions. So long as the Traders and trappers are permitted in the Indian country, the introduction of spirituous liquors will be inevitable, under any penalty the law may require ; and until its prohibition is certain and effectual, every effort of Government, through the most faithful and indefatigable agents, will be useless. It would be, in my humble opinion, better to give up every thing to the Traders, and let them have the sole and entire control of the Indians, than permit them to contend at every point, with the views of the Government ; and that contention made manifest, even to the most ignorant Indian.

" While the agent is advising the Indians to give up the chase and settle themselves, with a view to agricultural pursuits, the Traders are urging them on in search of skins.

" Far be it from me to be influenced or guided by improper or personal feeling, in the execution of my duty ; but, Sir, I submit my opinion to a candid world, in relation to the subject, and feel fully convinced you will be able to see at once the course which will ever place the Indian Trader, and the present policy of Government, in relation to the Indians, at eternal war.

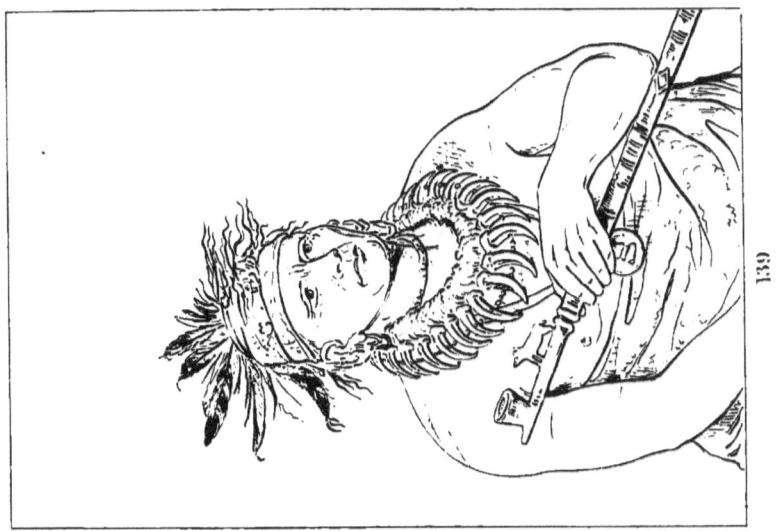

139

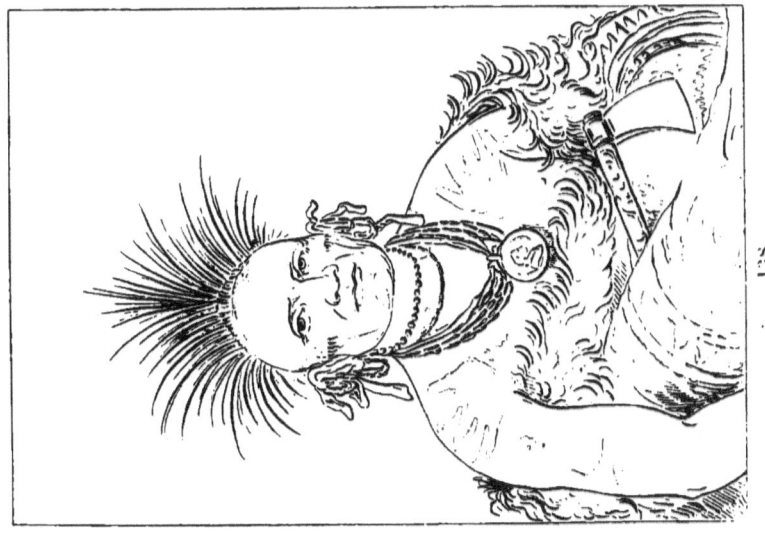

138

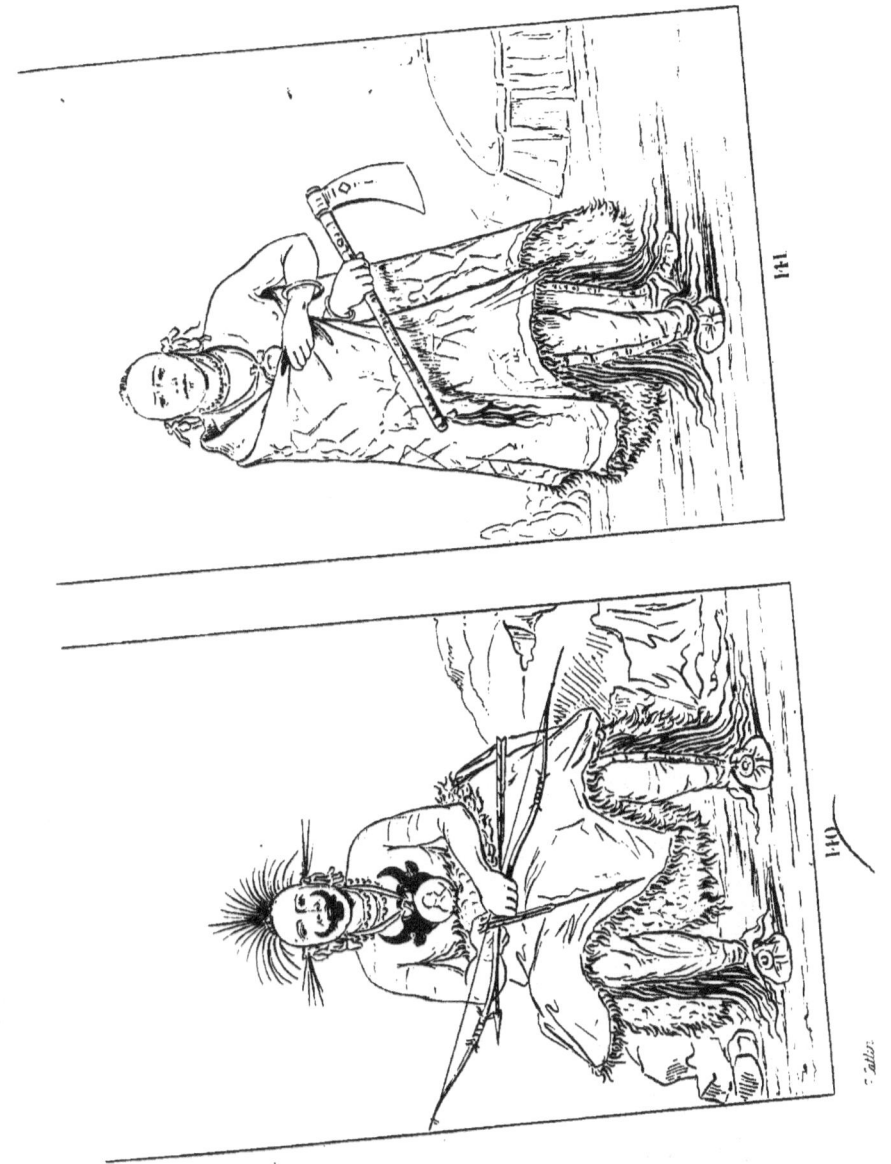

" The missionaries sent amongst the several tribes are, no doubt, sincere in their intentions. I believe them to be so, from what I have seen ; but, unfortunately, they commence their labours where they should end them. They should teach the Indians to work, by establishing schools of that description among them ; induce them to live at home, abandon their rest less and unsettled life, and live independent of the chase. After they are taught this, their intellectual faculties would be more susceptible of improvement of a moral and religious nature ; and their steps towards civilization would become less difficult."

The Pawnees are divided into four bands, or families—designated by the names of Grand Pawnees—Tappage Pawnees—Republican Pawnees, and Wolf Pawnees.

Each of these bands has a chief at its head ; which chiefs, with all the nation, acknowledge a superior chief at whose voice they all move.

At the head of the Grand Pawnees, is *Shon-ka-ki-he-ga* (the horse chief, PLATE 138) ; and by the side of him, *Haw-che-ke-sug-ga* (he who kills the Osages, PLATE 139), the aged chief of the Missouries, of whom I have spoken, and shall yet say more.

La-doo-ke-a (the buffalo bull, PLATE 140), with his *medicine* or *totem* (the head of a buffalo) painted on his breast and his face, with bow and arrows in his hands, is a warrior of great distinction in the same band.

Le-shaw-loo-lah-le-hoo (the big elk, PLATE 141), chief of the Wolf Pawnees, is another of the most distinguished of this tribe

In addition to the above, I have also painted of this tribe, for my Museum, *Ah-shaw-wah-rooks-te* (the medicine horse) ; *La-kee-too-wi-ra-sha* (the little chief); *Loo-ra-we-re-coo* (the bird that goes to war); *Ah-sha-la-coots-a* (mole in the forehead) ; *La-shaw-le-staw-hix* (the man chief) ; *Te-ah-ke-ra-le-re-coo* (the Chayenne) ; *Lo-loch-to-hoo-la* (the big chief) ; *La-wah-ee-coots-la-shaw-no* (the brave chief) ; and *L'har-e-tar-rushe* (the ill-natured man).

The Pawnees live in four villages, some few miles apart, on the banks of the Platte river, having their allies the Omahas und Ottoes so near to them as easily to act in concert, in case of invasion from any other tribe ; and from the fact that half or more of them are supplied with guns and ammunition, they are able to withstand the assaults of any tribe that may come upon them.

Of the Ottoes, *No-way-ke-sug-ga* (he who strikes two at once, PLATE 143); and *Raw-no-way-woh-krah* (the loose pipe-stem, PLATE 144), I have painted at full length, in beautiful costumes—the first with a necklace of grizzly bear's claws, and his dress profusely fringed with scalp-locks ; the second, in a tunic made of the entire skin of a grizzly bear, with a head-dress of the war-eagle's quills.

Besides these, I painted, also, *Wah-ro-nee-aah* (the surrounder); *Non-je-ning-a* (no heart); and *We-ke-ru-law* (he who exchanges).

Of the Omahas, *Ki-ho-ga-waw-shu-shee* (the brave chief, PLATE 145), is the head chief; and next to him in standing and reputation, is *Om-pu-ton-ga* (the big elk, PLATE 146), with his tomahawk in his Land, and his face painted black, for war.

Besides these, I painted *Man-sha-qui-ta* (the little soldier), a brave; *Shaw-da-mon-nee* (there he goes) ; and *Nom-ba-mon-nee* (the double walker).

Of these wild tribes I have much more in store to say in future, and shall certainly make another budget of Letters from this place, or from other regions from whence I may wish to write, and *possibly, lack material !* All of these tribes, as well as the numerous semi-civilized remnants of tribes, that have been thrown out from the borders of our settlements, have missionary establishments and schools, as well as agricultural efforts amongst them ; and will furnish valuable evidence as to the success that those philanthropic and benevolent exertions have met with, contending (as thay have had to do) with the contaminating influences of whiskey-sellers, and other mercenary men, catering for their purses and their unholy appetites.

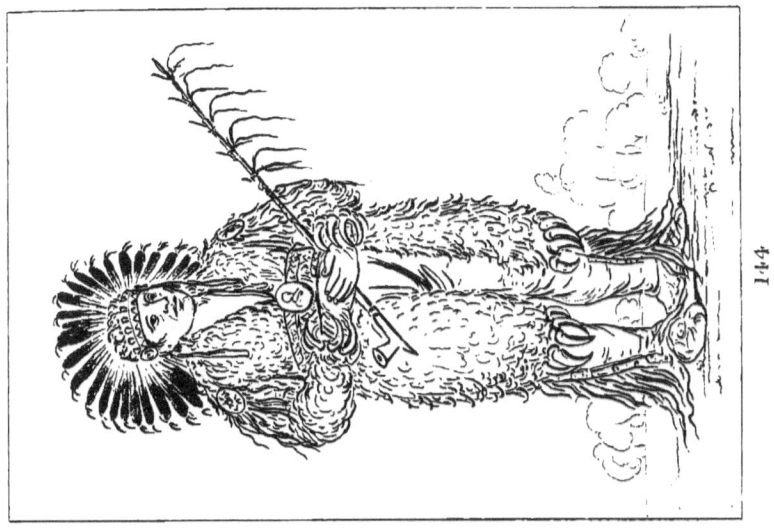

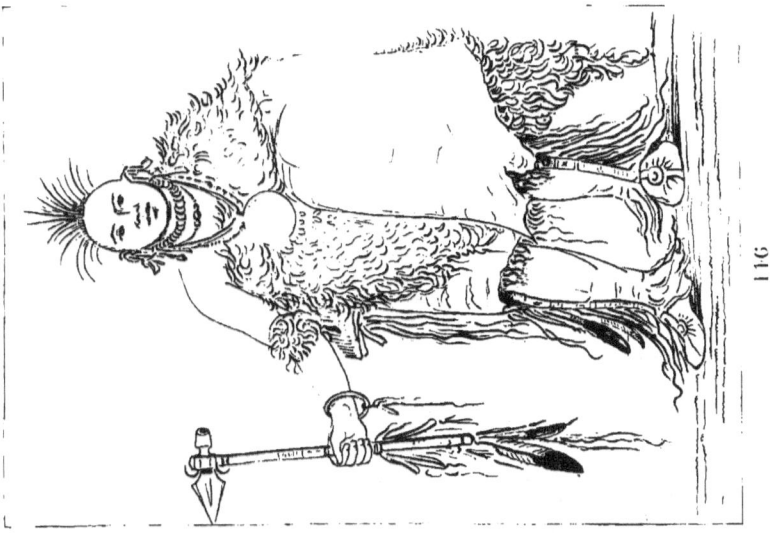

116

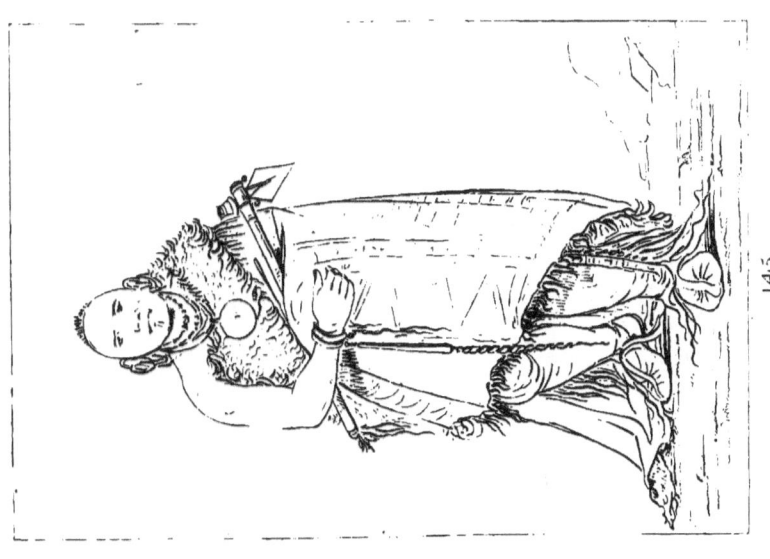

145

LETTER—No. 35.

My little bark has been soaked in the water again, and Ba'tiste and Bogard have paddled, and I have steered and dodged our little craft amongst the snags and sawyers, until at last we landed the humble little thing amongst the huge steamers and floating palaces at the wharf of this bustling and growing city.

And first of all, I must relate the fate of my little boat, which had borne us safe over two thousand miles of the Missouri's turbid and boiling current, with no fault, excepting two or three instances, when the waves became too saucy, she, like the best of boats of her size, went to the bottom, and left us soused, to paddle our way to the shore, and drag out our things and dry them in the sun.

When we landed at the wharf, my luggage was all taken out, and removed to my hotel; and when I returned a few hours afterwards, to look for my little boat, to which I had contracted a peculiar attachment (although I had left it in special charge of a person at work on the wharf); some *mystery* or *medicine* operation had relieved me from any further anxiety or trouble about it—it had gone and never returned, although it had safely passed the countries of mysteries, and had often laid weeks and months at the villages of red men, with no laws to guard it; and where it had also often been taken out of the water by *mystery-men*, and carried up the bank, and turned against my wigwam; and by them again safely carried to the river's edge, and put afloat upon the water, when I was ready to take a seat in it.

St. Louis, which is 1400 miles west of New York, is a flourishing town, of 15,000 inhabitants, and destined to be the great emporium of the West—the greatest inland town in America. Its location is on the Western bank of the Mississippi river, twenty miles below the mouth of the Missouri, and 1400 above the entrance of the Mississippi into the Gulf of Mexico.

This is the great depôt of all the Fur Trading Companies to the Upper Missouri and Rocky Mountains, and their starting-place; and also for the Santa Fe, and other Trading Companies, who reach the Mexican borders overland, to trade for silver bullion, from the extensive mines of that rich country.

I nave also made it *my* starting-point, and place of deposit, to which I send from different quarters, my packages of paintings and Indian articles minerals, fossils, &c., as I collect them in various regions, here to be stored till my return ; and where on my *last return*, if I ever make it, I shall hustle them altogether, and remove them to the East.

To this place I had transmitted by steamer and other conveyance, about twenty boxes and packages at different times, as my note-book shewed ; and I have, on looking them up and enumerating them, been lucky enough to recover and recognize about fifteen of the twenty, which is a pretty fair proportion for this wild and desperate country, and the very *conscientious hands* they often are doomed to pass through.

Ba'tiste and Bogard (poor fellows) I found, after remaining here a few days, had been about as unceremoniously snatched off, as my little canoe ; and Bogard, in particular, as he had made show of a few hundred dollars, which he had saved of his hard earnings in the Rocky Mountains.

He came down with a liberal heart, which he had learned in an Indian life of ten years, with a strong taste, which he had acquired, for whiskey, in a country where it was sold for twenty dollars per gallon ; and with an independent feeling, which illy harmonized with rules and regulations of a country of laws ; and the consequence soon was, that by the " Hawk and Buzzard" system, and Rocky Mountain liberality, and Rocky Mountain prodigality, the poor fellow was soon "jugged up;" where he could deliberately dream of beavers, and the free and cooling breezes of the mountain air, without the pleasure of setting his trap for the one, or even indulging the hope of ever again having the pleasure of breathing the other.

I had imbibed rather less of these delightful passions in the Indian country, and consequently indulged less in them when I came back ; and of course, was rather more fortunate than poor Bogard, whose feelings I soothed as far as it laid in my power, and prepared to " lay my course" to the South, with colours and canvass in readiness for another campaign.

In my sojourn in St. Louis, amongst many other kind and congenial friends whom I met, I have had daily interviews with the venerable Governor Clark, whose whitened locks are still shaken in roars of laughter, and good jests among the numerous citizens, who all love him, and continually rally around him in his hospitable mansion.

Governor Clark, with Captain Lewis, were the first explorers across the Rocky Mountains, and down the Colombia to the Pacific Ocean thirty-two years ago ; whose tour has been published in a very interesting work, which has long been before the world. My works and my design have been warmly approved and applauded by this excellent patriarch of the Western World ; and kindly recommended by him in such ways as have been of great service to me. Governor Clark is now Superintendant of Indian Affairs for all the Western and North Western regions ; and surely, their interests could never have been intrusted to better or abler hands.[*]

[*] Some year or two after writing the above, I saw the announcement of the death of this

So long have I been recruiting, and enjoying the society of friends in this town, that the navigation of the river has suddenly closed, being entirely frozen over; and the earth's surface covered with eighteen inches of drifting snow, which has driven me to the only means, and I start in a day or two, with a tough little pony and a packhorse, to trudge through the snow drifts from this to New Madrid, and perhaps further; a distance of three or four hundred miles to the South—where I must venture to meet a warmer climate—the river open, and steamers running, to waft me to the Gulf of Mexico. Of the fate or success that waits me, or of the incidents of that travel, as they have not transpired, I can as yet say nothing; and I close my book for further time and future entries.

veteran, whose life has been one of faithful service to his country, and, at the same time, of strictest fidelity as the guardian and friend of the red men.

LETTER—No. 36.

PENSACOLA, *WEST FLORIDA*.

From my long silence of late, you will no doubt have deemed me out of the *civil* and perhaps out of the *whole world*.

I have, to be sure, been a great deal of the time *out of the limits* of one and, at times, nearly *out of* the other. Yet I am *living*, and hold in my possession a number of epistles which passing events had dictated, but which I neglected to transmit at the proper season. In my headlong transit through the Southern tribes of Indians, I have *"popped out"* of the woods upon this glowing land, and I cannot forego the pleasure of letting you into a few of the secrets of this delightful place.

" *Flos—floris*," &c. every body knows the meaning of; and *Florida*, in Spanish, is a country of flowers.—*Perdido* is *perdition*, and Rio Perdido, *River* of *Perdition*. Looking down its perpendicular banks into its black water, its depth would seem to be *endless*, and the doom of the unwary to be gloomy in the extreme. Step not accidentally or wilfully over its fatal brink, and Nature's opposite extreme is spread about you. You are *literally* in the land of the " cypress and myrtle"—where the ever-green live oak and lofty magnolia dress the forest in a perpetual mantle of green.

The sudden transition from the ice-bound regions of the North to this mild climate, in the midst of winter, is one of peculiar pleasure. At a half-way of the distance, one's cloak is thrown aside; and arrived on the ever-verdant borders of Florida, the bosom is opened and bared to the soft breeze from the ocean's wave, and the congenial warmth of a summer's sun.

Such is the face of Nature here in the rude month of February ; green peas are served on the table—other garden vegetables in great perfection, and garden flowers, as well as wild, giving their full and sweetest perfume to the winds.

I looked into the deep and bottomless *Perdido*, and beheld about it the thousand charms which Nature has spread to allure the unwary traveller to its brink. 'Twas not enough to entangle him in a web of sweets upon its borders, but *Nature* seems to have used an *art* to draw him to its *bottom*, by the voluptuous buds which blossom under its black waters, and whose vivid colours are softened and enriched the deeper they are seen below its surface The sweetest of wild flowers enamel the shores and spangle the dark green tapestry which hangs over its bosom—the stately *magnolia* towers fearlessly over its black waters, and sheds (with the myrtle and jessamine) the richest perfume over this chilling pool of death.

How exquisitely pure and sweet are the delicate tendrils which Nature has hung over these scenes of melancholy and gloom! and how strong, also, has she fixed in man's breast the passion to possess and enjoy them! I could have hung by the tree tops over that fatal stream, or blindly staggered over its thorny brink to have culled the sweets which are found only in its bosom; but the *poisonous fang*, I was told, was continually aimed at my heel, and I left the sweetened atmosphere of its dark and gloomy, yet enamelled shores.

Florida is, in a great degree, a dark and sterile wilderness, yet with spots of beauty and of loveliness, with charms that cannot be forgotten. Her swamps and everglades, the dens of alligators, and lurking places of the desperate savage, gloom the thoughts of the wary traveller, whose mind is cheered and lit to admiration, when in the solitary pine woods, where he hears nought but the echoing notes of the *sand-hill cranes*, or the howling wolf, he suddenly breaks out into the open savannahs, teeming with their myriads of wild flowers, and palmettos (PLATE 147); or where the winding path through which he is wending his lonely way, suddenly brings him out upon the beach, where the rolling sea has thrown up her thousands of hills and mounds of sand as white as the drifted snow, over which her green waves are lashing, and sliding back again to her deep green and agitated bosom (PLATE 148). This sketch was made on *Santa Rosa Island*, within a few miles of Pensacola, of a favourite spot for *tea* (and other convivial) *parties*, which are often held there. The hills of sand are as *purely white as snow*, and fifty or sixty feet in height, and supporting on their tops, and in their sides, clusters of magnolia bushes—of myrtle—of palmetto and heather, all of which are evergreens, forming the most vivid contrast with the snow-white sand in which they are growing. On the beach a family of Seminole Indians are encamped, catching and drying red fish, their chief article of food.

I have traversed the snow-white shores of Pensacola's beautiful bay, and I said to myself, "Is it possible that Nature has done so much in vain—or will the wisdom of man lead him to add to such works the embellishments of art, and thus convert to his own use and enjoyment the greatest luxuries of life?" As a travelling stranger through the place, I said "yes: it must be so." Nature has here formed the finest harbour in the world; and the dashing waves of the ocean have thrown around its shores the purest barriers of sand, as white as the drifted snow. Unlike all other Southern ports, it is surrounded by living fountains of the purest water, and its shores continually fanned by the refreshing breathings of the sea. To a Northern man, the winters in this place appear like a continual spring time; and the intensity of a summer's sun is cooled into comfort and luxury by the ever-cheering sea breeze.

This is the only place I have found in the Southern country to which Northern people can repair with safety in the summer season; and I know not of a place in the world where they can go with better guarantees of good health, and a reasonable share of the luxuries of life. The town of Pensacola is beautifully situated on the shore of the bay, and contains at present about fifteen hundred inhabitants, most of them Spanish Creoles. They live an easy and idle life, without any energy further than for the mere means of living. The bay abounds in the greatest variety of fish, which are easily taken, and the finest quality of oysters are found in profusion, even alongside of the wharves.

Government having fixed upon this harbour as the great naval depôt for all the Southern coast, the consequence will be, that a vast sum of public money will always be put into circulation in this place; and the officers of the navy, together with the officers of the army, stationed in the three forts built and now building at this place, will constitute the most polished and desirable society in our country.

What Pensacola *has been* or *is*, in a commercial point of view, little can be said; but what it *can be*, and most certainly *will be*, in a few years, the most sanguine can hardly predict. I would unhesitatingly recommend this to the enterprising capitalists of the North, as a place where they can *live*, and where (if nature has been kind, as experience has taught us) they *will* flourish.* A few such men have taken their stand here within a few months past; and, as a first step towards their aggrandizement, a plan of a rail-road has been projected, from Pensacola to Columbus, in Georgia; which needs only to be completed, to place Pensacola at once before any other town on the Southern coast, excepting New Orleans. Of the feasibility of such a work, there is not the slightest doubt; and, from the opinions advanced by Captain Chase and Lieutenant Bowman, two of the most distinguished engineers of the army, it would seem as if Nature had formed a level nearly the whole way, and supplied the best kind of timber on the spot for its erection. The route of this rail-road would be through or near the principal cotton-growing part of Alabama, and the quantity of produce from that state, as well as from a great part of the state of Georgia, which would seek this market, would be almost incalculable. Had this road been in operation during the past winter, it has been ascertained by a simple calculation, that the cotton-growers of Alabama, might have saved 2,000,000 of dollars on their crop; by being enabled to have got it early into market, and received the first price of 18¾ cents, instead of waiting six weeks or two months for a rise of water, enabling them to get it to Mobile—at which time it had fallen to nine cents per pound.

As a work also of *national utility*, it would rank amongst the most important in our country, and the Government might afford to appropriate the whole sum necessary for its construction. In a period of war, when in all probability, for a great part of the time, this port may be in

147

148

G. Catlin

state of blockade, such a communication with the interior of the country, would be of incalculable benefit for the transportation of men—of produce and munitions of war.

Of the few remnants of Indians remaining in this part of the country, I have little to say, at present, that could interest you. The sum total that can be learned or seen of them (like all others that are half civilized) is, that they are to be pitied.

The direful "*trump of war*" is blowing in East Florida, where I was "steering my course;" and I shall in a few days turn my steps in a different direction.

Since you last heard from me, I have added on to my former Tour " down the river," the remainder of the Mississippi (or rather Missouri), from St. Louis to New Orleans; and I find that, from its source to the Balize, the distance is 4500 *miles only!* I shall be on the wing again in a few days, for a shake of the hand with the Camanchees, Osages, Pawnees, Kioways, Arapahoes, &c.—some hints of whom I shall certainly give you from their different localities, provided I can keep the hair on my head.

This Tour will lead me up the Arkansas to its source, and into the Rocky Mountains, under the protection of the United States dragoons. You will begin to think ere long, that I shall acquaint myself pretty well with the manners and customs of our country—at least with the *out-land-ish* part of it.

I shall hail the day with pleasure, when I can again reach the free land of the lawless savage ; for far more agreeable to my ear is the Indian yell and war-whoop, than the civilized groans and murmurs about " *pressure,*" " *de-posites,*" " *bunks,*" " *boundary questions,*" &c.; and I vanish from the country with the sincere hope that these tedious words may become *obsolete* before I return. Adieu.

LETTER—No 37.

FORT GIBSON, *ARKANSAS TERRITORY*.

SINCE the date of my last Letter at Pensacola, in Florida, I travelled to New Orleans, and from thence up the Mississippi several hundred miles, to the mouth of the Arkansas; and up the Arkansas, 700 miles to this place. We wended our way up, between the pictured shores of this beautiful river, on the steamer " Arkansas," until within 200 miles of this post; when we got aground, and the water falling fast, left the steamer nearly on dry ground. Hunting and fishing, and whist, and sleeping, and eating, were our principal amusements to deceive away the time, whilst we were waiting for the water to rise. Lieutenant Seaton, of the army, was one of my companions in misery, whilst we lay two weeks or more without prospect of further progress —the poor fellow on his way to his post to join his regiment, had left his trunk, unfortunately, with all his clothes in it; and by hunting and fishing in shirts that I loaned him, or from other causes, we became yoked in amusements, in catering for our table—in getting fish and wild fowl; and, after that, as the " last kick" for amusement and pastime, with another good companion by the name of Chadwick, we clambered up and over the rugged mountains' sides, from day to day, turning stones to catch *centipedes* and *tarantulas*, of which poisonous reptiles we caged a number; and on the boat amused ourselves by betting on their battles, which were immediately fought, and life almost instantly taken, when they came together.*

In this, and fifty other ways, we whiled away the heavy time : but yet, at last we reached our destined goal, and here we are at present fixed. Fort Gibson is the extreme south-western outpost on the United States frontier; beautifully situated on the banks of the river, in the midst of an extensive and lovely prairie; and is at present occupied by the 7th regiment of United States infantry, heretofore under the command of General Arbuckle, one of the oldest officers on the frontier, and the original builder of the post.

Being soon to leave this little civilized world for a campaign in the Indian country, I take this opportunity to bequeath a few words before the moment of departure. Having sometime since obtained permission from the Secre-

---

* Several years after writing the above, I was shocked at the announcement of the death of this amiable and honourable young man, Lieutenant Seaton, who fell a victim to the deadly disease of that country ; severing another of the many fibres of my heart, which peculiar circumstances in these wild regions, had woven, but to be broken.

tary of War to accompany the regiment of the United States dragoons in their summer campaign, I *reported* myself at this place two months ago, where I have been waiting ever since for their organization.—After the many difficulties which they have had to encounter, they have at length all assembled—the grassy plains are resounding with the trampling hoofs of the prancing war-horse—and already the hills are echoing back the notes of the spirit-stirring trumpets, which are sounding for the onset. The *natives* are again "to be astonished," and I shall probably again be a witness to the scene. But whether the approach of eight hundred mounted dragoons amongst the Camanchees and Pawnees, will afford me a better subject for a picture of a *gaping* and *astounded multitude,* than did the first approach of our steam-boat amongst the Mandans, &c., is a question yet to be solved. I am strongly inclined to think that the scene will not be less wild and spirited, and I ardently wish it ; for I have become so much Indian of late, that my pencil has lost all appetite for subjects that savour of tameness. I should delight in seeing these red knights of the lance astonished, for it is then that they shew their brightest hues—and I care not how badly we frighten them, provided we hurt them not, nor frighten them out of *sketching distance.* You will agree with me, that I am going farther to get *sitters,* than any of my fellow-artists ever did ; but I take an indescribable pleasure in roaming through Nature's trackless wilds, and selecting my models, where I am free and unshackled by the killing restraints of society ; where a painter must modestly sit and breathe away in agony the edge and soul of his inspiration, waiting for the sluggish *calls* of the civil. Though the toil, the privations, and expense of travelling to these remote parts of the world to get subjects for my pencil, place almost insurmountable, and sometimes *painful* obstacles before me, yet I am encouraged by the continual conviction that I am practising in the *true School of the Arts* ; and that, though I should get as poor as Lazarus, I should deem myself rich in models and studies for the future occupation of my life. Of this much I am certain—that amongst these sons of the forest, where are continually repeated the feats and gambols equal to the Grecian Games, I have learned more of the essential parts of my art in the three last years, than I could have learned in New York in a life-time.

The landscape scenes of these wild and beautiful regions, are, of themselves, a rich reward for the traveller who can place them in his portfolio : and being myself the only one accompanying the dragoons for scientific purposes, there will be an additional pleasure to be derived from those pursuits. The regiment of eight hundred men, with whom I am to travel, will be an effective force, and a perfect protection against any attacks that will ever be made by Indians. It is composed principally of young men of respectable families, who would act, on all occasions, from feelings of pride and honour, in addition to those of the common soldier.

The day before yesterday the regiment of dragoons and the 7th regiment of infantry, stationed here, were reviewed by General Leavenworth, who has lately arrived at this post, superseding Colonel Arbuckle in the command.

Both regiments were drawn up in battle array, in *fatigue dress*, and passing through a number of the manœuvres of battle, of charge and repulse, &c., presenting a novel and thrilling scene in the prairie, to the thousands of Indians and others who had assembled to witness the display. The proud and manly deportment of these young men remind one forcibly of a regiment of Independent Volunteers, and the horses have a most beautiful appearance from the arrangement of colours. Each company of horses has been selected of one colour entire. There is a company of *bays*, a company of *blacks*, one of *whites*, one of *sorrels*, one of *greys*, one of *cream* colour, &c. &c., which render the companies distinct, and the effect exceedingly pleasing. This regiment goes out under the command of Colonel Dodge, and from his well tested qualifications, and from the beautiful equipment of the command, there can be little doubt but that they will do credit to themselves and an honour to their country ; so far as honours can be gained and laurels can be plucked from their wild stems in a savage country. The object of this summer's campaign seems to be to cultivate an acquaintance with the Pawnees and Camanchees. These are two extensive tribes of roaming Indians, who, from their extreme ignorance of us, have not yet recognized the United States in treaty, and have struck frequent blows on our frontiers and plundered our traders who are traversing their country. For this I cannot so much blame them, for the Spaniards are gradually advancing upon them on one side, and the Americans on the other, and fast destroying the furs and game of their country, which God gave them as their only wealth and means of subsistence. This movement of the dragoons *seems* to be one of the most humane in its views, and I heartily hope that it may prove so in the event, as well for our own sakes as for that of the Indian. I can see no reason why we should march upon them with an invading army carrying with it the spirit of chastisement. The object of Government undoubtedly is to effect a friendly meeting with them, that they may see and respect us, and to establish something like a system of mutual rights with them. To penetrate their country with the other view, that of chastising them, even with five times the number that are now going, would be entirely futile, and perhaps *disastrous* in the extreme. It is a pretty thing (and perhaps an easy one, in the estimation of the world) for an army of mounted men to be gaily prancing over the boundless green fields of the West, and it *is* so for a little distance—but it would be well that the world should be apprised of some of the actual difficulties that oppose themselves to the success of such a campaign, that they may not censure too severely, in case this command should fail to accomplish the objects for which they were organized.

In the first place, from the great difficulty of organizing and equipping, these troops are starting too late in the season for their summer's campaign, by two months. The journey which they have to perform is a very long one.

and although the first part of it will be picturesque and pleasing, the after part of it will be tiresome and fatiguing in the extreme. As they advance to the West, the grass (and consequently the game) will be gradually diminishing, and water in many parts of the county not to be found.

As the troops will be obliged to subsist themselves a great part of the way, it will be extremely difficult to do it under such circumstances, and at the same time hold themselves in readiness, with half-famished horses and men nearly exhausted, to contend with a numerous enemy who are at home, on the ground on which they were born, with horses fresh and ready for action. It is not probable, however, that the Indians will venture to take advantage of such circumstances; but I am inclined to think, that the expedition will be more likely to fail from another source : it is my opinion that the appearance of so large a military force in their country, will alarm the Indians to that degree, that they will fly with their families to their hiding-places amongst those barren deserts, which they themselves can reach only by great fatigue and extreme privation, and to which our half-exhausted troops cannot possibly follow them. From these haunts their warriors would advance and annoy the regiment as much as they could, by striking at their hunting parties and cutting off their supplies. To attempt to pursue them, if they cannot be called to a council, would be as useless as to follow the wind ; for our troops in such a case, are in a country where they are obliged to subsist themselves, and the Indians being on fresh horses, with a supply of provisions, would easily drive all the buffaloes ahead of them ; and endeavour, as far as possible, to decoy our troops into the barren parts of the country, where they could not find the means of subsistence.

The plan designed to be pursued, and the only one that can succeed, is to send runners to the different bands, explaining the friendly intentions of our Government, and to invite them to a meeting. For this purpose several Camanchee and Pawnee prisoners have been purchased from the Osages, who may be of great service in bringing about a friendly interview.

I ardently hope that this plan may succeed, for I am anticipating great fatigue and privation in the endeavour to see these wild tribes together ; that I may be enabled to lay before the world a just estimate of their manners and customs.

I hope that my suggestions may not be truly prophetic ; but I am constrained to say, that I doubt very much whether we shall see anything more of them than their trails, and the sites of their deserted villages.

Several companies have already started from this place ; and the remaining ones will be on their march in a day or two. General Leavenworth will accompany them 200 miles, to the mouth of False Washita, and I shall be attached to his staff. Incidents which may occur, I shall record. Adieu.

NOTE.—In the mean time, as it may be long before I can write again, I send you some account of the Osages ; whom I have been visiting and painting during the two months I have been staying here.

FORT GIBSON, *ARKANSAS.*

NEARLY two months have elapsed since I arrived at this post, on my way up the river from the Mississippi, to join the regiment of dragoons on their campaign into the country of the Camanchees and Pawnee Picts; during which time, I have been industriously at work with my brush and my pen, recording the looks and the deeds of the Osages, who inhabit the country on the North and the West of this.

The Osage, or (as they call themselves) *Wa-saw-see*, are a tribe of about 5200 in numbers, inhabiting and hunting over the head-waters of the Arkansas, and Neosho or Grand Rivers. Their present residence is about 700 miles West of the Mississippi river; in three villages, constituted of wigwams, built of barks and flags or reeds. One of these villages is within forty miles of this Fort; another within sixty, and the third about eighty miles. Their chief place of trade is with the sutlers at this post; and there are constantly more or less of them encamped about the garrison.

The Osages may justly be said to be the tallest race of men in North America, either of red or white skins; there being very few indeed of the men, at their full growth, who are less than six feet in stature, and very many of them six and a half, and others seven feet. They are at the same time well-proportioned in their limbs, and good looking; being rather narrow in the shoulders, and, like most all very tall people, a little inclined to stoop; not throwing the chest out, and the head and shoulders back, quite as much as the Crows and Mandans, and other tribes amongst which I have been familiar. Their movement is graceful and quick; and in war and the chase, I think they are equal to any of the tribes about them.

This tribe, though living, as they long have, near the borders of the civilized community, have studiously rejected everything of civilized customs; and are uniformly dressed in skins of their own dressing—strictly maintaining their primitive looks and manners, without the slightest appearance of innovations, excepting in the blankets, which have been recently admitted to their use instead of the buffalo robes, which are now getting scarce amongst them.

The Osages are one of the tribes who shave the head, as I have before described when speaking of the Pawnees and Konzas, and they decorate

150

151

and paint it with great care, and some considerable taste. There is a peculiarity in the heads of these people which is very striking to the eye of a traveller; and which I find is produced by artificial means in infancy. Their children, like those of all the other tribes, are carried on a board, and slung upon the mother's back. The infants are lashed to the boards, with their backs upon them, apparently in a very uncomfortable condition; and with the Osages, the head of the child bound down so tight to the board, as to force in the occipital bone, and create an unnatural deficiency on the back part, and consequently more than a natural elevation of the top of the head. This custom, they told me they practiced, because " it pressed out a bold and manly appearance in front." This I think, from observation, to be rather imaginary than real; as I cannot see that they exhibit any extraordinary development in the front; though they evidently shew a striking deficiency on the back part, and also an unnatural elevation on the top of the head, which is, no doubt, produced by this custom. The difference between this mode and the one practiced by the Flat-head Indians beyond the Rocky Mountains, consists in this, that the Flat-heads press the head *between* two boards; the one pressing the frontal bone down, whilst the other is pressing the occipital up, producing the most frightful deformity; whilst the Osages merely press the occipital in, and that, but to a moderate degree, occasioning but a slight, and in many cases, almost immaterial, departure from the symmetry of nature.

These people, like all those tribes who shave the head, cut and slit their ears very much, and suspend from them great quantities of wampum and tinsel ornaments. Their necks are generally ornamented also with a profusion of wampum and beads; and as they live in a warm climate where there is not so much necessity for warm clothing, as amongst the more Northern tribes, of whom I have been heretofore speaking; their shoulders, arms, and chests are generally naked, and painted in a great variety of picturesque ways, with silver bands on the wrists, and oftentimes a profusion of rings on the fingers.

The head-chief of the Osages at this time, is a young man by the name of Clermont (PLATE 150), the son of a very distinguished chief of that name, who recently died; leaving his son his successor, with the consent of the tribe. I painted the portrait of this chief at full length, in a beautiful dress, his leggings fringed with scalp-locks, and in his hand his favourite and valued war-club.

By his side I have painted also at full length, his wife and child (PLATE 151). She was richly dressed in costly cloths of civilized manufacture, which is almost a solitary instance amongst the Osages, who so studiously reject every luxury and every custom of civilized people; and amongst those, the use of whiskey, which is on all sides tendered to them—but almost uniformily rejected! This is an unusual and unaccountable thing, unless the influence which the missionaries and teachers have exercised over them, has induced them to abandon the pernicious and destructive habit of drinking to excess. From what I can learn, the Osages were once fond of whiskey; and, like all other tribes who have had the opportunity, were in the habit of using it to excess. Several very good and exemplary men have been for years past exerting their greatest efforts, with those of their families, amongst these people; having established schools and agricultural experiments amongst them. And I am fully of the opinion, that this decided anomaly in the Indian country, has resulted from the devoted exertions of these pious and good men.

Amongst the chiefs of the Osages, and probably the next in authority and respect in the tribe, is Tchong-tas-sab-bee, the black dog (PLATE 152), whom I painted also at full length, with his pipe in one hand, and his tomahawk in the other; his head shaved, and ornamented with a beautiful crest of deers' hair, and his body wrapped in a huge mackinaw blanket.

This dignitary, who is blind in the left eye, is one of the most conspicuous characters in all this country, rendered so by his huge size (standing in height and in girth, above all of his tribe), as well as by his extraordinary life. The Black Dog is familiarly known to all the officers of the army, as well as to Traders and all other white men, who have traversed these regions, and I believe, admired and respected by most of them.

His height, I think, is seven feet; and his limbs full and rather fat, making his bulk formidable, and weighing, perhaps, some 250 or 300 pounds. This man is chief of one of the three bands of the Osages, divided as they are into three families; occupying, as I before said, three villages, denominated, "Clermont's Village," "Black Dog's Village," and "White Hair's Village." The White Hair is another distinguished leader of the Osages; and some have awarded to him the title of *Head Chief;* but in the jealous feelings of rivalry which have long agitated this tribe, and some times, even endangered its peace, I believe it has been generally agreed that his claims are third in the tribe; though he justly claims the title of a chief, and a very gallant and excellent man. The portrait of this man, I regret to say, I did not get.

Amongst the many brave and distinguished warriors of the tribe, one of the most noted and respected is Tal-lee (PLATE 153), painted at full length, with his lance in his hand—his shield on his arm, and his bow and quiver slung upon his back.

In this portrait, there is a fair specimen of the Osage figure and dress, as well as of the facial outline, and shape and character of the head, and mode of dressing and ornamenting it with the helmet-crest, and the eagle's quill.

If I had the time at present, I would unfold to the reader some of the pleasing and extraordinary incidents of this gallant fellow's military life; and also the anecdotes that have grown out of the familiar life I have led with this handsome and high-minded *gentleman* of the wild woods and

G. Catlin.

G. Catlin.

prairies. Of the Black Dog I should say more also; and most assuredly will not fail to do justice to these extraordinary men, when I have leisure to write off all my notes, and turn biographer. At present, I shake hands with these two noblemen, and bid them good-bye; promising them, that if I never get time to say more of their virtues—I shall say nothing again.st them.

In PLATES 154, 155, 156, I have represented three braves, Ko-ha-tunk-a (the big crow); Nah-com-e-shee (the man of the bed), and Mun-ne-pus-kee (he who is not afraid). These portraits set forth fairly the modes of dress and ornaments of the young men of the tribe, from the tops of their heads to the soles of their feet. The only dress they wear in warm weather is the breech-cloth, leggings, and moccasins of dressed skins, and garters worn immediately below the knee, ornamented profusely with beads and wampum. *

These three distinguished and ambitious young men, were of the best families in the Osage nation; and as they explained to me, having formed a peculiar attachment to each other—they desired me to paint them all on one canvass, in which wish I indulged them.

Besides the above personages, I also painted the portraits of *Wa-ho-beck-ee* (———), a brave, and said to be the handsomest man in the Osage nation; *Moi-een-e-shee* (the constant walker); *Wa-mash-ee-sheek* (he who takes away); *Wa-chesh-uk* (war); *Mink-chesk* (———); *Wash-im-pe-shee* (the mad man), a distinguished warrior; *Shin-ga-wos-sa* (the handsome bird); *Cah-he-ga-shin-ga* (the little chief), and *Tcha-to-ga* (the mad buffalo); all of which will hang in my INDIAN MUSEUM for the inspection of the curious. The last mentioned of these was tried and convicted of the murder of two white men during Adams's administration, and was afterwards pardoned, and still lives, though in disgrace in his tribe, as one whose life had been forfeited, " but (as they say) not worth taking."

The Osages have been formerly, and until quite recently, a powerful and warlike tribe: carrying their arms fearlessly through all of these realms; and ready to cope with foes of any kind that they were liable to meet. At present, the case is quite different; they have been repeatedly moved and jostled along, from the head waters of the White river, and even from the shores of the Mississippi, to where they now are; and reduced by every war and every move. The small-pox has taken its share of them at two or three different times; and the Konzas, as they are now called, having been a

---

* These three young men, with eight or ten others, were sent out by the order of the Black Dog and the other chiefs, with the regiment of dragoons, as guides and hunters, for the expedition to the Camanchees, an account of which will be found in the following pages.

I was a fellow-traveller and hunter with these young men for several months, and therefore have related in the following pages some of the incidents of our mutual exploits whilst in the Camanchee country

part of the Osages, and receded from them, impaired their strength; and have at last helped to lessen the number of their warriors; so that their decline has been very rapid, bringing them to the mere handful that now exists of them; though still preserving their valour as warriors, which they are continually shewing off as bravely and as professionally as they can, with the Pawnees and the Camanchees, with whom they are waging incessant war; although they are the principal sufferers in those scenes which they fearlessly persist in, as if they were actually bent on their self-destruction. Very great efforts have been, and are being made amongst these people to civilize and christianize them; and still I believe with but little success. Agriculture they have caught but little of; and of religion and civilization still less. One good result has, however, been produced by these faithful labourers, which is the conversion of these people to temperance; which I consider the first important step towards the other results, and which of itself is an achievement that redounds much to the credit and humanity of those, whose lives have been devoted to its accomplishment.

Here I must leave the Osages for the present, but not the reader, whose company I still hope to have awhile longer, to hear how I get along amongst the wild and untried scenes, that I am to start upon in a few days, in company with the first regiment of dragoons, in the first grand *civilized foray,* into the country of the wild and warlike Camanchees.

154 155 156

LETTER—No. 39.

MOUTH OF FALSE WASHITA, *RED RIVER.*

UNDER the protection of the United States dragoons, I arrived at this place three days since, on my way again in search of the " Far West." How far I may *this time* follow the flying phantom, is uncertain. I am already again in the land of the *buffaloes* and the *fleet-bounding antelopes* : and I anticipate, with many other beating hearts, rare sport and amusement amongst the wild herds ere long.

We shall start from hence in a few days, and other epistles I may occasionally drop you from *terra incognita,* for such is the great expanse of country which we expect to range over; and names we are to give, and country to explore, as far as we proceed. We are, at this place, on the banks of the Red River, having Texas under our eye on the opposite bank. Our encampment is on the point of land between the Red and False Washita rivers, at their junction; and the country about us is a panorama too beautiful to be painted with a pen : it is, like most of the country in these regions, composed of prairie and timber, alternating in the most delightful shapes and proportions that the eye of a connoisseur could desire. The verdure is everywhere of the deepest green, and the plains about us are literally speckled with buffalo. We are distant from Fort Gibson about 200 miles, which distance we accomplished in ten days.

A great part of the way, the country is prairie, gracefully undulating— well watered, and continually beautified by copses and patches of timber. On our way my attention was rivetted to the tops of some of the prairie bluffs, whose summits I approached with inexpressible delight. I rode to the top of one of these noble mounds, in company with my friends Lieut. Wheelock and Joseph Chadwick, where we agreed that our *horses* instinctively *looked* and *admired.* They thought not of the rich herbage that was under their feet, but, with deep-drawn sighs, their necks were loftily curved, and their eyes widely stretched over the landscape that was beneath us. From this elevated spot, the horizon was bounded all around us by mountain streaks of blue, softening into azure as they vanished, and the pictured vales that intermediate lay, were deepening into green as the eye was returning from its roamings. Beneath us, and winding through the waving landscape was seen with peculiar effect, the " bold dragoons," marching in beautiful order forming a train of a mile in length. Baggage waggons and

Indians (*engagés*) helped to lengthen the procession. From the point where we stood, the line was seen in miniature : and the undulating hills over which it was bending its way, gave it the appearance of a huge black snake gracefully gliding over a rich carpet of green.

This picturesque country of 200 miles, over which we have passed, belongs to the Creeks and Choctaws, and affords one of the richest and most desirable countries in the world for agricultural pursuits.

Scarcely a day has passed, in which we have not crossed oak ridges, or several miles in breadth, with a sandy soil and scattering timber ; where the ground was almost literally covered with vines, producing the greatest profusion of delicious grapes, of five-eighths of an inch in diameter, and hanging in such endless clusters, as justly to entitle this singular and solitary wilderness to the style of a vineyard (and ready for the vintage), for many miles together.

The next hour we would be trailing through broad and verdant valleys of green prairies, into which we had descended ; and oftentimes find our progress completely arrested by hundreds of acres of small plum-trees, of four or six feet in height ; so closely woven and interlocked together, as entirely to dispute our progress, and sending us several miles around ; when every bush that was in sight was so loaded with the weight of its delicious wild fruit, that they were in many instances literally without leaves on their branches, and bent quite to the ground. Amongst these, and in patches, were intervening beds of wild roses, wild currants, and gooseberries. And underneath and about them, and occasionally interlocked with them, huge masses of the prickly pears, and beautiful and tempting wild flowers that sweetened the atmosphere above ; whilst an occasional huge yellow rattlesnake, or a copper-head, could be seen gliding over, or basking across their vari-coloured tendrils and leaves.

On the eighth day of our march we met, for the first time, a herd of buffaloes ; and being in advance of the command, in company with General Leavenworth, Colonel Dodge, and several other officers ; we all had an opportunity of testing the mettle of our horses and *our own tact* at the wild and spirited death. The inspiration of chase took at once, and alike, with the old and the young ; a beautiful plain lay before us, and we all gave spur for the onset. General Leavenworth and Colonel Dodge, with their pistols, gallantly and handsomely belaboured a fat cow, and were in together at the death. I was not quite so fortunate in my selection, for the one which I saw fit to gallant over the plain alone, of the same sex, younger and coy, led me a hard chase, and for a long time, disputed my near approach ; when, at length, the *full speed* of my horse forced us to close company, and she desperately assaulted his shoulders with her horns. My gun was aimed, but missing its fire, the muzzle entangled in her mane, and was instantly broke in two in my hands, and fell over my shoulder. My pistols were then brought to bear upon her ; and though severely wounded, she

succeeded in reaching the thicket and left me without "a deed of chivalry
to boast."—Since that day, the Indian hunters in our charge have supplied
us abundantly with buffalo meat; and report says, that the country ahead
of us will afford us continual sport, and an abundant supply.

We are halting here for a few days to recruit horses and men, after which
the line of march will be resumed; and if the Pawnees are as near to us as we
have strong reason to believe, from their recent trails and fires, it is probable
that within a few days we shall "thrash" them or "get thrashed;" unless
through their sagacity and fear, they elude our search by flying before us
to their hiding-places.

The prevailing policy amongst the officers seems to be, that of flogging
them first, and then establishing a treaty of peace. If this plan were *morally
right*, I do not think it *practicable*; for, as *enemies*, I do not believe they will
stand to meet us; but, as *friends*, I think we *may* bring them to a *talk*, if
the proper means are adopted. We are here encamped on the ground on
which Judge Martin and servant were butchered, and his son kidnapped by
the Pawnees or Camanchees, but a few weeks since; and the moment they
discover us in a large body, they will presume that we are relentlessly seeking for revenge, and they will probably be very shy of our approach. We
are over the Washita—the "Rubicon is passed." We are invaders of a
sacred soil. We are carrying war in our front,—and "we shall soon *see*,
what we *shall see*."

The cruel fate of Judge Martin and family has been published in the
papers; and it belongs to the regiment of dragoons to demand the surrender
of the murderers, and get for the information of the world, some authentic
account of the mode in which this horrid outrage was committed.

Judge Martin was a very respectable and independent man, living on the
lower part of the Red River, and in the habit of taking his children and a couple
of black men-servants with him, and a tent to live in, every summer, into
these wild regions; where he pitched it upon the prairie, and spent several
months in killing buffaloes and other wild game, for his own private amusement. The news came to Fort Gibson but a few weeks before we started, that
he had been set upon by a party of Indians and destroyed. A detachment of
troops was speedily sent to the spot, where they found his body horridly
mangled, and also of one of his negroes; and it is supposed that his son, a
fine boy of nine years of age, has been taken home to their villages by them.
Where they still retain him, and where it is our hope to recover him.

Great praise is due to General Leavenworth for his early and unremitted
efforts to facilitate the movements of the regiment of dragoons, by opening
roads from Gibson and Towson to this place. We found encamped two
companies of infantry from Fort Towson, who will follow in the rear of the
dragoons as far as necessary, transporting with waggons, stores and supplies,
and ready, at the same time, to co-operate with the dragoons in case of necessity. General Leavenworth will advance with us from this post, but how

far he may proceed is uncertain. We know not exactly the route which we shall take, for circumstances alone must decide that point. We shall probably reach Cantonment Leavenworth in the fall; and one thing is *certain* (in the opinion of one who has already seen something of Indian life and country), we shall meet with many severe privations and reach that place a jaded set of fellows, and as ragged as Jack Falstaff's famous band.

You are no doubt inquiring, who are these Pawnees, Camanchees, and Arapahoes, and why not tell us all about them ? Their history, numbers and limits are still in obscurity; nothing definite is yet known of them, but I hope I shall soon be able to give the world a clue to them.

If my life and health are preserved, I anticipate many a pleasing scene for my pencil, as well as incidents worthy of reciting to the world, which I shall occasionally do, as opportunity may occur.

LETTER—No. 40.

SINCE I wrote my last Letter from this place, I have been detained here with the rest of the cavalcade from the extraordinary sickness which is afflicting the regiment, and actually threatening to arrest its progress.

It was, as I wrote the other day, the expectation of the commanding officer that we should have been by this time recruited and recovered from sickness, and ready to start again on our march; but since I wrote nearly one half of the command, and included amongst them, several officers, with General Leavenworth, have been thrown upon their backs, with the prevailing epidemic, a slow and distressing bilious fever. The horses of the regiment are also sick, about an equal proportion, and seemingly suffering with the same disease. They are daily dying, and men are calling sick, and General Leavenworth has ordered Col. Dodge to select all the men, and all the horses that are able to proceed, and be off to-morrow at nine o'clock upon the march towards the Camanchees, in hopes thereby to preserve the health of the men, and make the most rapid advance towards the extreme point of destination.

General Leavenworth has reserved Col. Kearney to take command of the remaining troops and the little encampment; and promises Colonel Dodge that he will himself be well enough in a few days to proceed with a party on his trail and overtake him at the Cross Timbers.

I should here remark, that when we started from Fort Gibson, the regiment of dragoons, instead of the eight hundred which it was supposed it would contain, had only organized to the amount of 400 men, which was the number that started from that place; and being at this time half disabled, furnishes but 200 effective men to penetrate the wild and untried regions of the hostile Camanchees. All has been bustle and confusion this day, packing up and preparing for the start to-morrow morning. My canvass and painting apparatus are prepared and ready for the packhorse, which carries the goods and chattels of my esteemed companion Joseph Chadwick and myself, and we shall be the two only guests of the procession, and consequently the only two who will be at liberty to gallop about where we please, despite military rules and regulations, chasing the wild herds, or seeking our own amusements in any such modes as we chouse. Mr. Chadwick is a young man from St. Louis, with whom I have been long acquainted, and for whom I have the highest esteem. He has so far stood by me as a faithful friend, and I rely implicitly on his society during this campaign for much good company and amusement. Though I have an order from the Secretary at War to the commanding officer, to protect and supply me, I shall ask but for their protection ; as I have, with my friend Joe, laid in our own supplies for the campaign, not putting the Government to any expense on my account, in pursuit of my own private objects.

I am writing this under General Leavenworth's tent, where he has generously invited me to take up my quarters during our encampment here, and he promises to send it by his express, which starts to-morrow with a mail from this to Fort Towson on the frontier, some hundreds of miles below this. At the time I am writing, the General lies pallid and emaciated before me, on his couch, with a dragoon fanning him, whilst he breathes forty or fifty breaths a minute, and writhes under a burning fever, although he is yet unwilling even to admit that he is sick.

In my last Letter I gave a brief account of a buffalo chase, where General Leavenworth and Col. Dodge took parts, and met with pleasing success. The next day, while on the march, and a mile or so in advance of the regiment, and two days before we reached this place, General Leavenworth, Col. Dodge, Lieut. Wheelock and myself were jogging along, and all in turn complaining of the lameness of our bones, from the chase on the former day, when the General, who had long ago had his surfeit of pleasure of this kind on the Upper Missouri, remonstrated against further indulgence, in the following manner : " Well, Colonel, this running for buffaloes is bad business for us —we are getting too old, and should leave such amusements to the young men ; I have had enough of this fun in my life, and I am determined not to hazard my limbs or weary my horse any more with it—it is the height of folly for us, but will do well enough for boys." Col. Dodge assented at once to his resolves, and approved them ; whilst I, who had tried it in every form (and I had thought, to my heart's content), on the Upper Missouri, joined my assent to the folly of our destroying our horses, which had a long journey to perform, and agreed that I would join no more in the buffalo chase, however near and inviting they might come to me.

In the midst of this conversation, and these mutual declarations (or rather just at the end of them), as we were jogging along in " *Indian file*," and General Leavenworth taking the lead, and just rising to the top of a little hill over which it seems he had had an instant peep, he dropped himself suddenly upon the side of his horse and wheeled back ! and rapidly informed us with an agitated whisper, and an exceeding game contraction of the eye, that a snug little band of buffaloes were quietly grazing just over the knoll in a beautiful meadow for running, and that if I would take to the left ! and Lieut. Wheelock to the right ! and let him and the Colonel dash right into the midst of them! we could play the devil with them ! ! one half of this at least was said after he had got upon his feet and taken off his portmanteau and valise, in which we had all followed suit, and were mounting for the start! and I am almost sure nothing else was said, and if it had been I should not have heard it, for I was too far off! and too rapidly dashed over the waving grass! and too eagerly gazing and plying the whip, to hear or to see, anything but the trampling hoofs! and the blackened throng! and the darting steeds! and the flashing of guns! until I had crossed the beautiful lawn! and the limb of a tree, as my horse was darting into the timber, had crossed my horse's back, and had scraped me into the grass, from which I soon raised my head! and all was silent! and all out of sight! save the dragoon regiment, which I could see in distance creeping along on the top of a high hill. I found my legs under me in a few moments, and put them in their accustomed positions, none of which would for some time, answer the usual purpose; but I at last got them to work, and brought "Charley" out of the bushes, where he had "brought up" in the top of a fallen tree, without damage.

No buffalo was harmed in this furious assault, nor horse nor rider. Col. Dodge and Lieut. Wheelock had joined the regiment, and General Leavenworth joined me, with too much game expression *yet* in his eye to allow him more time than to say, "I'll have that calf before I quit!" and away he sailed, "up hill and down dale," in pursuit of a fine calf that had been hidden on the ground during the chase, and was now making its way over the prairies in pursuit of the herd. I rode to the top of a little hill to witness the success of the General's second effort, and after he had come close upon the little affrighted animal, it dodged about in such a manner as evidently to baffle his skill, and perplex his horse, which at last fell in a hole, and both were instantly out of my sight. I ran my horse with all possible speed to the spot, and found him on his hands and knees, endeavouring to get up. I dismounted and raised him on to his feet, when I asked him if he was hurt, to which he replied "no, but I might have been," when he instantly fainted, and I laid him on the grass. I had left my canteen with my portmanteau, and had nothing to administer to him, nor was there water near us. I took my lancet from my pocket and was tying his arm to open a vein, when he recovered, and objected to the operation, assuring me that he was not in the least injured. I caught his horse and soon got him mounted again, when we rode on together, and after two or three hours were enabled to join the regiment.

From that hour to the present, I think I have seen a decided change in the General's face; he has looked pale and feeble, and been continually troubled with a violent cough. I have rode by the side of him from day to day, and he several times told me that he was fearful he was badly hurt. He looks very feeble now, and I very much fear the result of the fever that has set in upon him.

We take up the line of march at bugle-call in the morning, and it may be a long time before I can send a Letter again, as there are no post-offices nor mail carriers in the country where we are now going. It will take a great deal to stop me from writing, however, and as I am now to enter upon one of the most interesting parts of the Indian country, inasmuch as it is one of the wildest and most hostile, I shall surely scribble an occasional Letter, if I have to carry them in my own pocket, and bring them in with with me on my return.

LETTER—No. 41.

GREAT CAMANCHEE VILLAGE.

WE are again at rest, and I am with subjects rude and almost infinite around me, for my pen and my brush. The little band of dragoons are encamped by a fine spring of cool water, within half a mile of the principal town of the Camanchees, and in the midst of a bustling and wild scene, I assure you; and before I proceed to give an account of things and scenes that are about me, I must return for a few moments to the place where I left the Reader, at the encampment at False Washita, and rapidly travel with him over the country that lies between that place and the Camanchee Village, where I am now writing.

On the morning after my last Letter was written, the sound and efficient part of the regiment was in motion at nine o'clock. And with them, my friend " Joe" and I, with our provisions laid in, and all snugly arranged on our packhorse, which we alternately led or drove between us.

Our course was about due West, on the divide between the Washita and Red Rivers, with our faces looking towards the Rocky Mountains. The country over which we passed from day to day, was inimitably beautiful ; being the whole way one continuous prairie of green fields, with occasional clusters of timber and shrubbery, just enough for the uses of cultivating-man, and for the pleasure of his eyes to dwell upon. The regiment was rather more than half on the move, consisting of 250 men, instead of 200 as I predicted in my Letter from that place. All seemed gay and buoyant at the fresh start, which all trusted was to liberate us from the fatal miasma which we conceived was hovering about the mouth of the False Washita. We advanced on happily, and met with no trouble until the second night of our encampment, in the midst of which we were thrown into " pie" (as printers would say,) in an instant of the most appalling alarm and confusion. We were encamped on a beautiful prairie, where we were every hour apprehensive of the lurking enemy. And in the dead of night, when all seemed to be sound asleep and quiet, the instant sound and flash of a gun within a few paces of us ! and then the most horrid and frightful groans that instantly followed it, brought us all upon our hands and knees in an instant, and our affrighted horses (which were breaking their lasos,) in full speed and fury over our heads, with the frightful and mingled din of snorting, and cries of " Indians ! Indians! Pawnees !" &c., which rang from every part of our little encampment! In a few moments the excitement was chiefly over, and silence restored; when we could hear the trampling hoofs of the horses, which were making off in all directions, (not unlike a drove of swine that once ran into the sea, when they were possessed of devils); and leaving but now and then an individual quadruped hanging at its stake within our little camp. The mode of our encampment was, uniformly in four lines, forming a square of fifteen or twenty rods in diameter. Upon these lines our saddles and packs were all laid, at the distance of five feet from each other; and each man, after grazing his horse, had it fastened with a rope or laso, to a stake driven in the ground at a little distance from his feet; thus enclosing the horses all within the square, for the convenience of securing them in case of attack or alarm. In this way we laid encamped, when we were awakened by the alarm that I have just mentioned; and our horses affrighted, dashed out of the camp, and over the heads of their masters in the desperate " *Stampedo*."

After an instant preparation for battle, and a little recovery from the fright, which was soon effected by waiting a few moments in vain, for the enemy to come on;—a general explanation took place, which brought all to our legs again, and convinced us that there was no decided obstacle, as yet, to our reaching the Camanchee towns; and after that, " sweet home," and the arms of our wives and dear little children, provided we could ever overtake and recover our horses, which had swept off in fifty directions, and with impetus enough to ensure us employment for a day or two to come.

At the proper moment for it to be made, there was a general enquiry for the cause of this *real misfortune*, when it was ascertained to have originated in the following manner. A " raw recruit," who was standing as one of the sentinels on that night, saw, as he says " he supposed," an Indian creeping out of a bunch of bushes a few paces in front of him, upon whom he levelled his rifle; and as the poor creature did not " *advance* and *give the countersign*' at his call, nor any answer at all, he " let off!" and popped a bullet through the heart of a poor dragoon horse, which had strayed away on the night before, and had faithfully followed our trail all the day, and was now, with a beastly misgiving, coming up, and slowly poking through a little thicket of bushes into camp, to join its comrades, in servitude again!

The sudden shock of a gun, and the most appalling groans of this poor dying animal, in the dead of night, and so close upon the heels of sweet sleep, created a long vibration of nerves, and a day of great perplexity and toil which followed, as we had to retrace our steps twenty miles or more, in pursuit of affrighted horses; of which some fifteen or twenty took up wild and free life upon the prairies, to which they were abandoned, as they could not be found. After a detention of two days in consequence of this disaster, we took up the line of march again, and pursued our course with vigour and success, over a continuation of green fields, enamelled with wild flowers, and pleasingly relieved with patches and groves of timber.

On the fourth day of our march, we discovered many fresh signs of buffaloes ; and at last, immense herds of them grazing on the distant hills. Indian trails were daily growing fresh, and their smokes were seen in various directions ahead of us.   And on the same day at noon, we discovered a large party at several miles distance, sitting on their horses and looking at us. From the glistening of the blades of their lances, which were blazing as they turned them in the sun, it was at first thought that they were Mexican cavalry, who might have been apprized of our approach into their country, and had advanced to contest the point with us.   On drawing a little nearer, however, and scanning them closer with our spy-glasses, they were soon ascertained to be a war-party of Camanchees, on the look out for their enemies.

The regiment was called to a halt, and the requisite preparations made and orders issued, we advanced in a direct line towards them until we had approached to within two or three miles of them, when they suddenly disappeared over the hill, and soon after shewed themselves on another mound farther off and in a different direction.   The course of the regiment was then changed, and another advance towards them was commenced, and as before, they disappeared and shewed themselves in another direction.   After several such efforts which proved ineffectual, Col. Dodge ordered the command to halt, while he rode forward with a few of his staff, and an ensign carrying a white flag. I joined this advance, and the Indians stood their ground until we had come within half a mile of them, and could distinctly observe all their numbers and movements.   We then came to a halt, and the white flag was sent a little in advance, and waved as a signal for them to approach ; at which one of their party galloped out in advance of the war-party, on a milk white horse, carrying a piece of white buffalo skin on the point of his long lance in reply to our flag.

This moment was the commencement of one of the most thrilling and beautiful scenes I ever witnessed.   All eyes, both from his own party and ours, were fixed upon the manœuvres of this gallant little fellow, and he well knew it.

The distance between the two parties was perhaps half a mile, and that a beautiful and gently sloping prairie ; over which he was for the space of a quarter of an hour, reining and spurring his maddened horse, and gradually approaching us by tacking to the right and the left, like a vessel beating against the wind.   He at length came prancing and leaping along till he met the flag of the regiment, when he leaned his spear for a moment against it, looking the bearer full in the face, when he wheeled his horse, and dashed up to Col. Dodge (PLATE 157), with his extended hand, which was instantly grasped and shaken.   We all had him by the hand in a moment, and the rest of the party seeing him received in this friendly manner, instead of being sacrificed, as they undoubtedly expected, started under " full whip" in a direct line towards us, and in a moment gathered, like a black cloud, around us ! The regiment then moved up in regular order, and a general shake of the hand ensued, which was accomplished by each warrior riding along the ranks, and shaking the hand of every one as he passed. This necessary form took up considerable time, and during the whole operation, my eyes were fixed upon the gallant and wonderful appearance of the little fellow who bore us the white flag on the point of his lance. He rode a fine and spirited wild horse, which was as white as the drifted snow, with an exuberant mane, and its long and bushy tail sweeping the ground. In his hand he tightly drew the reins upon a heavy Spanish bit, and at every jump, plunged into the animal's sides, till they were in a gore of blood, a huge pair of spurs, plundered, no doubt, from the Spaniards in their border wars, which are continually waged on the Mexican frontiers. The eyes of this noble little steed seemed to be squeezed out of its head; and its fright, and its agitation had brought out upon its skin a perspiration that was fretted into a white foam and lather. The warrior's quiver was slung on the warrior's back, and his bow grasped in his left hand, ready for instant use, if called for. His shield was on his arm, and across his thigh, in a beautiful cover of buckskin, his gun was slung—and in his right hand his lance of fourteen feet in length.

Thus armed and equipped was this dashing cavalier; and nearly in the same manner, all the rest of the party; and very many of them leading an extra horse, which we soon learned was the favourite war-horse; and from which circumstances altogether, we soon understood that they were a war-party in search of their enemy.

After a shake of the hand, we dismounted, and the pipe was lit, and passed around. And then a "talk" was held, in which we were aided by a Spaniard we luckily had with us, who could converse with one of the Camanchees, who spoke some Spanish.

Colonel Dodge explained to them the friendly motives with which we were penetrating their country—that we were sent by the President to reach their villages—to see the chiefs of the Camanchees and Pawnee Picts—to shake hands with them, and to smoke the pipe of peace, and to establish an acquaintance, and consequently a system of trade that would be beneficial to both.

They listened attentively, and perfectly appreciated; and taking Colonel Dodge at his word, relying with confidence in what he told them; they informed us that their great town was within a few days' march, and pointing in the direction—offered to abandon their war-excursion, and turn about and escort us to it, which they did in perfect good faith. We were on the march in the afternoon of that day, and from day to day they busily led us on, over hill and dale, encamping by the side of us at night, and resuming the march in the morning.

During this march, over one of the most lovely and picturesque countries in the world, we had enough continually to amuse and excite us. The whole country seemed at times to be alive with buffaloes, and bands of wild horses.

We had with us about thirty Osage and Cherokee, Seneca and Delaware Indians, employed as guides and hunters for the regiment; and with the war-party of ninety or a hundred Camanchees, we formed a most picturesque appearance while passing over the green fields, and consequently, sad havoc amongst the herds of buffaloes, which we were almost hourly passing. We were now out of the influence and reach of bread stuffs, and subsisted ourselves on buffaloes' meat altogether; and the Indians of the different tribes, emulous to shew their skill in the chase, and prove the mettle of their horses, took infinite pleasure in dashing into every herd that we approached; by which means, the regiment was abundantly supplied from day to day with fresh meat.

In one of those spirited scenes when the regiment were on the march, and the Indians with their bows and arrows were closely plying a band of these affrighted animals, they made a bolt through the line of the dragoons, and a complete breach, through which the whole herd passed, upsetting horses and riders in the most amusing manner (PLATE 158), and receiving such shots as came from those guns and pistols that were *aimed*, and not fired off into the empty air.

The buffaloes are very blind animals, and owing, probably in a great measure, to the profuse locks that hang over their eyes, they run chiefly by the nose, and follow in the tracks of each other, seemingly heedless of what is about them ; and of course, easily disposed to rush in a mass, and the whole tribe or gang to pass in the tracks of those that have first led the way.

The tract of country over which we passed, between the False Washita and this place, is stocked, not only with buffaloes, but with numerous bands of wild horses, many of which we saw every day. There is no other animal on the prairies so wild and so sagacious as the horse; and none other so difficult to come up with. So remarkably keen is their eye, that they will generally run "at the sight," when they are a mile distant; being, no doubt, able to distinguish the character of the enemy that is approaching when at that distance ; and when in motion, will seldom stop short of three or four miles. I made many attempts to approach them by stealth, when they were grazing and playing their gambols, without ever having been more than once able to succeed. In this instance, I left my horse, and with my friend Chadwick, skulked through a ravine for a couple of miles; until we were at length brought within gun-shot of a fine herd of them, when I used my pencil for some time, while we were under cover of a little hedge of bushes which effectually screened us from their view. In this herd we saw all the colours, nearly, that can be seen in a kennel of English hounds. Some were milk white, some jet black—others were sorrel, and bay, and cream colour—many were of an iron grey; and others were pied, containing a variety of colours on the same animal. Their manes were very profuse, and hanging in the wildest confusion over their necks and faces—and their long tails swept the ground (see PLATE 160).

After we had satisfied our curiosity in looking at these proud and playful animals, we agreed that we would try the experiment of "creasing" one, as it is termed in this country; which is done by shooting them through the gristle on the top of the neck, which stuns them so that they fall, and are secured with the hobbles on the feet; after which they rise again without fatal injury. This is a practice often resorted to by expert hunters, with good rifles, who are not able to take them in any other way. My friend Joe and I were armed on this occasion, each with a light fowling-piece, which have not quite the preciseness in throwing a bullet that a rifle has; and having both levelled our pieces at the withers of a noble, fine-looking iron grey, we pulled trigger, and the poor creature fell, and the rest of the herd were out of sight in a moment. We advanced speedily to him, and had the most inexpressible mortification of finding, that we never had thought of hobbles or halters, to secure him—and in a few moments more, had the still greater mortification, and even anguish, to find that one of our shots had broken the poor creature's neck, and that he was quite dead.

The laments of poor Chadwick for the wicked folly of destroying this noble animal, were such as I never shall forget; and so guilty did we feel that we agreed that when we joined the regiment, we should boast of all the rest of our hunting feats, but never make mention of this.

The usual mode of taking the wild horses, is, by throwing the *laso*, whilst pursuing them at full speed (PLATE 161), and dropping a noose over their necks, by which their speed is soon checked, and they are "choked down." The laso is a thong of rawhide, some ten or fifteen yards in length, twisted or braided, with a noose fixed at the end of it; which, when the coil of the laso is thrown out, drops with great certainty over the neck of the animal, which is soon conquered.

The Indian, when he starts for a wild horse, mounts one of the fleetest he can get, and coiling his laso on his arm, starts off under the "full whip," till he can enter the band, when he soon gets it over the neck of one of the number; when he instantly dismounts, leaving his own horse, and runs as fast as he can, letting the laso pass out gradually and carefully through his hands, until the horse falls for want of breath, and lies helpless on the ground; at which time the Indian advances slowly towards the horse's head, keeping his laso tight upon its neck, until he fastens a pair of hobbles on the animal's two forefeet, and also loosens the laso (giving the horse chance to breathe), and gives it a noose around the under jaw, by which he gets great power over the affrighted animal, which is rearing and plunging when it gets breath; and by which, as he advances, hand over hand, towards the horse's nose (PLATE 162), he is able to hold it down and prevent it from throwing itself over on its back, at the hazard of its limbs. By this means e gradually advances, until he is able to place his hand on the animal's nose, and over its eyes; and at length to breathe in its nostrils, when it soon becomes docile and conquered; so that he has little else to do than to remove the hobbles from its feet, and lead or ride it into camp.

161

162

This "breaking down" or taming, however, is not without the most desperate trial on the part of the horse, which rears and plunges in every possible way to effect its escape, until its power is exhausted, and it becomes covered with foam; and at last yields to the power of man, and becomes his willing slave for the rest of its life. By this very rigid treatment, the poor animal seems to be so completely conquered, that it makes no further struggle for its freedom; but submits quietly ever after, and is led or rode away with very little difficulty. Great care is taken, however, in this and in subsequent treatment, not to subdue the spirit of the animal, which is carefully preserved and kept up, although they use them with great severity; being, generally speaking, cruel masters.

The wild horse of these regions is a small, but very powerful animal; with an exceedingly prominent eye, sharp nose, high nostril, small feet and delicate leg; and undoubtedly, have sprung from a stock introduced by the Spaniards, at the time of the invasion of Mexico; which having strayed off upon the prairies, have run wild, and stocked the plains from this to Lake Winnepeg, two or three thousand miles to the North.*

This useful animal has been of great service to the Indians living on these vast plains, enabling them to take their game more easily, to carry their burthens, &c.; and no doubt, render them better and handier service than if they were of a larger and heavier breed. Vast numbers of them are also killed for food by the Indians, at seasons when buffaloes and other game are scarce. They subsist themselves both in winter and summer by biting at the grass, which they can always get in sufficient quantities for their food.

Whilst on our march we met with many droves of these beautiful animals, and several times had the opportunity of seeing the Indians pursue them, and take them with the laso. The first successful instance of the kind was effected by one of our guides and hunters, by the name of Beatte, a Frenchman, whose parents had lived nearly their whole lives in the Osage village; and who, himself had been reared from infancy amongst them; and in a continual life of Indian modes and amusements, had acquired all the skill and tact of his Indian teachers, and probably a little more; for he is reputed, without exception, the best hunter in these Western regions.

This instance took place one day whilst the regiment was at its usual halt of an hour, in the middle of the day.

When the bugle sounded for a halt, and all were dismounted, Beatte and several others of the hunters asked permission of Col. Dodge to pursue a drove of horses which were then in sight, at a distance of a mile or more from us. The permission was given, and they started off, and by following

* There are many very curious traditions about the first appearance of horses amongst the different tribes, and many of which bear striking proof of the above fact. Most of the tribes have some story about the first appearance of horses; and amongst the Sioux, they have beautifully recorded the fact, by giving it the name of Shonka-wakon (the medicine-dog).

a ravine, approached near to the unsuspecting animals, when they broke upon them and pursued them for several miles in full view of the regiment. Several of us had good glasses, with which we could plainly see every movement and every manœuvre. After a race of two or three miles, Beatte was seen with his wild horse down, and the band and the other hunters rapidly leaving him.

Seeing him in this condition, I galloped off to him as rapidly as possible, and had the satisfaction of seeing the whole operation of " breaking down," and bringing in the wild animal; and in PLATE 162, I have given a fair representation of the mode by which it was done. When he had conquered the horse in this way, his brother, who was one of the unsuccessful ones in the chase, came riding back, and leading up the horse of Beatte which he had left behind, and after staying with us a few minutes, assisted Beatte in leading his conquered wild horse towards the regiment, where it was satisfactorily examined and commented upon, as it was trembling and covered with white foam, until the bugle sounded the signal for marching, when all mounted; and with the rest, Beatte, astride of his wild horse, which had a buffalo skin girted on its back, and a halter, with a cruel noose around the under jaw. In this manner the command resumed its march, and Beatte astride of his wild horse, on which he rode quietly and without difficulty, until night; the whole thing, the capture, and breaking, all having been accomplished within the space of one hour, our usual and daily halt at midday.

Several others of these animals were caught in a similar manner during our march, by others of our hunters, affording us satisfactory instances of this most extraordinary and almost unaccountable feat.

The horses that were caught were by no means very valuable specimens, being rather of an ordinary quality; and I saw to my perfect satisfaction, that the finest of these droves can never be obtained in this way, as they take the lead at once, when they are pursued, and in a few moments will be seen half a mile or more ahead of the bulk of the drove, which they are leading off. There is not a doubt but there are many very fine and valuable horses amongst these herds; but it is impossible for the Indian or other hunter to take them, unless it be done by " creasing" them, as I have before described; which is often done, but always destroys the spirit and character of the animal.

After many hard and tedious days of travel, we were at last told by our Camanchee guides that we were near their village; and having led us to the top of a gently rising elevation on the prairie, they pointed to their village at several miles distance, in the midst of one of the most enchanting valleys that human eyes ever looked upon. The general course of the valley is from N. W. to S. E., of several miles in width, with a magnificent range of mountains rising in distance beyond; it being, without doubt, a huge " spur" of the Rocky Mountains, composed entirely of a reddish granite or gneis

corresponding with the other links of this stupendous chain. In the midst
of this lovely valley, we could just discern amongst the scattering shrubbery
that lined the banks of the watercourses, the tops of the Camanchee wigwams, and the smoke curling above them. The valley, for a mile distant
about the village, seemed speckled with horses and mules that were grazing
in it. The chiefs of the war-party requested the regiment to halt, until they
could ride in, and inform their people who were coming. We then dismounted for an hour or so; when we could see them busily running and
catching their horses; and at length, several hundreds of their braves and
warriors came out at full speed to welcome us, and forming in a line in front
of us, as we were again mounted, presented a formidable and pleasing appearance (PLATE 163). As they wheeled their horses, they very rapidly
formed in a line, and " dressed" like well-disciplined cavalry. The regiment
was drawn up in three columns, with a line formed in front, by Colonel
Dodge and his staff, in which rank my friend Chadwick and I were also
paraded; when we had a fine view of the whole manœuvre, which was picturesque and thrilling in the extreme.

In the centre of our advance was stationed a white flag, and the Indians
answered to it with one which they sent forward and planted by the side of it.*

The two lines were thus drawn up, face to face, within twenty or thirty
yards of each other, as inveterate foes that never had met; and, to the everlasting credit of the Camanchees, whom the world had always looked upon
as murderous and hostile, they had all come out in this manner, with their
heads uncovered, and without a weapon of any kind, to meet a war-party
bristling with arms, and trespassing to the middle of their country. They
had every reason to look upon us as their natural enemy, as they have been
in the habit of estimating all pale faces; and yet, instead of arms or defences,
or even of frowns, they galloped out and looked us in our faces, without an
expression of fear or dismay, and evidently with expressions of joy and impatient pleasure, to shake us by the hand, on the bare assertion of Colonel
Dodge, which had been made to the chiefs, that " we came to see them on
a friendly visit.

After we had sat and gazed at each other in this way for some half an
hour or so, the head chief of the band came galloping up to Colonel Dodge,
and having shaken him by the hand, he passed on to the other officers in
turn, and then rode alongside of the different columns, shaking hands with
every dragoon in the regiment; he was followed in this by his principal

---

* It is a fact which I deem to be worth noting here, that amongst all Indian tribes, that
I have yet visited, in their primitive, as well as improved state, the *white flag* is used as a
flag of truce, as it is in the civilized parts of the world, and held to be sacred and inviolable.
The chief going to war always carries it in some form or other, generally of a piece of white
skin or bark, rolled on a small stick, and carried under his dress, or otherwise; and also a
red flag, either to be unfurled when occasion requires the *white flag* as a truce, and the red
one for battle, or, as they say, " for blood."

chiefs and braves, which altogether took up nearly an hour longer, when the Indians retreated slowly towards their village, escorting us to the banks of a fine clear stream, and a good spring of fresh water, half a mile from their village, which they designated as a suitable place for our encampment, and we were soon bivouacked at the place from which I am now scribbling.

No sooner were we encamped here (or, in other words, as soon as our things were thrown upon the ground,) Major Mason, Lieutenant Wheelock, Captain Brown, Captain Duncan, my friend Chadwick and myself, galloped off to the village, and through it in the greatest impatience to the prairies, where there were at least three thousand horses and mules grazing; all of us eager and impatient to see and to appropriate the splendid *Arabian horses*, which we had so often heard were owned by the Camanchee warriors. We galloped around busily, and glanced our eyes rapidly over them ; and all soon returned to the camp, quite "crest fallen" and satisfied, that, although there were some tolerable nags amongst this medley group of all colours and all shapes, the beautiful Arabian we had so often heard of at the East, as belonging to the Camanchees, must either be a great ways further South than this, or else it must be a *horse of the imagination.*

The Camanchee horses are generally small, all of them being of the wild breed, and a very tough and serviceable animal; and from what I can learn here of the chiefs, there are yet, farther South, and nearer the Mexican borders, some of the noblest animals in use of the chiefs, yet I do not know that we have any more reason to rely upon this information, than that which had made our horse-jockeys that we have with us, to run almost crazy for the possession of those we were to find at this place. Amongst the immense herds we found grazing here, one-third perhaps are mules, which are much more valuable than the horses.

Of the horses, the officers and men have purchased a number of the best, by giving a very inferior blanket and butcher's knife, costing in all about four dollars ! These horses in our cities at the East, independent of the name, putting them upon their merits alone, would be worth from eighty to one hundred dollars each, and not more.

A vast many of such could be bought on such terms, and are hourly brought into camp for sale. If we had goods to trade for them, and means of getting them home, a great profit could be made, which can easily be learned from the following transaction that took place yesterday. A fine look-ing Indian was hanging about my tent very closely for several days, and con-tinually scanning an old and half-worn cotton umbrella, which I carried over me to keep off the sun, as I was suffering with fever and ague, and at last proposed to purchase it of me, with a very neat limbed and pretty pied horse which he was riding. He proposed at first, that I should give him a knife and the umbrella, but as I was not disposed for the trade (the umbrella being so useful an article to me, that I did not know how to part with it, not knowing whether there was another in the regiment) ; he came a second time, and

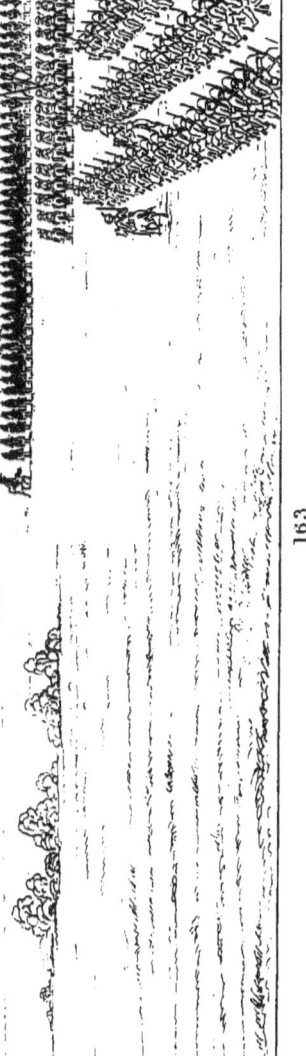

163

G. Cailan

offered me the horse for the umbrella alone, which offer I still rejected; and he went back to the village, and soon returned with another horse of a much better quality, supposing that I had not valued the former one equal to the umbrella.

With this he endeavoured to push the trade, and after I had with great difficulty made him understand that I was sick, and could not part with it, he turned and rode back towards the village, and in a short time returned again with one of the largest and finest mules I ever saw, proposing that, which I also rejected; when he *disappeared* again.

In a few moments my friend Captain Duncan, in whose hospitable tent I was quartered, came in, and the circumstance being related to him, started up some warm jockey feelings, which he was thoroughly possessed of, when he instantly sprang upon his feet, and exclaimed, " d———mn the fellow! where is he gone? here, Gosset! get my old umbrella out of the pack, I rolled it up with my *wiper* and the *frying-pan*—get it as quick as lightning!" with it in his hand, the worthy Captain soon overtook the young man, and escorted him into the village, and returned in a short time—not with the mule, but with the second horse that had been offered to me.

LETTER—No. 42.

GREAT CAMANCHEE VILLAGE.

THE village of the Camanchees by the side of which we are encamped, is composed of six or eight hundred skin-covered lodges, made of poles and buffalo skins, in the manner precisely as those of the Sioux and other Missouri tribes, of which I have heretofore given some account. This village with its thousands of wild inmates, with horses and dogs, and wild sports and domestic occupations, presents a most curious scene; and the manners and looks of the people, a rich subject for the brush and the pen.

In the view I have made of it (PLATE 164), but a small portion of the village is shewn; which is as well as to shew the whole of it, inasmuch as the wigwams, as well as the customs, are the same in every part of it. In the foreground is seen the wigwam of the chief; and in various parts, crotches and poles, on which the women are drying meat, and "*graining*" buffalo robes. These people, living in a country where buffaloes are abundant, make their wigwams more easily of their skins, than of anything else; and with them find greater facilities of moving about, as circumstances often require; when they drag them upon the poles attached to their horses, and erect them again with little trouble in their new residence.

We white men, strolling about amongst their wigwams, are looked upon with as much curiosity as if we had come from the moon; and evidently create a sort of chill in the blood of children and dogs, when we make our appearance. I was pleased to-day with the simplicity of a group which came out in front of the chief's lodge to scrutinize my faithful friend Chadwick and I, as we were strolling about the avenues and labyrinths of their village; upon which I took out my book and sketched as quick as lightning, whilst "Joe" rivetted their attention by some ingenious trick or other, over my shoulders, which I did not see, having no time to turn my head (PLATE 165). These were the juvenile parts of the chief's family, and all who at this moment were at home; the venerable old man, and his three or four wives, making a visit, like hundreds of others, to the encampment.

In speaking just above, of the mode of moving their wigwams, and changing their encampments, I should have said a little more, and should also have given to the reader, a sketch of one of these extraordinary scenes, which I have had the good luck to witness (PLATE 166); where several thousands

were on the march, and furnishing one of those laughable scenes which daily happen, where so many dogs, and so many squaws, are travelling in such a confused mass; with so many conflicting interests, and so many local and individual rights to be pertinaciously claimed and protected. Each horse drags his load, and each dog, *i. e.* each dog that *will* do it (and there are many that will *not*), also dragging his wallet on a couple of poles; and each squaw with her load, and all together (notwithstanding their burthens) cherishing their pugnacious feelings, which often bring them into general conflict, commencing usually amongst the dogs, and sure to result in fisti-cuffs of the women; whilst the men, riding leisurely on the right or the left, take infinite pleasure in overlooking these desperate conflicts, at which they are sure to have a laugh, and in which, as sure never to lend a hand.

The Camanchees, like the Northern tribes, have many games, and in pleasant weather seem to be continually practicing more or less of them, on the prairies, back of, and contiguous to, their village.

In their ball-plays, and some other games, they are far behind the Sioux and others of the Northern tribes; but, in racing horses and riding, they are not equalled by any other Indians on the Continent. Racing horses, it would seem, is a constant and almost incessant exercise, and their principal mode of gambling; and perhaps, a more finished set of jockeys are not to be found. The exercise of these people, in a country where horses are so abundant, and the country so fine for riding, is chiefly done on horseback; and it " stands to reason," that such a people, who have been practicing from their childhood, should become exceedingly expert in this wholesome and beautiful exercise. Amongst their feats of riding, there is one that has astonished me more than anything of the kind I have ever seen, or expect to see, in my life :—a stratagem of war, learned and practiced by every young man in the tribe; by which he is able to drop his body upon the side of his horse at the instant he is passing, effectually screened from his enemies' weapons (PLATE 167) as he lays in a horizontal position behind the body of his horse, with his heel hanging over the horses back; by which he has the power of throwing himself up again, and changing to the other side of the horse if necessary. In this wonderful condition, he will hang whilst his horse is at fullest speed, carrying with him his bow and his shield, and also his long lance of fourteen feet in length, all or either of which he will wield upon his enemy as he passes; rising and throwing his arrows over the horse's back, or with equal ease and equal success under the horse's neck.* This astonishing feat which the young men have been repeatedly playing off to our surprise as well as amusement, whilst they have

* Since writing the above, I have conversed with some of the young men of the Paw-nees, who practice the same feat, and who told me they could throw the arrow from under the horse's belly, and elevate it upon an enemy with deadly effect!

This feat I did not see performed, but from what I did see, I feel inclined to believe that these young men were boasting of no more than they were able to perform.

been galloping about in front of our tents, completely puzzled the whole of us; and appeared to be the result of magic, rather than of skill acquired by practice. · I had several times great curiosity to approach them, to ascertain by what means their bodies could be suspended in this manner, where nothing could be seen but the heel hanging over the horse's back. In these endeavours I was continually frustrated, until one day I coaxed a young fellow up within a little distance of me, by offering him a few plugs of tobacco, and he in a moment solved the difficulty, so far as to render it apparently more feasible than before; yet leaving it one of the most extraordinary results of practice and persevering endeavours. I found on examination, that a short hair halter was passed around under the neck of the horse, and both ends tightly braided into the mane, on the withers, leaving a loop to hang under the neck, and against the breast, which, being caught up in the hand, makes a sling into which the elbow falls, taking the weight of the body on the middle of the upper arm. Into this loop the rider drops suddenly and fearlessly, leaving his heel to hang over the back of the horse, to steady him, and also to restore him when he wishes to regain his upright position on the horse's back.

Besides this wonderful art, these people have several other feats of horsemanship, which they are continually showing off; which are pleasing and extraordinary, and of which they seem very proud. A people who spend so very great a part of their lives, actually on their horses' backs, must needs become exceedingly expert in every thing that pertains to riding—to war, or to the chase; and I am ready, without hesitation, to pronounce the Camanchees the most extraordinary horsemen that I have seen yet in all my travels, and I doubt very much whether any people in the world can surpass them.

The Camanchees are in stature, rather low, and in person, often approaching to corpulency. In their movements, they are heavy and ungraceful; and on their feet, one of the most unattractive and slovenly-looking races of Indians that I have ever seen; but the moment they mount their horses, they seem at once metamorphosed, and surprise the spectator with the ease and elegance of their movements. A Camanchee on his feet is out of his element, and comparatively almost as awkward as a monkey on the ground, without a limb or a branch to cling to; but the moment he lays his hand upon his horse, his *face*, even, becomes handsome, and he gracefully flies away like a different being.

Our encampment is surrounded by continual swarms of old and young—of middle aged—of male and female—of dogs, and every moving thing that constitutes their community; and our tents are lined with the chiefs and other worthies of the tribe. So it will be seen there is no difficulty of getting subjects enough for my brush, as well as for my pen, whilst residing in this place.

The head chief of this village, who is represented to us here, as the head of the nation, is a mild and pleasant looking gentleman, without anything striking or peculiar in his looks (PLATE 168); dressed in a very humble

168   169

170   171

manner, with very few ornaments upon him, and his hair carelessly falling about his face, and over his shoulders. The name of this chief is Ee-shah-ko-nee (the bow and quiver). The only ornaments to be seen about him were a couple of beautiful shells worn in his ears, and a boar's tusk attached to his neck, and worn on his breast.

For several days after we arrived at this place, there was a huge mass of flesh (PLATE 169), Ta-wah-que-nah (the mountain of rocks), who was put forward as head chief of the tribe; and all honours were being paid to him by the regiment of dragoons, until the above-mentioned chief arrived from the country, where it seems he was leading a war-party; and had been sent for, no doubt, on the occasion. When he arrived, this huge monster, who is the largest and fattest Indian I ever saw, stepped quite into the background, giving way to this admitted chief, who seemed to have the confidence and respect of the whole tribe.

This enormous man, whose flesh would undoubtedly weigh three hundred pounds or more, took the most wonderful strides in the exercise of his temporary authority; which, in all probability, he was lawfully exercising in the absence of his superior, as second chief of the tribe.

A perfect personation of Jack Falstaff, in size and in figure, with an African face, and a beard on his chin of two or three inches in length. His name, he tells me, he got from having conducted a large party of Camanchees through a secret and subterraneous passage, entirely through the mountain of granite rocks, which lies back of their village; thereby saving their lives from their more powerful enemy, who had "cornered them up" in such a way, that there was no other possible mode for their escape. The mountain under which he conducted them, is called *Ta-wah-que-nah* (the mountain of rocks), and from this he has received his name, which would certainly have been far more appropriate if it had been a *mountain of flesh*.

Corpulency is a thing exceedingly rare to be found in any of the tribes, amongst the men, owing, probably, to the exposed and active sort of lives they lead; and that in the absence of all the spices of life, many of which have their effect in producing this disgusting, as well as unhandy and awkward extravagance in civilized society.

Ish-a-ro-yeh (he who carries a wolf, PLATE 170); and Is-sa-wah-tam-ah (the wolf tied with hair, PLATE 171); are also chiefs of some standing in the tribe, and evidently men of great influence, as they were put forward by the head chiefs, for their likenesses to be painted in turn, after their own. The first of the two seemed to be the leader of the war-party which we met, and of which I have spoken; and in escorting us to their village, this man took the lead and piloted us the whole way, in consequence of which Colonel Dodge presented him a very fine gun.

His-oo-san-ches (the Spaniard, PLATE 172), a gallant little fellow, is represented to us as one of the leading warriors of the tribe; and no doubt is one of the most extraordinary men at present living in these regions.

He is half Spanish, and being a half-breed, for whom they generally have the most contemptuous feelings, he has been all his life thrown into the front of battle and danger; at which posts he has signalized himself, and commanded the highest admiration and respect of the tribe, for his daring and adventurous career. This is the man of whom I have before spoken, who dashed out so boldly from the war-party, and came to us with the white flag raised on the point of his lance, and of whom I have made a sketch in PLATE 157. I have here represented him as he stood for me, with his shield on his arm, with his quiver slung, and his lance of fourteen feet in length in his right hand. This extraordinary little man, whose figure was light, seemed to be all bone and muscle, and exhibited immense power, by the curve of the bones in his legs and his arms. We had many exhibitions of his extraordinary strength, as well as agility; and of his gentlemanly politeness and friendship, we had as frequent evidences. As an instance of this, I will recite an occurrence which took place but a few days since, when we were moving our encampment to a more desirable ground on another side of their village. We had a deep and powerful stream to ford, when we had several men who were sick, and obliged to be carried on litters. My friend "Joe" and I came up in the rear of the regiment, where the litters with the sick were passing, and we found this little fellow up to his chin in the muddy water, wading and carrying one end of each litter on his head, as they were in turn, passed over. After they had all passed, this gallant little fellow beckoned to me to dismount, and take a seat on his shoulders, which I declined; preferring to stick to my horse's back, which I did, as he took it by the bridle and conducted it through the shallowest ford. When I was across, I took from my belt a handsome knife and presented it to him, which seemed to please him very much.

Besides the above-named chiefs and warriors, I painted the portrait of *Kots-o-ko-ro-ko* (the hair of the bull's neck); and *Hah-nee* (the beaver); the first, a chief, and the second, a warrior of terrible aspect, and also of considerable distinction. These and many other paintings, as well as manufactures from this tribe, may be always seen in my MUSEUM, if I have the good luck to get them safe home from this wild and remote region.

From what I have already seen of the Camanchees, I am fully convinced that they are a numerous and very powerful tribe, and quite equal in numbers and prowess, to the accounts generally given of them.

It is entirely impossible at present to make a correct estimate of their numbers; but taking their own account of villages they point to in such numbers, South of the banks of the Red River, as well as those that lie farther West, and undoubtedly North of its banks, they must be a very numerous tribe; and I think I am able to say, from estimates that these chiefs have made me, that they number some 30 or 40,000—being able to shew some 6 or 7000 warriors, well-mounted and well-armed. This estimate I offer not as conclusive, for so little is as yet known of these people, that

no estimate can be implicitly relied upon other than that, which, in general terms, pronounces them to be a very numerous and warlike tribe

We shall learn much more of them before we get out of their country ; and I trust that it will yet be in my power to give something like a fair census of them before we have done with them.

They speak much of their allies and friends, the Pawnee Picts, living to the West some three or four days' march, whom we are going to visit in a few days, and afterwards return to this village, and then "bend our course" homeward, or, in other words, back to Fort Gibson. Besides the Pawnee Picts, there are the Kiowas and Wicos; small tribes that live in the same vicinity, and also in the same alliance, whom we shall probably see on our march. Every preparation is now making to be off in a few days—and I shall omit further remarks on the Camanchees, until we return, when I shall probably have much more to relate of them and their customs. So many of the men and officers are getting sick, that the little command will be very much crippled, from the necessity we shall be under, of leaving about thirty sick, and about an equal number of well to take care of and protect them; for which purpose, we are constructing a fort, with a sort of breast-work of timbers and bushes, which will be ready in a day or two; and the sound part of the command prepared to start with several Camanchee leaders, who have agreed to pilot the way.

LETTER—No. 43.

THE above Letter it will be seen, was written some time ago, and when all hands (save those who were too sick) were on the start for the Pawnee village. Amongst those exceptions was I, before the hour of starting arrived; and as the dragoons have made their visit there and returned in a most jaded condition, and I have again got well enough to write, I will render some account of the excursion, which is from the pen and the pencil of my friend Joe, who went with them and took my sketch and note-books in his pocket.

" We were four days travelling over a beautiful country, most of the way prairie, and generally along near the base of a stupendous range of mountains of reddish granite, in many places piled up to an immense height without tree or shrubbery on them; looking as if they had actually dropped from the clouds in such a confused mass, and all lay where they had fallen. Such we found the mountains enclosing the Pawnee village, on the bank of Red River, about ninety miles from the Camanchee town. The dragoon regiment was drawn up within half a mile or so of this village, and encamped in a square, where we remained three days. We found here a very numerous village, containing some five or six hundred wigwams, all made of long prairie grass, thatched over poles which are fastened in the ground and bent in at the top; giving to them, in distance, the appearance of straw beehives as in PLATE 173, which is an accurate view of it, shewing the Red River in front, and the *" mountains of rocks"* behind it.

" To our very great surprise, we have found these people cultivating quite extensive fields of corn (maize), pumpkins, melons, beans and squashes; so, with these aids, and an abundant supply of buffalo meat, they may be said to be living very well.

" The next day after our arrival here, Colonel Dodge opened a council with the chiefs, in the chief's lodge, where he had the most of his officers around him. He first explained to them the friendly views with which he came to see them; and of the wish of our Government to establish a lasting peace with them, which they seemed at once to appreciate and highly to estimate.

. " The head chief of the tribe is a very old man, and he several times replied

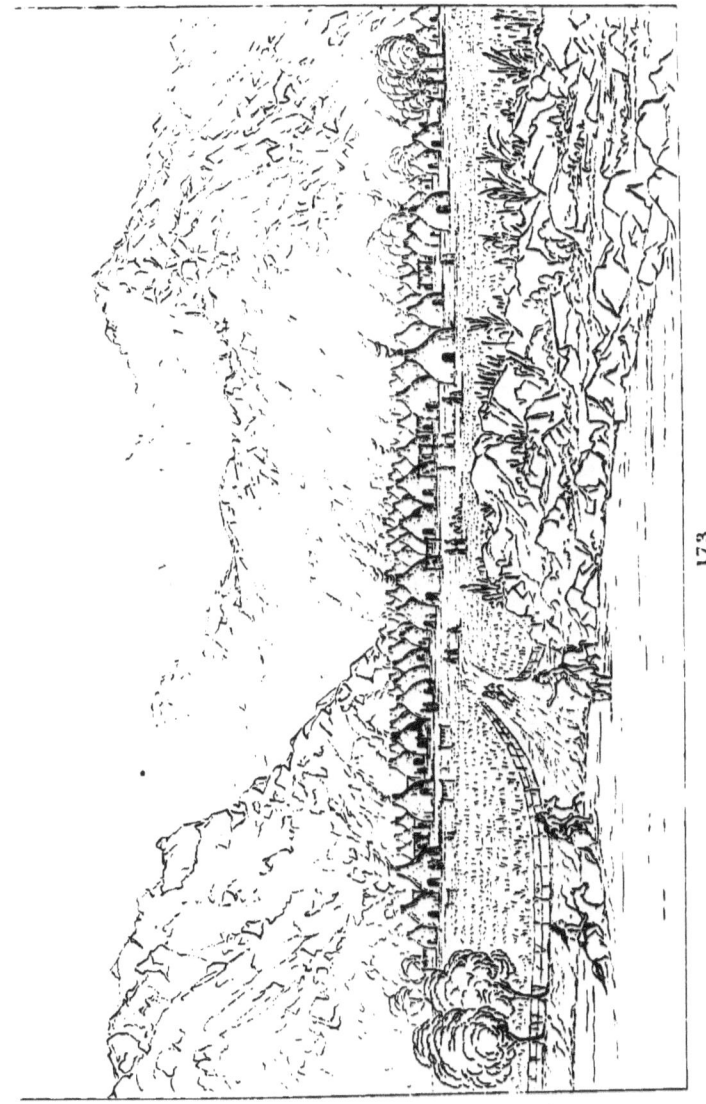

173

to Colonel Dodge in a very eloquent manner; assuring him of the friendly feelings of his chiefs and warriors towards the pale faces, in the direction from whence we came.

"After Colonel Dodge had explained in general terms, the objects of our visit, he told them that he should expect from them some account of the foul murder of Judge Martin and his family on the False Washita, which had been perpetrated but a few weeks before, and which the Camanchees had told us was done by the Pawnee Picts. The Colonel told them, also, that he learned from the Camanchees, that they had the little boy, the son of the murdered gentleman, in their possession; and that he should expect them to deliver him up, as an indispensable condition of the friendly arrangement that was now making. They positively denied the fact, and all knowledge of it; firmly assuring us that they knew nothing of the murder, or of the boy. The demand was repeatedly made, and as often denied; until at length a negro-man was discovered, who was living with the Pawnees, who spoke good English; and coming into the council-house, gave information that such a boy had recently been brought into their village, and was now a prisoner amongst them. This excited great surprise and indignation in the council, and Colonel Dodge then informed the chiefs that the council would rest here; and certainly nothing further of a peaceable nature would transpire until the boy was brought in. In this alarming dilemma, all remained in gloomy silence for awhile; when Colonel Dodge further informed the chiefs, that as an evidence of his friendly intentions towards them, he had, on starting, purchased at a very great price, from their enemies the Osages, two Pawnee (and one Kiowa) girls; which had been held by them for some years as prisoners, and which he had brought the whole way home, and had here ready to be delivered to their friends and relations; but whom he certainly would never show, until the little boy was produced. He also made another demand, which was for the restoration of an United States ranger, by the name of Abbé, who had been captured by them during the summer before. They acknowledged the seizure of this man, and all solemnly declared that he had been taken by a party of the Camanchees, over whom they had no controul, and carried beyond the Red River into the Mexican provinces, where he was put to death. They held a long consultation about the boy, and seeing their plans defeated by the evidence of the negro; and also being convinced of the friendly disposition of the Colonel, by bringing home their prisoners from the Osages, they sent out and had the boy brought in, from the middle of a corn-field, where he had been secreted. He is a smart and very intelligent boy of nine years of age, and when he came in, he was entirely naked, as they keep their own boys of that age. There was a great excitement in the council when the little fellow was brought in; and as he passed amongst them, he looked around and exclaimed with some surprise, "What! are there white men here?" to which Colonel Dodge replied, and asked his name; and he promptly answered, "my name is Matthew Wright Martin."

He was then received into Colonel Dodge's arms; and an order was immediately given for the Pawnee and Kiowa girls to be brought forward; they were in a few minutes brought into the council-house, when they were at once recognized by their friends and relatives, who embraced them with the most extravagant expressions of joy and satisfaction. The heart of the venerable old chief was melted at this evidence of white man's friendship, and he rose upon his feet, and taking Colonel Dodge in his arms, and placing his left cheek against the left cheek of the Colonel, held him for some minutes without saying a word, whilst tears were flowing from his eyes. He then embraced each officer in turn, in the same silent and affectionate manner; which form took half an hour or more, before it was completed.*

" From this moment the council, which before had been a very grave and uncertain one, took a pleasing and friendly turn. And this excellent old man ordered the women to supply the dragoons with something to eat, as they were hungry.

" The little encampment, which heretofore was in a woeful condition, having eaten up their last rations twelve hours before, were now gladdened by the approach of a number of women, who brought their " back loads" of dried buffalo meat and green corn, and threw it down amongst them. This seemed almost like a providential deliverance, for the country between here and the Camanchees, was entirely destitute of game, and our last provisions were consumed.

" The council thus proceeded successfully and pleasantly for several days, whilst the warriors of the Kiowas and Wicos, two adjoining and friendly tribes living further to the West, were arriving; and also a great many from other bands of the Camanchees, who had heard of our arrival; until two thousand or more of these wild and fearless-looking fellows were assembled, and all, from their horses' backs, with weapons in hand, were looking into our pitiful little encampment, of two hundred men, all in a state of dependence and almost literal starvation; and at the same time nearly one half the number too sick to have made a successful resistance if we were to have been attacked."

* * * * * * * * * * *

The command returned to this village after an absence of fifteen days, in a fatigued and destitute condition, with scarcely anything to eat, or chance of getting anything here; in consequence of which, Colonel Dodge almost instantly ordered preparations to be made for a move to the head of the Canadian river, a distance of an hundred or more miles, where the Indians represented to us there would be found immense herds of buffaloes; a place where we could get enough to eat, and by lying by awhile, could restore the sick, who are now occupying a great number of litters. Some days have

---

* The little boy of whom I have spoken, was brought in the whole distance to Fort Gibson, in the arms of the dragoons, who took turns in carrying him; and after the command arrived there, he was transmitted to the Red River, by an officer, who had the enviable satisfaction of delivering him into the arms of his disconsolate and half-distracted mother.

174   175

176   177

178   179

180   181

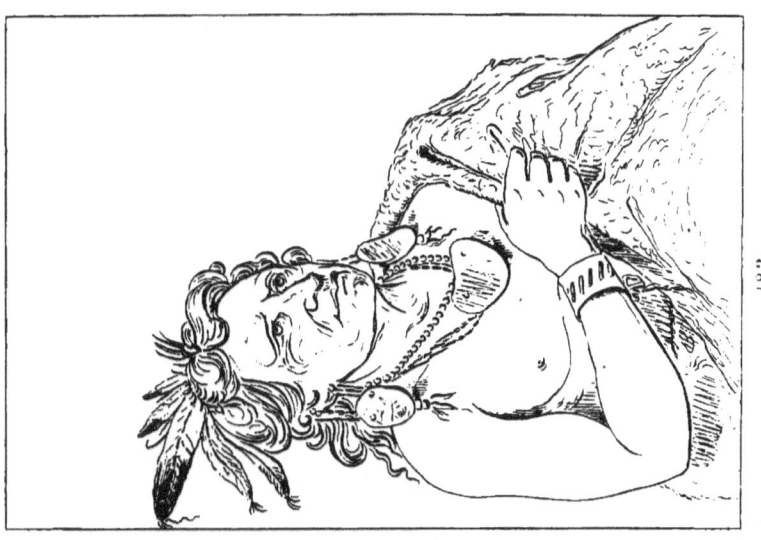

183

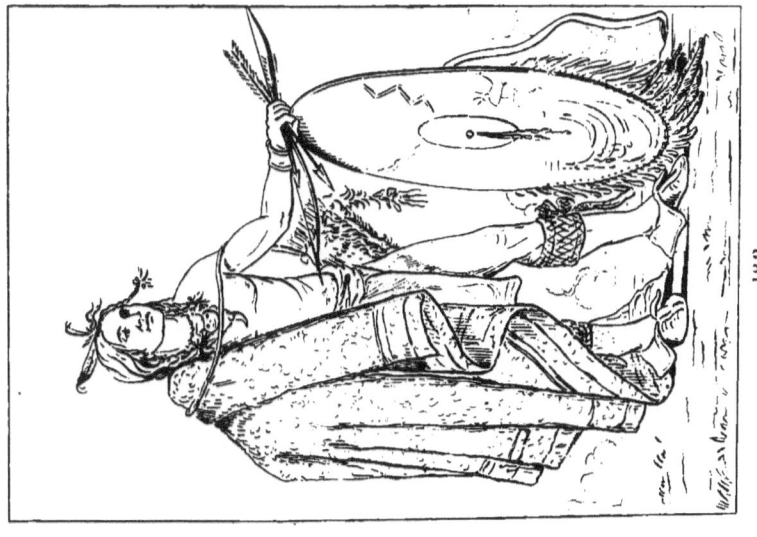

182

elapsed, however, and we are not quite ready for the start yet. And during that time, continual parties of the Pawnee Picts and Kioways have come up; and also Camanchees, from other villages, to get a look at us, and many of them are volunteering to go in with us to the frontier.

The world who know me, will see that I can scarcely be idle under such circumstances as these, where so many subjects for my brush and my pen are gathering about me.

The Pawnee Picts, Kioways, and Wicos are the subjects that I am most closely scanning at this moment, and I have materials enough around me.

The Pawnee Picts are undoubtedly a numerous and powerful tribe, occupying, with the Kioways and Wicos, the whole country on the head waters of the Red River, and quite into and through the southern part of the Rocky Mountains. The old chief told me by signs, enumerating with his hands and fingers, that they had altogether three thousand warriors; which if true, estimating according to the usual rule, one warrior to four, would make the whole number about twelve thousand; and, allowing a fair per-centage for boasting or bragging, of which they are generally a little guilty in such cases, there would be at a fair calculation from eight to ten thousand. These then, in an established alliance with the great tribe of Camanchees, hunting and feasting together, and ready to join in common defence of their country become a very formidable enemy when attacked on their own ground.

The name of the Pawnee Picts, we find to be in their own language, Towee-ahge, the meaning of which I have not yet learned. I have ascertained also, that these people are in no way related to the Pawnees of the Platte, who reside a thousand miles or more North of them, and know them only as enemies. There is no family or tribal resemblance; nor any in their language or customs. The Pawnees of the Platte shave the head, and the Pawnee Picts abominate the custom; allowing their hair to grow like the Camanchees and other tribes.

The old chief of the Pawnee Picts, of whom I have before spoken, and whose name is We-ta-ra-sha-ro (PLATE 174), is undoubtedly a very excellent and kind-hearted old man, of ninety or more years of age, and has consented to accompany us, with a large party of his people, to Fort Gibson; where Colonel Dodge has promised to return him liberal presents from the Government, for the friendship he has evinced on the present occasion.

The second chief of this tribe, Sky-se-ro-ka (PLATE 175), we found to be a remarkably clever man, and much approved and valued in his tribe.

The Pawnee Picts, as well as the Camanchees, are generally a very clumsy and ordinary looking set of men, when on their feet; but being fine horsemen, are equally improved in appearance as soon as they mount upon their horses' backs.

Amongst the women of this tribe, there were many that were exceedingly pretty in feature and in form; and also in expression, though their skins are very dark. The dress of the men in this tribe, as amongst the Camanchees, consists generally in leggings of dressed skins, and moccasins; with a flap or breech clout, made also of dressed skins or furs, and often very beautifully ornamented with shells, &c. Above the waist they seldom wear any drapery, owing to the warmth of the climate, which will rarely justify it; and their heads are generally uncovered with a head-dress, like the Northern tribes who live in a colder climate, and actually require them for comfort.

The women of the Camanchees and Pawnee Picts, are always decently and comfortably clad, being covered generally with a gown or slip, that reaches from the chin quite down to the ancles, made of deer or elk skins; often garnished very prettily, and ornamented with long fringes of elk's teeth, which are fastened on them in rows, and more highly valued than any other ornament they can put upon them.

In plates 176 and 177, I have given the portraits of two Pawnee girls, Kah-kee-tsee (the thighs), and She-de-a (wild sage), the two Pawnee women who had been held as prisoners by the Osages, and purchased by the Indian Commissioner, the Reverend Mr. Schemmerhom, and brought home to their own people, and delivered up in the Pawnee town, in the manner that I have just described.

The Kioways are a much finer looking race of men, than either the Camanchees or Pawnees—are tall and erect, with an easy and graceful gait— with long hair, cultivated oftentimes so as to reach nearly to the ground. They have generally the fine and Roman outline of head, that is so frequently found at the North,—and decidedly distinct from that of the Camanchees and Pawnee Picts. These men speak a language distinct from both of the others; and in fact, the Camanchees and Pawnee Picts—and Kioways, and Wicos, are all so distinctly different in their languages, as to appear in that respect as total strangers to each other.*

The head chief of the Kioways, whose name is Teh-toot-sah (plate 178), we found to be a very gentlemanly and high minded man, who treated the dragoons and officers with great kindness while in his country. His long hair, which was put up in several large clubs, and ornamented with a great many silver broaches, extended quite down to his knees. This distinguished man, as well as several others of his tribe, have agreed to join us on the march to Fort Gibson; so I shall have much of their company yet, and probably much more to say of them at a future period. Bon-son-gee (the new fire, plate 179) is another chief of this tribe, and called a very good man; the principal ornaments which he carried on his person were a boar's tusk and his war-whistle, which were hanging on his breast.

---

* I have several times, in former parts of this work, spoken of the great number of different Indian languages which I have visited, and given my opinion, as to the dissimilarity and distinctness of their character. And would refer the reader for further information on this subject, as well as for a vocabulary of several languages, to the Appendix to this Volume, letter B.

Quay-ham-kay (the stone shell, PLATE 180), is another fair specimen of the warriors of this tribe; and, if I mistake not, somewhat allied to the mysteries and arcana of the healing art, from the close company he keeps with my friend Dr. Findley, who is surgeon to the regiment, and by whom I have been employed to make a copy of my portrait of this distinguished personage.

In PLATE 181, Wun-pan-to-mee (the white weasel), a girl; and Tunkaht-oh-ye (the thunderer), a boy; who are brother and sister, are two Kioways who were purchased from the Osages, to be taken to their tribe by the dragoons. The girl was taken the whole distance with us, on horseback, to the Pawnee village, and there delivered to her friends, as I have before mentioned; and the fine little boy was killed at the Fur Trader's house on the banks of the Verdigris, near Fort Gibson, the day after I painted his portrait, and only a few days before he was to have started with us on the march. He was a beautiful boy of nine or ten years of age, and was killed by a ram, which struck him in the abdomen, and knocking him against a fence, killed him instantly.

Kots-a-to-ah (the smoked shield, PLATE 182), is another of the extraordinary men of this tribe, near seven feet in stature, and distinguished, not only as one of the greatest warriors, but the swiftest on foot, in the nation. This man, it is said, runs down a buffalo on foot, and slays it with his knife or his lance, as he runs by its side!

In PLATE 183, is the portrait of Ush-ee-kitz (he who fights with a feather) head chief of the Wi-co tribe, a very polite and polished Indian, in his manners, and remarkable for his mode of *embracing* the officers and others in council.

In the different talks and councils that we have had with these people, this man has been a conspicuous speaker; and always, at the end of his speeches, has been in the habit of stepping forward and embracing friends and foes, all that were about him, taking each one in turn, closely and affectionately in his arms, with his left cheek against theirs, and thus holding them tightly for several minutes.

All the above chiefs and braves, and many others, forming a very picturesque cavalcade, will move off with us in a day or two, on our way back to Fort Gibson, where it is to be hoped we may arrive more happy than we are in our present jaded and sickly condition.

LETTER—No. 44.

CAMP CANADIAN, *TEXAS.*

SIX days of severe travelling have brought us from the Camanchee village to the North bank of the Canadian, where we are snugly encamped on a beautiful plain, and in the midst of countless numbers of buffaloes; and halting a few days to recruit our horses and men, and dry meat to last us the remainder of our journey.

The plains around this, for many miles, seem actually speckled in distance, and in every direction, with herds of grazing buffaloes; and for several days, the officers and men have been indulged in a general licence to gratify their sporting propensities; and a scene of bustle and cruel slaughter it has been, to be sure! From morning till night, the camp has been daily almost deserted; the men have dispersed in little squads in all directions, and are dealing death to these poor creatures to a most cruel and wanton extent, merely for the pleasure of *destroying*, generally without stopping to cut out the meat. During yesterday and this day, several hundreds have undoubtedly been killed, and not so much as the flesh of half a dozen used. Such immense swarms of them are spread over this tract of country; and so divided and terrified have they become, finding their enemies in all directions where they run, that the poor beasts seem completely bewildered—running here and there, and as often as otherwise, come singly advancing to the horsemen, as if to join them for their company, and are easily shot down. In the turmoil and confusion, when their assailants have been pushing them forward, they have galloped through our encampment, jumping over our fires, upsetting pots and kettles, driving horses from their fastenings, and throwing the whole encampment into the greatest instant consternation and alarm. The hunting fever will be satiated in a few days amongst the young men, who are well enough to take parts in the chase; and the bilious fever, it is to be hoped, will be abated in a short time, amongst those who are invalid, and meat enough will be dried to last us to Fort Gibson, when we shall be on the march again, and wending our way towards that garrison.

Many are now sick and unable to ride, and are carried on litters between two horses. Nearly every tent belonging to the officers has been converted to hospitals for the sick; and sighs and groaning are heard in all directions.

From the Camanchee village to this place, the country has been entirely prairie ; and most of the way high and dry ground, without water, for which we sometimes suffered very much. From day to day we have dragged along exposed to the hot and burning rays of the sun, without a cloud to relieve its intensity, or a bush to shade us, or anything to cast a shadow, except the bodies of our horses. The grass for a great part of the way, was very much dried up, scarcely affording a bite for our horses ; and sometimes for the distance of many miles, the only water we could find, was in stagnant pools, lying on the highest ground, in which the buffaloes have been lying and wallowing like hogs in a mud-puddle. We frequently came to these dirty lavers, from which we drove the herds of wallowing buffaloes, and into which our poor and almost dying horses, irresistibly ran and plunged their noses, sucking up the dirty and poisonous draught, until, in some instances, they fell dead in their tracks—the men also (and oftentimes amongst the number, the writer of these lines) sprang from their horses, and laded up and drank to almost fatal excess, the disgusting and tepid draught, and with it filled their canteens, which were slung to their sides, and from which they were sucking the bilious contents during the day.

In our march we found many deep ravines, in the bottoms of which there were the marks of wild and powerful streams ; but in this season of drought they were all dried up, except an occasional one, where we found them dashing along in the coolest and clearest manner, and on trial, to our great agony, so *salt* that even here our horses could not drink from them ; so we had occasionally the tantalizing pleasure of hearing the roar of, and looking into, the clearest and most sparkling streams ; and after that the dire necessity of drinking from stagnant pools which lay from month to month exposed to the rays of the sun, till their waters become so poisonous and heavy, from the loss of their vital principle, that they are neither diminished by absorption, or taken into the atmosphere by evaporation.

This poisonous and indigestible water, with the intense rays of the sun in the hottest part of the summer, is the cause of the unexampled sickness of the horses and men. Both appear to be suffering and dying with the same disease, a slow and distressing bilious fever, which seems to terminate in a most frightful and fatal affection of the liver.

In these several cruel days' march, I have suffered severely, having had all the time (and having yet) a distracting fever on me. My real friend, Joe, has constantly rode by my side, dismounting and filling my canteen for me, and picking up minerals or fossils, which my jaundiced eyes were able to discover as we were passing over them ; or doing other kind offices for me, when I was too weak to mount my horse without aid. During this march over these dry and parched plains, we picked up many curious things of the fossil and mineral kind, and besides them a number of the horned frogs. In our portmanteaux we had a number of tin boxes in which we had carried Seidlitz powders, in which we caged a number of them safely, in hopes to carry them home alive. Several remarkable specimens my friend Joe has secured of these, with the horns of half and three-fourths of an inch in length, and very sharp at the points.

These curious subjects have so often fallen under my eye while on the Upper Missouri, that with me, they have lost their novelty in a great degree; but they have amused and astonished my friend Chadwick so much, that he declares he will take every one he can pick up, and make a sensation with them when ne gets home. In this way Joe's fancy for horned frogs has grown into a sort of *frog-mania*, and his eyes are strained all day, and gazing amongst the grass and pebbles as he rides along, for his precious little prizes, which he occasionally picks up and consigns to his pockets.*

On one of these hard day's march, and just at night, whilst we were looking out for water, and a suitable place to encamp, Joe and I galloped off a mile or two to the right of the regiment, to a point of timber, to look for water, where we found a small and sunken stagnant pool; and as our horses plunged their feet into it to drink, we saw to our great surprise, a number of frogs hopping across its surface, as our horses started them from the shore! Several of them stopped in the middle of the pool, sitting quite "high and dry" on the surface of the water; and when we approached them nearer, or jostled them, they made a leap into the air, and coming down head foremost—went under the water and secreted themselves at the bottom. Here was a subject for Joe, in his own line! frogs with horns, and frogs with *webbed feet*, that could hop about, and sit upon, the surface of the water! We rode around the pool and drove a number of them into it, and fearing that it would be useless to try to get one of them that evening; we rode back to the encampment, exulting very much in the curious discovery we had made for the naturalists; and by relating to some of the officers what we had seen, got excessively laughed at for our wonderful discovery! Nevertheless, Joe and I could not disbelieve what we had seen so distinctly "with our own eyes;" and we took to ourselves (or in other words, I acquiesced in Joe's taking to *himself*, as it was so peculiarly in his line) the most unequivocal satisfaction in the curious and undoubted discovery of this new variety; and we made our arrangements to ride back to the spot before "*bugle call*" in the morning; and by a thorough effort, to obtain a specimen or two of the web-footed frogs for Joe's pocket, to be by him introduced to the consideration of the knowing ones in the East. Well, our horses were saddled at an early hour, and Joe and I were soon on the spot—and he with a handkerchief at the end of a little pole, with which he had made a sort of scoop-net, soon dipped one up as it was hopping along on the surface of the water, and making unsuccessful efforts to dive through its surface. On examining its feet, we found, to our very great surprise,

* Several months after this, when I visited my friend Joe's room in St. Louis, he shewed me his horned frogs in their little tin boxes, in good flesh and good condition, where they had existed several months, without food of any kind.

that we had taken a great deal of pains to entrap an old and familiar little acquaintance of our boyhood ; but, somewhat like ourselves, unfortunately, from dire necessity, driven to a loathsome pool, where the water was so foul and slimy, that it could hop and dance about its surface with dry feet ; and where it oftentimes found difficulty in diving through the surface to hide itself at the bottom.

I laughed a great deal at poor Joe's most cruel expense, and we amused ourselves a few minutes about this filthy and curious pool, and rode back to the encampment. We found by taking the water up in the hollow of the hand, and dipping the finger in it, and drawing it over the side, thus conducting a little of it out ; it was so slimy that the whole would run over the side of the hand in a moment !

We were joked and teased a great deal about our *web-footed frogs ;* and after this, poor Joe has had repeatedly to take out and exhibit his little pets in his pockets, to convince our travelling companions that *frogs sometimes actually have horns.*

Since writing the above, an express has arrived from the encampment, which we left at the mouth of False Washita, with the melancholy tidings of the death of General Leavenworth, Lieutenant M'Clure, and ten or fifteen of the men left at that place ! This has cast a gloom over our little encampment here, and seems to be received as a fatal foreboding by those who are sick with the same disease ; and many of them, poor fellows, with scarce a hope left now for their recovery.

It seems that the General had moved on our trail a few days after we left the Washita, to the " Cross Timbers," a distance of fifty or sixty miles, where his disease at last terminated his existence ; and I am inclined to think, as I before mentioned, in consequence of the injury he sustained in a fall from his horse when running a buffalo calf. My reason for believing this, is, that I rode and ate with him every day after the hour of his fall ; and from that moment I was quite sure that I saw a different expression in his face, from that which he naturally wore ; and when riding by the side of him two or three days after his fall, I observed to him, " General, you have a very bad cough"—" Yes," he replied, " I have killed myself in running that devilish calf ; and it was a very lucky thing, Catlin, that you painted the portrait of me before we started, for it is all that my dear wife will ever see of me."

We shall be on the move again in a few days ; and I plainly see that I shall be upon a litter, unless my horrid fever leaves me, which is daily taking away my strength, and almost, at times, my senses. Adieu !

LETTER—No. 45.

FORT GIBSON, *ARKANSAS.*

THE last Letter was written from my tent, and out upon the wild prairies, when I was shaken and *terrified* by a burning fever, with home and my dear wife and little one, two thousand miles ahead of me, whom I was despairing of ever embracing again. I am now scarcely better off, except that I am in comfortable quarters, with kind attendance, and friends about me. I am yet sick and very feeble, having been for several weeks upon my back since I was brought in from the prairies. I am slowly recovering, and for the first time since I wrote from the Canadian, able to use my pen or my brush.

We drew off from that slaughtering ground a few days after my last Letter was written; with a great number sick carried upon litters—with horses giving out and dying by the way, which much impeded our progress over the long and tedious route that laid between us and Fort Gibson. Fifteen days, however, of constant toil and fatigue brought us here, but in a most crippled condition. Many of the sick were left by the way with attendants to take care of them, others were buried from their litters on which they breathed their last while travelling, and many others were brought in, to this place, merely to die and get the privilege of a decent burial.

Since the very day of our start into that country, the men have been constantly falling sick, and on their return, of those who are alive, there are not well ones enough to take care of the sick. Many are yet left out upon the prairies, and of those that have been brought in, and quartered in the hospital, with the soldiers of the infantry regiment stationed here, four or five are buried daily ; and as an equal number from the 9th regiment are falling by the same disease, I have the mournful sound of " Roslin Castle" with muffled drums, passing six or eight times a-day under my window, to the burying-ground ; which is but a little distance in front of my room, where I can lay in my bed and see every poor fellow lowered down into his silent and peaceful habitation. During the day before yesterday, no less than eight solemn processions visited that insatiable ground, and amongst them was carried the corpse of my intimate and much-loved friend Lieutenant West, who was aid-de-camp to General Leavenworth, on this disastrous campaign, and who has left in this place, a worthy and distracted widow, with her little ones to mourn for his untimely end. On the same day was buried also the Prussian Botanist, a most excellent and scientific gentleman, who had obtained an order from the Secretary at War to accompany the expedition for scientific purposes. He had at St. Louis, purchased a very comfortable dearborn waggon, and a snug span of little horses to convey himself and his servant with his collection of plants, over the prairies. In this he travelled in company with the regiment from St. Louis to Fort Gibson some five or six hundred miles and from that to the False Washita, and the Cross Timbers and back again. In this Tour he had made an immense, and no doubt, very valuable collection of plants, and at this place had been for some weeks indefatigably engaged in changing and drying them, and at last, fell a victim to the disease of the country, which seemed to have made an easy conquest of him, from the very feeble and enervated state he was evidently in, that of pulmonary consumption. This fine, gentlemanly and urbane, excellent man, to whom I became very much attached, was lodged in a room adjoining to mine, where he died, as he had lived, peaceably and smiling, and that when nobody knew that his life was in immediate danger. The surgeon who was attending me, (Dr. Wright,) was sitting on my bed-side in his morning-call at my room, when a negro boy, who alone had been left in the room with him, came into my apartment and said Mr. Beyrich was dying—we instantly stepped into his room and found him, not in the *agonies* of death, but quietly breathing his last, without a word or a struggle, as he had laid himself upon his bed with his clothes and his boots on. In this way perished this worthy man, who had no one here of kindred friends to drop tears for him ; and on the day previous to his misfortune, died also, and much in the same way, his devoted and faithful servant, a young man, a native of Germany. Their bodies were buried by the side of each other, and a general feeling of deep grief was manifested by the officers and citizens of the post, in the respect that was paid to their remains in the appropriate and decent committal of them to the grave.

After leaving the head waters of the Canadian, my illness continually increased, and losing strength every day, I soon got so reduced that I was necessarily lifted on to and off from, my horse; and at last, so that I could not ride at all. I was then put into a baggage-waggon which was going back empty, except with several soldiers sick, and in this condition rode eight days, most of the time in a delirious state, lying on the hard planks of the waggon, and made still harder by the jarring and jolting, until the skin from my elbows and knees was literally worn through, and I almost " *worn out ;*" when we at length reached this post, and I was taken to a bed, in comfortable quarters, where I have had the skilful attendance of my friend and old schoolmate Dr. Wright, under whose hands, thank God, I have been restored, and am now daily recovering my flesh and usual strength.

The experiment has thus been made, of sending an army of men from the North, into this Southern and warm climate, in the hottest months of the year, of July and August; and from this sad experiment I am sure a secret will be learned that will be of value on future occasions.

Of the 450 fine fellows who started from this place four months since, about one-third have already died, and I believe many more there are whose fates are sealed, and will yet fall victims to the deadly diseases contracted in that fatal country. About this post it seems to be almost equally unhealthy, and generally so during this season, all over this region, which is probably owing to an unusual drought which has been visited on the country, and unknown heretofore to the oldest inhabitants.

Since we came in from the prairies, and the sickness has a little abated, we have had a bustling time with the Indians at this place. Colonel Dodge sent *runners* to the chiefs of all the contiguous tribes of Indians, with an invitation to meet the Pawnees, &c. in council, at this place. Seven or eight tribes flocked to us, in great numbers on the first day of the month, when the council commenced; it continued for several days, and gave these semi-civilized sons of the forest a fair opportunity of shaking the hands of their wild and untamed red brethren of the West—of embracing them in their arms, with expressions of friendship, and of smoking the calumet together, as the solemn pledge of lasting peace and friendship.

Colonel Dodge, Major Armstrong (the Indian agent), and General Stokes (the Indian commissioner), presided at this council, and I cannot name a scene more interesting and entertaining than it was; where, for several days in succession, free vent was given to the feelings of men *civilized, half-civilized,* and *wild ;* where the three stages of man were fearlessly asserting their rights, their happiness, and friendship for each other. The vain orations of the half-polished (and half-breed) Cherokees and Choctaws, with all their finery and art, found their match in the brief and jarring gutturals of the wild and naked man.

After the council had adjourned, and the fumes of the peace-making calumet had vanished away, and Colonel Dodge had made them additional presents, they soon made preparations for their departure, and on the next day started, with an escort of dragoons, for their own country. This movement is much to be regretted; for it would have been exceedingly gratifying to the people of the East to have seen so wild a group, and it would have been of great service to them to have visited Washington—a journey, though, which they could not be prevailed upon to make.

We brought with us to this place, three of the principal chiefs of the Pawnees, fifteen Kioways, one Camanchee, and one Wico chief. The group was undoubtedly one of the most interesting that ever visited our frontier; and, I have taken the utmost pains in painting the portraits of all of them, as well as seven of the Camanchee chiefs, who came part of the way with us, and turned back. These portraits, together with other paintings which I have made, descriptive of their manners and customs—views of their villages—landscapes of the country, &c., will soon be laid before the amateurs of the East, and, I trust, will be found to be very interesting.

Although the achievement has been a handsome one, of bringing these unknown people to an acquaintance, and a general peace ; and at first sight would appear to be of great benefit to them—yet I have my strong doubts, whether it will better their condition, unless with the exercised aid of the strong arm of Government, they can be protected in the rights which by nature, they are entitled to.

There is already in this place a company of eighty men fitted out, who are to start to-morrow, to overtake these Indians a few miles from this place, and accompany them home, with a large stock of goods, with traps for catching beavers, &c., calculating to build a trading-house amongst them, where they will amass, at once, an immense fortune, being the first traders and trappers that have ever been in that part of the country.

I have travelled too much among Indian tribes, and seen too much, not to know the evil consequences of such a system. Goods are sold at such exorbitant prices, that the Indian gets a mere shadow for his peltries, &c. The Indians see no white people but traders and sellers of whiskey ; and of course, judge us all by them—they consequently hold us, and always will, in contempt; as inferior to themselves, as they have reason to do—and they neither fear nor respect us. When, on the contrary, if the Government would promptly prohibit such establishments, and invite these Indians to our frontier posts, they would bring in their furs, their robes, horses, mules, &c., to this place, where there is a good market for them all—where they would get the full value of their property—where there are several stores of goods —where there is an honourable competition, and where they would get four or five times as much for their articles of trade, as they would get from a trader in the village, out of the reach of competition, and out of sight of the civilized world.

At the same time, as they would be continually coming where they would see good and polished society, they would be gradually adopting our modes of living—introducing to their country our vegetables, our domestic animals, poultry, &c., and at length, our arts and manufactures ; they would see and estimate our military strength, and advantages, and would be led to fear and respect us. In short, it would undoubtedly be the quickest and surest way to a general acquaintance—to friendship and peace, and at last to civilization. If there is a law in existence for such protection of the Indian tribes, which may have been waived in the case of those nations with which we have long traded, it is a great pity that it should not be rigidly enforced in this new and important acquaintance, which we have just made with thirty or forty thousand strangers to the civilized world ; yet (as we have learned from their unaffected hospitality when in their villages), with hearts of human mould, *susceptible* of all the noble feelings . belonging to civilized man.

This acquaintance has cost the United States a vast sum of money, as well as the lives of several valuable and esteemed officers and more than

100 of the dragoons; and for the honour of the American name, I think we ought, in forming an acquaintance with these numerous tribes, to adopt and *enforce* some different system from that which has been generally practiced on and beyond our frontiers heretofore.

What the regiment of dragoons has suffered from sickness since they started on their summer's campaign is unexampled in this country, and almost incredible.—When we started from this place, ten or fifteen were sent back the first day, too sick to proceed; and so afterwards our numbers were daily diminished, and at the distance of 200 miles from this place we could muster, out of the whole regiment, but 250 men who were able to proceed, with which little band, and that again reduced some sixty or seventy by sickness, we pushed on, and accomplished all that was done. The beautiful and pictured scenes which we passed over had an alluring charm on their surface, but (as it would seem) a lurking poison within, that spread a gloom about our encampment whenever we pitched it.

We sometimes rode day after day, without a tree to shade us from the burning rays of a tropical sun, or a breath of wind to regale us or cheer our hearts—and with mouths continually parched with thirst, we dipped our drink from stagnant pools that were heated by the sun, and kept in fermentation by the wallowing herds of buffaloes that resort to them. In this way we dragged on, sometimes passing picturesque and broken country, with fine springs and streams, affording us the luxury of a refreshing shade and a cool draught of water.

Thus was dragged through and completed this most disastrous campaign; and to Colonel Dodge and Colonel Kearny, who so indefatigably led and encouraged their men through it, too much praise cannot be awarded.

During my illness while I have been at this post, my friend Joe has been almost constantly by my bedside; evincing (as he did when we were creeping over the vast prairies) the most sincere and intense anxiety for my recovery; whilst he has administered, like a brother, every aid and every comfort that lay in his power to bring. Such tried friendship as this, I shall ever recollect; and it will long hence and often, lead my mind back to retrace, at least, the first part of our campaign, which was full pleasant; and many of its incidents have formed pleasing impressions on my memory, which I would preserve to the end of my life.

When we started, we were fresh and ardent for the incidents that were before us—our little packhorse carried our bedding and culinary articles; amongst which we had a coffee-pot and a frying-pan—coffee in good store, and sugar—and wherever we spread our bear-skin, and kindled our fire in the grass, we were sure to take by ourselves, a delightful repast, and a refreshing sleep. During the march, as we were subject to no military subordination, . we galloped about wherever we were disposed, popping away at whatever we chose to spend ammunition upon—and running our noses into every wild nook and crevice, as we saw fit. In this way we travelled happily, until

our coffee was gone, and our bread; and even then we were happy upon
meat alone, until at last each one in his turn, like every other moving thing
about us, both man and beast, were vomiting and fainting, under the poisonous
influence of some latent enemy, that was floating in the air, and threatening
our destruction. Then came the " tug of war," and instead of catering for
our amusements, every one seemed desperately studying the means that were
to support him on his feet, and bring him safe home again to the bosoms of his
friends. In our start, our feelings were buoyant and light, and we had the
luxuries of life—the green prairies, spotted with wild flowers, and the clear
blue sky, were an earthly paradise to us, until fatigue and disease, and at
last despair, made them tiresome and painful to our jaundiced eyes.

On our way, and while we were in good heart, my friend Joe and I had
picked up many minerals and fossils of an interesting nature, which we put
in our portmanteaux and carried for weeks, with much pains, and some *pain*
also, until the time when our ardour cooled and our spirits lagged, and then
we discharged and threw them away; and sometimes we came across specimens again, still more wonderful, which we put in their place, and lugged
along till we were tired of *them*, and their weight, and we discharged them as
before; so that from our eager desire to procure, we lugged many pounds
weight of stones, shells, &c. nearly the whole way, and were glad that
their mother Earth should receive them again at our hands, which was done
long before we got back.

One of the most curious places we met in all our route, was a mountain
ridge of fossil shells, from which a great number of the above-mentioned
specimens were taken. During our second day's march from the mouth of
the False Washita, we were astonished to find ourselves travelling over a bed
of clam and oyster shells, which were all in a complete state of petrifaction.
This ridge, which seemed to run from N. E. to S.W. was several hundred feet
high, and varying from a quarter to half a mile in breadth, seemed to be composed of nothing but a concretion of shells, which, on the surface, exposed to
the weather for the depth of eight or ten inches, were entirely separated from
the cementing material which had held them together, and were lying on the
surface, sometimes for acres together, without a particle of soil or grass
upon them; with the colour, shapes and appearance exactly, of the natural
shells, lying loosely together, into which our horses' feet were sinking at every
step, above their fetterlocks. These I consider the most extraordinary
petrifactions I ever beheld. In any way they could be seen, individually
or in the mass together, they seemed to be nothing but the *pure shells
themselves*, both in colour and in shape. In many instances we picked
them up entire, never having been opened; and taking our knives out, and
splitting them open as we would an oyster, the fish was seen petrified in
perfect form, and by dipping it into water, it shewed all the colours and
freshness of an oyster just opened and laid on a plate to be eaten. Joe and
I had carefully tied up many of these, with which we felt quite sure we could

deceive our oyster-eating friends when we got back to the East; yet, like many other things we collected, they shared the fate that I have mentioned, without our bringing home one of them, though we brought many of them several hundreds of miles, and at last threw them away. This remarkable ridge is in some parts covered with grass, but generally with mere scattering bunches, for miles together, partially covering this compact mass of shells, forming (in my opinion) one of the greatest geological curiosities now to be seen in this country, as it lies evidently some thousands of feet above the level of the ocean, and seven or eight hundred miles from the nearest point on the sea-coast.

In another section of the country, lying between Fort Gibson and the Washita, we passed over a ridge for several miles, running parallel to this, where much of the way there was no earth or grass under foot, but our horses were travelling on a solid rock, which had on its surface a reddish or oxidized appearance; and on getting from my horse and striking it with my hatchet, I found it to contain sixty or eighty per cent of solid iron, which produced a ringing noise, and a rebounding of the hatchet, as if it were struck upon an anvil.

In other parts, and farther West, between the Camanchee village and the Canadian, we passed over a similar surface for many miles denuded, with the exception of here and there little bunches of grass and wild sage, a level and exposed surface of solid gypsum, of a dark grey colour; and through it, occasionally, as far as the eye could discover, to the East and the West streaks of three and five inches wide of snowy gypsum, which was literally as white as the drifted snow.

Of saltpetre and salt, there are also endless supplies; so it will be seen that the mineral resources of this wilderness country are inexhaustible and rich, and that the idle savage who never converts them to his use, must soon yield them to the occupation of enlightened and cultivating man.

In the vicinity of this post there are an immense number of Indians, most of whom have been removed to their present locations by the Government, from their Eastern original positions, within a few years past; and previous to my starting with the dragoons, I had two months at my leisure in this section of the country, which I used in travelling about with my canvass and note-book, and visiting all of them in their villages. I have made many paintings amongst them, and have a curious note-book to open at a future day, for which the reader may be prepared. The tribes whom I thus visited, and of whom my note-book will yet speak, are the *Cherokees, Choctaws, Creeks, Seminoles, Chickasaws, Quapaws, Senecas, Delawares,* and several others, whose customs are interesting, and whose history, from their proximity to, and dealings with the civilized community, is one of great interest, and some importance, to the enlightened world. Adieu.

LETTER—No. 46.

ALTON, *ILLINOIS.*

A FEW days after the date of the above Letter, I took leave of Fort Gibson, and made a transit across the prairies to this place, a distance of 550 miles, which I have performed entirely alone, and had the satisfaction of joining my wife, whom I have found in good health, in a family of my esteemed friends, with whom she has been residing during my last year of absence.

While at Fort Gibson, on my return from the Camanchees, I was quartered for a month or two in a room with my fellow-companion in misery, Captain Wharton, of the dragoons, who had come in from the prairies in a condition very similar to mine, and laid in a bed in the opposite corner of the room; where we laid for several weeks, like two grim ghosts, rolling our glaring and staring eyeballs upon each other, when we were totally unable to hold converse, other than that which was exchanged through the expressive language of our hollow, and bilious, sunken eyes.

The Captain had been sent with a company of dragoons to escort the Santa Fee Traders through the country of the Camanchees and Pawnees, and had returned from a rapid and bold foray into the country, with many of his men sick, and himself attacked with the epidemic of the country. The Captain is a gentleman of high and noble bearing, of one of the most respected families in Philadelphia, with a fine and chivalrous feeling; but with scarce physical stamina sufficient to bear him up under the rough vicissitudes of his wild and arduous sort of life in this country.

As soon as our respective surgeons had clarified our flesh and our bones with calomel, had brought our pulses to beat calmly, our tongues to ply gently, and our stomachs to digest moderately; we began to feel pleasure exquisitely in our convalescence, and draw amusement from mutual relations of scenes and adventures we had witnessed on our several marches. The Captain convalescing faster than I did, soon got so as to eat (but not to digest) enormous meals, which visited back upon him the renewed horrors of his disease; and I, who had got ahead of him in strength, but not in prudence, was thrown back in my turn, by similar indulgence; and so we were mutually and repeatedly, until he at length got so as to feel strength enough to ride, and resolution enough to swear that he would take leave of that deadly spot, and seek restoration and health in a cooler and more congenial latitude. So he had his horse brought up one morning, whilst he was so weak that he could scarcely mount upon its back, and with his servant, a small negro boy, packed on another, he steered off upon the prairies towards Fort Leavenworth, 500 miles to the North, where his company had long since marched.

I remained a week or two longer, envying the Captain the good luck to escape from that dangerous ground; and after I had gained strength sufficient to warrant it, I made preparations to take informal leave, and wend *my* way also over the prairies to the Missouri, a distance of 500 miles, and most of the way a solitary wilderness. For this purpose I had my horse " Charley" brought up from his pasture, where he had been in good keeping during my illness, and got so fat as to form almost an objectionable contrast to his master, with whom he was to embark on a long and tedious journey again, over the vast and almost boundless prairies.

I had, like the Captain, grown into such a dread of that place, from the scenes of death that were and had been visited upon it, that I resolved to be off as soon as I had strength to get on to my horse, and balance myself upon his back. For this purpose I packed up my canvass and brushes, and other luggage, and sent them down the river to the Mississippi, to be forwarded by steamer, to meet me at St. Louis. So, one fine morning, Charley was brought up and saddled, and a bear-skin and a buffalo robe being spread upon his saddle, and a coffee-pot and tin cup tied to it also— with a few pounds of hard biscuit in my portmanteau—with my fowling-piece in my hand, and my pistols in my belt—with my sketch-book slung on my back, and a small pocket compass in my pocket; I took leave of Fort Gibson, even against the advice of my surgeon and all the officers of the garrison, who gathered around me to bid me farewell. No argument could contend with the fixed resolve in my own mind, that if I could get out upon the prairies, and moving continually to the Northward, I should daily gain strength, and save myself, possibly, from the jaws of that voracious burial-ground that laid in front of my room; where I had for months laid and imagined myself going with other poor fellows, whose mournful dirges were played under my window from day to day. No one can imagine what was the dread I felt for that place ; nor the pleasure, which was extatic, when Charley was trembling under me, and I turned him around on the top of a prairie bluff at a mile distance, to take the last look upon it, and thank God, as I did audibly, that I was not to be buried within its enclosure. I said to myself, that " to die on the prairie, and be devoured by wolves; or to fall in combat and be scalped by an Indian, would be far more acceptable than the lingering death that would consign me to the jaws of that insatiable grave," for which, in the fever and weakness of my mind, I had contracted so destructive a terror.

So, alone, without other living being with me than my affectionate horse Charley, I turned my face to the North, and commenced on my long journey, with confidence full and strong, that I should gain strength daily; and no one can ever know the pleasure of that moment, which placed me alone, upon the boundless sea of waving grass, over which my proud horse was prancing, and I with my life in my own hands, commenced to steer my course to the banks of the Missouri.

For the convalescent, rising and escaping from the gloom and horrors of a sick bed, astride of his strong and trembling horse, carrying him fast and safely over green fields spotted and tinted with waving wild flowers; and through the fresh and cool breezes that are rushing about him, as he daily shortens the distance that lies between him and his wife and little ones, there is an exquisite pleasure yet to be learned, by those who never have felt it.

Day by day I thus pranced and galloped along, the whole way through waving grass and green fields, occasionally dismounting and lying in the grass an hour or so, until the grim shaking and chattering of an ague chill had passed off; and through the nights, slept on my bear-skin spread upon the grass, with my saddle for my pillow, and my buffalo robe drawn over me for my covering. My horse Charley was picketed near me at the end of his laso, which gave him room for his grazing; and thus we snored and nodded away the nights, and never were denied the doleful serenades of the gangs of sneaking wolves that were nightly perambulating our little encampment, and stationed at a safe distance from us at sun-rise in the morning—gazing at us, and impatient to pick up the crumbs and bones that were left, when we moved away from our feeble fire that had faintly flickered through the night, and in the absence of timber, had been made of dried buffalo dung, (PLATE 184).

This " *Charley*" was a noble animal of the Camanchee wild breed, of a clay bank colour; and from our long and tried acquaintance, we had become very much attached to each other, and acquired a wonderful facility both of mutual accommodation, and of construing each other's views and intentions. In fact, we had been so long tried together, that there would have seemed to the spectator almost an unity of *interest*; and at all events, an unity of feelings on the subject of attachment, as well as on that of mutual dependence and protection.

I purchased this very showy and well-known animal of Colonel Burbank, of the ninth regiment, and rode it the whole distance to the Camanchee villages and back again; and at the time when most of the horses of the regiment were drooping and giving out by the way—*Charley* flourished and came in in good flesh and good spirits.

On this journey, while he and I were twenty-five days alone, we had much time, and the best of circumstances, under which to learn what we had as yet overlooked in each other's characters, as well as to draw great pleasure and real benefit from what we already had learned of each other, in our former travels.

N

I generally halted on the bank of some little stream, at half an hour's sun, where feed was good for Charley, and where I could get wood to kindle my fire, and water for my coffee. The first thing was to undress " Charley" and drive down his picket, to which he was fastened, to graze over a circle that he could inscribe at the end of his laso. In this wise he busily fed himself until nightfall; and after my coffee was made and drank, I uniformly moved him up, with his picket by my head, so that I could lay my hand upon his laso in an instant, in case of any alarm that was liable to drive him from me. On one of these evenings when he was grazing as usual, he slipped the laso over his head, and deliberately took his supper at his pleasure, wherever he chose to prefer it, as he was strolling around. When night approached, I took the laso in hand and endeavoured to catch him, but I soon saw that he was determined to enjoy a little freedom ; and he continually evaded me until dark, when I abandoned the pursuit, making up my mind that I should inevitably lose him, and be obliged to perform the rest of my journey on foot. He had led me a chase of half a mile or more, when I left him busily grazing, and returned to my little solitary bivouac, and laid myself on my bear skin, and went to sleep.

In the middle of the night I waked, whilst I was lying on my back, and on half opening my eyes, I was instantly shocked to the soul, by the huge figure (as I thought) of an Indian, standing over me, and in the very instant of taking my scalp! The chill of horror that paralyzed me for the first moment, held me still till I saw there was no need of my moving—that my faithful horse " Charley" had "played shy" till he had " filled his belly," and had then moved up, from feelings of pure affection, or from instinctive fear, or possibly, from a due share of both, and taken his position with his forefeet at the edge of my bed, with his head hanging directly over me, while he was standing fast asleep !

My nerves, which had been most violently shocked, were soon quieted, and I fell asleep, and so continued until sunrise in the morning, when I waked, and beheld my faithful servant at some considerable distance, busily at work picking up his breakfast amongst the cane-brake, along the bank of the creek. I went as busily to work, preparing my own, which was eaten, and after it, I had another half-hour of fruitless endeavours to catch Charley, whilst he seemed mindful of success on the evening before, and continually tantalized me by turning around and around, and keeping out of my reach. I recollected the conclusive evidence of his attachment and dependence, which he had voluntarily given in the night, and I thought I would try them in another way. So I packed up my things and slung the saddle on my back, trailing my gun in my hand, and started on my route. After I had advanced a quarter of a mile, I looked back, and saw him standing with his head and tail very high, looking alternately at me and at the spot where I had been encamped, and left a little fire burning. In this condition he stood and surveyed the prairies around for a while, as I continued on. He,

at length, walked with a hurried step to the spot, and seeing everything gone, began to neigh very violently, and at last started off at fullest speed, and overtook me, passing within a few paces of me, and wheeling about at a few rods distance in front of me, trembling like an aspen leaf.

I called him by his familiar name, and walked up to him with the bridle in my hand, which I put over his head, as he held it down for me, and the saddle on his back, as he actually stooped to receive it. I was soon arranged, and on his back, when he started off upon his course as if he was well contented and pleased, like his rider, with the manœuvre which had brought us together again, and afforded us mutual relief from our awkward positions. Though this alarming freak of " Charley's" passed off and terminated so satisfactorily; yet I thought such rather dangerous ones to play, and I took good care after that night, to keep him under my strict authority; resolving to avoid further tricks and experiments till we got to the land of cultivated fields and steady habits.

On the night of this memorable day, Charley and I stopped in one of the most lovely little valleys I ever saw, and even far more beautiful than could have been *imagined* by mortal man. An enchanting little lawn of five or six acres, on the banks of a cool and rippling stream, that was alive with fish; and every now and then, a fine brood of young ducks, just old enough for delicious food, and too unsophisticated to avoid an easy and simple death. This little lawn was surrounded by bunches and copses of the most luxuriant and picturesque foliage, consisting of the lofty bois d'arcs and elms, spreading out their huge branches, as if offering protection to the rounded groups of cherry and plum-trees that supported festoons of grape-vines, with their purple clusters that hung in the most tempting manner over the green carpet that was everywhere decked out with wild flowers, of all tints and of various sizes, from the modest wild sun-flowers, with their thousand tall and drooping heads, to the lillies that stood, and the violets that crept beneath them. By the side of this cool stream, Charley was fastened, and near him my bear-skin was spread in the grass, and by it my little fire, to which I soon brought a fine string of perch from the brook; from which, and a broiled duck, and a delicious cup of coffee, I made my dinner and supper, which were usually united in one meal, at half an hour's sun. After this I strolled about this sweet little paradise, which I found was chosen, not only by myself, but by the wild deer, which were repeatedly rising from their quiet lairs, and bounding out, and over the graceful swells of the prairies which hemmed in, and framed this little picture of sweetest tints and most masterly touches.

The Indians also, I found, had loved it once, and left it; for here and there were their solitary and deserted graves, which told, though briefly, of former chaunts and sports; and perhaps, of wars and deaths, that have once rung and echoed through this little silent vale.

On my return to my encampment, I laid down upon my back, and looked awhile into the blue heavens that were over me, with their pure and milk white clouds that were passing—with the sun just setting in the West, and the silver moon rising in the East, and renewed the impressions of my own insignificance, as I contemplated the incomprehensible mechanism of that *wonderful clock*, whose time is infallible, and whose motion is eternity! I trembled, at last, at the dangerous expanse of my thoughts, and turned them again, and my eyes, upon the little and more comprehensible things that were about me. One of the first was a *newspaper*, which I had brought from the Garrison, the National Intelligencer, of Washington, which I had read for years, but never with quite the zest and relish that I now conversed over its familiar columns, in this clean and sweet valley of dead silence!

And while reading, I thought of (and laughed), what I had almost forgotten, the sensation I produced amongst the Minatarees while on the Upper Missouri, a few years since, by taking from amongst my painting apparatus an old number of the *New York Commercial Advertiser*, edited by my kind and tried friend Colonel Stone. The Minatarees thought that I was mad, when they saw me for hours together, with my eyes fixed upon its pages. They had different and various conjectures about it; the most current of which was, that I was looking at it to cure my sore eyes, and they called it the "*medicine cloth for sore eyes!*" I at length put an end to this and several equally ignorant conjectures, by reading passages in it, which were interpreted to them, and the objects of the paper fully explained; after which, it was looked upon as much greater mystery than before; and several liberal offers were made me for it, which I was obliged to refuse, having already received a beautifully garnished robe for it, from the hands of a young son of Esculapius, who told me that if he could employ a good interpreter to explain everything in it, he could travel about amongst the Minatarees and Mandans, and Sioux, and exhibit it after I was gone; getting rich with presents, and adding greatly to the list of his *medicines*, as it would make him a great *Medicine-Man*. I left with the poor fellow his painted robe, and the newspaper; and just before I departed, I saw him unfolding it to show to some of his friends, when he took from around it, some eight or ten folds of birch bark and deer skins; all of which were carefully enclosed in a sack made of the skin of a pole cat, and undoubtedly destined to become, and to be called, his mystery or *medicine-bag*.

The distance from Fort Gibson to the Missouri, where I struck the river, is about five hundred miles, and most of the way a beautiful prairie, in a wild and uncultivated state without roads and without bridges, over a great part of which I steered my course with my pocket-compass, fording and swimming the streams in the best manner I could; shooting prairie hens, and occasionally catching fish, which I cooked for my meals, and slept upon the ground at night. On my way I visited "Riqua's Village" of Osages, and lodged during the night in the hospitable cabin of my old friend Beatte, of whom I have often spoken heretofore, as one of the guides and hunters for the dragoons on their campaign in the Camanchee country. This was the most extraordinary hunter, I think, that I ever have met in all my travels. *To "hunt,"* was a phrase almost foreign to him, however, for when he went out with his rifle, it was *"for meat,"* or *"for cattle;"* and he never came in without it. He never told how many animals he had seen—how many he had wounded, &c.—but his horse was always loaded with meat, which was thrown down in camp without comment or words spoken. Riqua was an early pioneer of Christianity in this country, who has devoted many years of his life, with his interesting family, in endeavouring to civilize and christianize these people, by the force of pious and industrious examples, which he has successfully set them ; and, I think, in the most judicious way, by establishing a little village, at some miles distance from the villages of the Osages ; where he has invited a considerable number of families who have taken their residence by the side of him ; where they are following his virtuous examples in their dealings and modes of life, and in agricultural pursuits which he is teaching them, and showing them that they may raise the comforts and luxuries of life out of the ground, instead of seeking for them in the precarious manner in which they naturally look for them, in the uncertainty of the chase.

It was a source of much regret to me, that I did not see this pious man, as he was on a Tour to the East, when I was in his little village.

Beatte lived in this village with his aged parents, to whom he introduced me ; and with whom, altogether, I spent a very pleasant evening in conversation. They are both French, and have spent the greater part of their lives with the Osages, and seem to be familiar with their whole history. This Beatte was the hunter and guide for a party of rangers (the summer before our campaign), with whom Washington Irving made his excursion to the borders of the Pawnee country ; and of whose extraordinary character and powers, Mr. Irving has drawn a very just and glowing account, excepting one error which I think he has inadvertently fallen into, that of calling him a " *half breed.*" Beatte had complained of this to me often while out on the prairies ; and when I entered his hospitable cabin, he said he was glad to see me, and almost instantly continued, " Now you shall see, Monsieur Catline, I am not ' *half breed,*' here I shall introduce you to my father and my mother, who you see are two very nice and good old French people."

From this cabin where I fared well and slept soundly, I started in the morning, after taking with them a good cup of coffee, and went smoothly on over the prairies on my course.

About the middle of my journey, I struck a road leading into a small civilized settlement, called the " *Kickapoo prairie,*" to which I " bent my course ;" and riding up to a log cabin which was kept as a sort of an hotel or tavern, I met at the door, the black boy belonging to my friend Captain Wharton, who I have said took his leave of Fort Gibson a few weeks before me ; I asked the boy where his master was, to which he replied, " My good massa, Massa Wharton, in dese house, jist dead ob de libber compliment !"

I dismounted and went in, and to my deepest sorrow and anguish, I found him, as the boy said, nearly dead, without power to raise his head or his voice—his eyes were rolled upon me, and as he recognized me he took me by the hand, which he firmly gripped, whilst both shed tears in profusion. By placing my ear to his lips, his whispers could be heard, and he was able in an imperfect manner to make his views and his wishes known. His disease seemed to be a repeated attack of his former malady, and a severe affection of the liver, which was to be (as his physician said) the proximate cause of his death. I conversed with his physician who seemed to be a young and inexperienced man, who told me that he certainly could not live more than ten days. I staid two days with him, and having no means with me of rendering him pecuniary or other aid amongst strangers, I left him in kind hands, and started on my course again. My health improved daily, from the time of my setting out at Fort Gibson; and I was now moving along cheerfully, and in hopes soon to reach the end of my toilsome journey. I had yet vast prairies to pass over, and occasional latent difficulties, which were not apparent on their smooth and deceiving surfaces. Deep sunken streams, like ditches, occasionally presented themselves suddenly to my view, when I was within a few steps of plunging into them from their perpendicular sides, which were overhung with long wild grass, and almost obscured from the sight. The bearings of my compass told me that I must cross them, and the only alternative was to plunge into them, and get out as well as I could. They were often muddy, and I could not tell whether they were three or ten feet deep, until my horse was in them; and sometimes he went down head foremost, and I with him, to scramble out on the opposite shore in the best condition we could. In one of these canals, which I had followed for several miles in the vain hope of finding a shoal, or an accustomed ford, I plunged, with Charley, where it was about six or eight yards wide (and God knows how deep, for we did not go to the bottom), and swam him to the opposite bank, on to which I clung; and which, being perpendicular and of clay, and three or four feet higher than the water, was an insurmountable difficulty to Charley; and I led the poor fellow at least a mile, as I walked on the top of the bank, with the bridle in my hand, holding his head above the water as he was swimming; and I at times almost inextricably entangled in the long grass that was often higher than my head, and hanging over the brink, filled and woven together, with ivy and wild pea-vines. I at length (and just before I was ready to drop the rein of faithful Charley, in hopeless despair), came to an old buffalo ford, where the banks were graded down, and the poor exhausted animal, at last got out, and was ready and willing to take me and my luggage (after I had dried them in the sun) on the journey again.

The Osage river which is a powerful stream, I struck at a place which seemed to stagger my courage very much. There had been heavy rains but a few days before, and this furious stream was rolling along its wild and turbid waters, with a freshet upon it, that spread its waters, in many places over its banks, as was the case at the place where I encountered it. There seemed to be but little choice in places with this stream, which, with its banks full, was sixty or eighty yards in width. with a current that was sweeping along at a rapid rate. I stripped everything from Charley, and tied him with his laso, until I travelled the shores up and down for some distance, and collected drift wood enough for a small raft, which I constructed, to carry my clothes and saddle, and other things, safe over. This being completed, and my clothes taken off, and they with other things, laid upon the raft, I took Charley to the bank and drove him in and across, where he soon reached the opposite shore, and went to feeding on the bank. Next was to come the " *great white medicine ;*" and with him, saddle, bridle, saddle-bags, sketch-book, gun and pistols, coffee and coffee-pot, powder, and his clothes, all of which were placed upon the raft, and the raft pushed into the stream, and the "*medicine man*" swimming behind it, and pushing it along before him, until it reached the opposite shore, at least half a mile below ! From this, his things were carried to the top of the bank, and in a little time, Charley was caught and dressed, and straddled, and on the way again.

These are a few of the incidents of that journey of 500 miles, which I performed entirely alone, and which at last brought me out at Boonville on the Western bank of the Missouri. While I was crossing the river at that place, I met General Arbuckle, with two surgeons, who were to start the next day from Boonville for Fort Gibson, travelling over the route that I had just passed. I instantly informed them of the condition of poor Wharton, and the two surgeons were started off that afternoon at fullest speed, with orders to reach him in the shortest time possible, and do everything to save his life. I assisted in purchasing for him, several little things that he had named to me, such as jellies—acids—apples, &c. &c.; and saw them start; and (God knows), I shall impatiently hope to hear of their timely assistance, and of his recovery.*

From Boonville, which is a very pretty little town, building up with the finest style of brick houses, I crossed the river to New Franklin, where I laid by several days, on account of stormy weather; and from thence proceeded with success to the end of my journey, where I now am, under the roof of kind and hospitable friends, with my dear wife, who has patiently waited one year to receive me back, a wreck, as I now am; and who is to start in a few days with me to the coast of Florida, 1400 miles South of this, to spend the winter in patching up my health, and fitting me for future campaigns.

On this Tour (from which I shall return in the spring, if my health will

* I have great satisfaction in informing the reader, that I learned a year or so after the above date, that those two skilful surgeons hastened on with all possible speed to the assistance of this excellent gentleman, and had the satisfaction of conducting him to his post after he had entirely and permanently recovered his health.

admit of it), I shall visit the Seminoles in Florida,—the Euchees—the Creeks in Alabama and Georgia, and the Choctaws and Cherokees, who are yet remaining on their lands, on the East side of the Mississippi.

We take steamer for New Orleans to morrow, so, till after another campaign, Adieu

LETTER—No. 47.

SAINT LOUIS.

SINCE the date of my last Letter, a whole long winter has passed off, which I have whiled away on the Gulf of Mexico and about the shores of Florida and Texas. My health was soon restored by the congenial climate I there found, and my dear wife was my companion the whole way. We visited the different posts, and all that we could find to interest us in these delightful realms, and took steamer from New Orleans to this place, where we arrived but a few days since.

Supposing that the reader by this time may be somewhat tired of following me in my erratic wanderings over these wild regions, I have resolved to sit down awhile before I go further, and open to him my *sketch-book*, in which I have made a great many entries, as I have been dodging about, and which I have not as yet shewed to him, for want of requisite time and proper opportunity.

In opening this book, the reader will allow me to turn over leaf after leaf, and describe to him, tribe after tribe, and chief after chief, of many of those whom I have visited, without the tediousness of travelling too minutely over the intervening distances; in which I fear I might lose him as a fellow-traveller, and leave him fagged out by the way-side, before he would see all that I am anxious to show him.

About a year since I made a visit to the

KICKAPOOS,

At present but a small tribe, numbering six or 800, the remnant of a once numerous and warlike tribe. They are residing within the state of Illinois, near the south end of Lake Michigan, and living in a poor and miserable condition, although they have one of the finest countries in the world. They have been reduced in numbers by whiskey and small-pox, and the game being destroyed in their country, and having little industry to work, they are exceedingly poor and dependent. In fact, there is very little inducement for them to build houses and cultivate their farms, for they own so large and so fine a tract of country, which is now completely surrounded by civilized settlements, that they know, from experience, they will soon be obliged to sell out their country for a trifle, and move to the West.

This system of moving has already commenced with them, and a considerable party have located on a tract of lands offered to them on the West bank of the Missouri river, a little north of Fort Leavenworth.*

The Kickapoos have long lived in alliance with the Sacs and Foxes, and speak a language so similar that they seem almost to be of one family. The present chief of this tribe, whose name is *Kee-an-ne-kuk* (the foremost man, PLATE 185), usually called the *Shawnee Prophet*, is a very shrewd and talented man. When he sat for his portrait, he took his attitude as seen in the picture, which was that of prayer. And I soon learned that he was a very devoted Christian, regularly holding meetings in his tribe, on the sabbath, preaching to them and exhorting them to a belief in the Christian religion, and to an abandonment of the fatal habit of whiskey-drinking, which he strenuously represented as the bane that was to destroy them all, if they did not entirely cease to use it. I went on the sabbath, to hear this eloquent man preach, when he had his people assembled in the woods; and although I could not understand his language, I was surprised and pleased with the natural ease and emphasis, and gesticulation, which carried their own evidence of the eloquence of his sermon.

I was singularly struck with the noble efforts of this champion of the mere remnant of a poisoned race, so strenuously labouring to rescue the remainder of his people from the deadly bane that has been brought amongst them by enlightened Christians. How far the efforts of this zealous man have succeeded in christianizing, I cannot tell, but it is quite certain that his exemplary and constant endeavours have completely abolished the practice of drinking whiskey in his tribe; which alone is a very praiseworthy achievement, and the first and indispensable step towards all other improvements. I was some time amongst these people, and was exceedingly pleased, and surprised also, to witness their sobriety, and their peaceable conduct; not having seen an instance of drunkenness, or seen or heard of any use made of spirituous liquors whilst I was amongst the tribe.

Ah-ton-we-tuck (the cock turkey, PLATE 186), is another Kickapoo of some distinction, and a disciple of the Prophet; in the attitude of prayer also, which he is reading off from characters cut upon a stick that he holds in his hands. It was told to me in the tribe by the Traders (though I am afraid to vouch for the whole truth of it), that while a Methodist preacher was soliciting him for permission to preach in his village, the Prophet refused him the privilege, but secretly took him aside and supported him until he learned from him his creed, and his system of teaching it to others; when he discharged him, and commenced preaching amongst his people himself; pretending to have had an interview with some superhuman mission, or inspired personage; ingeniously resolving, that if there was any honour or emolument, or influence to be gained by the promulgation of it, he might as well

* Since the above was written, the whole of this tribe have been removed beyond the Missouri, having sold out their lands in the state of Illinois to the Government.

185   186

187   188

have it as another person; and with this view he commenced preaching and instituted a prayer, which he ingeniously carved on a maple-stick of an inch and a half in breadth, in characters somewhat resembling Chinese letters. These sticks, with the prayers on them, he has introduced into every family of the tribe, and into the hands of every individual; and as he has necessarily the manufacturing of them all, he sells them at his own price; and has thus added lucre to fame, and in two essential and effective ways, augmented his influence in his tribe. Every man, woman and child in the tribe, so far as I saw them, were in the habit of saying their prayer from this stick when going to bed at night, and also when rising in the morning; which was invariably done by placing the fore-finger of the right hand under the upper character, until they repeat a sentence or two, which it suggests to them; and then slipping it under the next, and the next, and so on, to the bottom of the stick, which altogether required about ten minutes, as it was sung over in a sort of a chaunt, to the end.

Many people have called all this an ingenious piece of hypocrisy on the part of the Prophet, and whether it be so or not, I cannot decide; yet one thing I can vouch to be true, that whether his motives and his life be as pure as he pretends or not, his example has done much towards correcting the habits of his people, and has effectually turned their attention from the destructive habits of dissipation and vice, to temperance and industry, in the pursuits of agriculture and the arts. The world may still be unwilling to allow him much credit for this, but I am ready to award him a great deal, who can by his influence thus far arrest the miseries of dissipation and the horrid deformities of vice, in the descending prospects of a nation who have so long had, and still have, the white-skin teachers of vices and dissipation amongst them.

Besides these two chiefs, I have also painted *Ma-shee-na* (the elk's horn) *Ke-chim-qua* (the big bear), warriors, and *Ah-tee-wot-o-mee*, and *She-nah-wee*, women of the same tribe, whose portraits are in the Gallery.

WEE-AHS.

These are also the remnant of a once powerful tribe, and reduced by the same causes, to the number of 200. This tribe formerly lived in the State of Indiana, and have been moved with the Piankeshaws, to a position forty or fifty miles south of Fort Leavenworth.

Go-to-kow-pah-a (he who stands by himself, PLATE 187), and *Wa-pon-je-a* (the swan), are two of the most distinguished warriors of the tribe, both with intelligent European heads.

POT-O-WAT-O-MIES.

The remains of a tribe who were once very numerous and warlike, but reduced by whiskey and small-pox, to their present number, which is not more than 2700. This tribe may be said to be semi-civilized, inasmuch as they have so long lived in contiguity with white people, with whom their blood is considerably mixed, and whose modes and whose manners they have in many respects copied. From a similarity of language as well as of customs and personal appearance, there is no doubt that they have formerly been a part of the great tribe of Chippeways or Ot-ta-was. living neighbours and adjoining to them, on the North. This tribe live within the state of Michigan, and there own a rich and very valuable tract of land ; which, like the Kickapoos, they are selling out to the Government, and about to remove to the west bank of the Missouri, where a part of the tribe have already gone and settled, in the vicinity of Fort Leavenworth. Of this tribe I have painted the portraits of *On-saw-kie* (the Sac, PLATE 189), in the attitude of prayer, and *Na-pow-sa* (the Bear travelling in the night,) PLATE 190, one of the principal chiefs of the tribe. These people have for some time lived neighbours to, and somewhat under the influence of the Kickapoos ; and very many of the tribe have become zealous disciples of the Kickapoo prophet, using his prayers most devoutly, and in the manner that I have already described, as is seen in the first of the two last-named portraits.

KAS-KAS-KI-AS.

This is the name of a tribe that formerly occupied, and of course owned, a vast tract of country lying on the East of the Mississippi, and between its banks and the Ohio, and now forming a considerable portion of the great and populous state of Illinois. History furnishes us a full and extraordinary account of the once warlike character and numbers of this tribe; and also of the disastrous career that they have led, from their first acquaintance with civilized neighbours ; whose rapacious avarice in grasping for their fine lands—with the banes of whiskey and small-pox, added to the unexampled cruelty of neighbouring hostile tribes, who have struck at them in the days of their adversity, and helped to erase them from existence.

Perhaps there has been no other tribe on the Continent of equal power with the Kas-kas-ki-as, that have so suddenly sank down to complete annihilation and disappeared. The remnant of this tribe have long since merged into the tribe of Peorias of Illinois ; and it is doubtful whether one dozen of them are now existing. With the very few remnants of this tribe will die in a few years a beautiful language, entirely distinct from all others about it, unless some enthusiastic person may preserve it from the lips of those few who are yet able to speak it. Of this tribe I painted *Kee-mon-saw* (the little chief), half-civilized, and, I should think, half-breed (PLATE 191 ;) and *Wah-pe-seh-see* (PLATE 192), a very aged woman, mother of the same.

This young man is chief of the tribe ; and I was told by one of the Traders, that his mother and his son, were his only subjects ! Whether this be true or not, I cannot positively say, though I can assert with safety

189

190

191

192

193   194

G. Catlin

195   196

that there are but a very few of them left, and that those, like all of the last of tribes, will soon die of dissipation or broken hearts.

PE-O-RI-AS.

The name of another tribe inhabiting a part of the state of Illinois; and, like the above tribes, but a remnant and civilized (or *cicatrized*, to speak more correctly). This tribe number about 200, and are, like most of the other remnants of tribes on the frontiers, under contract to move to the West of the Missouri. Of this tribe I painted the portrait of *Pah-me-cow-e-tah* (the man who tracks, PLATE 193); and *Kee-mo-ra-ni-a* (no English, PLATE 194). These are said to be the most influential men in the tribe, and both were very curiously and *well* dressed, in articles of civilized manufacture.

PI-AN-KE-SHAWS.

The remnant of another tribe, of the states of Illinois and Indiana, who have also recently sold out their country to Government, and are under contract to move to the West of the Missouri, in the vicinity of Fort Leavenworth. *Ni-a-co-mo* (to fix with the foot, PLATE 195), a brave of distinction; and *Men-son-se-ah* (the left hand, PLATE 196), a fierce-looking and very distinguished warrior, with a stone-hatchet in his hand, are fair specimens of this reduced and enfeebled tribe, which do not number more than 170 persons at this time.

DELAWARES.

The very sound of this name has carried terror wherever it has been heard in the Indian wilderness; and it has travelled and been known, as well as the people, over a very great part of the Continent. This tribe originally occupied a great part of the Eastern border of Pennsylvania, and great part of the states of New Jersey and Delaware. No other tribe on the Continent has been so much moved and jostled about by civilized invasions; and none have retreated so far, or fought their way so desperately, as they have honourably and bravely contended for every foot of the ground they have passed over. From the banks of the Delaware to the lovely Susquehana, and *my native valley*, and to the base of and over, the Alleghany mountains, to the Ohio river—to the Illinois and the Mississippi, and at last to the West of the Missouri, they have been moved by Treaties after Treaties with the Government, who have now assigned to the mere handful of them that are left, a tract of land, as has been done a dozen times before, in *fee simple, for ever!* In every move the poor fellows have made, they have been thrust against their wills from the graves of their fathers and their children; and planted as they now are, on the borders of new enemies, where their first occupation has been to take up their weapons in self-defence, and fight for the ground they have been planted on. There is no tribe, perhaps, amongst which greater and more continued exertions have been made for their conversion to Christianity; and that ever since the zealous efforts of the Moravian missionaries, who first began with them; nor any, amongst whom those pious and zealous efforts have been squandered more in vain; which has, probably, been owing to the bad faith with which they have so often and so continually been treated by white people, which has excited prejudices that have stood in the way of their mental improvement.

This scattered and reduced tribe, which once contained some 10 or 15,000, numbers at this time but 800; and the greater part of them have been for the fifty or sixty years past, residing in Ohio and Indiana. In these states, their reservations became surrounded by white people, whom they dislike for neighbours, and their lands too valuable for Indians—and the certain consequence has been, that they have sold out and taken lands West of the Mississippi; on to which they have moved, and on which it is, and always will be, almost impossible to find them, owing to their desperate disposition for roaming about, indulging in the chase, and in wars with their enemies.

The wild frontier on which they are now placed, affords them so fine an opportunity to indulge both of these propensities, that they will be continually wandering in little and desperate parties over the vast buffalo plains, and exposed to their enemies, till at last the new country, which is given to them, in " fee simple, for ever," and which is destitute of game, will be deserted, and they, like the most of the removed remnants of tribes, will be destroyed; and the faith of the Government well preserved, which has offered *this* as their *last move*, and these lands as *theirs in fee simple, for ever*.

In my travels on the Upper Missouri, and in the Rocky Mountains, I learned to my utter astonishment, that little parties of these adventurous myrmidons, of only six or eight in numbers, had visited those remote tribes, at 2000 miles distance; and in several instances, after having cajoled a whole tribe—having been feasted in their villages—having solemnized the articles of everlasting peace with them, and received many presents at their hands, and taken affectionate leave, have brought away six or eight scalps with them; and nevertheless, braved their way, and defended themselves as they retreated in safety out of their enemies' country, and through the regions of other hostile tribes, where they managed to receive the same honours, and come off with similar trophies.

Amongst this tribe there are some renowned chiefs, whose lives, if correctly written, would be matter of the most extraordinary kind for the reading world; and of which, it may be in my power at some future time, to give a more detailed account. In PLATE 197 will be seen the portrait of one of the leading chiefs of the tribe, whose name is *Ni-co-man* (the answer), with his bow and arrows in his hand. *Non-on-da-gon* (PLATE 198), with a

197   198

199   200

G.Catlin.

silver ring in his nose, is another of the chiefs of distinction, whose history I admired very much, and whom, from his very gentlemanly attentions to me, I became much attached to. In both of these instances, their dresses were principally of stuffs of civilized manufacture; and their heads were bound with vari-coloured handkerchiefs or shawls, which were tastefully put on like a Turkish turban.

MO-HEE-CON-NEUHS, or MOHEGANS (THE GOOD CANOEMEN).

There are 400 of this once powerful and still famous tribe, residing near Green Bay, on a rich tract of land given to them by the Government, in the territory of Wisconsin, near Winnebago lake—on which they are living very comfortably; having brought with them from their former country, in the state of Massachusetts, a knowledge of agriculture, which they had there effectually learned and practiced.

This tribe are the remains, and all that are left, of the once powerful and celebrated tribe of Pequots of Massachusetts. History tells us, that in their wars and dissensions with the whites, a considerable portion of the tribe moved off under the command of a rival chief, and established a separate tribe or band, and took the name of Mo-hee-con-neuhs, which they have preserved until the present day; the rest of the tribe having long since been extinct.

The chief of this tribe, *Ee-tow-o-kaum* (both sides of the river, PLATE 199), which I have painted at full length, with a psalm-book in one hand, and a cane in the other, is a very shrewd and intelligent man, and a professed, and I think, sincere Christian. *Waun-naw-con* (the dish), John W. Quinney (PLATE 200), in civilized dress, is a civilized Indian, well-educated—speaking good English—is a Baptist missionary preacher, and a very plausible and eloquent speaker.

O-NEI-DA'S.

The remnant of a numerous tribe that have been destroyed by wars with the whites—by whiskey and small-pox, numbering at present but five or six hundred, and living in the most miserable poverty, on their reserve in the state of New York, near Utica and the banks of the Mohawk river. This tribe was one of the confederacy, called the Six Nations, and much distinguished in the early history of New York. The present chief is known by the name of *Bread* (PLATE 201). He is a shrewd and talented man, well educated,—speaking good English—is handsome, and a polite and gentlemanly man in his deportment.

TUS-KA-RO-RA'S.

Another of the tribes in the confederacy of the Six Nations, once numerous, but reduced at present to the number of 500. This little tribe are living on their reserve, a fine tract of land, near Buffalo, in the state of New York, and surrounded by civilized settlements. Many of them are good farmers, raising abundant and fine crops.

The chief of the tribe is a very dignified man, by the name of *Cu-sick*, and his son, of the same name, whom I have painted (PLATE 202), is a very talented man—has been educated for the pulpit in some one of our public institutions, and is now a Baptist preacher, and I am told a very eloquent speaker.

SEN-E-CA'S.

One thousand two hundred in numbers at present, living on their reserve. near Buffalo, and within a few miles of Niagara Falls, in the state of New York. This tribe formerly lived on the banks of the Seneca and Cayuga lakes ; but, like all the other tribes who have stood in the way of the " march of civilization," have repeatedly bargained away their country, and removed to the West ; which easily accounts for the origin of the familiar phrase that is used amongst them, that " they are going to the setting sun."

This tribe, when first known to the civilized world, contained some eight or ten thousand ; and from their position in the centre of the state of New York, held an important place in its history. The Senecas were one of the most numerous and effective tribes, constituting the compact called the " Six Nations ;" which was a confederacy formed by six tribes, who joined in a league as an effective mode of gaining strength, and preserving themselves by combined efforts which would be sufficiently strong to withstand the assaults of neighbouring tribes, or to resist the incursions of white people in their country. This confederacy consisted of the Senecas, Oneidas, Onondagas, Cayugas, Mohawks, and Tuskaroras ; and until the innovations of white people, with their destructive engines of war—with whiskey and small-pox, they held their sway in the country, carrying victory, and consequently terror and dismay, wherever they warred. Their war-parties were fearlessly sent into Connecticut and Massachusetts, to Virginia, and even to the Carolinas. and victory everywhere crowned their efforts. Their combined strength, however, in all its might, poor fellows, was not enough to withstand the siege of their insidious foes—a destroying flood that has risen and advanced, like a flood-tide upon them, and covered their country ; has broken up their strong holds, has driven them from land to land ; and in their retreat, has drowned the most of them in its waves.

The Senecas are the most numerous remnant of this compact ; and have at their head an aged and very distinguished chief, familiarly known throughout the United States, by the name of *Red Jacket* (PLATE 205). I painted this portrait from the life, in the costume in which he is represented ; and indulged him also, in the wish he expressed, " that he might be seen standing on the Table Rock, at the Falls of Niagara ; about which place he thought his spirit would linger after he was dead."

Good Hunter (PLATE 203), and *Hard Hickory* (PLATE 204), are fair

201   202

203   204

G. Catlin.

205

specimens of the warriors of this tribe or rather hunters; or perhaps, still more correctly speaking, *farmers;* for the Senecas have had no battles to fight lately, and very little game to kill, except squirrels and pheasants; and their hands are turned to the plough, having become, most of them, tolerable farmers; raising the necessaries, and many of the luxuries of life, from the soil.

Of this interesting tribe, the visitors to my Gallery will find several other portraits and paintings of their customs; and in books that have been written, and are being compiled, a much more able and faithful account than I can give in an epistle of this kind.

The fame as well as the face of Red Jacket, is generally familiar to the citizens of the United States and the Canadas; and for the information of those who have not known him, I will briefly say, that he has been for many years the head chief of the scattered remnants of that once powerful compact, the Six Nations; a part of whom reside on their reservations in the vicinity of the Senecas, amounting perhaps in all, to about four thousand, and owning some two hundred thousand acres of fine lands. Of this Confederacy, the Mohawks and Cayugas, chiefly emigrated to Canada, some fifty years ago, leaving the Senecas, the Tuskaroras, Oneidas, and Onondagas in the state of New York, on fine tracts of lands, completely surrounded with white population; who by industry and enterprize, are making the Indian lands too valuable to be long in their possession, who will no doubt be induced to sell out to the Government, or, in other words, to exchange them for lands West of the Mississippi, where it is the avowed intention of the Government to remove all the border tribes.*

Red Jacket has been reputed one of the greatest orators of his day; and, no doubt, more distinguished for his eloquence and his influence in council, than as a warrior, in which character I think history has not said much of him. This may be owing, in a great measure, to the fact that the wars of his nation were chiefly fought before his fighting days; and that the greater part of his life and his talents have been spent with his tribe, during its downfall; where, instead of the horrors of Indian wars, they have had a more fatal and destructive enemy to encounter, in the insidious encroachments of pale faces, which he has been for many years exerting his eloquence and all his talents to resist. Poor old chief—not all the eloquence of Cicero and Demosthenes would be able to avert the calamity, that awaits his declining nation—to resist the despoiling hand of mercenary white man, that opens and spreads liberally, but to entrap the unwary and ignorant within its withering grasp.

This talented old man has for many years past, strenuously remonstrated

* Since the above was written, the Senecas and all the other remnants of the Six Nations residing in the state of New York, have agreed in Treaties with the United States to remove to tracts of country assigned them, West of the Mississippi, twelve hundred miles from their reservations in the state of New York.

both to the Governor of New York, and the President of the United States, against the continual encroachments of white people; whom he represented as using every endeavour to wrest from them their lands—to destroy their game, introducing vices of a horrible character, and unknown to his people by nature ! and most vehemently of all, has he continually remonstrated against the preaching of missionaries in his tribe; alleging, that the " black coats" (as he calls the clergymen), did more mischief than good in his tribe, by creating doubts and dissensions amongst his people ! which are destructive of his peace, and dangerous to the success, and even *existence* of his tribe. Like many other great men who endeavour to soothe broken and painful feelings, by the kindness of the bottle, he has long since taken up whiskey-drinking to excess; and much of his time, lies drunk in his cabin, or under the corner of a fence, or wherever else its *kindness* urges the necessity of his dropping his helpless body and limbs, to indulge in the delightful *spell*. He is as great a drunkard as some of our most distinguished lawgivers and law-makers; and yet *ten times more culpable*, as he has little to do in life, and wields the destinies of a nation in his hands !*

There are no better people to be found, than the Seneca Indians—none that I know of that are by Nature more talented and ingenious: nor any that would be found to be better neighbours, if the arts and abuses of white men and whiskey, could be kept away from them. They have mostly laid down their hunting habits, and become efficient farmers, raising fine crops of corn, and a great abundance of hogs, cattle and horses, and other necessaries and luxuries of life.

I-ROQUOIS.

One of the most numerous and powerful tribes that ever existed in the Northern regions of our country, and now one of the most completely annihilated. This tribe occupied a vast tract of country on the River St. Lawrence, between its banks and Lake Champlain; and at times, by conquest, actually over-run the whole country, from that to the shores of Lakes Erie, Huron, and Michigan. But by their continual wars with the French, English, and Indians, and dissipation and disease, they have been almost entirely annihilated. The few remnants of them have long since merged into other tribes, and been mostly lost sight of.† Of this tribe I have

---

* This celebrated chief died several years since, in his village near Buffalo; and since his death our famous comedian, Mr. Placide, has erected a handsome and appropriate monument over his grave; and I am pleased also to learn, that my friend Wm. L. Stone, Esq., is building him a still more lasting one in history, which he is compiling, of the life of this extraordinary man, to an early perusal of which, I can confidently refer the world for much curious and valuable information.

† The whole of the Six Nations have been by some writers denominated Iroquois—how correct this may be, I am not quite able to say; one thing is certain, that is, that the Iroquois tribe did not all belong to that Confederacy, their original country was on the shores of the St. Lawrence; and, although one branch of their nation, the Mohawks, formed a part, and the most effective portion of that compact, yet the other members of it spoke

painted but one, *Not-o-way* (the thinker, PLATE 206). This was an excellent man, and was handsomely dressed for his picture. I had much conversation with him, and became very much attached to him. He seemed to be quite ignorant of the early history of his tribe, as well as of the position and condition of its few scattered remnants, who are yet in existence. He told me, however, that he had always learned that the Iroquois had conquered nearly all the world; but the Great Spirit being offended at the great slaughters by his favourite people, resolved to punish them; and he sent a dreadful disease amongst them, that carried the most of them off, and all the rest that could be found, were killed by their enemies—that though he was an Iroquois, which he was proud to acknowledge to me, as I was to "make him live after he was dead;" he wished it to be generally thought, that he was a Chippeway, that he might live as long as the Great Spirit had wished it when he made him.*

different languages; and a great part of the Iroquois moved their settlements further North and East, instead of joining in the continual wars carried on by the Six Nations. It is of this part of the tribe that I am speaking, when I mention them as nearly extinct: and it is from this branch of the family that I got the portrait which I have introduced above.

* Since the above Letter was written, all the tribes and remnants of tribes mentioned in it have been removed by the Government, to lands West of the Mississippi and Missouri, given to them, in addition to considerable annuities, in consideration for the immense tracts of country they have left on the frontier, and within the States. The present positions of these tribes, and their relative locations to the civilized frontier and the wild, unjostled tribes, can be seen on a map in the beginning of this Volume. There are also other tribes there laid down, who have also been removed by Treaty stipulations, in the same way, which are treated of in subsequent Letters. The Government, under General Jackson, strenuously set forth and carried out, the policy of removing all the semi-civilized and border Indians, to a country West of the Mississippi; and although the project had many violent opponents, yet there were very many strong reasons in favour of it, and the thing *has been at last done*; and a few years will decide, by the best of all arguments, whether the policy was a good one or not. I may have occasion to say more on this subject hereafter; and in the mean time recommend the reader to examine their relative positions, and contemplate their prospects between their mortal foes on the West, and their acquisitive *friends* following them up from the East.

ST. LOUIS.

WHILST I am thus taking a hasty glance at the tribes on the Atlantic Coast, on the borders of Mexico, and the confines of Canada, the reader will pardon me for taking him for a few minutes to the mouth of the Columbia, on the Pacific Coast; which place I have not yet quite reached myself, in my wild rambles, but most undoubtedly shall ere long, if my strolling career be not suddenly stopped. I scarcely need tell the reader where the Columbia River is, since its course and its character have been so often, and so well described, by recent travellers through those regions. I can now but glance at this remote country and its customs ; and revert to it again after I shall have examined it in all its parts, and collected my materials for a fuller account.

FLAT HEADS.

These are a very numerous people, inhabiting the shores of the Columbia River, and a vast tract of country lying to the South of it, and living in a country which is exceedingly sterile and almost entirely, in many parts, destitute of game for the subsistence of the savage; they are mostly obliged to live on roots, which they dig from the ground, and fish which they take from the streams; the consequences of which are, that they are generally poor and miserably clad; and in no respect equal to the Indians of whom I have heretofore spoken, who live on the East of the Rocky Mountains, in the ranges of the buffaloes; where they are well-fed, and mostly have good horses to ride, and materials in abundance for manufacturing their beautiful and comfortable dresses.

The people generally denominated Flat Heads, are divided into a great many bands, and although they have undoubtedly got their name from the custom of flattening the head ; yet there are but very few of those so denominated, who actually practice that extraordinary custom.

The *Nez Percés* who inhabit the upper waters and mountainous parts of the Columbia, are a part of this tribe, though they are seldom known to flatten the head like those lower down, and about the mouth of the river. *Hee-oh'ks-te-kin* (the rabbit skin leggings, PLATE 207), and *H'co-a-h'co a-h'cotes-min* (no horns on his head, PLATE 208), are young men of this tribe. These two young men, when I painted them, were in beautiful Sioux dresses,

207

208

209

210

which had been presented to them in a talk with the Sioux, who treated them very kindly, while passing through the Sioux country. These two men were part of a delegation that came across the Rocky Mountains to St. Louis, a few years since, to enquire for the truth of a representation which they said some white man had made amongst them, " that our religion was better than theirs, and that they would all be lost if they did not embrace it."

Two old and venerable men of this party died in St. Louis, and I travelled two thousand miles, companion with these two young fellows, towards their own country, and became much pleased with their manners and dispositions.

The last mentioned of the two, died near the mouth of the Yellow Stone River on his way home, with disease which he had contracted in the civilized district; and the other one I have since learned, arrived safely amongst his friends, conveying to them the melancholy intelligence of the deaths of all the rest of his party; but assurances at the same time, from General Clark, and many Reverend gentlemen, that the report which they had heard was well founded ; and that missionaries, good and religious men, would soon come amongst them to teach this religion, so that they could all understand and have the benefits of it.

When I first heard the report of the object of this extraordinary mission across the mountains, I could scarcely believe it ; but on conversing with General Clark on a future occasion, I was fully convinced of the fact; and I, like thousands of others, have had the satisfaction of witnessing the complete success that has crowned the bold and daring exertions of Mr. Lee and Mr. Spalding, two Reverend gentlemen who have answered in a Christian manner to this unprecedented call ; and with their wives have crossed the most rugged wilds and wildernesses of the Rocky Mountains, and triumphantly proved to the world, that the Indians, in their native wilds are a kind and friendly people, and susceptible of mental improvement.

I had long been of the opinion, that to ensure success, the exertions of pious men should be carried into the heart of the wilderness, beyond the reach and influence of civilized vices ; and I so expressed my opinion to the Reverend Mr. Spalding and his lady, in Pittsburgh, when on their way, in their first Tour to that distant country. I have seen the Reverend Mr. Lee and several others of the mission, several years since the formation of their school; as well as several gentlemen who have visited their settlement, and from all, I am fully convinced of the complete success of these excellent and persevering gentlemen, in proving to the world the absurdity of the assertion that has been often made, " that the Indian can never be civilized or christianized." Their uninterrupted transit over such a vast and wild journey, also, with their wives on horseback, who were everywhere on their way, as well as amongst the tribes where they have located, treated with the utmost kindness and respect, bears strong testimony to the assertions so often made by travellers in those countries, that these are, in their native state, a kind and excellent people.

I hope I shall on a future occasion, be able to give the reader some further detailed account of the success of these zealous and excellent men, whose example, of penetrating to the *heart* of the Indian country, and *there* teaching the Indian in the true and effective way, will be a lasting honour to themselves, and I fully believe, a permanent benefit to those ignorant and benighted people.

THE CHINOOKS,

Inhabiting the lower parts of the Columbia, are a small tribe, and correctly come under the name of Flat Heads, as they are almost the only people who strictly adhere to the custom of squeezing and flattening the head. PLATE 209, is the portrait of a Chinook boy, of fifteen or eighteen years of age, on whose head that frightful operation has never been performed. And in PLATE 210, will be seen the portrait of a Chinook woman, with her child in her arms, her own head flattened, and the infant undergoing the process of flattening; which is done by placing its back on a board, or thick plank, to which it is lashed with thongs, to a position from which it cannot escape, and the back of the head supported by a sort of pillow, made of moss or rabbit skins, with an inclined piece (as is seen in the drawing), resting on the forehead of the child; being every day drawn down a little tighter by means of a cord, which holds it in its place, until it at length touches the nose; thus forming a straight line from the crown of the head to the end of the nose.

This process is seemingly a very cruel one, though I doubt whether it causes much pain; as it is done in earliest infancy, whilst the bones are soft and cartilaginous, and easily pressed into this distorted shape, by forcing the occipital up, and the frontal down; so that the skull at the top, in profile, will show a breadth of not more than an inch and a half, or two inches; when in a front view it exhibits a great expansion on the sides, making it at the top, nearly the width of one and a half natural heads.

By this remarkable operation, the brain is singularly changed from its natural shape; but in all probability, not in the least diminished or injured in its natural functions. This belief is drawn from the testimony of many credible witnesses, who have closely scrutinized them; and ascertained that those who have the head flattened, are in no way inferior in intellectual powers to those whose heads are in their natural shapes.

In the process of flattening the head, there is often another form of crib or cradle, into which the child is placed, much in the form of a small canoe, dug out of a log of wood, with a cavity just large enough to admit the body of the child, and the head also, giving it room to expand in width; while from the head of the cradle there is a sort of lever, with an elastic spring to it that comes down on the forehead of the child, and produces the same effects as the one I have above described.

The child is wrapped in rabbits' skins, and placed in this little coffin-like

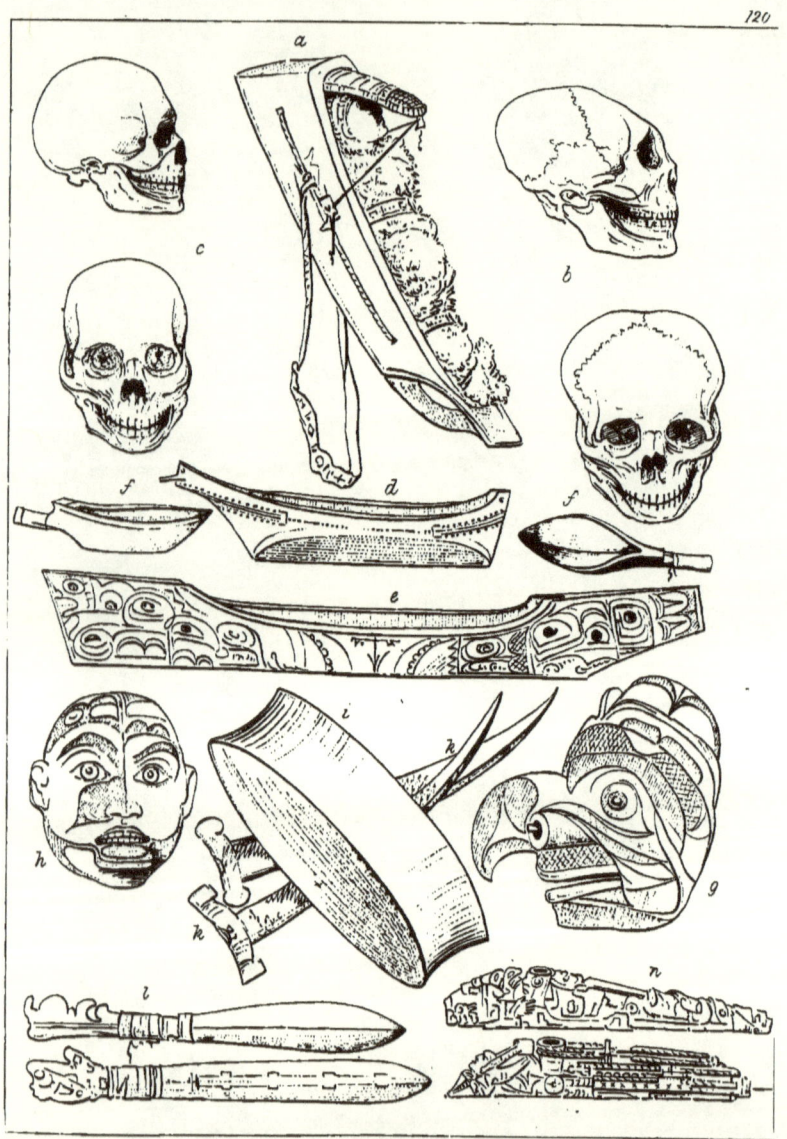

210½

G. Catlin

looking cradle, from which it is not, in some instances, taken out for several weeks. The bandages over and about the lower limbs, and as high up as the breast, are loose, and repeatedly taken off in the same day, as the child may require cleansing; but the head and shoulders are kept strictly in the same position, and the breast given to the child by holding it up in the cradle, loosing the outer end of the lever that comes over the nose, and raising it up of turning it aside, so as to allow the child to come at the breast, without moving its head.

The length of time that the infants are generally carried in these cradles is three, five, or eight weeks, until the bones are so formed as to keep their shapes, and preserve this singular appearance through life.

This little cradle has a strap, which passes over the woman's forehead whilst the cradle rides on her back; and if the child dies during its subjection to this rigid mode, its cradle becomes its coffin, forming a little canoe, in which it lies floating on the water in some sacred pool, where they are often in the habit of fastening the canoes, containing the dead bodies of the old and the young; or which is often the case, elevated into the branches of trees, where their bodies are left to decay, and their bones to dry; whilst they are bandaged in many skins, and curiously packed in their canoes, with paddles to propel, and ladles to bail them out, and provisions to last, and pipes to smoke, as they are performing their " long journey after death, to their contemplated hunting-grounds," which these people think is to be performed in their canoes.

In PLATE 210½ letter *a*, is an accurate drawing of the above-mentioned cradle, perfectly exemplifying the custom described ; and by the side of it (letter *b*,) the drawing of a Chinook skull, giving the front and profile view of it. Letter *c*, in the same plate, exhibits an Indian skull in its *natural* shape, to contrast with the *artificial*.*

This mode of flattening the head is certainly one of the most unaccountable, as well as unmeaning customs, found amongst the North American Indians. What it could have originated in, or for what purpose, other than a mere useless fashion, it could have been invented, no human being can probably ever tell. The Indians have many curious and ridiculous fashions, which have come into existence, no doubt, by accident, and are of no earthly use (like many silly fashions in enlightened society), yet they are perpetuated much longer, and that only because their ancestors practiced them in ages gone by. The greater part of Indian modes, however, and particularly those that are accompanied with much pain or trouble in their enactment, are most wonderfully adapted to the production of some good or useful results; for which the inquisitive world, I am sure, may for ever look in vain to this stupid and useless fashion, that has most unfortunately been engendered on these ignorant people, whose superstition forbids them to lay it down.

* Besides these, there are a number of other skulls in the Collection, most interesting specimens, from various tribes.

It is a curious fact, and one that should be mentioned here, that these people have not been alone in this strange custom; but that it existed and was practiced precisely the same, until recently, amongst the Choctaws and Chickasaws; who occupied a large part of the states of Mississippi and Alabama, where they have laid their bones, and hundreds of their skulls have been procured, bearing incontrovertible evidence of a similar treatment, with similar results.

The Choctaws who are now living, do not flatten the head; the custom, like that of the *medicine-bag*, and many others, which the Indians have departed from, from the assurances of white people, that they were of no use, and were utterly ridiculous to be followed. Whilst amongst the Choctaws, I could learn little more from the people about such a custom, than that " their old men recollected to have heard it spoken of"—which is much less satisfactory evidence than inquisitive white people get by referring to the grave, which the Indian never meddles with. The distance of the Choctaws from the country of the Chinooks, is certainly between two and three thousand miles; and there being no intervening tribes practicing the same custom—and no probability that any two tribes in a state of Nature, would ever hit upon so peculiar an absurdity, we come, whether willingly or not, to the conclusion, that these tribes must at some former period, have lived neighbours to each other, or have been parts of the same family; which time and circumstances have gradually removed to such a very great distance from each other. Nor does this, in my opinion (as many suppose), furnish any very strong evidence in support of the theory, that the different tribes have all sprung from one stock; but carries a strong argument to the other side, by furnishing proof of the very great tenacity these people have for their peculiar customs; many of which are certainly not general, but often carried from one end of the Continent to the other, or from ocean to ocean, by bands or sections of tribes, which often get "run off" by their enemies in wars, or in hunting, as I have before described; where to emigrate to a vast distance is not so unaccountable a thing, but almost the *inevitable result*, of a tribe that have got set in motion, all the way amongst deadly foes, in whose countries it would be fatal to stop.

I am obliged therefore, to believe, that either the Chinooks emigrated from the Atlantic, or that the Choctaws came from the West side of the Rocky Mountains; and I regret exceedingly that I have not been able as yet, to compare the languages of these two tribes, in which I should expect to find some decided resemblance. They might, however, have been near neighbours, and practicing a copied custom where there was no resemblance in their language.

Whilst among the Choctaws I wrote down from the lips of one of their chiefs, the following tradition, which seems strongly to favour the supposition that they came from a great distance in the West, and probably from beyond the Rocky Mountains:—*Tradition.* " The Choctaws, a great many winters ago, commenced moving from the country where they then lived, which was a great distance to the West of the great river, and the mountains of snow; and they were a great many years on their way. A great medicine-man led them the whole way, by going before with a red pole, which he stuck in the ground every night where they encamped. This pole was every morning found leaning to the East; and he told them that they must continue to travel to the East, until the pole would stand upright in their encampment, and that there the Great Spirit had directed that they should live. At a place which they named *Nah-ne-wa-ye* (the sloping hill); the pole stood straight up, where they pitched their encampment, which was one mile square, with the men encamped on the outside, and the women and children in the centre; which is the centre of the old Choctaw nation to 'this day.'"

In the vicinity of the mouth of the Columbia, there are, besides the *Chinooks*, the *Klick-a-tacks*, *Cheehaylas*, *Na-as*, and many other tribes, whose customs are interesting, and of whose manufactures, my Museum contains many very curious and interesting specimens, from which I have inserted a few outlines in PLATE 210½, to which the reader will refer. Letter *d*, is a correct drawing of a Chinook canoe—*e*, a Na-as war-canoe, curiously carved and painted—*f*, two dishes or ladles for baling their canoes—*g*, a Stikeen mask, curiously carved and painted, worn by the mystery-men when in councils, for the purpose of calling up the Great or Evil Spirits to consult on the policy of peace or war—*h*, custom of the *Na-as* women of wearing a block of wood in the under lip, which is almost as unaccountable as the custom of flattening the head. Letter *i*, is a drawing of the block, and the exact dimensions of one in the Collection, taken out of the lip of a deceased *Na-as* woman—*k*, "wapito diggers," instruments used by the women for digging the wapito, a bulbous root, much like a turnip, which the French Traders call *pomme blanche*, and which I have before described. Letter *l*, *pau-to-mau-gons*, or *po-ko-mo-kons*, war-clubs, the one made by the Indians from a piece of native copper, the other of the bone of the sperm whale. Letter *n*, two very curiously carved pipes, made of black slate and highly polished.

Besides these, the visitor will find in the Collection a great number of their very ingenious articles of dress; their culinary, war, and hunting implements, as well as specimens of their spinning and weaving, by which they convert dog's hair and the wool of the mountain-sheep into durable and splendid robes, the production of which, I venture to say, would bid defiance to any of the looms in the American or British Factories.

The Indians who inhabit the rugged wildernesses of the Rocky Mountains, are chiefly the Blackfeet and Crows, of whom I have heretofore spoken, and the Shoshonees or Snakes, who are a part of the Camanchees, speaking the same language, and the Shoshokies or root diggers, who inhabit the southern parts of those vast and wild realms, with the Arapohoes and Navahoes, who are neighbours to the Camanchees on the West, having Santa Fe on the

South, and the coast of California on the West. Of the Shoshonees and Shoshokies, all travellers who have spoken of them, give them a good character, as a kind and hospitable and harmless people ; to which fact I could cite the unquestionable authorities of the excellent Rev. Mr. Parker, who has published his interesting Tour across the Rocky Mountains—Lewis and Clarke—Capt. Bonneville and others; and I allege it to be a truth, that the reason why we find them as they are uniformly described, a kind and inoffensive people, is, that they have not as yet been abused—that they are in their primitive state, as the Great Spirit made and endowed them with good hearts and kind feelings, unalloyed and untainted by the vices of the money-making world.

To the same fact, relative to the tribes on the Columbia river, I have been allowed to quote the authority of H. Beaver, a very worthy and kind Reverend Gentleman of England, who has been for several years past living with these people, and writes to me thus :—

" I shall be always ready, with pleasure, to testify my perfect accordance with the sentiments I have heard you express, both in your public lectures, and private conversation, relative to the much-traduced character of our Red brethren, particularly as it relates to their *honesty, hospitality* and *peaceableness,* throughout the length and breadth of the Columbia. Whatever of a contrary disposition has at any time, in those parts, been displayed by them, has, I am persuaded been exotic, and forced on them by the depravity and impositions of the white Traders.'"

LETTER—No. 49

ST. LOUIS.

In one of my last Letters from Fort Gibson, written some months since, I promised to open my note-book on a future occasion, to give some further account of tribes and remnants of tribes located in that vicinity, amongst whom I had been spending some time with my pen and my pencil; and having since that time extended my rambles over much of that ground again, and also through the regions of the East and South East, from whence the most of those tribes have emigrated; I consider this a proper time to say something more of them, and their customs and condition, before I go farther.

The most of these, as I have said, are tribes or parts of tribes which the Government has recently, by means of Treaty stipulations, removed to that wild and distant country, on to lands which have been given to them in exchange for their valuable possessions within the States, ten or twelve hundred miles to the East.

Of a number of such reduced and removed tribes, who have been located West of the Missouri, and North of St. Louis, I have already spoken in a former Letter, and shall yet make brief mention of another, which has been conducted to the same region—and then direct the attention of the reader to those which are settled in the neighbourhood of Fort Gibson, who are the Cherokees—Creeks—Choctaws—Chickasaws—Seminoles, and Euchees.

The people above alluded to are the

SHA-WA-NO'S.

The history of this once powerful tribe is so closely and necessarily connected with that of the United States, and the revolutionary war, that it is generally pretty well understood. This tribe formerly inhabited great parts of the states of Pennsylvania, New Jersey, (and for the last sixty years,) a part of the states of Ohio and Indiana, to which they had removed; and now, a considerable portion of them, a tract of country several hundred miles West of the Mississippi, which has been conveyed to them by Government in exchange for their lands in Ohio, from which it is expected the remainder of the tribe will soon move. It has been said that this tribe came formerly from Florida, but I do not believe it. The mere fact, that there is found in East Florida a river by the name of *Su wa-nee*, which bears some resemblance to *Sha-wa-no*, seems, as far as I can learn, to be the principal evidence that has been adduced for the fact. They have evidently been known, and that within the scope of our authenticated history, on the Atlantic coast—on the Delaware and Chesapeak bays. And after that, have fought their way against every sort of trespass and abuse—against the bayonet and disease, through the states of Pennsylvania, Delaware and Ohio, Indiana, Illinois and Missouri, to their present location near the Kon-zas River, at least 1500 miles from their native country.

This tribe and the Delawares, of whom I have spoken, were neighbours on the Atlantic coast, and alternately allies and enemies, have retrograded and retreated together—have fought their enemies united, and fought each other, until their remnants that have outlived their nation's calamities, have now settled as neighbours together in the Western wilds; where, it is probable, the sweeping hand of death will soon relieve *them* from further necessity of warring or moving; and the *Government*, from the necessity or policy of proposing to them a yet more distant home. In their long and disastrous pilgrimage, both of these tribes laid claim to, and alternately occupied the beautiful and renowned valley of Wy-ô-ming; and after strewing the Susquehana's lovely banks with their bones, and their tumuli, they both yielded at last to the dire necessity, which follows all civilized intercourse with natives, and fled to the Alleghany, and at last to the banks of the Ohio; where necessity soon came again, and again, and again, until the great "*Guardian*" *of all* "*red children*" placed them where they now are.

There are of this tribe remaining about 1200; some few of whom are agriculturists, and industrious and temperate, and religious people; but the greater proportion of them are miserably poor and dependent, having scarcely the ambition to labour or to hunt, and a passion for whiskey-drinking, that sinks them into the most abject poverty, as they will give the last thing they possess for a drink of it.

There is not a tribe on the Continent whose history is more interesting than that of the Shawanos, nor any one that has produced more extraordinary men.

The great Tecumseh, whose name and history I can but barely allude to at this time, was the chief of this tribe, and perhaps the most extraordinary Indian of his age.

The present chief of the tribe *Lay-law-she-kaw* (he who goes up the river, PLATE 211), is a very aged, but extraordinary man, with a fine and intelligent head, and his ears slit and stretched down to his shoulders, a custom highly valued in this tribe; which is done by severing the rim of the ear with a knife, and stretching it down by wearing heavy weights attached to it at times, to elongate it as much as possible, making a large orifice, through which, on parades, &c. they often pass a bunch of arrows or quills, and wear them as ornaments.

In this instance (which was not an unusual one), the rims of the ears were so extended down, that they touched the shoulders, making a ring through which the whole hand could easily be passed. The daughter of this old chief, *Ka-te-qua* (the female eagle, PLATE 212), was an agreeable-looking girl, of fifteen years of age, and much thought of by the tribe. *Pah-te-coo-saw* (the straight man, PLATE 213), a warrior of this tribe, has distinguished himself by his exploits; and when he sat for his picture, had painted his face in a very curious manner with black and red paint.

Ten-squa-ta-way (the open door, PLATE 214), called the " *Shawnee Prophet*," is perhaps one of the most remarkable men, who has flourished on these frontiers for some time past. This man is brother of the famous Tecumseh, and quite equal in his *medicines* or mysteries, to what his brother was in arms; he was blind in his left eye, and in his right hand he was holding his " *medicine fire*," and his " *sacred string of beans*" in the other. With these mysteries he made his way through most of the North Western tribes, enlisting warriors wherever he went, to assist Tecumseh in effecting his great scheme, of forming a confederacy of all the Indians on the frontier, to drive back the whites and defend the Indians' rights; which he told them could never in any other way be protected. His plan was certainly a correct one, if not a very great one; and his brother, the Prophet, exercised his astonishing influence in raising men for him to fight his battles, and carry out his plans. For this purpose, he started upon an embassy to the various tribes on the Upper Missouri, nearly all of which he visited with astonishing success; exhibiting his mystery fire, and using his sacred string of beans, which every young man who was willing to go to war, was to touch; thereby taking the solemn oath to start when called upon, and not to turn back.

In this most surprising manner, this ingenious man entered the villages of most of his inveterate enemies, and of others who never had heard of the name of his tribe; and manœuvred in so successful a way, as to make his medicines a safe passport for him to all of their villages; and also the means of enlisting in the different tribes, some eight or ten thousand warriors, who had solemnly sworn to return with him on his way back; and to assist in the wars that Tecumseh was to wage against the whites on the frontier. I found, on my visit to the Sioux—to the Puncahs, to the Riccarees and the Mandans, that he had been there, and even to the Blackfeet; and everywhere told them of the potency of his mysteries, and assured them, that if they allowed the fire to go out in their wigwams, it would prove fatal to them in every case. He carried with him into every wigwam that he visited, the image of a dead person of the size of life; which was made ingeniously of some light material, and always kept concealed under bandages of thin white muslin cloths and not to be opened; of this he made great mystery, and got his recruits to swear by touching a sacred string of white beans, which he had attached to its neck or some other way secreted about it. In this way, by his extraordinary cunning, he had carried terror into the country as far as he went; and had actually enlisted some eight or ten thousand men, who were sworn to follow him home; and in a few days would have been on their way with him, had not a couple of his political enemies in his own tribe, followed on his track, even to those remote tribes, and defeated his plans, by pronouncing him an impostor; and all of his forms and plans an imposition upon them, which they would be fools to listen to. In this manner, this great recruiting officer was defeated in his plans, for raising an army of men to fight his brother's battles; and to save his life, he discharged his medicines as suddenly as possible, and secretly travelled his way home, over those vast regions, to his own tribe, where the death of Tecumseh, and the opposition of enemies, killed all his splendid prospects, and doomed him to live the rest of his days in silence, and a sort of disgrace; like all men in Indian communities who pretend to *great medicine*, in any way, and fail; as they all think such failure an evidence of the displeasure of the Great Spirit, who always judges right.

This, no doubt, has been a very shrewd and influential man, but circumstances have destroyed him, as they have many other great men before him; and he now lives respected, but silent and melancholy in his tribe. I conversed with him a great deal about his brother Tecumseh, of whom he spoke frankly, and seemingly with great pleasure; but of himself and his own great schemes, he would say nothing. He told me that Tecumseh's plans were to embody all the Indian tribes in a grand confederacy, from the province of Mexico, to the Great Lakes, to unite their forces in an army that would be able to meet and drive back the white people, who were continually advancing on the Indian tribes, and forcing them from their lands towards the Rocky Mountains—that Tecumseh was a great general, and that nothing but his premature death defeated his grand plan.

The Shawanos, like most of the other remnants of tribes, in whose countries the game has been destroyed, and by the use of whiskey, have been reduced to poverty and absolute want, have become, to a certain degree, agriculturists; raising corn and beans, potatoes, hogs, horses, &c., so as to be enabled, if they could possess anywhere on earth, a country which they could have a certainty of holding in perpetuity, as their own, to plant and raise their own crops, and necessaries of life from the ground.

The Government have effected with these people, as with most of the other dispersed tribes, an arrangement by which they are to remove West of the Mississippi, to lands assigned them; on which they are solemnly promised a home *for ever;* the uncertain definition of which important word, time and circumstances alone will determine.

Besides the personages whom I have above-mentioned, I painted the portraits of several others of note in the tribe; and amongst them *Lay-loo-ah-pe-ai shee-kaw* (the grass-bush and blossom), whom I introduce in this place, rather from the very handy and poetical name, than from any great personal distinction known to have been acquired by him.

211   212

213   214

Living in the vicinity of, and about Fort Gibson, on the Arkansas, and 700 miles west of the Mississippi river, are a third part or more of the once very numerous and powerful tribe who inhabited and still inhabit, a considerable part of the state of Georgia, and under a Treaty made with the United States Government, have been removed to those regions, where they are settled on a fine tract of country; and having advanced some-what in the arts and agriculture before they started, are now found to be mostly living well, cultivating their fields of corn and other crops, which they raise with great success.

Under a serious difficulty existing between these people (whom their for-mer solemn Treaties with the United States Government, were acknowledged a free and independent nation, with powers to make and enforce their own laws), and the state of Georgia, which could not admit such a Government within her sovereignty, it was thought most expedient by the Government of the United States, to propose to them, for the fourth or fifth time, to enter into Treaty stipulations again to move; and by so doing to settle the difficult question with the state of Georgia, and at the same time, to place them in peaceable possession of a large tract of fine country, where they would for ever be free from the continual trespasses and abuses which it was supposed they would be subjected to, if they were to remain in the state of Georgia, under the present difficulties and the high excited feelings which were then existing in the minds of many people along their borders.

John Ross, a civilized and highly educated and accomplished gentleman, who is the head-chief of the tribe, (ᴘʟᴀᴛᴇ 215), and several of his leading subordinate chiefs, have sternly and steadily rejected the proposition of such a Treaty; and are yet, with a great majority of the nation remaining on their own ground in the state of Georgia, although some six or 7000 of the tribe have several years since removed to the Arkansas, under the guidance and con-troul of an aged and dignified chief by the name of *Jol-lee* (ᴘʟᴀᴛᴇ 217).

This man, like most of the chiefs, as well as a very great proportion of the Cherokee population, has a mixture of white and red blood in his veins, of which, in this instance, the first seems decidedly to predominate. Another chief, and second to this, amongst this portion of the Cherokees, by the name of Teh-ke-neh-kee (the black coat), I have also painted and placed in my Collection, as well as a very interesting specimen of the Cherokee women (ᴘʟᴀᴛᴇ 216).

I have travelled pretty generally through the several different locations of this interesting tribe, both in the Western and Eastern divisions, and have found them, as well as the Choctaws and Creeks, their neighbours, very far advanced in the arts; affording to the world the most satisfactory evidences that are to be found in America, of the fact, that the Indian was not made to shun and evade good example, and necessarily to live and die a brute, as many speculating men would needs record them and treat them, until they are robbed and trampled into the dust ; that no living evidences might give the lie to their theories, or draw the cloak from their cruel and horrible iniquities.

As I have repeatedly said to my readers, in the course of my former epistles, that the greater part of my time would be devoted to the condition and customs of the tribes that might be found in their primitive state, they will feel disposed to pardon me for barely introducing the Cherokees, and several others of these very interesting tribes, and leaving them and their customs and histories (which are of themselves enough for volumes), to the reader, who is, perhaps, nearly as familiar as I am myself, with the full and fair accounts of these people, who have had their historians and biographers.

The history of the Cherokees and other numerous remnants of tribes, who are the exhabitants of the finest and most valued portions of the United States, is a subject of great interest and importance, and has already been woven into the most valued histories of the country, as well as forming material parts of the archives of the Government, which is my excuse for barely introducing the reader to them, and beckoning him off again to the native and untrodden wilds, to teach him something new and unrecorded. Yet I leave the subject, as I left the people (to whom I became attached, for their kindness and friendship), with a heavy heart, wishing them success and the blessing of the Great Spirit, who alone can avert the *doom* that would almost seem to be fixed for their unfortunate race.

The Cherokees amount in all to about 22,000, 16,000 of whom are yet living in Georgia, under the Government of their chief, John Ross, whose name I have before mentioned ; with this excellent man, who has been for many years devotedly opposed to the Treaty stipulations for moving from their country, I have been familiarly acquainted ; and, notwithstanding the bitter invective and animadversions that have been by his political enemies heaped upon him, I feel authorized, and bound, to testify to the unassuming and gentlemanly urbanity of his manners, as well as to the rigid temperance of his habits, and the purity of his language, in which I never knew him to transgress for a moment, in public or private interviews.

At this time, the most strenuous endeavours are making on the part of the Government and the state of Georgia, for the completion of an arrangement for the removal of the whole of this tribe, as well as of the Choctaws and Seminoles ; and I have not a doubt of their final success, which seems, from all former experience, to attend every project of the kind made by the Government to their red children.*

* Since writing the above, the Government have succeeded in removing the remainder of the Cherokees beyond the Mississippi, where they have taken up their residence along side of their old friends, who emigrated several years since under *Jol-lee*, as I have before mentioned. In the few years past, the Government has also succeeded in stipulating with, and removing West of the Mississippi, nearly every remnant of tribes spoken of in

215   216

217   218

Catlin.

It is not for me to decide, nor in this place to reason, as to the justice or injustice of the treatment of these people at the hands of the Government or individuals; or of the wisdom of the policy which is to place them in a new, though vast and fertile country, 1000 miles from the land of their birth, in the doubtful dilemma whether to break the natural turf with their rusting ploughshares, or string their bows, and dash over the boundless prairies, beckoned on by the alluring dictates of their nature, seeking laurels amongst the ranks of their new enemies, and subsistence amongst the herds of buffaloes.

Besides the Cherokees in Georgia, and those that I have spoken of in the neighbourhood of Fort Gibson, there is another band or family of the same tribe, of several hundreds, living on the banks of the Canadian river, an hundred or more miles South West of Fort Gibson, under the Government of a distinguished chief by the name of *Tuch-ee* (familiarly called by the white people, " *Dutch*," PLATE 218). This is one of the most extraordinary men that lives on the frontiers at the present day, both for his remarkable history, and for his fine and manly figure, and character of face.

This man was in the employment of the Government as a guide and hunter for the regiment of dragoons, on their expedition to the Camanchees, where I had him for a constant companion for several months, and opportunities in abundance, for studying his true character, and of witnessing his wonderful exploits in the different varieties of the chase. The history of this man's life has been very curious and surprising; and I sincerely hope that some one, with more leisure and more talent than myself, will take it up, and do it justice. I promise that the life of this man furnishes the best materials for a popular tale, that are now to be procured on the Western frontier.

He is familiarly known, and much of his life, to all the officers who have been stationed at Fort Gibson, or at any of the posts in that region of country.

Some twenty years or more since, becoming fatigued and incensed with civilized encroachments, that were continually making on the borders of the Cherokee country in Georgia, where he then resided, and probably, foreseeing the disastrous results they were to lead to, he beat up for volunteers to emigrate to the West, where he had designed to go, and colonize in a wild country beyond the reach and contamination of civilized innovations; and succeeded in getting several hundred men, women, and children, whom he led over the banks of the Mississippi, and settled upon the head waters of White River, where they lived until the appearance of white faces, which began to peep through the forests at them, when they made another move of 600 miles to the banks of the Canadian, where they now reside; and where, by

this and the two last Letters, so that there are at this time but a few hundreds of the red men East of the Mississippi; and it is probable, that a few months more will effect the removal of the remainder of them. See their present locations West of the Mississippi, on the map at the beginning of this Volume.

the system of desperate warfare, which he has carried on against the Osages and the Camanchees, he has successfully cleared away from a large tract of fine country, all the enemies that could contend for it, and now holds it, with his little band of myrmidons, as their own undisputed soil, where they are living comfortably by raising from the soil fine crops of corn and potatoes, and other necessaries of life ; whilst they indulge whenever they please, in the pleasures of the chase amongst the herds of buffaloes, or in the natural propensity for ornamenting their dresses and their war-clubs with the scalp-locks of their enemies.

The CREEKS (or MUS-KO-GEES).

Of 20,000 in numbers, have, until quite recently, occupied an immense tract of country in the states of Mississippi and Alabama ; but by a similar arrangement (and for a similar purpose) with the Government, have exchanged their possessions there for a country, adjoining to the Cherokees, on the South side of the Arkansas, to which they have already all removed, and on which, like the Cherokees, they are laying out fine farms, and building good houses, in which they live ; in many instances, surrounded by immense fields of corn and wheat. There is scarcely a finer country on earth than that now owned by the Creeks ; and in North America, certainly no Indian tribe more advanced in the arts and agriculture than they are. It is no uncommon thing to see a Creek with twenty or thirty slaves at work on his plantation, having brought them from a slave-holding country, from which, in their long journey, and exposure to white man's ingenuity, I venture to say, that most of them got rid of one-half of them, whilst on their long and disastrous crusade.

The Creeks, as well as the Cherokees and Choctaws, have good schools and churches established amongst them, conducted by excellent and pious men, from whose example they are drawing great and lasting benefits.

In PLATES 219 and 220, I have given the portraits of two distinguished men, and I believe, both chiefs. The first by the name of *Stee-cha-co-me-co* (the great king), familiarly called " Ben Perryman ;" and the other, *Hol-te-mal-te-tez-te-neehk-ee* (——), called " Sam Perryman." These two men are brothers, and are fair specimens of the tribe, who are mostly clad in calicoes, and other cloths of civilized manufacture ; tasselled and fringed off by themselves in the most fantastic way, and sometimes with much true and picturesque taste. They use a vast many beads, and other trinkets, to hang upon their necks, and ornament their moccasins and beautiful belts.

The CHOCTAWS,

Of fifteen thousand, are another tribe, removed from the Northern parts of Alabama, and Mississippi, within the few years past, and now occupying a large and rich tract of country, South of the Arkansas and the Canadian

219   220

221   222

G Catlin

223

rivers ; adjoining to the country of the Creeks and the Cherokees, equally civilized, and living much in the same manner.

In this tribe I painted the portrait of their famous and excellent chief, *Mo-sho-la-tub-bee* (he who puts out and kills, PLATE 221), who has since died of the small-pox. In the same plate will also be seen, the portrait of a distinguished and very gentlemanly man, who has been well-educated, and who gave me much curious and valuable information, of the history and traditions of his tribe. The name of this man, is *Ha-tchoc-tuck-nee* (the snapping turtle, PLATE 222), familiarly called by the whites *"Peter Pinchlin."*

These people seem, even in their troubles, to be happy ; and have, like all the other remnants of tribes, preserved with great tenacity their different games, which it would seem they are everlastingly practicing for want of other occupations or amusements in life. Whilst I was staying at the Choctaw agency in the midst of their nation, it seemed to be a sort of season of amusements, a kind of holiday ; when the whole tribe almost, were assembled around the establishment, and from day to day we were entertained with some games or feats that were exceedingly amusing : horse-racing, dancing, wrestling, foot-racing, and ball-playing, were amongst the most exciting ; and of all the catalogue, the most beautiful, was decidedly that of ball-playing. This wonderful game, which is the favourite one amongst all the tribes, and with these Southern tribes played exactly the same, can never be appreciated by those who are not happy enough to see it.

It is no uncommon occurrence for six or eight hundred or a thousand of these young men, to engage in a game of ball, with five or six times that number of spectators, of men, women and children, surrounding the ground, and looking on. And I pronounce such a scene, with its hundreds of Nature's most beautiful models, denuded, and painted of various colours, running and leaping into the air, in all the most extravagant and varied forms, in the desperate struggles for the ball, a school for the painter or sculptor, equal to any of those which ever inspired the hand of the artist in the Olympian games or the Roman forum.

I have made it an uniform rule, whilst in the Indian country, to attend every ball-play I could hear of, if I could do it by riding a distance of twenty or thirty miles ; and my usual custom has been on such occasions, to straddle the back of my horse, and look on to the best advantage. In this way I have sat, and oftentimes reclined, and almost dropped from my horse's back, with irresistible laughter at the succession of droll tricks, and kicks and scuffles which ensue, in the almost superhuman struggles for the ball. These plays generally commence at nine o'clock, or near it, in the morning ; and I have more than once balanced myself on my pony, from that time till near sundown, without more than one minute of intermission at a time, before the game has been decided.

It is impossible for pen and ink alone, or brushes, or even with their combined efforts, to give more than a *caricature* of such a scene ; but such as I have been able to do, I have put upon the canvass, and in the slight outlines which I have here attached in PLATES 224, 225, 226, taken from those paintings, (for the colouring to which the reader must look to my pen,) I will convey as correct an account as I can, and leave the reader to imagine the rest ; or look to *other books* for what I may have omitted.

While at the Choctaw agency it was announced, that there was to be a great play on a certain day, within a few miles, on which occasion I attended, and made the three sketches which are hereto annexed ; and also the following entry in my note-book, which I literally copy out.

" Monday afternoon at three, o'clock, I rode out with Lieutenants S. and M., to a very pretty prairie, about six miles distant, to the ball-play-ground of the Choctaws, where we found several thousand Indians encamped. There were two points of timber about half a mile apart, in which the two parties for the play, with their respective families and friends, were encamped ; and lying between them, the prairie on which the game was to be played. My companions and myself, although we had been apprised, that to see the whole of a ball-play, we must remain on the ground all the night previous, had brought nothing to sleep upon, resolving to keep our eyes open, and see what transpired through the night. During the afternoon, we loitered about amongst the different tents and shantees of the two encampments, and afterwards, at sundown, witnessed the ceremony of measuring out the ground, and erecting the " byes" or goals which were to guide the play. Each party had their goal made with two upright posts, about 25 feet high and six feet apart, set firm in the ground, with a pole across at the top. These goals were about forty or fifty rods apart ; and at a point just half way between, was another small stake, driven down, where the ball was to be thrown up at the firing of a gun, to be struggled for by the players. All this preparation was made by some old men, who were, it seems, selected to be the judges of the play, who drew a line from one bye to the other ; to which directly came from the woods, on both sides, a great concourse of women and old men, boys and girls, and dogs and horses, where bets were to be made on the play. The betting was all done across this line, and seemed to be chiefly left to the women, who seemed to have martialled out a little of everything that their houses and their fields possessed. Goods and chattels—knives—dresses—blankets—pots and kettles—dogs and horses, and guns ; and all were placed in the possession of *stake-holders*, who sat by them, and watched them on the ground all night, preparatory to the play.

The sticks with which this tribe play, are bent into an oblong hoop at the end, with a sort of slight web of small thongs tied across, to prevent the ball from passing through. The players hold one of these in each hand, and by leaping into the air, they catch the ball between the two nettings and throw it, without being allowed to strike it, or catch it in their hands.

The mode in which these sticks are constructed and used, will be seen in the portrait of *Tullock-chish-ko* (he who drinks the juice of the stone), the

most distinguished ball-player of the Choctaw nation (PLATE 223), represented in his ball-play dress, with his ball-sticks in his hands. In every ball-
play of these people, it is a rule of the play, that no man shall wear moccasins on his feet, or any other dress, than his breech-cloth around his waist,
with a beautiful bead belt, and a " tail," made of white horsehair or quills,
and a " mane" on the neck, of horsehair dyed of various colours.

This game had been arranged and "made up," three or four months before the parties met to play it, and in the following manner :—The two
champions who led the two parties, and had the alternate choosing of the
players through the whole tribe, sent runners, with the ball-sticks most fantastically ornamented with ribbons and red paint, to be touched by each one
of the chosen players ; who thereby agreed to be on the spot at the appointed
time and ready for the play. The ground having been all prepared and
preliminaries of the game all settled, and the bettings all made, and goods
all " staked," night came on without the appearance of any players on the
ground. But soon after dark, a procession of lighted flambeaux was seen
coming from each encampment, to the ground where the players assembled
around their respective byes ; and at the beat of the drums and chaunts of
the women, each party of players commenced the "ball-play dance" (PLATE
224). Each party danced for a quarter of an hour around their respective
byes, in their ball-play dress ; rattling their ball-sticks together in the most
violent manner, and all singing as loud as they could raise their voices;
whilst the women of each party, who had their goods at stake, formed into
two rows on the line between the two parties of players, and danced also, in
an uniform step, and all their voices joined in chaunts to the Great Spirit ;
in which they were soliciting his favour in deciding the game to their advantage ; and also encouraging the players to exert every power they possessed,
in the struggle that was to ensue. In the mean time, four old medicine-men,
who were to have the starting of the ball, and who were to be judges of the
play, were seated at the point where the ball was to be started ; and busily
smoking to the Great Spirit for their success in judging rightly, and impartially, between the parties in so important an affair.

This dance was one of the most picturesque scenes imaginable, and was
repeated at intervals of every half hour during the night, and exactly in the
same manner; so that the players were certainly awake all the night, and
arranged in their appropriate dress, prepared for the play which was to commence at nine o'clock the next morning. In the morning, at the hour, the
two parties and all their friends, were drawn out and over the ground ; when
at length the game commenced, by the judges throwing up the ball at the
firing of a gun ; when an instant struggle ensued between the players, who
were some six or seven hundred in numbers, and were mutually endeavouring
to catch the ball in their sticks, and throw it home and between their respective stakes ; which, whenever successfully done, counts one for game. In this
game every player was dressed alike, that is, divested of all dress, except the

girdle and the tail, which I have before described; and in these desperate struggles for the ball, when it is *up* (PLATE 225, where hundreds are running together and leaping, actually over each other's heads, and darting between their adversaries' legs, tripping and throwing, and foiling each other in every possible manner, and every voice raised to the highest key, in shrill yelps and barks)! there are rapid successions of feats, and of incidents, that astonish and amuse far beyond the conception of any one who has not had the singular good luck to witness them. In these struggles, every mode is used that can be devised, to oppose the progress of the foremost, who is likely to get the ball; and these obstructions often meet desperate individual resistance, which terminates in a violent scuffle, and sometimes in fisticuffs; when their stricks are dropped, and the parties are unmolested, whilst they are settling it between themselves; unless it be by a general *stampedo*, to which they are subject who are down, if the ball happens to pass in their direction. Every weapon, by a rule of all ball-plays, is laid by in their respective encampments, and no man allowed to go for one; so that the sudden broils that take place on the ground, are presumed to be as suddenly settled without any probability of much personal injury; and no one is allowed to interfere in any way with the contentious individuals.

There are times, when the ball gets to the ground (PLATE 226), and such a confused mass rushing together around it, and knocking their sticks together, without the possibility of any one getting or seeing it, for the dust that they raise, that the spectator loses his strength, and everything else but his senses; when the condensed mass of ball-sticks, and shins, and bloody noses, is carried around the different parts of the ground, for a quarter of an hour at a time, without any one of the mass being able to see the ball; and which they are often thus scuffling for, several minutes after it has been thrown off, and played over another part of the ground.

For each time that the ball was passed between the stakes of either party, one was counted for their game, and a halt of about one minute; when it was again started by the judges of the play, and a similar struggle ensued; and so on until the successful party arrived to 100, which was the limit of the game, and accomplished at an hour's sun, when they took the stakes; and then, by a previous agreement, produced a number of jugs of whiskey, which gave all a wholesome drink, and sent them all off merry and in good humour, but not drunk.

After this exciting day, the concourse was assembled in the vicinity of the agency house, where we had a great variety of dances and other amusements; the most of which I have described on former occasions. One, however, was new to me, and I must say a few words of it: this was the *Eagle Dance*, a very pretty scene, which is got up by their young men, in honour of that bird, for which they seem to have a religious regard. This picturesque dance was given by twelve or sixteen men, whose bodies were chiefly naked and painted white, with white clay, and each

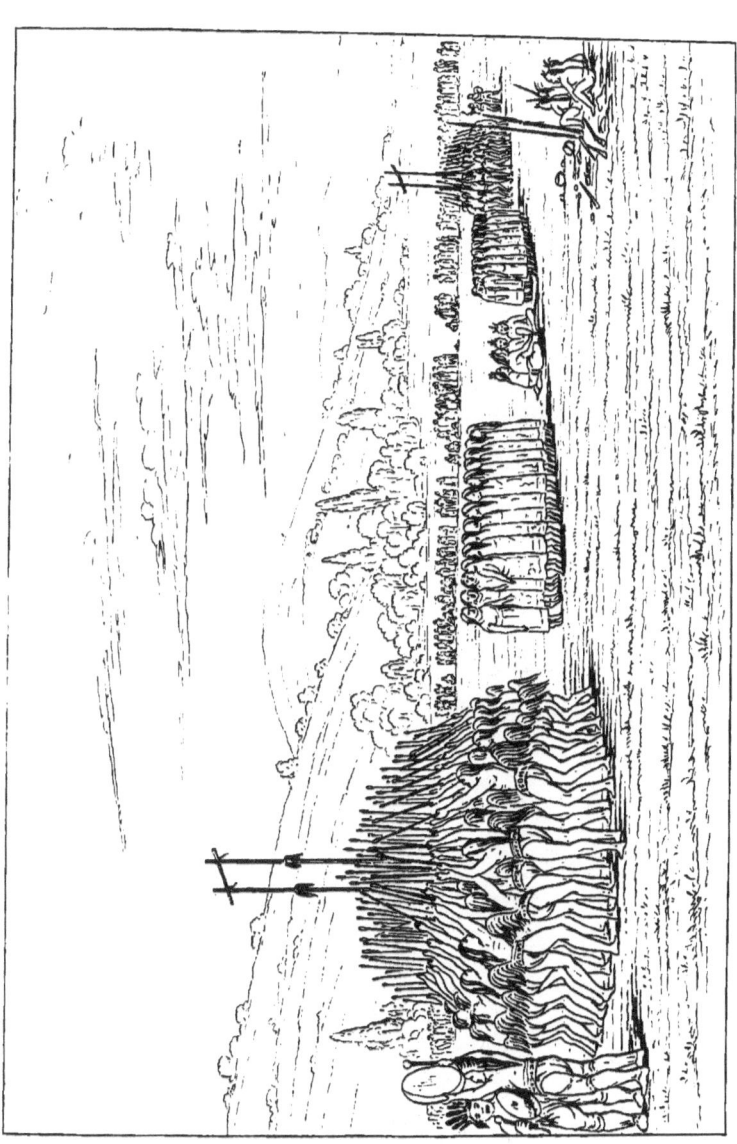

Catlin.

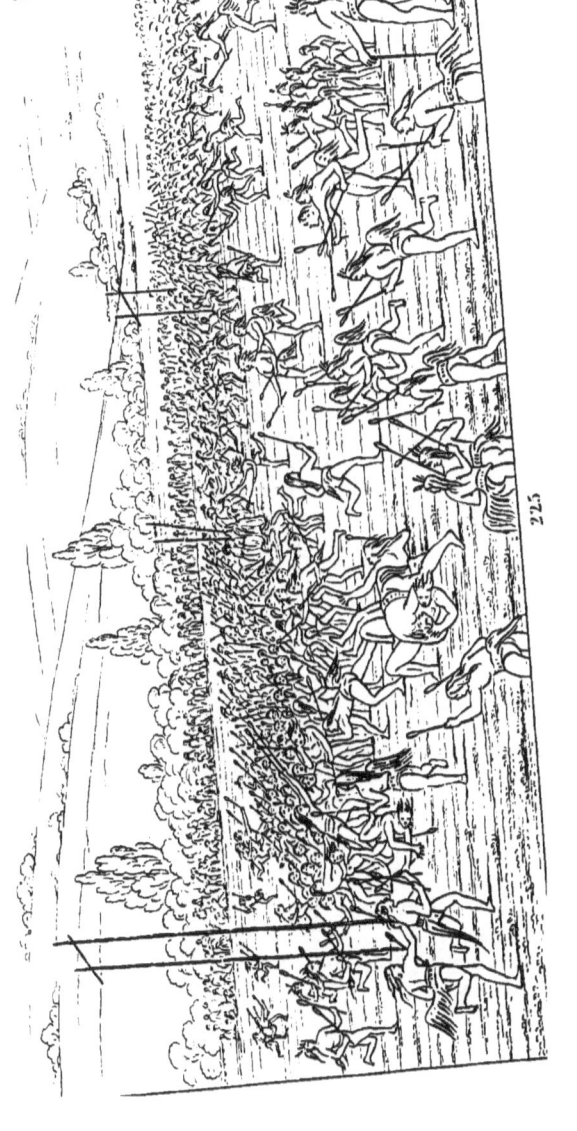

225

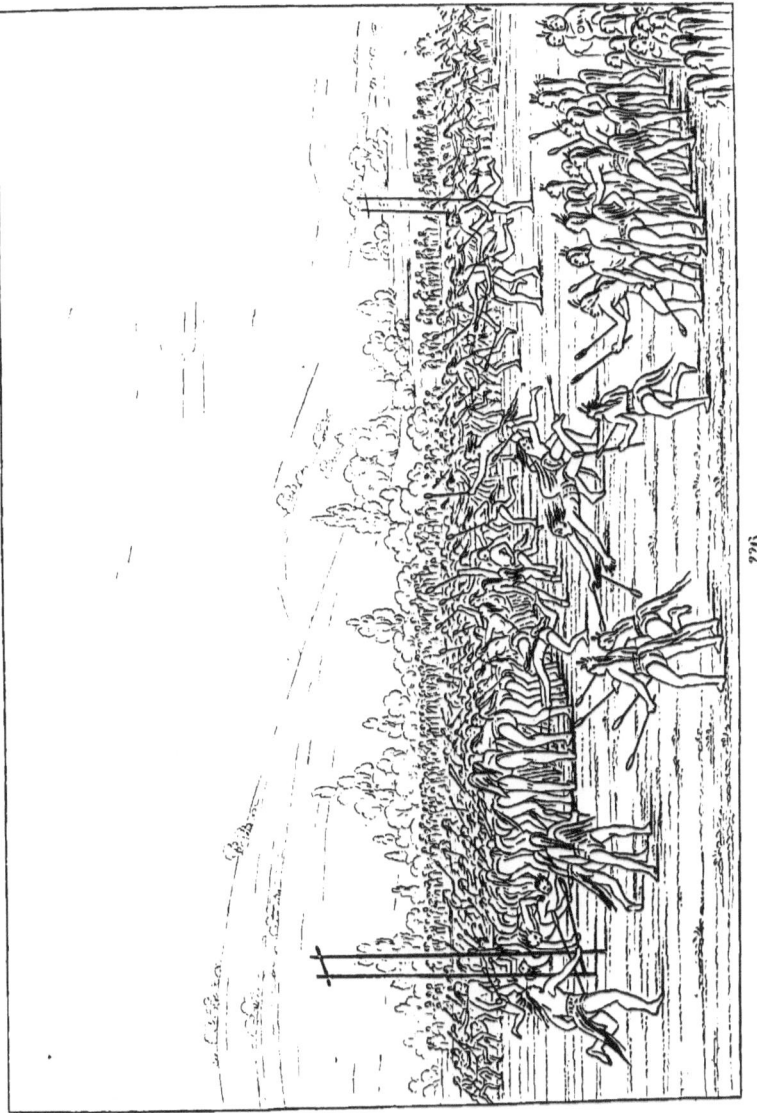

one holding in his hand the tail of the eagle, while his head was also decorated with an eagle's quill (PLATE 227). Spears were stuck in the ground, around which the dance was performed by four men at a time, who had simultaneously, at the beat of the drum, jumped up from the ground where they had all sat in rows of four, one row immediately behind the other, and ready to take the place of the first four when they left the ground fatigued, which they did by hopping or jumping around behind the rest, and taking their seats, ready to come up again in their turn, after each of the other sets had been through the same forms.

In this dance, the steps or rather jumps, were different from anything I had ever witnessed before, as the dancers were squat down, with their bodies almost to the ground, in a severe and most difficult posture, as will have been seen in the drawing.

I have already, in a former Letter, while speaking of the ancient custom of flattening the head, given a curious tradition of this interesting tribe, accounting for their having come from the West, and I here insert another or two, which I had, as well as the former one, from the lips of Peter Pinchlin, a very intelligent and influential man in the tribe, of whom I have spoken in page 123.

The Deluge. "Our people have always had a tradition of the Deluge, which happened in this way :—there was total darkness for a great time over the whole of the earth ; the Choctaw doctors or mystery-men looked out for daylight for a long time, until at last they despaired of ever seeing it, and the whole nation were very unhappy. At last a light was discovered in the North, and there was great rejoicing, until it was found to be great mountains of water rolling on, which destroyed them all, except a few families who had expected it and built a great raft, on which they were saved."

Future State. "Our people all believe that the spirit lives in a future state—that it has a great distance to travel after death towards the West—that it has to cross a dreadful deep and rapid stream, which is hemmed in on both sides by high and rugged hills—over this stream, from hill to hill, there lies a long and slippery pine-log, with the bark peeled off, over which the dead have to pass to the delightful hunting-grounds. On the other side of the stream there are six persons of the good hunting-grounds, with rocks in their hands, which they throw at them all when they are on the middle of the log. The good walk on safely, to the good hunting-grounds, where there is one continual day—where the trees are always green—where the sky has no clouds—where there are continual fine and cooling breezes—where there is one continual scene of feasting, dancing and rejoicing—where there is no pain or trouble, and people never grow old, but for ever live young and enjoy the youthful pleasures.

"The wicked see the stones coming, and try to dodge, by which they fall from the log, and go down thousands of feet to the water, which is dashing over the rocks, and is stinking with dead fish, and animals, where they are carried around and brought continually back to the same place in whirl-pools—where the trees are all dead, and the waters are full of toads and lizards, and snakes—where the dead are always hungry, and have nothing to eat—are always sick, and never die—where the sun never shines, and where the wicked are continually climbing up by thousands on the sides of a high rock from which they can overlook the beautiful country of the good hunting-grounds, the place of the happy, but never can reach it."

Origin of the *Craw-fish band*. " Our people have amongst them a band which is called, the *Craw-fish band*. They formerly, but at a very remote period, lived under ground, and used to come up out of the mud—they were a species of craw-fish; and they went on their hands and feet, and lived in a large cave deep under ground, where there was no light for several miles. They spoke no language at all, nor could they understand any. The entrance to their cave was through the mud—and they used to run down through that, and into their cave; and thus, the Choctaws were for a long time unable to molest them. The Choctaws used to lay and wait for them to come out into the sun, where they would try to talk to them, and cultivate an acquaintance.

" One day, a parcel of them were run upon so suddenly by the Choctaws, that they had no time to go through the mud into their cave, but were driven into it by another entrance, which they had through the rocks. The Choctaws then tried a long time to smoke them out, and at last suc-ceeded—they treated them kindly—taught them the Choctaw language—taught them to walk on two legs—made them cut off their toe nails, and pluck the hair from their bodies, after which they adopted them into their nation—and the remainder of them are living under ground to this day."

LETTER—No. 50.

HAVING recruited my health during the last winter. in recreation and amusements on the Coast of Florida, like a *bird of passage* I started, at the rallying notes of the swan and the wild goose, for the cool and freshness of the North, but the gifted passengers soon left me behind. I found them here, their nests built—their eggs hatched—their offspring fledged and figuring in the world, before I arrived.

The majestic river from the Balize to the Fall of St. Anthony, I have just passed over; with a high-wrought mind filled with amazement and wonder, like other travellers who occasionally leave the stale and profitless routine of the " Fashionable Tour," to gaze with admiration upon the wild and native grandeur and majesty of this great Western world. The Upper Mississippi, like the Upper Missouri, must be approached to be appreciated ; for all that can be seen on the Mississippi below St. Louis, or for several hundred miles above it, gives no hint or clue to the magnificence of the scenes which are continually opening to the view of the traveller, and riveting him to the deck of the steamer, through sunshine, lightning or rain, from the mouth of the Ouisconsin to the Fall of St. Anthony.

The traveller in ascending the river, will see but little of picturesque beauty in the landscape, until he reaches Rock Island ; and from that point he will find it growing gradually more interesting, until he reaches Prairie du Chien ; and from that place until he arrives at Lake Pepin, every reach and turn in the river presents to his eye a more immense and magnificent scene of grandeur and beauty. From day to day, the eye is riveted in listless, tireless admiration, upon the thousand bluffs which tower in majesty above the river on either side, and alternate as the river bends, into countless fascinating forms.

The whole face of the country is covered with a luxuriant growth of grass, whether there is timber or not ; and the magnificent bluffs, studding the sides of the river, and rising in the forms of immense cones, domes and ramparts, give peculiar pleasure, from the deep and soft green in which they are clad up their broad sides, and to their extreme tops, with a carpet of grass, with spots and clusters of timber of a deeper green ; and apparently in many places, arranged in orchards and pleasure-grounds by the hands of art.

The scenes that are passed between Prairie du Chien and St. Peters, including Lake Pepin, between whose magnificently turretted shores one passes for twenty-two miles, will amply reward the tourist for the time and expense of a visit to them. And to him or her of too little relish for Nature's rude works, to profit as they pass, there will be found a redeeming pleasure at the mouth of St. Peters and the Fall of St. Anthony. This scene has often been described, and I leave it for the world to come and gaze upon for themselves; recommending to them at the same time, to denominate the next " Fashionable Tour," a trip to St. Louis; thence by steamer to Rock Island, Galena, Dubuque, Prairie du Chien, Lake Pepin, ·St. Peters, Fall of St. Anthony, back to Prairie du Chien, from thence to Fort Winnebago, Green Bay, Mackinaw, Sault de St. Mary, Detroit, Buffalo, Niagara, and home. This Tour would comprehend but a small part of the great "Far West;" but it will furnish to the traveller a fair sample, and being a part of it which is now made so easily accessible to the world, and the only part of it to which *ladies* can have access, I would recommend to all who have time and inclination to devote to the enjoyment of so splendid a Tour, to wait not, but make it while the subject is new, and capable of producing the greatest degree of pleasure. To the world at large, this trip is one of surpassing interest—to the artist it has a double relish, and to *me*, still further inducements; inasmuch as, many of the tribes of Indians which I have met with, furnish manners and customs which have awakened my enthusiasm, and afforded me interesting materials for my Gallery.

To give to the reader a better idea of the character of the scenes which I have above described, along the stately shores of the Upper Mississippi, I have here inserted a river view taken about one hundred miles below this place (PLATE 228); and another of "Dubuque's Grave" (PLATE 229), about equi-distant between this and St. Louis; and both fairly setting forth the predominant character of the shores of the Upper Mississippi, which are every where covered, as far as the eye can behold, with a green turf, and occasional forest trees, as seen in the drawings.

Dubuque's Grave is a place of great notoriety on this river, in consequence of its having been the residence and mining place of the first lead mining pioneer of these regions, by the name of Dubuque, who held his title under a grant from the Mexican Government (I think), and settled by the side of this huge bluff, on the pinnacle of which he erected the tomb to receive his own body, and placed over it a cross with his own inscription on it. After his death, his body was placed within the tomb, at his request, lying in state (and uncovered except with his winding-sheet), upon a large flat stone, where it was exposed to the view, as his bones now are, to the gaze, of every traveller who takes the pains to ascend this beautiful, grassy and lilly-covered mound to th top, and peep through the gratings of two little windows, which have admitted the eyes, but stopped the sacrilegious *hands* of thousands who have taken a walk to it.

At the foot of this bluff, there is now an extensive smelting furnace, where vast quantities of lead are melted from the ores which are dug out of the hills in all directions about it.

228

229

C Catlin

230

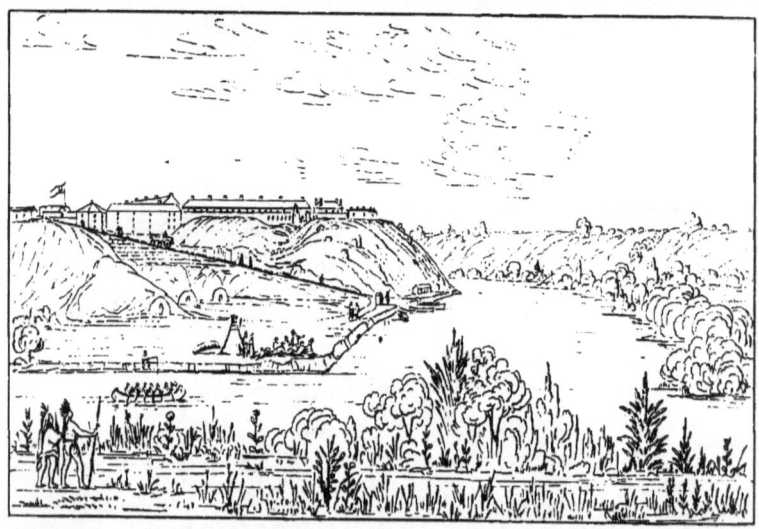

G. Catlin

231

The *Fall of St. Anthony* (PLATE 230), which is 900 miles above St. Louis, is the natural curiosity of this country, and nine miles above the mouth of St. Peters, from whence I am at this time writing. At this place, on the point of land between the Mississippi and the St. Peters rivers, the United States' Government have erected a strong Fort, which has taken the name of Fort Snelling, from the name of a distinguished and most excellent officer of that name, who superintended the building of it. The site of this Fort is one of the most judicious that could have been selected in the country, both for health and defence; and being on an elevation of 100 feet or more above the water, has an exceedingly bold and picturesque effect, as seen in PLATE 231.

This Fort is generally occupied by a regiment of men placed here to keep the peace amongst the Sioux and Chippeways, who occupy the country about it, and also for the purpose of protecting the citizens on the frontier.

The Fall of St. Anthony is about nine miles above this Fort, and the junction of the two rivers; and, although a picturesque and spirited scene, is but a pigmy in size to Niagara, and other cataracts in our country—the actual perpendicular fall being but eighteen feet, though of half a mile or so in extent, which is the width of the river; with brisk and leaping rapids above and below, giving life and spirit to the scene.

The Sioux who live in the vicinity of the Falls, and occupy all the country about here, West of the Mississippi, are a part of the great tribe on the Upper Missouri; and the same in most of their customs, yet very dissimilar in personal appearance, from the changes which civilized examples have wrought upon them. I mentioned in a former Letter, that the country of the Sioux, extended from the base of the Rocky Mountains to the banks of the Mississippi; and for the whole of that way, it is more or less settled by this immense tribe, bounding the East side of their country by the Mississippi River.

The Sioux in these parts, who are out of reach of the beavers and buffaloes, are poor and very meanly clad, compared to those on the Missouri, where they are in the midst of those and other wild animals, whose skins supply them with picturesque and comfortable dresses. The same deterioration also is seen in the morals and constitutions of these, as amongst all other Indians, who live along the frontiers, in the vicinity of our settlements, where whiskey is sold to them, and the small-pox and other diseases are introduced to shorten their lives.

The principal bands of the Sioux that visit this place, and who live in the vicinity of it, are those known as the Black Dog's band—Red Wing's band, and Wa-be-sha's band; each band known in common parlance, by the name of its chief, as I have mentioned. The Black Dog's band reside but a few miles above Fort Snelling, on the banks of the St. Peters, and number some five or six hundred. The Red Wing's band are at the head of Lake Pepin, sixty miles below this place on the West side of the river. And

Wa-be-sha's band and village are some sixty or more miles below Lake Pepin on the West side of the river, on a beautiful prairie, known (and ever will be) by the name of "Wa-be-sha's prairie." Each of these bands, and several others that live in this section of country, exhibit considerable industry in their agricultural pursuits, raising very handsome corn-fields, laying up their food, thus procured, for their subsistence during the long and tedious winters.

The greater part of the inhabitants of these bands are assembled here at this time, affording us, who are visitors here, a fine and wild scene of dances, amusements, &c. They seem to take great pleasure in "showing off" in these scenes, to the amusement of the many fashionable visitors, both ladies and gentlemen, who are in the habit of reaching this post, as steamers are arriving at this place every week in the summer from St. Louis.

Many of the customs of these people create great surprise in the minds of the travellers of the East, who here have the first satisfactory opportunity of seeing them ; and none, I observe, has created more surprise, and pleasure also, particularly amongst the ladies, than the mode of carrying their infants, slung on their backs, in their beautifully ornamented cradles.

The custom of carrying the child thus is not peculiar to this tribe, but belongs alike to all, as far as I have yet visited them ; and also as far as I have been able to learn from travellers, who have been amongst tribes that I have not yet seen. The child in its earliest infancy, has its back lashed to a straight board, being fastened to it by bandages, which pass around it in front, and on the back of the board they are tightened to the necessary degree by lacing strings, which hold it in a straight and healthy position, with its feet resting on a broad hoop, which passes around the foot of the cradle, and the child's position (as it rides about on its mother's back, supported by a broad strap that passes across her forehead), that of standing erect, which, no doubt, has a tendency to produce straight limbs, sound lungs, and long life. In PLATE 232, letter a, is a correct drawing of a Sioux cradle, which is in my Collection, and was purchased from a Sioux woman's back, as she was carrying her infant in it, as is seen in letter d of the same plate.

In this instance, as is often the case, the bandages that pass around the cradle, holding the child in, are all the way covered with a beautiful embroidery of porcupine quills, with ingenious figures of horses, men, &c. A broad hoop of elastic wood passes around in front of the child's face, to protect it in case of a fall, from the front of which is suspended a little toy of exquisite embroidery, for the child to handle and amuse itself with. To this and other little trinkets hanging in front of it, there are attached many little tinselled and tinkling things, of the brightest colours, to amuse both the eyes and the ears of the child. Whilst travelling on horseback, the arms of the child are fastened under the bandages, so as not to be endangered if the cradle falls ; and when at rest, they are generally taken out,

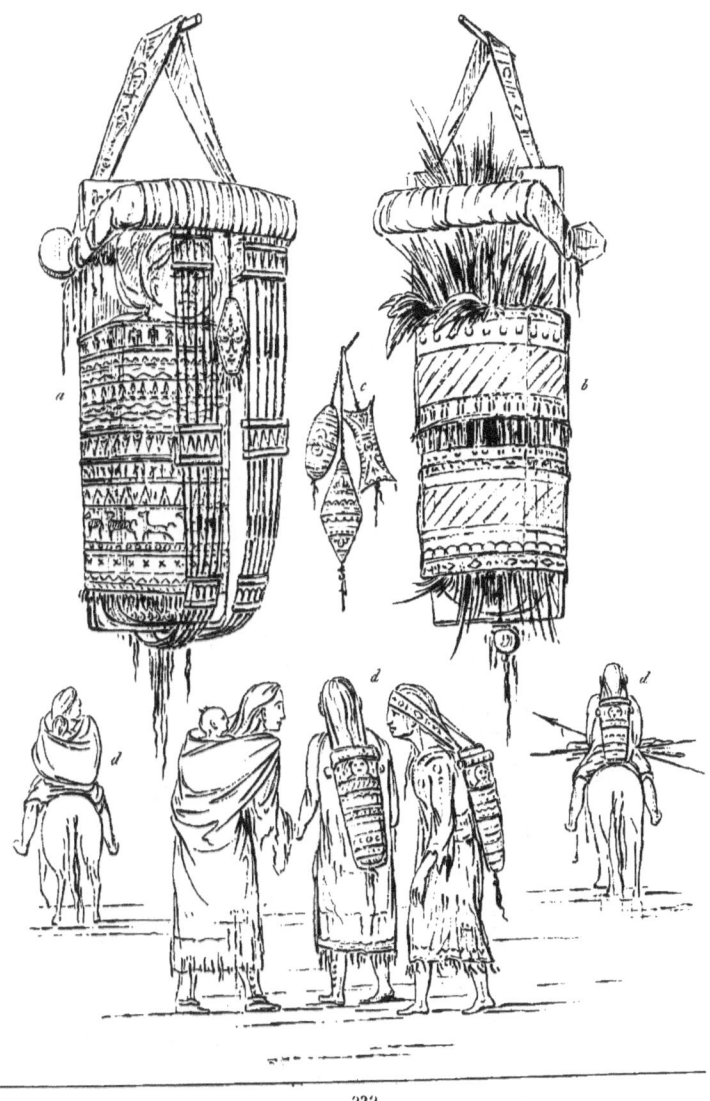

232

allowing the infant to reach and amuse itself with the little toys and trinkets that are placed before it, and within its reach. This seems like a cruel mode, but I am inclined to believe that it is a very good one for the people who use it, and well adapted to the circumstances under which they live; in support of which opinion, I offer the universality of the custom, which has been practiced for centuries amongst all the tribes of North America, as a legitimate and very strong reason. It is not true that amongst all the tribes the cradle will be found so much ornamented as in the present instance; but the model is essentially the same, as well as the mode of carrying it.

Along the frontiers, where the Indians have been ridiculed for the custom, as they are for everything that is not *civil* about them, they have in many instances departed from it; but even there, they will generally be seen lugging their child about in this way, when they have abandoned almost every other native custom, and are too poor to cover it with more than rags and strings, which fasten it to its cradle.

The infant is carried in this manner until it is five, six or seven months old, after which it is carried on the back, in the manner represented in two of the figures of the same plate, and held within the folds of the robe or blanket.

The modes of carrying the infant when riding, are also here shewn, and the manner in which the women ride, which, amongst all the tribes, is *astride*, in the same manner as that practiced by the men.

Letter *b* in the same plate is a *mourning cradle*, and opens to the view of the reader another very curious and interesting custom. If the infant dies during the time that is allotted to it to be carried in this cradle, it is buried, and the disconsolate mother fills the cradle with black quills and feathers, in the parts which the child's body had occupied, and in this way carries it around with her wherever she goes for a year or more, with as much care as if her infant were alive and in it; and she often lays or stands it leaning against the side of the wigwam, where she is all day engaged in her needle-work, and chatting and talking to it as familiarly and affectionately as if it were her loved infant, instead of its shell, that she was talking to. So lasting and so strong is the affection of these women for the lost child, that it matters not how heavy or cruel their load, or how rugged the route they have to pass over, they will faithfully carry this, and carefully from day to day, and even more strictly perform their duties to it, than if the child were alive and in it.

In the little toy that I have mentioned, and which is suspended before the child's face, is carefully and superstitiously preserved the *umbilicus*, which is always secured at the time of its birth, and being rolled up into a little wad of the size of a pea, and dried, it is enclosed in the centre of this little bag, and placed before the child's face, as its protector and its security for "*good luck*" and long life. Letter *c*, same plate, exhibits a number of forms and different tastes of several of these little toys, which I have purchased from the women, which they were very willing to sell for a trifling present; but in every instance, they cut them open, and removed from within a bunch of cotton or moss, the little sacred *medicine*, which, to part with, would be to " endanger the health of the child"—a thing that no consideration would have induced them in any instance to have done.

My brush has been busily employed at this place, as in others ; and amongst the dignitaries that I have painted, is, first and foremost, *Wa-nah-de-tunck-a* the big eagle), commonly called the "Black Dog" (PLATE 234). This is a very noted man, and chief of the *O-hah-kas-ka-toh-y-an-te* (long avenue) band.

By the side of him *Toh-to-wah-kon-da-pee* (the blue medicine—PLATE 233), a noted medicine-man, of the Ting-tah-to-a band ; with his medicine or mystery drum, made of deer-skins; and his mystery rattles made of antelopes' hoofs, in his hands. This notorious old man was professionally a doctor in his tribe, but not very distinguished, until my friend Dr. Jarvis, who is surgeon for the post, very liberally dealt out from the public medicine-chest, occasional " odds and ends" to him, and with a *professional concern* for the poor old fellow's success, instructed him in the modes of their application ; since which, the effects of his prescriptions have been so decided amongst his tribe, whom he holds in ignorance of his aid in his mysterious operations ; that he has risen quite rapidly into notice, within the few last years, in the vicinity of the Fort ; where he finds it most easy to carry out his new mode of practice, for reasons above mentioned.

In PLATES 235 and 236, there are portraits of the two most distinguished ball-players in the Sioux tribe, whose names are *Ah-no-je-nahge* (he who stands on · both sides), and *We-chush-ta-doo-ta* (the red man). Both of these young men stood to me for their portraits, in the dresses precisely in which they are painted ; with their ball-sticks in their hands, and in the attitudes of the play. We have had several very spirited plays here within the few past days ; and each of these young men came from the ball-play ground to my painting-room, in the dress in which they had just struggled in the play.

It will be seen by these sketches, that the custom in this tribe, differs in some respects from that of the Choctaws and other Southern tribes, of which I have before spoken ; and I there showed that they played with a stick in each hand, when the Sioux use but one stick, which is generally held in both hands, with a round hoop at the end, in which the ball is caught and thrown with wonderful tact ; a much more difficult feat, I should think, than that of the Choctaws, who catch the ball between two sticks. The tail also, in this tribe, differs, inasmuch as it is generally made of quills, instead of white horsehair, as described amongst the Choctaws. In other respects, the rules and manner of the game are the same as amongst those tribes.

Several others of the *distingués* of the tribe, I have also painted here, and must needs refer the reader to the Museum for further information of them.

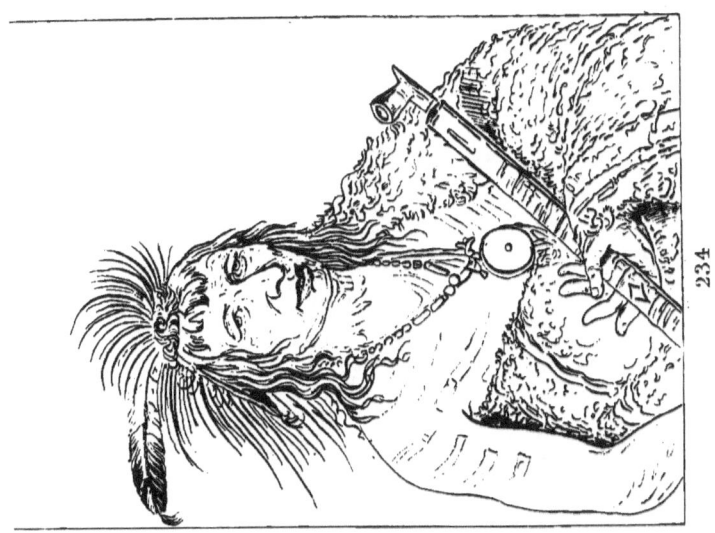

234

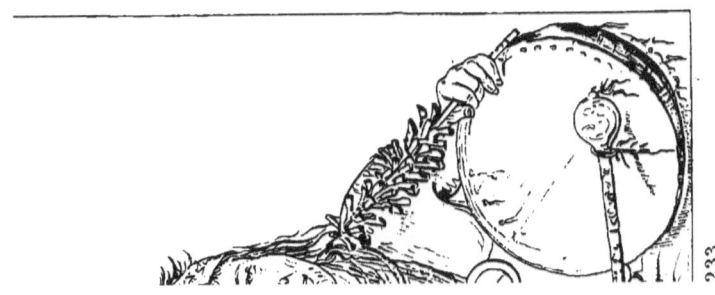

233

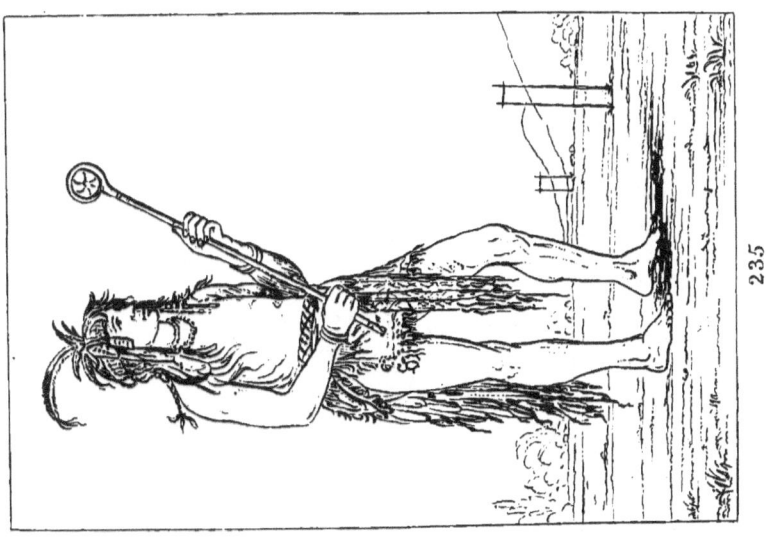

236

235

LETTER—No. 51.

The fourth of July was hailed and celebrated by us at this place, in an unusual, and not uninteresting manner. With the presence of several hundreds of the wildest of the Chippeways, and as many hundreds of the Sioux; we were prepared with material in abundance for the novel—for the wild and grotesque,—as well as for the grave and ludicrous. Major Talliafferro, the Indian agent, to aid my views in procuring sketches of manners and customs, represented to them that I was a great *medicine-man,* who had visited, and witnessed the sports of, a vast many Indians of different tribes, and had come to see whether the Sioux and Chippeways were equal in a ball-play, &c. to their neighbours; and that if they would come in on the *next* day (fourth of July), and give us a ball-play, and some of their dances, in their best style, he would have the *big gun* fired twenty-one times (the customary salute for that day), which they easily construed into a high compliment to themselves. This, with still stronger inducements, a barrel of flour—a quantity of pork and tobacco, which I gave them, brought the scene about on the day of independence, as follows :—About eleven o'clock (the usual time for Indians to make their appearance on any great occasion), the young men, who were enlisted for ball-play, made their appearance on the ground with ball-sticks in hand—with no other dress on than the flap, and attached to a girdle or ornamental sash, a tail, extending nearly to the ground, made of the choicest arrangement of quills and feathers, or of the hair of white horses' tails. After an excited and warmly contested play of two hours, they adjourned to a place in front of the agent's office, where they entertained us for two or three hours longer, with a continued variety of their most fanciful and picturesque dances. They gave us the *beggar's dance*—the *buffalo-dance*—the *bear-dance*—the *eagle-dance*—and *dance of the braves.* This last is peculiarly beautiful, and exciting to the feelings in the highest degree.

At intervals they stop, and one of them steps into the ring, and vociferates as loud as possible, with the most significant gesticulations, the feats of bravery which he has performed during his life—he boasts of the scalps he has taken—of the enemies he has vanquished, and at the same time carries his body through all the motions and gestures, which have been used during these scenes when they were transacted. At the end of his boasting, all assent to the truth of his story, and give in their approbation by the guttural "*waugh!*" and the dance again commences. At the next interval, another makes his boasts, and another, and another, and so on.

During this scene, a little trick was played off in the following manner, which produced much amusement and laughter. A woman of goodly size, and in woman's attire, danced into the ring (which seemed to excite some surprise, as women are never allowed to join in the dance), and commenced " sawing the air," and boasting of the astonishing feats of bravery she had performed—of the incredible number of horses she had stolen—of the scalps she had taken, &c. &c.; until her feats surpassed all that had ever been heard of—sufficient to put all the warriors who had boasted, to the blush. They all gave assent, however, to what she had said, and apparently *credence* too ; and to reward so extraordinary a feat of female prowess, they presented to her a kettle, a cradle, beads, ribbons, &c. After getting her presents, and placing them safely in the hands of another matron for safe keeping, she commenced disrobing herself; and, almost instantly divesting herself of a loose dress, in the presence of the whole company, came out in a *soldier's coat* and *pantaloons!* and laughed at them excessively for their mistake ! She then commenced dancing and making her boasts of her exploits, assuring them that she was a man, and a great brave. They all gave unqualified assent to this, acknowledged their error, and made her other presents of a gun, a horse, of tobacco, and a war-club. After her boasts were done, and the presents secured as before, she deliberately threw off the pantaloons and coat, and presented herself at once, and to their great astonishment and confusion, in a beautiful woman's dress. The tact with which she performed these parts, so uniformily pleased, that it drew forth thundering applause from the Indians, as well as from the spectators ; and the chief stepped up and crowned her head with a beautiful plume of the eagle's quill, rising from a crest of the swan's down. My wife, who was travelling this part of the country with me, was a spectator of these scenes, as well as the ladies and officers of the garrison, whose polite hospitality we are at this time enjoying.

Several days after this, the plains of St. Peters and St. Anthony, rang with the continual sounds of drums and rattles, in time with the thrilling yells of the dance, until it had doubly ceased to be novelty. General Patterson, of Philadelphia, and his family arrived about this time, however, and a dance was got up for their amusement; and it proved to be one of an unusual kind, and interesting to all. Considerable preparation was made for the occasion, and the Indians informed me, that if they could get a couple of dogs that were of no use about the garrison, they would give us their favourite, the "*dog dance.*" The two dogs were soon produced by the officers, and in presence of the whole assemblage of spectators, they butchered them and placed their two hearts and livers entire and uncooked, on a couple of crotches about as high as a man's face (PLATE 237). These were then

G. Catlin.

cut into strips, about an inch in width, and left hanging in this condition, with the blood and smoke upon them. A spirited dance then ensued; and, in a confused manner, every one sung forth his own deeds of bravery m ejaculatory gutturals, which were almost deafening; and they danced up, two at a time to the stakes, and after spitting several times upon the liver and hearts, catched a piece in their mouths, bit it off, and swallowed it. This was all done without losing the step (which was in time to their music), or interrupting the times of their voices.

Each and every one of them in this wise bit off and swallowed a piece of the livers, until they were demolished; with the exception of the two last pieces hanging on the stakes, which a couple of them carried in their mouths, and communicated to the mouths of the two musicians who swallowed them. This is one of the most valued dances amongst the Sioux, though by no means the most beautiful or most pleasing. The beggar's dance, the discovery dance, and the eagle dance, are far more graceful and agreeable. The *dog dance* is one of *distinction*, inasmuch as it can only be danced by those who have taken scalps from the enemy's heads, and come forward boasting, that they killed their enemy in battle, and swallowed a piece of his heart in the same manner.

As the Sioux own and occupy all the country on the West bank of the river in this vicinity; so do the Chippeways claim all lying East, from the mouth of the Chippeway River, at the outlet of Lake Pepin, to the source of the Mississippi; and within the month past, there have been one thousand or more of them encamped here, on business with the Indian agent and Sioux, with whom they have recently had·some difficulty. These two hostile foes, who have, time out of mind, been continually at war, are now encamped here, on different sides of the Fort; and all difficulties having been arranged by their agent, in whose presence they have been making their speeches, for these two weeks past, have been indulging in every sort of their amusements, uniting in their dances, ball-plays and other games; and feasting and smoking together, only to raise the war-cry and the tomahawk again, when they get upon their hunting grounds.

Major Talliafferro is the Government agent for the Sioux at this place, and furnishes the only instance probably, of a public servant on these frontiers, who has performed the duties of his office, strictly and faithfully, as well as kindly, for fifteen years. The Indians think much of him, and call him Great Father, to whose advice they listen with the greatest attention.

The encampment of the Chippeways, to which I have been a daily visitor, was built in the manner seen in PLATE 238; their wigwams made of birch bark, covering the frame work, which was of slight poles stuck in the ground, and bent over at the top, so as to give a rooflike shape to the lodge, best calculated to ward off rain and winds.

Through this curious scene I was strolling a few days since with my wife, and I observed the Indian women gathering around her, anxious to shake hands with her, and shew her their children, of which she took especial notice; and they literally filled her hands and her arms, with *muk-kuks* of maple sugar which they manufacture, and had brought in, in great quantities for sale.

After the business and amusements of this great Treaty between the Chippeways and Sioux were all over, the Chippeways struck their tents by taking them down and rolling up their bark coverings, which, with their bark canoes seen in the picture, turned up amongst their wigwams, were carried to the water's edge; and all things being packed in, men, women, dogs, and all, were swiftly propelled by paddles to the Fall of St. Anthony, where we had repaired to witness their mode of passing the cataract, by *"making* (as it is called) *the portage,"* which we found to be a very curious scene; and was done by running all their canoes into an eddy below the Fall, and as near as they could get by paddling; when all were landed, and every thing taken out of the canoes (PLATE 239), and with them carried by the women, around the Fall, and half a mile or so above, where the canoes were put into the water again; and goods and chattels being loaded in, and all hands seated, the paddles were again put to work, and the light and bounding crafts upon their voyage.

The bark canoe of the Chippeways is, perhaps, the most beautiful and light model of all the water crafts that ever were invented. They are generally made complete with the rind of one birch tree, and so ingeniously shaped and sewed together, with roots of the tamarack, which they call *wut-tap,* that they are water-tight, and ride upon the water, as light as a cork. They gracefully lean and dodge about, under the skilful balance of an Indian, or the ugliest squaw; but like everything wild, are timid and treacherous under the guidance of white man; and, if he be not an experienced equilibrist, he is sure to get two or three times soused, in his first endeavours at familiar acquaintance with them. In PLATE 240, letter *a,* the reader will see two specimens of these canoes correctly drawn; where he can contrast them and their shapes, with the log canoe, letter *b,* (or "dug out," as it is often called in the Western regions) of the Sioux, and many other tribes; which is dug out of a solid log, with great labour, by these ignorant people, who have but few tools to work with.

In the same plate, letter *c,* I have also introduced the skin canoes of the Mandans, (of the Upper Missouri, of whom I have spoken in Volume I), which are made almost round like a tub, by straining a buffalo's skin over a frame of wicker work, made of willow or other boughs. The woman in paddling these awkward tubs, stands in the bow, and makes the stroke with the paddle, by reaching it forward in the water and drawing it to her, by which means she pulls the canoe along with some considerable speed. These very curious and rudely constructed canoes, are made in the form of the *Welsh coracle*; and, if I mistake not, propelled in the same manner, which is a very curious circumstance; inasmuch as they are found in the heart of

238

G. Catlin

239

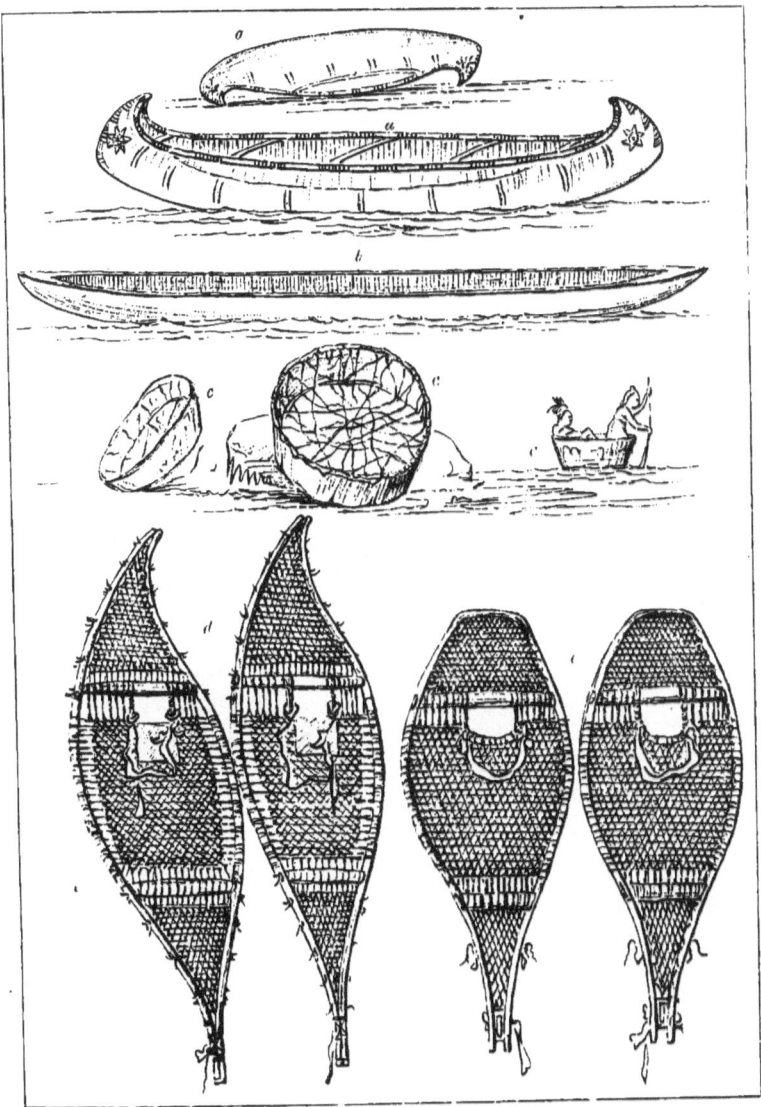

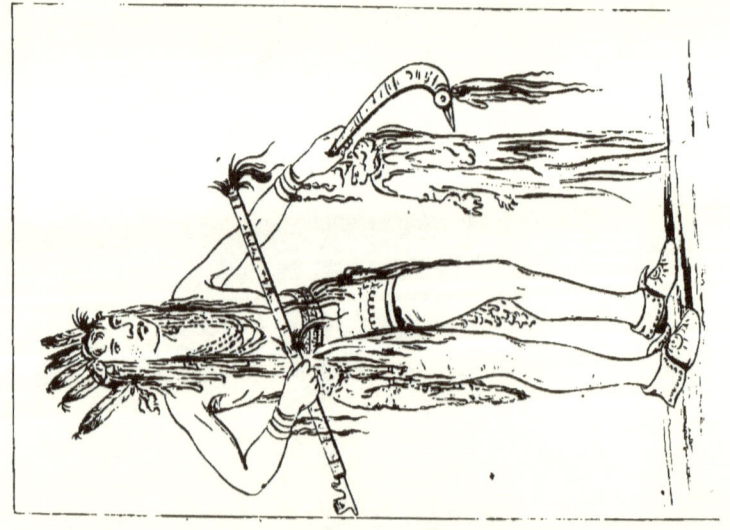

the great wilderness of America. when all the other surrounding tribes construct their canoes in decidedly different forms, and of different materials.

In the same plate. letter *d.* is a pair of Sioux (and in letter *e,* of Chippeway) *snow shoes,* which are used in the deep snows of the winter, under the Indians' feet. to buoy him up as he runs in pursuit of his game. The hoops or frames of these are made of elastic wood. and the webbing, of strings of rawhide. which form such a resistance to the snow. as to carry them over without sinking into it ; and enabling them to come up with their game, which is wallowing through the drifts, and easily overtaken ; as in the buffalo hunt, in PLATE 109, Volume I.

Of the portraits of chiefs and others I have painted amongst the Chippeways at this place, two distinguished young men will be seen in PLATES 241, 242. The first by the name of *Ka-bes-kunk* (he who travels everywhere). the other. *Ka-be-mub-be* (he who sits everywhere), both painted at full length, in full dress, and just as they were adorned and equipped, even to a quill and a trinket.

The first of these two young men is, no doubt, one of the most remarkable of his age to be found in the tribe. Whilst he was standing for his portrait, which was in one of the officer's quarters in the Fort. where there were some ten or fifteen of his enemies the Sioux, seated on the floor around the room ; he told me to take particular pains in representing eight quills which were arranged in his head-dress. which he said stood for so many Sioux scalps that he had taken with his left hand, in which he was grasping his war-club, with which hand he told me he was in the habit of making all his blows.

In PLATE 244, is the portrait of a warrior by the name of *Ot-ta-wa* (the otaway), ——— with his pipe in his hand ; and in PLATE 245, the portrait of a Chippeway woman, *Ju-ah-kis-gaw,* with her child in its crib or cradle. In a former Letter I gave a minute account of the Sioux cradle. and here the reader sees the very similar mode amongst the Chippeways ; and as in all instances that can be found. the *ni-ahkust-ahg* (or umbilicus) hanging before the child's face for its supernatural protector.

This woman's dress was mostly made of civilized manufactures, but curiously decorated and ornamented according to Indian taste

Many were the dances given to me on different places. of which I may make further use and further mention on future occasions ; but of which I shall name but one at present. the *snow-shoe dance* (PLATE 243). which is exccedingly picturesque. being danced with the snow shoes under the feet, at the falling of the first snow in the beginning of winter ; when they sing a song of thanksgiving to the Great Spirit for sending them a return of snow, when they can run on their snow shoes in their valued hunts and easily take the game for their food.

About this lovely spot I have whiled away a few months with great pleasure, and having visited all the curiosities, and all the different villages of
Indians in the vicinity, I close my note-book and start in a few days for
Prairie du Chien, which is 300 miles below this; where I shall have new
subjects for my brush and new themes for my pen, when I may continue my
epistles. Adieu.

244   245

LETTER—No. 52.

CAMP DES MOINES.

Soon after the date of my last Letter, written at St. Peters, having placed my wife on board of the steamer, with a party of ladies, for Prairie du Chien, I embarked in a light bark canoe, on my homeward course, with only one companion, Corporal Allen, from the garrison ; a young man of considerable taste, who thought he could relish the transient scenes of a voyage in company with a painter, having gained the indulgence of Major Bliss, the commanding officer, with permission to accompany me.

With stores laid in for a ten days' voyage, and armed for any emergency —with sketch-book and colours prepared, we shoved off and swiftly glided away with paddles nimbly plied, resolved to see and relish every thing curious or beautiful that fell in our way. We lingered along, among the scenes of grandeur which presented themselves amid the thousand bluffs, and arrived at Prairie du Chien in about ten days, in good plight, without accident or incident of a thrilling nature, with the exception of one instance which happened about thirty miles below St. Peters, and on the first day of our journey. In the after part of the day, we discovered three lodges of Sioux Indians encamped on the bank, all hallooing and waving their blankets for us to come in, to the shore. We had no business with them, and resolved to keep on our course, when one of them ran into his lodge, and coming out with his gun in his hand, levelled it at us, and gave us a charge of buck-shot about our ears. One of them struck in my canoe, passing through several folds of my cloak, which was folded, and lying just in front of my knee, and several others struck so near on each side as to spatter the water into our faces. There was no fun in this, and I then ran my canoe to the shore as fast as possible—they all ran, men, women, and children, to the water's edge, meeting us with yells and laughter as we landed. As the canoe struck the shore, I rose violently from my seat, and throwing all the infuriated demon I could into my face—thrusting my pistols into my belt—a half dozen bullets into my mouth—and my double-barrelled gun in my hand —I leaped ashore and chased the lot of them from the beach, throwing myself, by a nearer route, between them and their wigwams, where I kept them for some time at a stand, with my barrels presented, and threats (corroborated with looks which they could not misunderstand) that I would annihilate the whole of them in a minute. As the gun had been returned to the lodge, and the man who fired it could not be identified, the rascal's life was thereby probably prolonged. We stood for some time in this position, and no explanation could be made, other than that which could be read from the lip and the brow, a language which is the same, and read alike, among all nations. I slipped my sketch-book and pencil into my hand, and under the muzzle of my gun, each fellow stood for his likeness, which I made them 'understand, by signs, were to be sent to "Muzzabucksa" (iron cutter), the name they gave to Major Talliafferro, their agent at St. Peters.

This threat, and the continued vociferation of the corporal from the canoe, that I was a "Grande Capitaine," seemed considerably to alarm them. I at length gradually drew myself off, but with a lingering eye upon the sneaking rascals, who stood in sullen silence, with one eye upon me, and the other upon the corporal; who I found had held them at bay from the bow of his canoe, with his musket levelled upon them—his bayonet fixed—his cartouch box slung, with one eye in full blaze over the barrel, and the other drawn down within two parts of an inch of the upper corner of his mouth. At my approach, his muscles were gradually (but somewhat reluctantly) relaxed. We seated ourselves, and quietly dipped our paddles again on our way.

Some allowance must be made for this outrage, and many others that could be named, that have taken place amongst that part of the Sioux nation; they have been for many years past made drunkards, by the solicitations of white men, and then abused, and their families also; for which, when they are drunk (as in the present instance), they are often ready, and disposed to retaliate and to return insult for injuries.

We went on peaceably and pleasantly during the rest of our voyage, having ducks, deer, and bass for our game and our food; our bed was generally on the grass at the foot of some towering bluff, where, in the melancholy stillness of night, we were lulled to sleep by the liquid notes of the whip-poor-will; and after his warbling ceased, roused by the mournful complaints of the starving wolf, or *surprised* by the startling interrogation, "who! who! who!" by the winged monarch of the dark.

There is a something that fills and feeds the mind of an enthusiastic man, when he is thrown upon natural resources, amidst the rude untouched scenes of nature, which cannot be described; and I leave the world to imagine the feelings of pleasure with which I found myself again out of the din of artful life, among scenes of grandeur worthy the whole soul's devotion, and admiration.

When the morning's dew was shaken off, our coffee enjoyed—our light bark again launched upon the water, and the chill of the morning banished by the quick stroke of the paddle, and the busy chaunt of the corporal's boat-song, our ears and our eyes were open to the rude scenes of romance that were about us—our light boat ran to every ledge—dodged into every slough or *cut-off*" to be seen—every mineral was examined—every cave ex-

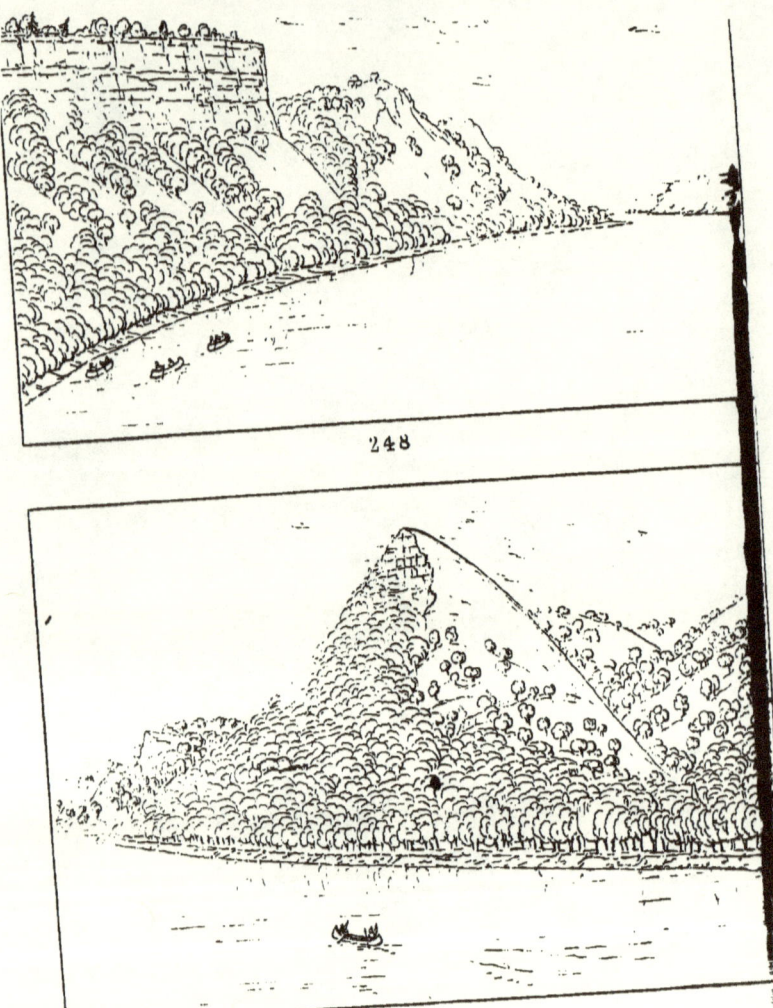

248

249

G. Catlin

plored—and almost every bluff of grandeur ascended to the top. These towering edifices of nature, which will stand the admiration of thousands and tens of thousands, unchanged and unchangeable, though grand and majestic to the eye of the passing traveller, will be found to inspire new ideas of magnitude when attempted to be travelled to the top. From the tops of many of them I have sketched for the information of the world, and for the benefit of those who travel much, I would recommend a trip to the summit of " Pike's Tent" (the highest bluff on the river), 100 miles above Prairie du Chien ; to the top also of " La Montaigne qui tromps a l'eau"—the summit of Bad Axe Mountain—and a look over Lake Pepin's turretted shores from the top of the bluff opposite to the " Lover's Leap," being the highest on the lake, and the point from which the greater part of its shores can be seen.

Along the shores of this beautiful lake we lingered for several days, and our canoe was hauled a hundred times upon the pebbly beach, where we spent hours and days, robbing it of its precious gems, which are thrown up by the waves. We found many rich agates, carnelians, jaspers, and porphyrys. The agates are many of them peculiarly beautiful, most of them water-waved—their colours brilliant and beautifully striated. " Point aux Sables" has been considered the most productive part of the lake for these gems ; but owing to the frequent landings of the steam-boats and other craft on that point, the best specimens of them have been picked up; and the traveller will now be best remunerated for his trouble, by tracing the shore around into some of its coves, or on some of its points less frequented by the footsteps of man.

The *Lover's Leap* (PLATE 248), is a bold and projecting rock, of six or seven hundred feet elevation on the East side of the lake, from the summit of which, it is said, a beautiful Indian girl, the daughter of a chief, threw herself off in presence of her tribe, some fifty years ago, and dashed herself to pieces, to avoid being married to a man whom her father had decided to be her husband, and whom she would not marry. On our way, after we had left the beautiful shores of Lake Pepin, we passed the magnificent bluff called " *Pike's Tent*" (PLATE 249), and undoubtedly, the highest eminence on the river, running up in the form of a tent; from which circumstance, and that of having first been ascended by Lieutenant Pike, it has taken the name of Pike's Tent, which it will, doubtless, for ever retain.

The corporal and I run our little craft to the base of this stupendous pyramid, and spent half a day about its sides and its pinnacle, admiring the lovely and almost boundless landscape that lies beneath it.

To the top of this grass-covered mound I would advise every traveller in the country, who has the leisure to do it, and sinew enough in his leg, to stroll awhile, and enjoy what it may be difficult for him to see elsewhere.

" *Cap au l'ail*" (Garlic Cape, PLATE 250), about twenty miles above Prairie du Chien is another beautiful scene—and the " Cornice Rocks"

(PLATE 251), on the West bank, where my little bark rested two days, till the corporal and I had taken bass from every nook and eddy about them, where our hooks could be dipped. To the lover of fine fish, and fine sport in fishing, I would recommend an encampment for a few days on this picturesque ledge, where his appetite and his passion will be soon gratified.

Besides these picturesque scenes, I made drawings also of all the Indian villages on the way, and of many other interesting points, which are curious in my Collection, but too numerous to introduce in this place.

In the midst, or half-way of Lake Pepin, which is an expansion of the river of four or five miles in width, and twenty-five miles in length, the corporal and I hauled our canoe out upon the beach of Point aux Sables, where we spent a couple of days, feasting on plums and fine fish and wild fowl, and filling our pockets with agates and carnelions we were picking up along the pebbly beach; and at last, started on our way for the outlet of the lake, with a fair North West wind, which wafted us along in a delightful manner, as I sat in the stern and steered, while the corporal was "catching the breeze" in a large umbrella, which he spread open and held in the bow. We went merrily and exultingly on in this manner, until at length the wind increased to anything but a gale; and the waves were foaming white, and dashing on the shores where we could not land without our frail bark being broken to pieces. We soon became alarmed, and saw that our only safety was in keeping on the course that we were running at a rapid rate, and that with our sail full set, to brace up and steady our boat on the waves, while we kept within swimming distance of the shore, resolved to run into the first cove, or around the first point we could find for our protection. We kept at an equal distance from the shore—and in this most critical condition, the wind drove us ten or fifteen miles, without a landing-place, till we exultingly steered into the mouth of the Chippeway river, at the outlet of the lake, where we soon found quiet and safety; but found our canoe in a sinking condition, being half full of water, and having three of the five of her beams or braces broken out, with which serious disasters, a few rods more of the fuss and confusion would have sent us to the bottom. We here laid by part of a day, and having repaired our disasters, wended our way again pleasantly and successfully on.

At Prairie du Chien, which is near the mouth of the Ouisconsin River, and 600 miles above St. Louis, where we safely landed my canoe, I found my wife enjoying the hospitality of Mrs. Judge Lockwood, who had been a schoolmate of mine in our childhood, and is now residing with her interesting family in that place. Under her hospitable roof we spent a few weeks with great satisfaction, after which my wife took steamer for Dubuque, and I took to my little bark canoe alone (having taken leave of the corporal), which I paddled to this place, quite leisurely—cooking my own meat, and having my own fun as I passed along.

Prairie du Chien (PLATE 253) has been one of the earliest and principal

250

251

253

Gérôme

trading posts of the Fur Company, and they now have a large establishment at that place ; but doing far less business than formerly, owing to the great mortality of the Indians in its vicinity, and the destruction of the game, which has almost entirely disappeared in these regions. The prairie is a beautiful elevation above the river, of several miles in length, and a mile or so in width, with a most picturesque range of grassy bluffs encompassing it in the rear. The Government have erected there a substantial Fort, in which are generally stationed three or four companies of men, for the purpose (as at the Fall of St. Anthony) of keeping the peace amongst the hostile tribes, and also of protecting the frontier inhabitants from the attacks of the excited savages. There are on the prairie some forty or fifty families, mostly French, and some half-breeds, whose lives have been chiefly spent in the arduous and hazardous occupations of trappers, and traders, and voyageurs; which has well qualified them for the modes of dealing with Indians, where they have settled down and stand ready to compete with one another for their shares of annuities, &c. which are dealt out to the different tribes who concentrate at that place, and are easily drawn from the poor Indians' hands by whiskey and useless gew-gaws.

The consequence of this system is, that there is about that place, almost one continual scene of wretchedness, and drunkenness, and disease amongst the Indians, who come there to trade and to receive their annuities, that disgusts and sickens the heart of every stranger that extends his travels to it.

When I was there, Wa-be-sha's band of the Sioux came there, and remained several weeks to get their annuities, which, when they received them, fell (as they always will do), far short of paying off the account, which the Traders take good care to have standing against them for goods furnished them on a year's credit. However, whether they pay off or not, they can always get whiskey enough for a grand carouse and a brawl, which lasts for a week or two, and almost sure to terminate the lives of some of their numbers.

At the end of one of these a few days since, after the men had enjoyed their surfeit of whiskey, and wanted a little more amusement, and felt disposed to indulge the weaker sex in a little recreation also ; it was announced amongst them, and through the village, that the women were going to have a ball-play!

For this purpose the men, in their very liberal trades they were making and filling their canoes with goods delivered to them on a year's credit, laid out a great quantity of ribbons and calicoes, with other presents well adapted to the wants and desires of the women ; which were hung on a pole resting on crotches, and guarded by an old man, who was to be judge and umpire of the play which was to take place amongst the women, who were divided into two equal parties, and were to play a desperate game of ball, for the valuable stakes that were hanging before them (PLATE 252).

U

In the ball-play of the women, they have two balls attached to the ends of a string, about a foot and a half long; and each woman has a short stick in each hand, on which she catches the string with the two balls, and throws them, endeavouring to force them over the goal of her own party. The men are more than half drunk, when they feel liberal enough to indulge the women in such an amusement; and take infinite pleasure in rolling about on the ground and laughing to excess, whilst the women are tumbling about in all attitudes, and scuffling for the ball. The game of "*hunt the slipper*," even, loses its zest after witnessing one of these, which sometimes last for hours together; and often exhibits the hottest contest for the balls, exactly over the heads of the men; who, half from whiskey, and half from inclination, are laying in groups and flat upon the ground.

Prairie du Chien is the concentrating place of the Winnebagoes and Menomonies, who inhabit the waters of the Ouisconsin and Fox Rivers, and the chief part of the country lying East of the Mississippi, and West of Green Bay.

The *Winnebagoes* are the remnant of a once powerful and warlike tribe, but are now left in a country where they have neither beasts or men to war with; and are in a most miserable and impoverished condition. The numbers of this tribe do not exceed four thousand; and the most of them have sold even their guns and ammunition for whiskey. Like the Sioux and Menomonies that come in to this post, they have several times suffered severely with the small-pox, which has in fact destroyed the greater proportion of them

In PLATE 254, will be seen the portrait of an old chief, who died a few years since; and who was for many years the head chief of the tribe, by the name of *Naw-kaw* (wood). This man has been much distinguished in his time, for his eloquence; and he desired me to paint him in the attitude of an orator, addressing his people.

PLATE 255, is a distinguished man of the Winnebago tribe, by the name of *Wah-chee-hahs-ka* (the man who puts all out of doors), commonly called the " boxer." The largest man of the tribe, with rattle-snakes' skins on his arms, and his war-club in his hand.*

In PLATE 256 is seen a warrior, *Kaw-kaw-ne-choo-a*; and in PLATE 257 another, Wa-kon-zee-kaw (the snake), both at full length; and fair specimens of the tribe, who are generally a rather short and thick-set, square shouldered set of men, of great strength, and of decided character as brave and desperate in war.

Besides the chief and warriors above-named, I painted the portraits of *Won-de-tow-a* (the wonder), *Wa-kon-chash-kaw* (he who comes on the

* This man died of the small-pox the next summer after this portrait was painted. Whilst the small-pox was raging so bad at the Prairie, he took the disease, and in a rage plunged into the river, and swam across to the island where he dragged his body out upon the beach, and there died, and his bones were picked by dogs, without any friend to give him burial.

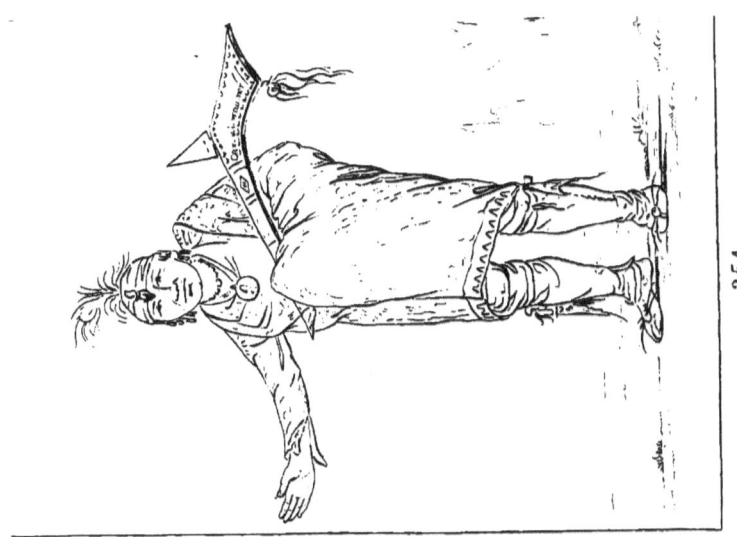

254

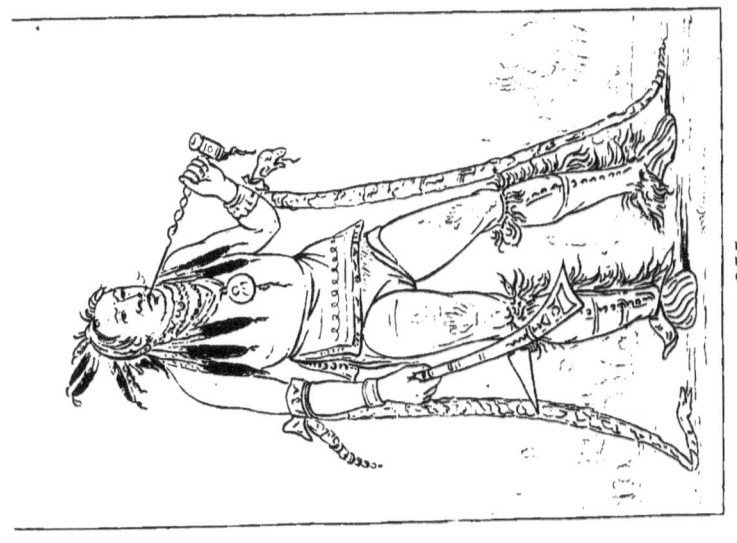

255

257

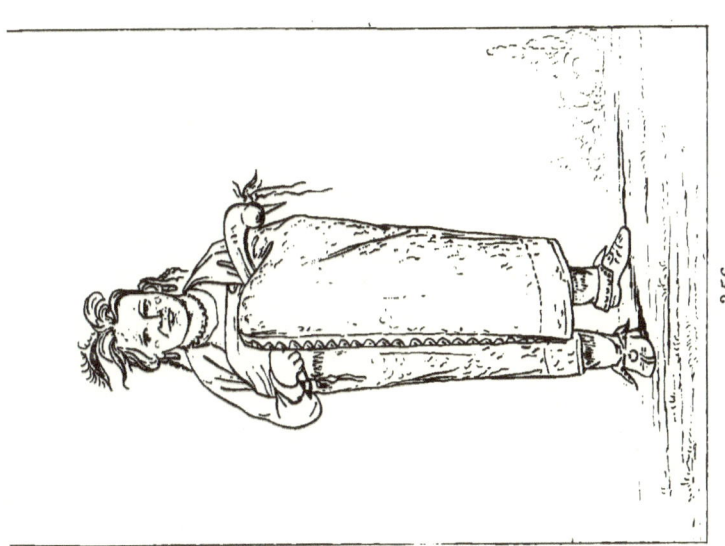

256

G. Catlin.

258   259

260   261

G Catlin.

thunder), *Nau-naw-pay-ee* (the soldier), *Span-e-o-nee-kaw* (the Spaniard) Hoo-wan-ee-kaw (the little elk), *No-ah-choo-she-kaw* (he who breaks the bushes), and *Naugh-haigh-ke-kaw* (he who moistens the wood), all distinguished men of the tribe ; and all at full length, as they will be seen standing in my Collection.

The MENOMONIES,

Like the Winnebagoes, are the remnant of a much more numerous and in dependent tribe, but have been reduced and enervated by the use of whiskey and the ravages of the small-pox, and number at this time, something like three thousand, living chiefly on the banks of Fox River, and the Western shore of Green Bay. They visit Prairie du Chien, where their annuities are paid them ; and they indulge in the *bane*, like the tribes that I have mentioned.

Of this tribe, I have painted quite a number of their leading characters, and at the head of them all, *Mah-kee-me-teuv* (the grizzly bear, PLATE 258), with a handsome pipe in his hand ; and by the side of him his wife *Me-cheet-e-neuh* (the wounded bear's shoulder, PLATE 259). Both of these have died since their portraits were painted. This dignified chief led a delegation of fifteen of his people to Washington City, some years since, and there commanded great respect for his eloquence, and dignity of deportment.

In PLATE 260 is the portrait of *Chee-me-na-na-quet* (the great cloud), son of the chief—an ill-natured and insolent fellow who has since been killed for some of his murderous deeds. PLATE 261, is the portrait of a fine boy, whose name is *Tcha-kauks-o-ko-maugh* (the great chief). This tribe living out of the reach of buffaloes, cover themselves with blankets, instead of robes, and wear a profusion of beads and wampum, and other trinkets.

In PLATE 262, is Coo-coo-coo (the owl), a very aged and emaciated chief, whom I painted at Green Bay, in Fort Howard. He had been a distinguished man, but now in his dotage, being more than 100 years old— and a great pet of the surgeon and officers of the post.

In PLATE 263, are two Menominee youths at full length, in beautiful dresses, whose names I did not get—one with his war-club in his hand, and the other blowing on his "courting flute," which I have before described.

In addition to these I have painted of this tribe, and placed in my Collection, the portraits of *Ko-man-i-kin-o-shaw* (the little whale) ; *Sha-wa-no* (the South) ; *Mash-kee-wet* (the thought) ; *Pah-shee-nau-shaw* (———) ; *Au-nah-quet-o-hau-pay-o* (the one sitting in the clouds) ; *Auh-ka-na-paw-wah* (earth standing) ; *Ko-man-ni-kin* (the big wave) ; *O-ho-pa-sha* (the small whoop) ; *Au-wah-shew-kew* (the female bear) ; and *Chesh-ko-tong* (he who sings the war-song).

It will be seen by the reader, from the above facts, that I have been laying up much curious and valuable record of people and customs in these regions; and it will be seen at the same time, from the brief manner in which I have treated of these semi-civilized tribes, which every body can see, and thousands have seen, that my enthusiasm, as I have before explained, has led me more into minuteness and detail amongst those tribes which are living in their unchanged native modes, whose customs I have been ambitious to preserve for ages to come, before the changes that civilized acquaintance will soon work upon them.

The materials which I am daily gathering, however, are interesting; and I may on a future occasion use them—but in an epistle of this kind, there is not room for the incidents of a long voyage, or for a minute description of the country and the people in it; so, what I have said must suffice for the present. I lingered along the shores of this magnificent river then, in my fragile bark, to Prairie du Chien—Dubuque—Galena, to Rock Island, and lastly to this place.

During such a Tour between the almost endless banks, carpeted with green, with one of the richest countries in the world, extending back in every direction, the mind of a contemplative man is continually building for posterity splendid seats, cities, towers and villas, which a few years of rolling time will bring about, with new institutions, new states, and almost empires; for it would seem that this vast region of rich soil and green fields, was almost enough for a world of itself.

I hauled my canoe out of the water at Dubuque, where I joined my wife again in the society of kind and hospitable friends, and found myself amply repaid for a couple of weeks' time spent in the examination of the extensive lead mines; walking and creeping through caverns, some eighty or one hundred feet below the earth's surface, decked in nature's pure livery of stalactites and spar—with walls, and sometimes ceilings, of glistening massive lead. And I hold yet (and ever shall) in my mind, without loss of a fraction of feature or expression, the image of one of my companions, and the scene that at one time was about him. His name is Jeffries. We were in "Lockwood's Cave," my wife and another lady were behind, and he advancing before me; *his* ribs, more elastic than mine, gave him entrance through a crevice, into a chamber yet unexplored; he dared the pool, for there was one of icy water, and translucent as the air itself. We stood luckless spectators, to gaze and envy, while he advanced. The lighted flambeau in his hand brought the splendid furniture of this tesselated palace into view; the surface of the jostled pool laved his sides as he advanced, and the rich stalagmites that grew up from the bottom reflected a golden light through the water, while the walls and ceiling were hung with stalactites which glittered like diamonds.

In this wise he stood in silent gaze, in awe and admiration of the hidden works of Nature; his figure, as high as the surface of the water, was magnified into a giant—and his head and shoulders not unfit for a cyclop. In fact, he was a perfect figure of Vulcan. The water in which he stood was

263

262

a lake of liquid fire—he held a huge hammer in his right hand, and a flaming thunderbolt in his left, which he had just forged for Jupiter. There was but one thing wanting, it was the "sound of the hammer!" which was soon given in peals upon the beautiful pendents of stalactite and spar, which sent back and through the cavern, the hollow tones of thunder.

A visit of a few days to Dubuque will be worth the while of every traveller; and for the speculator and man of enterprize, it affords the finest field now open in our country. It is a small town of 200 houses, built entirely within the last two years, on one of the most delightful sites on the river, and in the heart of the richest and most productive parts of the mining region; having this advantage over most other mining countries, that immediately over the richest (and in fact all) of the lead mines; the land on the surface produces the finest corn, and all other vegetables that may be put into it. This is certainly the richest section of country on the Continent, and those who live a few years to witness the result, will be ready to sanction my assertion, that it is to be the *mint of our country*.

From Dubuque, I descended the river on a steamer, with my bark canoe laid on its deck, and my wife was my companion, to Camp Des Moines, from whence I am now writing.

After arriving at this place, which is the wintering post of Colonel Kearney, with his three companies of dragoons, I seated my wife and two gentlemen of my intimate acquaintance, in my bark canoe, and paddled them through the Des Moine's Rapids, a distance of fourteen miles, which we performed in a very short time; and at the foot of the Rapids, placed my wife on the steamer for St. Louis, in company with friends, when I had some weeks to return on my track, and revert back again to the wild and romantic life that I occasionally love to lead. I returned to Camp Des Moines, and in a few days joined General Street, the Indian Agent, in a Tour to Ke-o-kuck's village of Sacs and Foxes.

Colonel Kearney gave us a corporal's command of eight men, with horses, &c. for the journey; and we reached the village in two days' travel, about sixty miles up the Des Moines. The whole country that we passed over was like a garden, wanting only cultivation, being mostly prairie, and we found their village beautifully situated on a large prairie, on the bank of the Des Moines River. They seemed to be well supplied with the necessaries of life, and with some of its luxuries. I found Ke-o-kuck to be a chief of fine and portly figure, with a good countenance, and great dignity and grace in his manners.

General Street had some documents from Washington, to read to him, which he and his chiefs listened to with great patience; after which he placed before us good brandy and good wine, and invited us to drink, and to lodge with him; he then called up five of his *runners* or *criers*, communicated to them in a low, but emphatic tone, the substance of the talk from the agent, and of the letters read to him, and they started at full gallop—

one of them proclaiming it through his village, and the others sent express to the other villages, comprising the whole nation. Ke-o-kuck came in with us, with about twenty of his principal men—he brought in all his costly wardrobe, that I might select for his portrait such as suited me best; but at once named (of his own accord) the one that was purely Indian. In that he paraded for several days, and in it I painted him at full length. He is a man of a great deal of pride, and makes truly a splendid appearance on his black horse. He owns the finest horse in the country, and is excessively vain of his appearance when mounted, and arrayed, himself and horse, in all their gear and trappings. He expressed a wish to see himself represented on horseback, and I painted him in that plight. He rode and nettled his prancing steed in front of my door, until its sides were in a gore of blood. I succeeded to *his* satisfaction, and his vanity is increased, no doubt, by seeing himself immortalized in that way. After finishing him, I painted his favourite wife (the favoured one of seven), his favourite boy, and eight or ten of his principal men and women; after which, he and all his men shook hands with me, wishing me well, and leaving, as tokens of regard, the most valued article of his dress, and a beautiful string of wampum, which he took from his wife's neck.

They then departed for their village in good spirits, to prepare for their *fall hunt.*

Of this interesting interview and its incidents, and of these people, I shall soon give the reader a further account, and therefore close my note-book for the present. Adieu.

LETTER--No 53.

SAINT LOUIS.

It will be seen by the heading of this Letter that I am back again to " head-quarters," where I have joined my wife, and being seated down by a comfortable fire, am to take a little retrospect of my rambles, from the time of my last epistle.

The return to the society of old friends again, has been delightful, and amongst those whom I more than esteem, I have met my kind and faithful friend Joe Chadwick, whom I have often mentioned, as my companion in distress whilst on that disastrous campaign amongst the Camanchees. Joe and I have taken great pleasure in talking over the many curious scenes we have passed together, many of which are as yet unknown to others than ourselves. We had been separated for nearly two years, and during that time I had passed many curious scenes worthy of Joe's knowing, and while he sat down in the chair for a portrait I painted of him to send to his mother, on leaving the States, to take an appointment from Governor Houston in the Texan army; I related to him one or two of my recent *incidents*, which were as follow, and pleased Joe exceedingly :—

" After I had paddled my bark canoe through the rapids, with my wife and others in it, as I mentioned, and had put them on board a steamer for St. Louis, I dragged my canoe up the east shore of the rapids, with a line, for a distance of four miles, when I stopped and spent half of the day in collecting some very interesting minerals, which I had in the bottom of my canoe, and ready to get on the first steamer passing up, to take me again to Camp Des Moines, at the head of the rapids.

" I was sitting on a wild and wooded shore, and waiting, when I at length discovered a steamer several miles below me, advancing through the rapids, and in the interim I set too and cleaned my fowling-piece and a noble pair of pistols, which I had carried in a belt at my side, through my buffalo and other sports of the West, and having put them in fine order and deposited them in the bottom of the canoe before me, and taken my paddle in hand, with which my long practice had given me unlimited confidence, I put off from the shore to the middle of the river, which was there a mile and a half in width, to meet the steamer, which was stemming the opposing torrent, and slowly moving up the rapids. I made my signal as I neared the steamer, and desired my old friend Captain Rogers, not to stop his engine; feeling full confidence that I could, with an *Indian touch* of the paddle, toss my little bark around, and gently grapple to the side of the steamer, which was loaded down, with her gunnels near to the water's edge. Ol, that my skill had been equal to my imagination, or that I could have had at that moment the balance and the skill of an Indian *woman*, for the sake of my little craft and what was in it! I had *brought it about*, with a master hand, however, but the waves of the rapids and the foaming of the waters by her sides were too much for my peaceable adhesion, and at the moment of wheeling, to part company with her, a line, with a sort of "laso throw," came from an awkward hand on the deck, and falling over my shoulder and around the end of my canoe, with a simultaneous "haul" to it, sent me down head foremost to the bottom of the river; where I was tumbling along with the rapid current over the huge rocks on the bottom, whilst my gun and pistols, which were emptied from my capsised boat, were taking their permanent position amongst the rocks; and my trunk, containing my notes of travel for several years, and many other valuable things, was floating off upon the surface. If I had drowned, my death would have been witnessed by at least an hundred ladies and gentlemen who were looking on, but I *did not*. —I soon took a peep, by the side of my trunk &c., above the water, and for the first time in my life was "collared," and that by my friend Captain Rogers, who undoubtedly saved me from making further explorations on the river bottom, by pulling me into the boat, to the amusement of all on deck, many of whom were my old acquaintance, and not knowing the preliminaries, were as much astounded at my sudden appearance, as if I had been disgorged from a whale's belly. A small boat was sent off for my trunk, which was picked up about half a mile below and brought on board full of water, and consequently, clothes, and sketch-books and everything else entirely wet through. My canoe was brought on board, which was several degrees dearer to me now than it had been for its long and faithful service; but my gun and pistols are there yet, and at the service of the lucky one who may find them. I remained on board for several miles, till we were passing a wild and romantic rocky shore, on which the sun was shining warm, and I launched my little boat into the water, with my trunk in it and put off to the shore, where I soon had every paper and a hundred other things spread in the sun, and at night in good order for my camp, which was at the mouth of a quiet little brook, where I caught some fine bass and fared well, till a couple of hours paddling the next morning brought me back to Camp Des Moines."

Here my friend Joe laughed excessively, but said not a word, as I kept on painting—and told him also, that a few days after this, I put my little canoe on the deck of a steamer ascending the river, and landed at Rock Island, ninety miles above, on some business with General Street, the Indian Agent—after which I "put off" in my little bark, descending the river alone, to Camp Des Moines, with a fine double-barrelled fowling-piece, which I had purchased at the garrison, lying in the canoe before me as the means of procuring wild fowl, and other food on my passage. "Egad!"

said Joe, " how I should like to have been with you !" " Sit still," said I, " or I shall lose your likeness." So Joe kept his position, and I proceeded·

"I left Rock Island about eleven o'clock in the morning, and at half-past three in a pleasant afternoon, in the cool month of October, run my canoe to the shore of *Mas-co-tin* Island, where I stepped out upon its beautiful pebbly beach, with my paddle in my hand, having drawn the bow of my canoe, as usual, on to the beach, so as to hold it in its place. This beautiful island, so called from a band of the Illinois Indians of that name, who once dwelt upon it, is twenty-five or thirty miles in length, without habitation on or in sight of it, and the whole way one extended and lovely prairie ; with high banks fronting the river, and extending back a great way, covered with a high and luxuriant growth of grass. To the top of this bank I went with my paddle in my hand, quite innocently, just to range my eye over its surface, and to see what might be seen ; when, in a minute or two, I turned towards the river, and, to my almost annihilating surprise and vexation, I saw my little canoe some twenty or thirty rods from the shore, and some distance below me, with its head aiming across the river, and steadily gliding along in that direction, where the wind was roguishly wafting it ! What little swearing I had learned in the whole of my dealings with the *civilized* world, seemed then to concentrate in two or three involuntary exclamations, which exploded as I was running down the beach, and throwing off my garments one after the other, till I was denuded—and dashing through the deep and boiling current in pursuit of it, I swam some thirty· rods in a desperate rage, resolving that this *must be* my remedy, as there was no other mode ; but at last found, to my great mortification and *alarm*, that the canoe, having got so far from the shore, was more in the wind, and travelling at a speed quite equal to my own ; so that the only safe alternative was to turn and make for the shore with all possible despatch. This I did—and had but just strength to bring me where my feet could reach the bottom, and I waded out with the appalling conviction, that if I had swam one rod farther into the stream, my strength would never have brought me to the shore ; for it was in the fall of the year, and the water so cold as completely to have benumbed me, and paralyzed my limbs. I hastened to pick up my clothes, which were dropped at intervals as I had run on the beach, and having adjusted them on my shivering limbs, I stepped to the top of the bank, and took a deliberate view of my little canoe, which was steadily making its way to the other shore—with my gun, with my provisions and fire apparatus, and sleeping apparel, all snugly packed in it.

"The river at that place is near a mile wide ; and I watched the mischievous thing till it ran quite into a bunch of willows on the opposite shore, and out of sight. I walked the shore awhile, alone and solitary as a Zealand penguin, when I at last sat down, and in one minute passed the following resolves from premises that were before me, and too imperative to be evaded or unappreciated. ' I am here on a desolate island, with no·

thing to eat, and destitute of the means of procuring anything : and if I pass the night, or half a dozen of them here, I shall have neither fire or clothes to make me comfortable ; and nothing short of *having my canoe* will answer me at all.' For this, the only alternative struck me, and I soon commenced upon it. An occasional log or limb of drift wood was seen along the beach and under the bank, and these I commenced bringing together from all quarters, and some I had to lug half a mile or more, to form a raft to float me up and carry me across the river. As there was a great scarcity of materials, and I had no hatchet to cut anything ; I had to use my scanty materials of all lengths and of all sizes and all shapes, and at length ventured upon the motley mass, with paddle in hand, and carefully shoved it off from the shore, finding it just sufficient to float me up. I took a seat in its centre on a bunch of barks which I had placed for a seat, and which, when I started, kept me a few inches above the water, and consequently dry, whilst my feet were resting on the raft, which in most parts was sunk a little below the surface. The only alternative was *to go*, for there was no more timber to be found ; so I balanced myself in the middle, and by reaching forward with my paddle, to a little space between the timbers of my raft, I had a small place to dip it, and the only one, in which I could make but a feeble stroke—propelling me at a very slow rate *across*, as I was floating rapidly *down* the current. I sat still and worked patiently, however, content with the little gain ; and at last reached the opposite shore about three miles below the place of my embarkation ; having passed close by several huge snags, which I was lucky enough to escape, without the power of having cleared them except by kind accident.

" My craft was ' unseaworthy' when I started, and when I had got to the middle of the river, owing to the rotten wood, with which a great part of it was made, and which had now become saturated with water, it had sunk entirely under the surface, letting me down nearly to the waist, in the water. In this critical way I moved slowly along, keeping the sticks together under me ; and at last, when I reached the shore. some of the long and awkward limbs projecting from my raft, having reached it before me, and being suddenly resisted by the bank, gave the instant signal for its dissolution, and my sudden debarkation, when I gave one grand leap in the *direction* of the bank, yet some yards short of it, and into the water, from head to foot ; but soon crawled out, and wended my way a mile or two up the shore, where I found my canoe snugly and safely moored in the willows, where I stepped into it, and paddled back to the island, and to the same spot where my misfortunes commenced, to enjoy the pleasure of exultations, which were to flow from contrasting my present with my former situation.

"Thus, the Island of Mas-co-tin soon lost its horrors, and I strolled two days and encamped two nights upon its silent shores—with prairie hens and wild fowl in abundance for my meals. From this lovely ground, which shews the peaceful graves of hundreds of red men, who have valued it before me, I paddled off in my light bark, and said, as I looked back, ‘Sleep there in peace, ye brave fellows ! until the sacrilegious hands of white man, and the unsympathizing ploughshare shall turn thy bones from their quiet and beautiful resting-place !

" Two or three days of strolling, brought me again to the Camp Des Moines, and from thence, with my favourite little bark canoe, placed upon the deck of the steamer, I embarked for St. Louis, where I arrived in good order, and soon found the way to the comfortable quarters from whence I am now writing. "

When I finished telling this story to Joe, his portrait was done, and I rejoiced to find that I had given to it all the fire and all the *game look* that had become so familiar and pleasing to me in our numerous rambles in the far distant wilds of our former campaigns.*

When I had landed from the steamer Warrior, at the wharf, I left all other considerations to hasten and report myself to my dear wife, leaving my little canoe on deck and in the especial charge of the Captain, till I should return for it in the afternoon, and remove it to safe storage with my other Indian articles, to form an interesting part of my Museum. On my return to the steamer it was "*missing*," and like one that I have named on a former occasion, by some *medicine* operation, for ever severed from my sight, though not from my recollections, where it will long remain, and also in a likeness which I made of it (PLATE 240, *a*), just after the trick it played me on the shore of the Mascotin Island.

After I had finished the likeness of my friend Joe, and had told him the two stories, I sat down and wrote thus in my note-book, and now copy it into my Letter :—

The West—not the " Far West," for that is a phantom, travelling on its tireless wing : but the *West*, the simple West—the vast and vacant wilds which lie between the trodden haunts of present savage and civil life—the great and almost boundless garden-spot of earth ! This is the theme at present. The " antres vast and deserts idle," where the tomahawk sleeps with the bones of the savage, as yet untouched by the trespassing ploughshare— the pictured land of silence, which, in its melancholy alternately echoes backward and forward the plaintive yells of the vanished red men, and the busy chaunts of the approaching pioneers. I speak of the boundless plains of beauty, and Nature's richest livery, where the waters of the " great deep" parted in peace, and gracefully passed off without leaving deformity behind them. Over whose green, enamelled fields, as boundless and free as the ocean's wave, Nature's proudest, noblest men have pranced on their wild horses, and extended, through a series of ages, their long arms in orisons of praise and gratitude to the Great Spirit in the sun, for the freedom and

* Poor Chadwick ! a few days after the above occasion, he sent his portrait to his mother, and started for Texas, where he joined the Texan army, with a commission from Governor Houston ; was taken prisoner in the first battle that he fought, and was amongst the four hundred prisoners who were shot down in cold blood by the order of Santa Anna.

happiness of their existence.—The land that was beautiful and famed, but had no chronicler to tell—where, while "civilized" was yet in embryo, dwelt the valiant and the brave, whose deeds of chivalry and honour have passed away like themselves, unembalmed and untold—where the plumed war horse has pranced in time with the shrill sounding war-cry, and the eagle calumet as oft sent solemn and mutual pledges in fumes to the skies. I speak of the *neutral ground* (for such it may be called), where the smoke of the wigwam is no longer seen, but the bleaching bones of the buffaloes, and the graves of the savage, tell the story of times and days that are passed —the land of stillness, on which the red man now occasionally re-treads in sullen contemplation, amid the graves of his fathers, and over which civilized man advances, filled with joy and gladness.

Such is the great valley of the Mississippi and Missouri, over almost every part of which I have extended my travels, and of which and of its future wealth and improvements, I have had sublime contemplations.

I have viewed man in the artless and innocent simplicity of nature, in the full enjoyment of the luxuries which God had bestowed upon him. I have seen him happier than kings or princes *can* be ; with his pipe and little ones about him. I have seen him shrinking from civilized approach, which came *with all its vices*, like the *dead of night*, upon him : I have seen raised, too, in that *darkness, religion's torch*, and seen him gaze and then retreat like the frightened deer, that are blinded by the light ; I have seen him shrinking from the soil and haunts of his boyhood, bursting the strongest ties which bound him to the earth, and its pleasures ; I have seen him set fire to his wigwam, and smooth over the graves of his fathers ; I have seen him ('tis the only thing that will bring them) with tears of grief sliding over his cheeks, clap his hand in silence over his mouth, and take the *last look* over his fair hunting grounds, and turn his face in sadness to the setting sun. All this I have seen performed in Nature's silent dignity and grace, which forsook him not in the last extremity of misfortune and despair ; and I have seen as often, the approach of the bustling, busy, talking, whistling, hopping, elated and exulting white man, with the first dip of the ploughshare, making sacrilegious trespass on the bones of the valiant dead. I have seen the *skull*, the *pipe*, and the *tomahawk* rise from the ground together, in interrogations which the sophistry of the world can never answer. I have seen thus, in all its forms and features, the grand and irresistible march of civilization. I have seen this splendid Juggernaut rolling on, and beheld its sweeping desolation ; and held converse with the happy thousands, living, as yet, beyond its influence, who have not been crushed, nor yet have dreamed of its approach.

I have stood amidst these unsophisticated people, and contemplated with feelings of deepest regret, the certain approach of this overwhelming system, which will inevitably march on and prosper, until reluctant tears shall have watered every rod of this fair land ; and from the towering cliffs of the Rocky Mountains, the luckless savage will turn back his swollen eye, over the blue

and illimitable hunting grounds from whence he has fled, and there contemplate, like Caius Marius on the ruins of Carthage, their splendid desolation.

Such is the vast expanse of country from which Nature's men are at this
time rapidly vanishing, giving way to the *modern crusade* which is following
the thousand allurements, and stocking with myriads, this world of green
fields. This splendid area, denominated the " Valley of the Mississippi," embraced between the immutable barriers on either side, the Alleghany and Rocky
Mountains ; with the Gulf of Mexico on the South, and the great string of
lakes on the North, and the mighty Mississippi rolling its turbid waters
through it, for the distance of four thousand miles, receiving its hundred
tributaries, whose banks and plateaus are capable of supporting a population
of one hundred millions, covered almost entirely with the richest soil in the
world, with lead, iron, and coal, sufficient for its population—with twelve
thousand miles of river navigation for steamers, within its embrace, besides
the coast on the South, and the great.expanse of lakes on the North—with
a population of five millions, already sprinkled over its nether half, and a
greater part of the remainder of it, inviting the world to its possession, for one
dollar and 25 cents (five shillings) per acre !

I ask, who can contemplate, without amazement, this *mighty river alone*,
eternally rolling its boiling waters through the richest of soil, for the distance
of four thousand miles ; over three thousand five hundred of which, I have
myself been wafted on mighty steamers, ensconced within " curtains dam-
asked, and carpets ingrain ;" and on its upper half, gazed with tireless admiration upon its thousand hills and mounds of grass and green, sloping
down to the water's edge, in all the grace and beauty of Nature's loveliest
fabrication. On its lower half, also, whose rich alluvial shores are studded
with stately cotton wood and elms, which echo back the deep and hollow
cough of the puffing steamers. I have contemplated the bed of this vast
river, sinking from its natural surface ; and the alligator driven to its bosom,
abandoning his native bog and fen, which are drying and growing into beauty
and loveliness under the hand of the husbandman.

I have contemplated these boundless forests melting away before the fatal
axe, until the expanded waters of this vast channel, and its countless tributaries, will yield their surplus to the thirsty sunbeam, to which their shorn
banks will expose them ; and I have contemplated, also, the never-ending
transit of steamers, ploughing up the sand and deposit from its bottom,
which its turbid waters are eternally hurrying on to the ocean, sinking its
channel, and thereby raising its surrounding alluvions for the temptations
and enjoyment of man.

All this is *certain*. Man's increase, and the march of human improvements in this New World, are as true and irresistible as the laws of nature,
and he who could rise from his grave and speak, or would speak from the
life some half century from this, would proclaim my prophecy true and ful-
filled. I said above, (and I again say it,) that these are subjects for " sublime

contemplation !" At all events they are so to the traveller, who has wandered over and seen this vast subject in all its parts, and able to appreciate—who has seen the frightened *herds*, as well as *multitudes of human*, giving way and shrinking from the mountain wave of civilization, which is busily rolling on behind them.

From Maine to Florida on the Atlantic coast, the forefathers of those hardy sons who are now stocking this fair land, have, from necessity, in a hard and stubborn soil, inured their hands to labour, and their habits and taste of life to sobriety and economy, which will ensure them success in the new world.

This rich country which is now alluring the enterprising young men from the East, being commensurate with the whole Atlantic States, holds out the extraordinary inducement that every emigrant can enjoy a richer soil, and that too in his own native latitude. The sugar planter, the rice, cotton, and tobacco growers—corn, rye, and wheat producers, from Louisiana to Montreal, have only to turn their faces to the West, and there are waiting for them the same atmosphere to breathe, and green fields already cleared, and ready for the plough, too tempting to be overlooked or neglected.

As far west as the banks of the Mississippi, the great wave of emigration has rolled on, and already in its rear the valley is sprinkled with towns und cities, with their thousand spires pointing to the skies. For several hundred miles West, also, have the daring pioneers ventured their lives and fortunes, with their families, testing the means and luxuries of life, which Nature has spread before them ; in the country where the buried tomahawk is scarce rusted, and the war-cry has scarcely died on the winds. Among these people have I roamed. On the Red River I have seen the rich Louisianian chequering out his cotton and sugar plantations, where the sunbeam could be seen reflected from the glistening pates of his hundred negroes, making first trespass with the hoe. I have sat with him at his hospitable table in his log cabin, sipping sherry and champaigne. *He* talks of "*hogsheads* and *price of stocks*," or "goes in for cotton."

In the western parts of Arkansas and Missouri, I have shared the genuine cottage hospitality of the abrupt, yet polite and honourable Kentuckian ; the easy, affable and sociable Tennesseean ; *this* has "a smart chance of corn ;" the *other*, perhaps, "a power of cotton ;" and then, occasionally, (from the "Old Dominion,") "I *reckon* I shall have a *mighty heap* of tobacco this season," &c.

Boys in this country are "*peart*," fever and ague renders one "*powerful weak*," and sometimes it is almost impossible to get "*shet*" of it. Intelligence, hospitality, and good cheer reign under all of these humble roofs, and the traveller who knows how to appreciate those things, with a good cup of coffee, "*corn** bread," and fresh butter, can easily enjoy moments of bliss in converse with the humble pioneer.

On the Upper Mississippi and Missouri, for the distance of seven or eight

* Maize.

nundred miles above St. Louis, is one of the most beautiful champaigne countries in the world, continually alternating into timber and fields of the softest green, calculated, from its latitude, for the people of the northern and eastern states, and "Jonathan" is already here—and almost every body else from "down East"—with fences of white, drawn and drawing, like chalk lines, over the green prairie. "By gosh, this ere is the biggest clearin I ever see." "I expect we had'nt ought to raise nothin but wheat and rye here."—"I guess you've come arter land, ha'nt you?"

Such is the character of this vast country, and such the manner in which it is filled up, with people from all parts, tracing their own latitudes, and carrying with them their local peculiarities and prejudices. The mighty Mississippi, however, the great and everlasting highway on which these people are for ever to intermingle their interests and manners, will effectually soften down those prejudices, and eventually result in an amalgamation of feelings and customs, from which this huge mass of population will take one new and general appellation.

It is here that the true character of the *American* is to be formed—here where the peculiarities and incongruities which detract from his true character are surrendered for the free, yet lofty principle that strikes between meanness and prodigality—between *literal democracy* and *aristocracy*—between low cunning and self-engendered ingenuousness. Such will be found to be the true character of the Americans when jostled awhile together, until their local angles are worn off; and such may be found and already pretty well formed, in the genuine Kentuckian, the first brave and daring pioneer of the great West; he is the true model of an American—the nucleus around which the character must form, and from which it is to emanate to the world. This is the man who first relinquished the foibles and fashions of Eastern life, trailing his rifle into the forest of the Mississippi, taking simple Nature for his guide. From necessity (as well as by nature), bold and intrepid, with the fixed and unfaltering brow of integrity, and a hand whose very grip (without words) tells you welcome.

And yet, many people of the East object to the Mississippi, "that it is too far off—is out of the world." But how strange and insufficient is such an objection to the traveller who has seen and enjoyed its hospitality, and reluctantly retreats from it with feelings of regret; pronouncing it a "world of itself, equal in luxuries and amusements to any other." How weak is such an objection to him who has ascended the Upper Mississippi to the Fall of St. Anthony, traversed the States of Missouri, Illinois, and Michigan, and territory of Ouisconsin; over all of which nature has spread her green fields, smiling and tempting man to ornament with painted house and fence, with prancing steed and tasseled carriage—with countless villages, silvered spires and domes, denoting march of intellect and wealth's refinement. The sun is sure to look upon these scenes, and we, perhaps, "*may hear the tinkling from our graves.*" Adieu.

LETTER—No 54.

RED PIPE STONE QUARRY, CÔTEAU DES PRAIRIES.

THE reader who would follow me from the place where my last epistle was written, to where I now am, must needs start, as I did, from St. Louis, and cross the Alleghanny mountains, to my own native state; where I left my wife with my parents, and wended my way to Buffalo, on Lake Erie, where I deposited my Collection ; and from thence trace, as I did, the zig-zag course of the Lakes, from Buffalo to Detroit—to the Sault de St. Marys —to Mackinaw—to Green Bay, and thence the tortuous windings of the Fox and Ouisconsin Rivers, to Prairie du Chien ; and then the mighty Mississippi (for the second time), to the Fall of St. Anthony—then the sluggish, yet decorated and beautiful St. Peters, towards its source ; and thence again (on horseback) the gradually and gracefully rising terraces of the shorn, yet green and carpeted plains, denominated the " *Côteau des Prairies*" (being the high and dividing ridge between the St. Peters and the Missouri Rivers), where I am bivouacked, at the " *Red Pipe Stone Quarry.*" The distance of such a Tour would take the reader 4,000 miles; but I save him the trouble by bringing him, in a moment, on the spot.

This journey has afforded me the opportunity of seeing, on my way, *Mackinaw*—the *Sault de St. Marys*, and *Green Bay*—points which I had not before visited ; and also of seeing many distinguished Indians among the Chippeways, Menomonies and Winnebagoes, whom I had not before painted or seen.

I can put the people of the East at rest, as to the hostile aspect of this part of the country, as I have just passed through the midst of these tribes, as well as of the Sioux, in whose country I now am, and can, without contradiction, assert, that, as far as can be known, they are generally well-disposed, and have been so, towards the whites.

There have been two companies of United States dragoons, ordered and marched to Green Bay, where I saw them ; and three companies of infantry from Prairie du Chien to Fort Winnebago, in anticipation of difficulties; but in all probability, without any real cause or necessity, for the Winnebago chief answered the officer, who asked him if they wanted to fight, " that they *could* not, had they been so disposed; for," said he, " we have no guns, no ammunition, nor anything to eat ; and, what is worst of all, one half

264

G.Catlin.

265

of our men are dying with the small-pox. If you will give us guns and ammunition, and pork, and flour, and feed and take care of our squaws and children, we will fight you; nevertheless, we will *try* to fight if you want us to, as it is."

There is, to appearance (and there is no doubt of the truth of it), the most humble poverty and absolute necessity for peace among these people at present, that can possibly be imagined. And, amidst their poverty and wretchedness, the only war that suggests itself to the eye of the traveller through their country, is the *war of sympathy and pity*, which wages in the breast of a feeling, thinking man.

The small-pox, whose ravages have now pretty nearly subsided, has taken off a great many of the Winnebagoes and Sioux. The famous Wa-be-sha, of the Sioux, and more than half of his band, have fallen victims to it within a few weeks, and the remainder of them, blackened with its frightful distortions, look as it they had just emerged fiom the sulphurous regions below. At Prairie du Chien, a considerable number of the half-breeds, and French also, suffered death by this baneful disease ; and at that place I learned one fact, which may be of service to science, which was this : that in all cases of vaccination, which had been given several years ago, it was an efficient protection ; but in those cases where the vaccine had been recent (and there were many of them), it had not the effect to protect, and in almost every instance of such, death ensued.

At the Sault de St. Marys on Lake Superior, I saw a considerable number of Chippeways, living entirely on fish, which they catch with great ease at that place.

I need not detain the reader a moment with a description of St. Marys, or of the inimitable summer's paradise, which can always be seen at Mackinaw ; and which, like the other, has been an hundred times described. I shall probably have the chance of seeing about 3,000 Chippeways at the latter place on my return home, who are to receive their annuities at that time through the hands of Mr. Schoolcraft, their agent.

In PLATE 264, I have given a distant view of *Mackinaw*, as seen approaching it from the East ; and in PLATE 265, a view of the *Sault de St Marys*, taken from the Canada shore, near the missionary-house, which is seen in the fore-ground of the picture, and in distance, the United States Garrison, and the Rapids ; and beyond them the Capes at the outlet of Lake Superior.

I mentioned that the Chippeways living in the vicinity of the Sault, live entirely on fish ; and it is almost literally true also, that the French and English, and Americans, who reside about there live on fish, which are caught in the greatest abundance in the rapids at that place, and are, perhaps, one of the greatest luxuries of the world. The *white fish*, which is in appearance much like a salmon, though smaller, is the luxury I am speaking of, and is caught in immense quantities by the scoop-nets of the Indians and

Frenchmen, amongst the foaming and dashing water of the rapids (PLATE 266), where it gains strength and flavour not to be found in the same fish in any other place. This unequalled fishery has long been one of vast importance to the immense numbers of Indians, who have always assembled about it; but of late, has been found by *money-making men,* to be too valuable a spot for the exclusive occupancy of the savage, like hundreds of others, and has at last been filled up with adventurers, who have dipped *their* nets till the poor Indian is styled an intruder; and his timid bark is seen dodging about in the coves for a scanty subsistence, whilst he scans and envies insatiable white man filling his barrels and boats, and sending them to market to be converted into money.

In PLATE 267 is seen one of their favourite amusements at this place, which I was lucky enough to witness a few miles below the Sault, when high bettings had been made, and a great concourse of Indians had assembled to witness an *Indian regatta* or *canoe race,* which went off with great excitement, firing of guns, yelping, &c. The Indians in this vicinity are all Chippeways, and their canoes all made of birch bark, and chiefly of one model; they are exceedingly light, as I have before described, and propelled with wonderful velocity.

Whilst I stopped at the Sault, I made excursions on Lake Superior, and through other parts of the country, both on the Canada and United States sides, and painted a number of Chippeways; amongst whom were *On-daig* (the crow, PLATE 268), a young man of distinction, in an extravagant and beautiful costume; and *Gitch-ee-gaw-ga-osh* (the point that remains for ever), PLATE 269, an old and respected chief.* And besides these, *Gaw-zaw-que-dung* (he who hallows; *Kay-ee-qua-da-kum-ee-gish-kum* (he who tries the ground with his foot); and *I-an-be-wa-dick* (the male carabou.)

From Mackinaw I proceeded to Green Bay, which is a flourishing beginning of a town, in the heart of a rich country, and the head-quarters of land speculators.

From thence, I embarked in a large bark canoe, with five French voyageurs at the oars, where happened to be grouped and *messed* together, five "jolly companions" of us, bound for Fort Winnebago and the Mississippi. All our stores and culinary articles were catered for by, and bill rendered to, mine host, Mr. C. Jennings (quondam of the city hotel in New York), who was one of our party, and whom we soon elected "*Major*" of the expedition; and shortly after, promoted to "*Colonel*"—from the philosophical dignity and patience with which he met the difficulties and exposure which we had to encounter, as well as for his extraordinary skill and taste displayed in the culinary art. Mr. Irving, a relative of W. Irving, Esq., and Mr. Robert Serril Wood, an Englishman (both travellers of European realms, with fund inexhaustible

* This very distinguished old chief, I have learned, died a few weeks after I painted his portrait.

266

267

for amusement and entertainment) ; Lieutenant Reed, of the army, and my-self, forming the rest of the party. The many amusing little incidents which enlivened our transit up the sinuous windings of the Fox river, amid its rapids, its banks of loveliest prairies and " oak openings," and its boundless shores of wild rice, with the thrilling notes of Mr. Wood's guitar, and " *chansons pour rire*," from our tawny boatmen, &c. were too good to be thrown away, and have been registered, perhaps for a future occasion. Suffice it for the present, that our fragile bark brought us in good time to Fort Winnebago, with impressions engraven on our hearts which can never be erased, of this sweet and beautiful little river, and of the fun and fellowship which kept us awake during the nights, almost as well as during the days. At this post, after remaining a day, our other companions took a different route, leaving Mr. Wood and myself to cater anew, and to buy a light bark canoe for our voyage down the Ouisconsin, to Prairie du Chien ; in which we embarked the next day, with paddles in hand, and hearts as light as the zephyrs, amid which we propelled our little canoe. Three days' paddling, embracing two nights' encampment, brought us to the end of our voyage. We entered the mighty Mississippi, and mutually acknowledged ourselves paid for our labours, by the inimitable scenes of beauty and romance, through which we had passed, and on which our untiring eyes had been riveted during the whole way.

The Ouisconsin, which the French most appropriately denominate " La belle riviere," may certainly vie with any other on the Continent or in the world, for its beautifully skirted banks and prairie bluffs. It may justly be said to be equal to the Mississippi about the Prairie du Chien in point of sweetness and beauty, but not on quite so grand a scale.

My excellent and esteemed fellow-traveller, like a true Englishman, has untiringly stuck by me through all difficulties, passing the countries above-mentioned, and also the Upper Mississippi, the St. Peters, and the overland route to our present encampment on this splendid plateau of the Western world. *   *   *   *   *   *

   *   Thus far have I strolled, within the space of a few weeks, for the purpose of reaching *classic ground*.

Be not amazed if I have sought, in this distant realm, the Indian *Muse*, for here she dwells, and here she must be invoked—nor be offended if my narratives from this moment should savour of poetry or appear like romance.

If I can catch the inspiration, I may sing (or yell) a few epistles from this famed ground before I leave it ; or at least I will *prose* a few of its leading characteristics and mysterious legends. This place is great (not in history, for there is none of it, but) in traditions, and stories, of which this Western world is full and rich.

" Here (according to their traditions), happened the mysterious birth of the red pipe, which has blown its fumes of peace and war to the remotest corners of the Continent ; which has visited every warrior, and passed through its reddened stem the irrevocable oath of war and desolation. And here also, the peace-breathing calumet was born, and fringed with the eagle's quills, which has shed its thrilling fumes over the land, and soothed the fury of the relentless savage.

" The Great Spirit at an ancient period, here called the Indian nations together, and standing on the precipice of the red pipe stone rock, broke from its wall a piece, and made a huge pipe by turning it in his hand, which he smoked over them, and to the North, the South, the East, and the West, and told them that this stone was red—that it was their flesh—that they must use it for their pipes of peace—that it belonged to them all, and that the war-club and scalping knife must not be raised on its ground. At the last whiff of his pipe his head went into a great cloud, and the whole surface of the rock for several miles was melted and glazed; two great ovens were opened beneath, and two women (guardian spirits of the place), entered them in a blaze of fire; and they are heard there yet (Tso-mec-cos-tee, and Tso-me-cos-te-won-dee), answering to the invocations of the high priests or medicine-men, who consult them when they are visitors to this sacred place."

Near this spot, also, on a high mound, is the " *Thunder's nest*," (*nid-du-Tonnere*), where " a very small bird sits upon her eggs during fair weather, and the skies are rent with bolts of thunder at the approach of a storm, which is occasioned by the hatching of her brood !"

" This bird is eternal, and incapable of reproducing her own species : she has often been seen by the medicine-men, and is about as large as the end of the little finger ! Her mate is a serpent, whose fiery tongue destroys the young ones as they are hatched, and the fiery noise darts through the skies."

Such are a few of the stories of this famed land, which of itself, in its beauty and loveliness, without the aid of traditionary fame, would be appropriately denominated a paradise. Whether it has been an Indian Eden or not, or whether the thunderbolts of Indian Jupiter are actually forged here, it is nevertheless a place renowned in Indian heraldry and tradition, which I hope I may be able to fathom and chronicle, as explanatory of many of my anecdotes and traditionary superstitions of Indian history, which I have given, and *am giving*, to the world.

With my excellent companion, I am encamped on, and writing from, the very rock where "the Great Spirit stood when he consecrated the *pipe of peace*, by moulding it from the rock, and smoking it over the congregated nations that were assembled about him." (See PLATE 270.)

Lifted up on this stately mound, whose top is fanned with air as light to breathe as nitrous oxide gas—and bivouacked on its very ridge, (where nought on earth is seen in distance save the thousand *treeless, bushless, weedless* hills of grass and vivid green which all around me vanish into an infinity of blue and azure), stretched on our bears'-skins, my fellow-

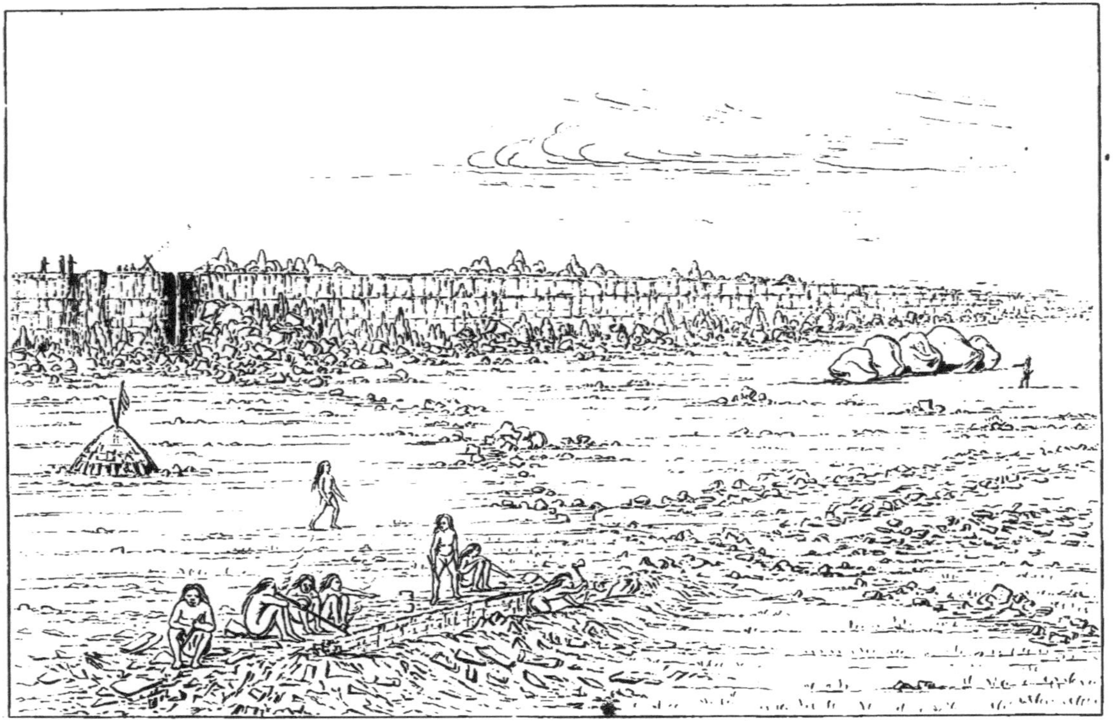

270

traveller, Mr. Wood, and myself, have laid and contemplated the splendid orrery of the heavens. With *sad delight*, that shook me with a terror, have I watched the swollen sun *shoving down* (too fast for time) upon the mystic horizon; whose line was lost except as it was marked in blue across his blood-red disk. Thus have we laid night after night (two congenial spirits who could draw pleasure from sublime contemplation), and descanted on our own insignificance; we have closely drawn our buffalo robes about us, talked of the ills of life—of friends we had lost—of projects that had failed —and of the painful steps we had to retrace to reach our own dear native lands again. We have sighed in the melancholy of twilight, when the busy winds were breathing their last, the chill of sable night was hovering around us, and nought of noise was heard but the silvery tones of the howling wolf, and the subterraneous whistle of the busy gophirs that were ploughing and vaulting the earth beneath us. Thus have we seen *wheeled down* in the *West*, the glories of day; and at the next moment, in the East, beheld her *silver majesty* jutting up above the horizon, with splendour in her face that seemed again to fill the world with joy and gladness. We have seen here, too, in all its sublimity, the blackening thunderstorm—the lightning's glare, and stood amidst the jarring thunder-bolts, that tore and broke in awful rage about us, as they rolled over the smooth surface, with nought but empty air to vent their vengeance on. There is a sublime grandeur in these scenes as they are presented here, which must be seen and felt, to be understood. There is a majesty in the very ground that we tread upon, that inspires with awe and reverence; and he must have the soul of a brute, who could gallop his horse for a whole day over swells and terraces of green that rise continually a-head, and tantalize (where hills peep over hills, and Alps on Alps arise), without feeling his bosom swell with awe and admiration, and himself as well as his thoughts, lifted up in sublimity when he rises the last terrace, and sweeps his eye over the wide spread, blue and pictured infinity that lies around and beneath him.*

Man feels here, and startles at the thrilling sensation, the force of *illimitable freedom*—his body and his mind both seem to have entered a new element—the former as free as the very wind it inhales, and the other as expanded and infinite as the boundless imagery that is spread in distance around him. Such is (and it is feebly told) the *Côteau du Prairie.* The rock on which I sit to write, is the summit of a precipice thirty feet high, extending two miles in length and much of the way polished, as if a liquid glazing had been poured over its surface. Not far from us, in the solid rock, are the deep impressed "footsteps of the Great Spirit (in the form of a track of a large bird), where he formerly stood when the blood of the buffaloes that he was devouring, ran into the rocks and turned them red." At a few yards from us, leaps a beautiful little stream, from the top of the precipice, into a deep basin

* The reader and traveller who may have this book with him, should follow the Côteau a few miles to the North of the Quarry, for the highest elevation and greatest sublimity of view.

below. Here, amid rocks of the loveliest hues, but wildest contour, is seen the poor Indian performing ablution ; and at a little distance beyond, on the plain, at the base of five huge granite boulders, he is humbly propitiating the guardian spirits of the place, by sacrifices of tobacco, entreating for permission to take away a small piece of the red stone for a pipe. Farther along, and over an extended plain are seen, like gophir hills, their excavations, ancient and recent, and on the surface of the rocks, various marks and their sculptured hieroglyphics—their wakons, totems and medicines—subjects numerous and interesting for the antiquary or the merely curious. Graves, mounds, and ancient fortifications that lie in sight—the *pyra mid* or *leaping-rock*, and its legends ; together with traditions, novel and numerous, and a description, graphical and geological, of this strange place, have all been subjects that have passed rapidly through my contemplation, and will be given in future epistles.

On our way to this place, my English companion and myself were arrested by a rascally band of the Sioux, and held in *durance vile*, for having dared to approach the sacred *fountain of the pipe!* While we had halted at the trading-hut of " Le Blanc," at a place called *Traverse des Sioux*, on the St. Peters river, and about 150 miles from the Red Pipe, a murky cloud of dark-visaged warriors and braves commenced gathering around the house, closing and cramming all its avenues, when one began his agitated and insulting harangue to us, announcing to us in the preamble, that we were prisoners, and could not go ahead. About twenty of them spoke in turn ; and we were doomed to sit nearly the whole afternoon, without being allowed to speak a word in our behalf, until they had all got through. We were compelled to keep our seats like culprits, and hold our tongues, till all had brandished their fists in our faces, and vented all the threats and invective which could flow from Indian malice, grounded on the presumption that we had come to trespass on their dearest privilege,—their religion.

There was some allowance to be made, and some excuse, surely, for the rashness of these poor fellows, and we felt disposed to pity, rather than resent, though their *unpardonable stubbornness* excited us almost to desperation. Their superstition was sensibly touched, for we were persisting, in the most peremptory terms, in the determination to visit this, their greatest medicine (mystery) place ; where, it seems, they had often resolved no white man should ever be allowed to go. They took us to be "officers sent by Government to see what this place was worth," &c. As " this red stone was a part of their flesh," it would be sacrilegious for white man to touch or take it away"—" a hole would be made in their flesh, and the blood could never be made to stop running." My companion and myself were here in a *fix*, one that demanded the use of every energy we had about us ; astounded at so unexpected a rebuff, and more than ever excited to go ahead, and see what was to be seen at this strange place ; in this emergency, we mutually agreed to go forward, even if it should be at the hazard of our lives; we heard all they had to say, and then made our own speeches—and at length had our horses brought, which we mounted and rode off without further molestation; and having arrived upon this interesting ground, have found it quite equal in interest and beauty to our sanguine expectations, abundantly repaying us for all our trouble in traveling to it.

I had long ago heard many curious descriptions of this spot given by the Indians, and had contracted the most impatient desire to visit it.* It will be seen by some of the traditions inserted in this Letter, from my notes taken on the Upper Missouri four years since, that those tribes have visited this place freely in former times; and that it has once been held and owned in common, as neutral ground, amongst the different tribes who met here to renew their pipes, under some superstition which stayed the tomahawk of natural foes, always raised in deadly hate and vengeance in other places. It will be seen also, that within a few years past (and that, probably, by the instigation of the whites, who have told them that by keeping off other tribes, and manufacturing the pipes themselves, and trading them to other adjoining nations, they can acquire much influence and wealth), the Sioux have laid entire claim to this quarry; and as it is in the centre of their country, and they are more powerful than any other tribes, they are able successfully to prevent any access to it.

That this place should have been visited for centuries past by all the neighbouring tribes, who have hidden the war-club as they approached it, and stayed the cruelties of the scalping-knife, under the fear of the vengeance of the Great Spirit, who overlooks it, will not seem strange or unnatural, when their religion and superstitions are known.

That such has been the custom, there is not a shadow of doubt; and that even so recently as to have been witnessed by hundreds and thousands of Indians of different tribes, now living, and from many of whom I have personally drawn the information, some of which will be set forth in the following traditions; and as an additional (and still more conclusive) evidence of the above position, here are to be seen (and will continue to be seen for

---

* I have in former epistles, several times spoken of the red pipes of the Indians which are found in almost every tribe of Indians on the Continent; and in every instance have, I venture to say, been brought from the Côteau des Prairies, inasmuch as no tribe of Indians that I have yet visited, have ever apprized me of any other source than this; and the stone from which they are all manufactured, is of the same character exactly, and different from any known mineral compound ever yet discovered in any part of Europe, or other parts of the American Continent. This may be thought a broad assertion—yet it is one I have ventured to make (and one I should have had no motive for making, except for the purpose of eliciting information, if there be any, on a subject so curious and so exceedingly interesting). In my INDIAN MUSEUM there can always be seen a great many beautiful specimens of this mineral selected on the spot, by myself, embracing all of its numerous varieties; and I challenge the world to produce anything like it, except it be from the same locality. In a following Letter will be found a further account of it, and its chemical analysis.

ages to come), the *totems* and *arms* of the different tribes, who have visit e this place for ages past, deeply engraved on the quartz rocks, where they are to be recognized in a moment (and not to be denied) by the passing traveller, who has been among these tribes, and acquired even but a partial knowledge of them and their respective modes.*

The thousands of inscriptions and paintings on the rocks at this place, as well as the ancient diggings for the pipe-stone, will afford amusement for the world who will visit it, without furnishing the least data, I should think, of the time at which these excavations commenced, or of the period at which the Sioux assumed the exclusive right to it.

Among the many traditions which I have drawn personally from the different tribes, and which go to support the opinion above advanced, is the following one, which was related to me by a distinguished Knisteneaux, on the Upper Missouri, four years since, on occasion of presenting to me a handsome red stone pipe. After telling me that he had been to this place—and after describing it in all its features, he proceeded to say :—

" That in the time of a great freshet, which took place many centuries ago, and destroyed all the nations of the earth, all the tribes of the red men assembled on the Côteau du Prairie, to get out of the way of the waters. After they had all gathered here from all parts, the water continued to rise, until at length it covered them all in a mass, and their flesh was converted into red pipe stone. Therefore it has always been considered neutral ground —it belonged to all tribes alike, and all were allowed to get it and smoke it together.

" While they were all drowning in a mass, a young woman, K-wap-tah-w (a virgin), caught hold of the foot of a very large bird that was flying over, and was carried to the top of a high cliff, not far off, that was above the water. Here she had twins, and their father was the war-eagle, and her children have since peopled the earth.

" The pipe stone, which is the flesh of their ancestors, is smoked by them as the symbol of peace, and the eagle's quill decorates the head of the brave."

Tradition of the Sioux.—" Before the creation of man, the Great Spirit (whose tracks are yet to be seen on the stones, at the Red Pipe, in form of the tracks of a large bird) used to slay the buffaloes and eat them on the ledge of the Red Rocks, on the top of the Côteau des Prairies, and their blood running on to the rocks, turned them red. One day when a large snake had crawled

---

* I am aware that this interesting fact may be opposed by subsequent travellers, who will find nobody but the Sioux upon this ground, who now claim exclusive right to it ; and for the satisfaction of those who doubt, I refer them to Lewis and Clark's Tour thirty-three years since, before the influence of Traders had deranged the system and truth of things, in these regions. I have often conversed with General Clark, of St. Louis, on this subject, and he told me explicitly, and authorized me to say it to the world, that every tribe on the Missouri told him they had been to this place, and that the Great Spirit kept the peace amongst his red children on that ground, where they had smoked with their enemies.

into the nest of the bird to eat his eggs, one of the eggs hatched out in a clap of thunder, and the Great Spirit catching hold of a piece of the pipe stone to throw at the snake, moulded it into a man.' This man's feet grew fast in the ground where he stood for many ages, like a great tree, and therefore he grew very old ; he was older than an hundred men at the present day ; and at last another tree grew up by the side of him, when a large snake ate them both off at the roots, and they wandered off together ; from these have sprung all the people that now inhabit the earth."

The above tradition I found amongst the Upper Missouri Sioux, but which, when I related to that part of the great tribe of Sioux who inhabit the Upper Mississippi, they seemed to know nothing about it. The reason for this may have been, perhaps, as is often the case, owing to the fraud or excessive ignorance of the interpreter, on whom we are often entirely dependent in this country ; or it is more probably owing to the very vague and numerous fables which may often be found, cherished and told by different bands or families in the same tribe, and relative to the same event.

I shall on a future occasion, give you a Letter on traditions of this kind, which will be found to be very strange and amusing ; establishing the fact at the same time, that theories respecting their origin, creation of the world, &c. &c., are by no means uniform throughout the different tribes, nor even through an individual tribe ; and that very many of these theories are but the vagaries, or the ingenious systems of their medicine or mystery-men, conjured up and taught to their own respective parts of a tribe, for the purpose of gaining an extraordinary influence over the minds and actions of the remainder of the tribe, whose superstitious minds, under the supernatural controul and dread of these self-made magicians, are held in a state of mysterious vassalage.

Amongst the Sioux of the Mississippi, and who live in the region of the Red Pipe Stone Quarry, I found the following and not less strange tradition on the same subject. " Many ages after the red men were made, when all the different tribes were at war, the Great Spirit sent runners and called them all together at the ' Red Pipe.'—He stood on the top of the rocks, and the red people were assembled in infinite numbers on the plains below. He took out of the rock a piece of the red stone, and made a large pipe ; he smoked it over them all ; told them that it was part of their flesh ; that though they were at war, they must meet at this place as friends ; that it belonged to them all ; that they must make their calumets from it and smoke them to him whenever they wished to appease him or get his good-will—the smoke from his big pipe rolled over them all, and he disappeared in its cloud ; at the last whiff of his pipe a blaze of fire rolled over the rocks, and melted their surface—at that moment two squaws went in a blaze of fire under the two medicine rocks, where they remain to this day, and must be consulted and propitiated whenever the pipe stone is to be taken away."

The following speech of a Mandan, which was made to me in the Mandan village four years since, after I had painted his picture, I have copied from my note-book as corroborative of the same facts :

"My brother—You have made my picture and I like it much. My friends tell me they can see the eyes move, and it must be very good—it must be partly alive. I am glad it is done—though many of my people are afraid. I am a young man, but my heart is strong. I have jumped on to the medicine-rock—I have placed my arrow on it and no Mandan can take it away.* The red stone is slippery, but my foot was true—it did not slip. My brother, this pipe which I give to you, I brought from a high mountain, it is toward the rising sun—many were the pipes that we brought from there—and we brought them away in peace. We left our *totems* or marks on the rocks—we cut them deep in the stones, and they are there now. The Great Spirit told all nations to meet there in peace, and all nations hid the war-club and the tomahawk. The *Dah-co-tahs*, who are our enemies, are very strong—they have taken up the tomahawk, and the blood of our warriors has run on the rocks. My friend, we want to visit our medicines—our pipes are old and worn out. My friend, I wish you to speak to our Great Father about this."

The chief of the Puncahs, on the Upper Missouri, also made the following allusion to this place, in a speech which he made to me on the occasion of presenting me a very handsome pipe about four years since :—

"My friend, this pipe, which I wish you to accept, was dug from the ground, and cut and polished as you now see it, by my hands. I wish you to keep it, and when you smoke through it, recollect that this red stone is a part of our flesh. This is one of the last things we can ever give away. Our enemies the Sioux, have raised the red flag of blood over the Pipe Stone Quarry, and our medicines there are trodden under foot by them. The Sioux are many, and we cannot go to the mountain of the red pipe. We have seen all nations smoking together at that place—but, my brother, it is not so now."†

* The medicine (or leaping) rock is a part of the precipice which has become severed from the main part, standing about seven or eight feet from the wall, just equal in height, and about seven feet in diameter.

It stands like an immense column of thirty-five feet high, and highly polished on its top and sides. It requires a daring effort to leap on to its top from the main wall, and back again, and many a heart has sighed for the honour of the feat without daring to make the attempt. Some few have tried it with success, and left their arrows standing in its crevice, several of which are seen there at this time ; others have leapt the chasm and fallen from the slippery surface on which they could not hold, and suffered instant death upon the craggy rocks below. Every young man in the nation is ambitious to perform this feat ; and those who have successfully done it are allowed to boast of it all their lives. In the sketch already exhibited, there will be seen, a view of the "leaping rock ;" and in the middle of the picture, a mound, of a conical form, of ten feet height, which was erected over the body of a distinguished young man who was killed by making this daring effort, about two years before I was there, and whose sad fate was related to me by a Sioux chief, who was father of the young man, and was visiting the Red Pipe Stone Quarry, with thirty others of his tribe, when we were there, and cried over the grave, as he related the story to Mr. Wood and myself, of his son's death.

† On my return from the Pipe Stone Quarry, one of the old chiefs of the Sacs, on seeing

Such are a few of the stories relating to this curious place, and many others might be given which I have procured, though they amount to nearly the same thing, with equal contradictions and equal absurdities.

The position of the Pipe Stone Quarry, is in a direction nearly West from the Fall of St. Anthony, at a distance of three hundred miles, on the summit of the dividing ridge between the St. Peters and the Missouri rivers, being about equi-distant from either. This dividing ridge is denominated by the French, the " Côteau des Prairies," and the " Pipe Stone Quarry" is situated near its southern extremity, and consequently not exactly on its highest elevation, as its general course is north and south, and its southern extremity terminates in a gradual slope.

Our approach to it was from the East, and the ascent, for the distance of fifty miles, over a continued succession of slopes and terraces, almost imperceptibly rising one above another, that seemed to lift us to a great height. The singular character of this majestic mound, continues on the West side, in its descent toward the Missouri. There is not a tree or bush to be seen from the highest summit of the ridge, though the eye may range East and West, almost to a boundless extent, over a surface covered with a short grass, that is green at one's feet, and about him, but changing to blue in distance, like nothing but the blue and vastness of the ocean.

The whole surface of this immense tract of country is hard and smooth, almost without stone or gravel, and coated with a green turf of grass of three or four inches only in height. Over this the wheels of a carriage would run as easily, for hundreds of miles, as they could on a Mc Adamized road, and its graceful gradations would in all parts, admit of a horse to gallop, with ease to himself and his rider.

The full extent and true character of these vast prairies are but imperfectly understood by the world yet; who will agree with me that they are a subject truly sublime, for contemplation, when I assure them, that " a coach and four" might be driven with ease, (with the exception of rivers and ravines, which are in many places impassable), over unceasing fields of green, from the Fall of St. Anthony to Lord Selkirk's Establishment on the Red

some specimens of the stone which I brought with me from that place, observed as follows :—

" My friend, when I was young, I used to go with our young men to the mountain of the Red Pipe, and dig out pieces for our pipes. We do not go now ; and our red pipes as you see, are few. The Dah-co-tah's have spilled the blood of red men on that place, and the Great Spirit is offended. The white traders have told them to draw their bows upon us when we go there; and they have offered us many of the pipes for sale, but we do not want to smoke them, for we know that the Great Spirit is offended. My mark is on the rocks in many places, but I shall never see them again. They lie where the Great Spirit sees them, for his eye is over that place, and he sees everything that is here.".

Ke-o-kuck chief of the Sacs and Foxes, when I asked him whether he had ever been there, replied—

" No, I have never seen it; it is in our enemies' country,—I wish it was in ours—I would sell it to the whites for a great many boxes of money."

River, sir the North; from that to the mouth of Yellow Stone on the Missouri—thence to the Platte—to the Arkansas, and Red Rivers of the South, and through Texas to the Gulf of Mexico, a distance of more than three thousand miles.

I mentioned in a former Letter, that we had been arrested by the Sioux, on our approach to this place, at the trading-post of Le Blanc, on the banks of the St. Peters; and I herein insert the most important part of the speeches made, and talks held on that momentous occasion, as near as my friend and I could restore them, from partial notes and recollection. After these copper-visaged advocates of their country's rights had assembled about us, and filled up every avenue of the cabin, the grave council was opened in the following manner:—

Te-o-kun-hko (the swift man), first rose and said—

" My friends, I am not a chief, but the son of a chief—I am the son of my father—he is a chief—and when he is gone away, it is my duty to speak for him—he is not here—but what I say is the talk of his mouth. We have been told that you are going to the Pipe Stone Quarry. We come now to ask for what purpose you are going, and what business you have to go there." (' How ! how !' vociferated all of them, thereby approving what was said, giving assent by the word *how*, which is their word for yes).

" *Brothers*—I am a brave, but not a chief—my arrow stands in the top of the leaping-rock; all can see it, and all know that Te-o-kun-hko's foot has been there. (' How ! how !')

" *Brothers*—We look at you and we see that you are Che-mo-ke-mon capitains (white men officers): we know that you have been sent by your Government, to see what that place is worth, and we think the white people want to buy it. (' How, how').

" *Brothers*—We have seen always that the white people, when they see anything in our country that they want, send officers to value it, and then if they can't buy it, they will get it some other way. (' How ! how !')

" *Brothers*—I speak strong, my heart is strong, and I speak fast; this red pipe was given to the red men by the Great Spirit—it is a part of our flesh, and therefore is great *medicine*. (' How ! how !')

" *Brothers*—We know that the whites are like a great cloud that rises in the East, and will cover the whole country. We know that they will have all our lands; but, if ever they get our Red Pipe Quarry they will have to pay very dear for it. (' How ! how ! how !')

" *Brothers*—We know that no white man has ever been to the Pipe Stone Quarry, and our chiefs have often decided in council that no white man shall ever go to it. (' How ! how !')

" *Brothers*—You have heard what I have to say, and you can go no further, but you must turn about and go back. (' How ! how ! how !')

" *Brothers*—You see that the sweat runs from my face, for I am troubled."

Then I commenced to reply in the following manner:—

" My friends, I am sorry that you have mistaken us so much, and the object of our visit to your country. We are not officers—we are not sent by any one—we are two poor men travelling to see the Sioux and shake hands with them, and examine what is curious or interesting in their country. This man who is with me is my friend ; he is a *Sa-ga-nosh* (an Englishman).

(' How ! how ! how !')

(All rising and shaking hands with him, and a number of them taking out and showing British medals which were carried in their bosoms.)

" We have heard that the Red Pipe Quarry was a great curiosity, and we have started to go to it, and we will not be stopped." (Here I was interrupted by a grim and black-visaged fellow, who shook his long shaggy locks as he rose, with his sunken eyes fixed in direst hatred on me, and his fist brandished within an inch of my face.)

" *Pale faces !* you cannot speak till we have all done ; you are our *prisoners*—our young men (our soldiers) are about the house, and you must listen to what we have to say. What has been said to you is true, you must go back. (' How ! how !')

" We heard the word *Saganosh*, and it makes our hearts glad ; we shook hand with our brother—his father is our father—he is our Great Father—he lives across the big lake—his son is here, and we are glad—we wear our Great Father the sag-a-nosh on our bosoms, and we keep his face bright*— we shake hands, but no white man has been to the red pipe and none shall go. (' How !')

* Many and strong are the recollections of the Sioux and other tribes, of their alliance with the British in the last and revolutionary wars, of which I have met many curious instances, one of which was correctly reported in the London Globe, from my Lectures, and I here insert it.—

THE GLOBE AND TRAVELLER.

" *Indian Knowledge of English Affairs*—Mr. Catlin, in one of his Lectures on the manners and customs of the North American Indians, during the last week, related a very curious occurrence, which excited a great deal of surprise and some considerable mirth amongst his highly respectable and numerous audience. Whilst speaking of the great and warlike tribe of Sioux or Dahcotas, of 40,000 or 50,000, he stated that many of this tribe, as well as of several others, although living entirely in the territory of the United States, and several hundred miles south of her Majesty's possessions, were found cherishing a lasting friendship for the English, whom they denominate Saganosh. And in very many instances they are to be seen wearing about their necks large silver medals, with the portrait of George III. in bold relief upon them. These medals were given to them as badges of merit during the last war with the United States, when these warriors were employed in the British service.

" The Lecturer said, that whenever the word Saganosh was used, it seemed to rouse them at once ; that on several occasions when Englishmen had been in his company as fellow-travellers, they had marked attentions paid them by these Indians as Saganoshes. And on one occasion, in one of his last rambles in that country, where he had painted several portraits in a small village of Dahcotas, the chief of the band positively refused to sit ; alleging as his objection that the pale faces, who were not to be trusted, might do some injury to his portrait, and his health or his life might be affected by it. The painter,

" You see (holding a red pipe to the side of his naked arm) that this pipe is a part of our flesh. The red men are a part of the red stone. ('How, how !')

" If the white men take away a piece of the red pipe stone, it is a hole made in our flesh, and the blood will always run. We cannot stop the blood from running. ('How, how !')

" The Great Spirit has told us that the red stone is only to be used for pipes, and through them we are to smoke to him. ('How !')

" Why do the white men want to get there ? You have no good object in view ; we know you have none, and the sooner you go back, the better." ("How, how !")

Muz-za (the iron) spoke next.

" My friends, we do not wish to harm you ; you have heard the words of our chief men, and you now see that you must go back. (' How, how !')

" *Tchan-dee-pah-sha-kah-free* (the red pipe stone) was given to us by the Great Spirit, and no one need ask the price of it, for it is *medicine*. ('How, how !')

" My friends, I believe what you have told us ; I think your intentions are good ; but our chiefs have always told us, that no white man was allowed to go there—and you cannot go." ("How, how !")

as he was about to saddle his horse for his departure, told the Indian that he was a Saganosh, and was going across the Big Salt Lake, and was very sorry that he could not carry the picture of so distinguished a man. At this intelligence the Indian advanced, and after a hearty grip of the hand, very carefully and deliberately withdrew from his bosom, and next to his naked breast, a large silver medal, and turning his face to the painter, pronounced with great vehemence and emphasis the word Sag-a-nosh ! The artist, supposing that he had thus gained his point with the Indian Sagamore, was making preparation to proceed with his work, when the Indian still firmly denied him the privilege— holding up the face of his Majesty (which had got a superlative brightness by having been worn for years against his naked breast), he made this singular and significant speech :—' When you cross the Big Salt Lake, tell my Great Father that you saw his face, and it was bright !' To this the painter replied, ' I can never see your Great Father, he is dead !' The poor Indian recoiled in silence, and returned his medal to his bosom, entered his wigwam, at a few paces distant, where he seated himself amidst his family around his fire, and deliberately lighting his pipe, passed it around in silence.

" When it was smoked out he told them the news he had heard, and in a few moments returned to the traveller again, who was preparing with his party to mount their horses, and enquired whether the Saganoshes had no chief. The artist replied in the affirmative, saying that the present chief of the Saganoshes is a *young* and *very beautiful woman*. The Sagamore expressed great surprise and some incredulity at this unaccountable information ; and being fully assured by the companions of the artist that his assertion was true, the Indian returned again quite hastily to his wigwam, called his own and the neighbouring families into his presence, lit and smoked another pipe, and then communicated the intelligence to them, to their great surprise and amusement ; after which he walked out to the party about to start off, and advancing to the painter (or Great Medicine as they called him), with a sarcastic smile on his face, in due form, and with much grace and effect, he carefully withdrew again from his bosom the polished silver medal, and turning the face to the painter, said, ' Tell my *Great Mother*, that you saw our Great Father, and that we keep his face bright !' "

Another.—" My friends, you see I am a young man; you see on my war-club two scalps from my enemies' heads; my hands have been dipped in blood, but I am a good man. I am a friend to the whites, to the traders; and they are your friends. I bring them 3000 muskrat skins every year, which I catch in my own traps. ('How, how!')

" We love to go to the Pipe Stone, and get a piece for our pipes; but we ask the Great Spirit first. If the white men go to it, they will take it out, and not fill up the holes again, and the Great Spirit will be offended." ("How, how, how!")

Another.—" My friends, listen to me! what I am to say will be the truth. —('How!')

" I brought a large piece of the pipe stone, and gave it to a white man to make a pipe; he was our trader, and I wished him to have a good pipe. The next time I went to his store, I was unhappy when I saw that stone made into a dish! ('Eugh!')

" This is the way the white men would use the red pipe stone, if they could get it. Such conduct would offend the Great Spirit, and make a red man's heart sick. ('How, how!')

" *Brothers*, we do not wish to harm you—if you turn about and go back, you will be well, both you and your *horses*—you cannot go forward. ('How, how!')

" We know that if you go to the pipe stone, the Great Spirit looks upon you—the white people do not think of that. ('How, how!')

" I have no more to say."

These, and a dozen other speeches to the same effect, having been pronounced, I replied in the following manner :

" *My friends*, you have entirely mistaken us; we are no officers, nor are we sent by any one—the white men do not want the red pipe—it is not worth their carrying home so far, if you were to give it all to them. Another thing, they don't use pipes—they don't know how to smoke them.

' How, how!'

" *My friends*, I think as you do, that the Great Spirit has given that place to the red men for their pipes.

' How, how, how!'

" I give you great credit for the course you are taking to preserve and protect it; and I will do as much as any man to keep white men from taking it away from you.

' How, how!'

" But we have started to go and see it; and we cannot think of being stopped."

Another rose (interrupting me) :—

" White men! your words are very smooth; you have some object in view or you would not be so determined to go—you have no good design, and the quicker you turn back the better; there is no use of talking any

more about it—if you think best to go, try it; that's all I have to say."
("How, how!")

During this scene, the son of Monsr. Le Blanc was standing by, and seeing this man threatening me so hard by putting his fist near my face: he several times stepped up to him, and told him to stand back at a respectful distance, or that he would knock him down. After their speaking was done, I made a few remarks, stating that we should go ahead, which we did the next morning, by saddling our horses and riding off through the midst of them, as I have before described.

Le Blanc told us, that these were the most disorderly and treacherous part of the Sioux nation, that they had repeatedly threatened his life, and that he expected they would take it. He advised us to go back as they ordered; but we heeded not his advice.

On our way we were notified at several of their villages which we passed, that we must go back; but we proceeded on, and over a beautiful prairie country, of one hundred miles or more, when our Indian guide brought us to the trading-house of an old acquaintance of mine, Monsieur La Fromboise, who lives very comfortably, and in the employment of the American Fur Company, near the base of the Côteau, and forty or fifty miles from the Pipe Stone Quarry.

We rode up unexpectedly, and at full gallop, to his door, when he met us and addressed us as follows:—

"Ha! Monsr. how do you do?—Quoi! ha, est ce vous, Monsr. Cataline—est il possible? Oui, oui, vraiment le meme—mon ami, Cataline—comment se va-t-il? et combien (pardon me though, for I can speak Engglish). How have you been since I saw you last season? and how under Heaven, have you wandered into this wild region, so far from civilization? Dismount, dismount, gentlemen, and you are welcome to the comforts, such as they are, of my little cabin."

"Monsr. La Fromboise, allow me to introduce to your acquaintance, my friend, and travelling companion, Mr. Wood, of England."

"Monsr. Wood, I am happy to see you, and I hope you will make allowance for the rudeness of my cabin, and the humble manner in which I shall entertain you."

"I assure you, my dear sir, that no apology is necessary; for your house looks as delightful as a palace, to Mr. Catlin and myself, who have so long been tenants of the open air."

"Gentlemen, walk in; we are surrounded with red folks here, and you will be looked upon by them with great surprise."

"That's what we want to see exactly. Catlin! that's fine—oh! how lucky we are."

"Well, gentlemen, walk into the other room; you see I have two rooms to my house (or rather cabin), but they are small and unhandy. Such as I have shall be at your service heartily; and I assure you, gentlemen, that this is the happiest moment of my life. I cannot give you feather-beds to sleep on ; but I have a plenty of new robes, and you, at all events, Monsr. Cataline, know by this time how to make a bed of them. We can give you plenty of buffalo meat, buffalo tongues, wild geese, ducks, prairie hens, venison, trout, young swan, beaver tails, pigeons, plums, grapes, young bear, some green corn, squash, onions, water-melons, and pommes des terres, some coffee and some tea."

" My good friend, one-half or one-third of these things (which are all luxuries to us) would render us happy ; put yourself to no trouble on our account, and we shall be perfectly happy under your roof."

" I am very sorry, gentlemen, that I cannot treat you as I would be glad to do ; but you must make up for these things if you are fond of sporting, for there are plenty of buffaloes about ; at a little distance the prairies are speckled with them ; and our prairies and lakes abound with myriads of prairie hens, ducks geese and swan. You shall make me a long visit, gentlemen, and we will have sport in abundance. I assure you, that I shall be perfectly happy whilst you are with me. Pardon me a little, while I order you some dinner, and attend to some Indians who are in my store, trading, and taking their fall credits."

" That's a fine fellow I'll engage you," said my companion.

" Yes, he is all that. I have known him before ; he is a gentleman, and a polished one too, every ounce of him. You see in this instance how durable and lasting are the manners of a true gentleman, and how little a life-time of immersion in the wilderness, amid the reckless customs of savage life, will extinguish or efface them. I could name you a number of such, whose surface seems covered with a dross, which once rubbed of, shows a polish brighter than ever."

We spent a day or two very pleasantly with this fine and hospitable fellow, until we had rested from the fatigue of our journey ; when he very kindly joined us with fresh horses, and piloted us to the Pipe Stone Quarry, where he is now encamped with us, a jolly companionable man, and familiar with most of the events and traditions of this strange place, which he has visited on former occasions.*

La Fromboise has some good Indian blood in his veins, and from his modes of life, as well as from a natural passion that seems to belong to the French adventurers in these wild regions, he has a great relish for songs and stories, of which he gives us many, and much pleasure ; and furnishes us one of the most amusing and gentlemanly companions that could possibly be found. My friend Wood sings delightfully, also, and as I cannot sing, but can tell, now and then, a story, with tolerable effect, we manage to pass away

* This gentleman, the summer previous to this, while I was in company with him at Prairie du Chien, gave me a very graphic account of the Red Pipe Stone Quarry, and made for me, from recollection, a chart of it, which I yet possess, and which was drawn with great accuracy.

our evenings, in our humble bivouack, over our buffalo meat and prairie hens, with much fun and amusement. In these nocturnal amusements, I have done *my* part, by relating anecdotes of my travels on the Missouri, and other parts of the Indian country which I have been over; and occasionally reading from my note-book some of the amusing entries I had formerly made in it, but never have had time to transcribe for the world.

As I can't write music, and *can* (in my own way) write a story, the readers will acquit me of egotism or partiality, in reporting only *my own part* of the entertainments; which was generally the mere reading a story or two from my notes which I have with me, or relating some of the incidents of life which my old travelling companion " *Batiste*" and I had witnessed in former years.

Of these, I read one last evening, that pleased my good friend La Fromboise so exceedingly, that I am constrained to copy it into my Letter and send it home.

This amusing story is one that my man Ba'tiste used to tell to Bogard, and others with great zest; describing his adventure one night, in endeavouring to procure a *medicine-bag*, which I had employed him to obtain for me on the Upper Missouri; and he used to prelude it thus :—

" Je commence—"

" Dam your commonce, (said Bogard), tell it in English—"

" Pardón, Monsieur, en Americaine—"

" Well, American then, if you please; anything but your darned ' *parlez vous.*' "

" Bien, excusez—now Monsieur Bogard, you must know first place, de ' *Medicine-Bags*' is mere humbug, he is no *medicine* in him—no pills; he is someting mysterieux. Some witchcraft, súppose. You must know que tous les sauvages have such tings about him, pour for good luck. Ce n'est que (pardón) it is only *hocus pocus*, to keep off witch, súppose. You must know ces articles can nevare be sold, of course you see dey cannot be buy. So my friend here, Monsieur Cataline, who have collect all de curiosités des pays sauvages, avait made strong applique to me pour for to get one of dese *medicine-bags* for his Collection curieux, et I had, pour moimeme, le curiosité extreme pour for to see des quelques choses ces étranges looking tings was composi.

" I had learn much of dese strange custom, and I know wen de Ingin die, his *medicine-bags* is buried wis him.

" Oui, Monsieur, so it never can be got by any boday. Bien. I hap to tink one day wen we was live in de mous of Yellow Stone, now is time, and I avait said to Monsieur Cataline, que pensez vous ? *Kon-te-wonda* (un des chefs du) (pardón, one of de chiefs, of de Knisteneux) has die tó-day. Il avait une *medicine-bag* magnifique, et extremement curieux ; il est composé d'un, it is made (pardón, si vous plait) of de wite wolf skin, ornement et stuff

wid tousand tings wich we shall see, ha ? Good luck! Suppose Monsieur
Cataline, I have seen him just now. I av see de *medicine-bag* laid on his
breast avec his hands crossed ovare it. Que pensez vous ? I can get him
to-night, ha ? If you will keep him, if you shall not tell, ha ? 'Tis no harm
—'tis no steal—he is dead, ha ? Well, you shall see. But, would you not
be afraid, Ba'tiste, (said Monsieur Cataline), to take from dis poor fellow
his medicines (or mysteries) on which he has rest all his hopes in dis world,
and de world to come ? Pardón, je n'ai pas peur ; non, Monsieur, ne rien de
peur. I nevare saw ghost—I have not fear, mais, súppose, it is not right,
éxact ; but I have grand disposition pour for to obligé my friend, et le curiosité moimeme, pour to see wat it is made of ; suppose tó-night I shall go,
ha ? ‘Well, Ba'tiste, I have no objection (said Monsieur Cataline) if your
heart does not fail you, for I will be very glads to get him, and will make you
a handsome present for it, but I think it will·be a cold and gloomy kind of
business.’ Nevare mind, Monsieur Cataline (I said) provide he is well dead,
perfect dead! Well, I had see les Knisteneux when dey ave bury de chap
—I ave watch close, and I ave see how de medicine-bags was put. It was
fix pretty tight by some cord around his bellay, and den some skins was
wrap many times áround him—he was put down in de hole dug for him, and
some flat stones and some little dirt was laid on him, only till next day,
wen some grand ceremonays was to be pérform ovare him, and den de hole
was to be fill up ; now was de only time possibe for de *medicine-bag*, ha ? I
ave very pretty little wife at dat times, Assinneboin squaw, and we sleep in
one of de stores inside of de Fort, de Trade-house, you know, ha ?

“ So you may súppose I was all de day perplex to know how I should
go, somebody may watch—súppose, he may not be dead! not quite
dead, ha ? nevare mind—le jour was bien long, et le nuit dismal, *dismal*! oh by gar *it was dismal*! plien, plien (pardón) full of apprehension, mais sans *peur*, je *n'avais pas peur*! So some time aftere
midnights, wen it was bout right time pour go, I made start, very light,
so my wife must not wake. Oh diable l'imagination! quel solitude! well, I
have go very well yet, I am pass de door, and I am pass de gate, and I am
at lengts arrive at de grave! súppose ‘ now Ba'tiste, courage, courage!
now is de times come.’ Well, súppose, I am not fraid of *dead man*, mais,
perhaps, dese *medicine-bag* is give by de Grande Esprit to de Ingin for someting? possibe! I will let him keep it. I shall go back! No, Monsieur
Cataline will laughs at me. I must have him, ma foi, mon courage! so I
climb down very careful into de grave, mais, as I déscend, my heart rise up
into my mouse! Oh mon Dieu! courage Ba'tiste, courage! ce n'est pas
l'homme dat I fear, mais ie *medicine*, le *medicine*. So den I ave lift out de
large stones, I ave put out my head in de dark, and I ave look all de contré
round ; ne personne, ne personne—no bodé in sight! Well, I ave got softly
down on my knees ovare him, (oh, courage! courage! oui) and wen I ave
unwrap de robe, I ave all de time say, ‘ pardon, courage! pardon, courage!

untill I ad got de skins all off de bodé ; I ave den take hold of de cord to untie, mais !! (dans l'instant) two cold hands seize me by de wrists! and I was just dead—I was petrifact in one instant. Oh St. Esprit! I could just see in de dark two eyes glaring like fire sur upon me! and den, (oh, eugh!) it spoke to me, 'Who are you?' (Sacré, vengeance! it will not do to deceive him, no,) 'I am Ba'tiste, *poor* Ba'tiste!' 'Then thou art surely mine, (as he clenched both arms tight around my boday) lie still Ba'tiste.' Oh, holy Vierge! St. Esprit! O mon Dieu! I could not breathe! miserable! je sui perdu! oh pourquoi have I been such fool to get into dese cold, cold arms! 'Ba'tiste? (drawing me some tighter and tighter!) do you not belong to me, Ba'tiste?' Yes, súppose! oh diable! belong? Oui, oui, je suis certainment perdu, lost, lost, for evare! *Oh! can you not possibe let me go*? 'No, Ba'tiste, we must never part.' Grand Dieu! c'est finis, finis, finis avec moi! "Then you do not love me any more, Ba'tiste?" Quel! quoi! what!! est ce vous, *Wee-ne-on-ka*? 'Yes, Ba'tiste, it is the *Bending Willow* who holds you, she that loves you and will not let you go? Are you dreaming Ba'tiste?' Oui, diable, ———!"

" Well, Ba'tiste, that's a very good story, and very well told; I presume you never tried again to get a medicine-bag ?"

" Non, Monsieur Bogard, je vous assure, I was satisfy wis de mistakes dat night, pour for je crois qu'il fut l'Esprit, le Grand Esprit."

After this, my entertaining companions sung several amusing songs, and then called upon me for another story. Which Mr. Wood had already heard me tell several times, and which he particularly called for; as

" THE STORY OF THE DOG,"

and which I began as follows :—

" Well, some time ago, when I was drifting down the mighty Missouri, in a little canoe, with two hired men, Bogard and Ba'tiste, (and in this manner *did* we glide along) amid all the pretty scenes and ugly, that decked the banks of that river, from the mouth of the Yellow Stone, to St. Louis, a distance of *only* two thousand miles; Bogard and Ba'tiste plied their paddles and I *steered*, amid snag and sand-bar—amongst drift logs and herds of swimming buffaloes—our beds were uniformly on the grass, or upon some barren beach, which we often chose, to avoid the suffocating clouds of musquitos; our fire was (by the way we had none at night) kindled at sundown, under some towering bluff—our supper cooked and eaten, and we off again, floating some four or five miles after nightfall, when our canoe was landed at random, on some unknown shore. In whispering silence and darkness our buffalo robes were drawn out and spread upon the grass, and our bodies stretched upon them ; our pistols were belted to our sides, and our rifles always slept in our arms. In this way we were encamped, and another robe drawn over us, head and foot, under which our iron slumbers were secure from the tread of all foes saving that of the sneaking gangs of wolves, who were nightly serenading us with their harmonics, and often quarrelling for the privilege of chewing off the corners of the robe, which served us as a blanket. 'Caleb' (the grizzly bear) was often there too, leaving the print of his deep impressed footsteps where he had perambulated, reconnoitring, though not disturbing us. Our food was simply buffalo meat from day to day, and from morning till night, for coffee and bread we had not. The fleece (hump) of a fat cow, was the luxury of luxuries; and for it we would step ashore, or as often level our rifles upon the 'slickest' of the herds from our canoe, as they were grazing upon the banks. Sometimes the antelope, the mountain-sheep, and so the stately elk contributed the choicest cuts for our little larder; and at others, while in the vicinity of war-parties, where we dared not to fire our guns, our boat was silently steered into some little cove or eddy, our hook and line dipped, and we trusted to the bite of a catfish for our suppers: if we got him, he was sometimes too large and tough; and if we got him not, we would swear, (not at all) and go to bed.

"Our meals were generally cooked and eaten on piles of driftwood, where our fire was easily kindled, and a peeled log (which we generally straddled) did admirably well for a seat, and a table to eat from.

"In this manner did we glide away from day to day, with anecdote and fun to shorten the time, and just enough of the *spice of danger* to give vigour to our stomachs, and keenness to our appetites—making and meeting accident and incident sufficient for a 'book.' Two hundred miles from the mouth of Yellow Stone brought us to the village of the kind and gentlemanly Mandans. With them I lived for some time—was welcomed—taken gracefully by the arm, by their plumed dignitaries, and feasted in their hospitable lodges. Much have I already said of these people, and more of them, a great deal, I may say at a future day; but now, to our '*story.*' As *preamble*, however, having launched our light canoe at the Mandan village, shook hands with the chiefs and braves, and took the everlasting farewell glance at those *models*, which I wept to turn from; we dipped our paddles, and were again gliding off upon the mighty water, on our way to St. Louis. We travelled fast, and just as the village of the Mandans, and the bold promontory on which it stands, were changing to blue, and 'dwindling into nothing,' we heard the startling yells, and saw in distance behind us, the troop that was gaining upon us! their red shoulders were bounding over the grassy bluffs—their hands extended, and robes waving with signals for us to stop! In a few moments they were opposite to us on the bank, and I steered my boat to the shore. They were arranged for my reception, with amazement and orders imperative stamped on every brow. 'Mi-neek-e-sunk-te-ka' (the mink), they exclaimed, 'is dying! the picture which you made of her is too much like her—you put so much of her into it, that when your boat took it away from. our village, it drew a part of her life away with it—she is bleeding from her mouth—she is puking up all her blood; by taking that away, you are drawing the strings out of her heart, and they will soon break ; we must take her picture back, and then she will get well—your *medicine* is great, it is too great; but we wish you well.' Mr. Kipp, their Trader, came with the party, and interpreted as above. I unrolled my bundle of portraits, and though I was unwilling to part with it (for she was a beautiful girl), yet I placed it in their hands, telling them that I wished her well ; and I was exceedingly glad to get my boat peaceably under way again, and into the current, having taken another and everlasting shake of the hands. They rode back at full speed with the portrait ; but intelligence which I have since received from there, informs me that the girl died ; and that I am for ever to be considered as the cause of her misfortunes. This is not *the* ' story,' however, but I will tell it as soon as I can come to it. We dropped off, and down the rolling current again, from day to day, until at length the curling smoke of the Riccarees announced their village in view before us !

"We trembled and quaked, for all boats not stoutly armed, steal by them in the dead of night. We muffled our paddles, and instantly dropped under some willows, where we listened to the yelping, barking rabble, until sable night had drawn her curtain around (though it was not *sable*, for the moon arose, to our great mortification and alarm, in full splendour and brightness), when, at eleven o'clock, we put out to the middle of the stream—silenced our paddles, and trusted to the current to waft us by them. We lay close in our boat with a pile of green bushes over us, making us nothing in the world but a ' floating tree-top.' On the bank, in front of the village, was enacting at that moment, a scene of the most frightful and thrilling nature. An hundred torches were swung about in all directions, giving us a full view of the group that were assembled, and some fresh scalps were hung on poles, and were then going through the nightly ceremony that is performed about them for a certain number of nights, composed of the frightful and appalling shrieks, and yells, and gesticulations of the *scalp-dance.**

"In addition to this multitude of demons (as they looked), there were some hundreds of cackling women and girls bathing in the river on the edge of a sand-bar, at the lower end of the village ; at which place the stream drifted our small craft in, close to the shore, till the moon lit their shoulders, their foreheads, chins, noses ! and they stood, half-merged, like mermaids, and gazed upon us ! singing ' *Chee-na-see-nun, chee-na-see-nun ke-mon-shoo kee-ne-he-na, ha-way-tah ? shee-sha, shee-sha ;*' ' How do you do, how do you do ? where are you going, old tree ? Come here, come here.' ' *Lah-kee-hoon ! lah-kee-hoon ! natoh, catogh* !' (' A canoe, a canoe ! see the paddle ! !') In a moment the songs were stopped ! the lights were out—

* But a few weeks before I left the mouth of Yellow Stone, the news arrived at that place, that a party of trappers and traders had burnt two Riccarees to death, on the prairies, and M'Kenzie advised me not to stop at the Riccarree village, but to pass them in the night ; and after I had got some hundreds of miles below them, I learned that they were dancing two white men's scalps taken in revenge for that inhuman act.

the village in an instant was in darkness, and dogs were muzzled! and nimbly did our paddles ply the water, till spy-glass told us at morning's dawn, that the bank and boundless prairies of grass and green that were all around us, were free from following footsteps of friend or foe. A sleepless night had passed, and lightly tripped our bark, and swift, over the swimming tide during *that* day ; which was one, not of pleasure, but of trembling excitement ; while our eyes were continually scanning the distant scenes that were behind us, and our muscles throwing us forward with tireless energy.

* * * * * * *

* * Night came upon us again, and we landed at the foot of a towering bluff, where the musquitoes met us with ten thousand kicks and cuffs, and importunities, until we were choked and strangled into almost irrevocable despair and madness.*

"A '*snaggy bend*' announced its vicinity just below us by its roaring ; and hovering night told us, that we could not with safety ' undertake it.'

" The only direful alternative was now in full possession of us, (I am not going to tell the ' *story*' yet), for just below us was a stately bluff of 200 feet in height, rising out of the water, at an angle of forty-five degrees, entirely denuded in front, and constituted of clay. ' Montons, montons !' said Ba'tiste, as he hastily clambered up its steep inclined plane on his hands and feet, over its parched surface, which had been dried in the sun, ' essayez vous, essayez ! ce'n'est pas difficile Monsr. Cataline,' exclaimed he, from an elevation of about 100 feet from the water, where he had found a level platform, of some ten or fifteen feet in diameter, and stood at its brink, waving his hand over the twilight landscape that lay in partial obscurity beneath him.

" ' Nous avons ici une belle place pour for to get some *slips*, some *coot slips*, vare de dam Riccaree et de dam muskeet shall nevare get si haut, by Gar ! montez, montez en haut.'

" Bogard and I took our buffalo robes and our rifles, and with difficulty hung and clung along in the crevices with fingers and toes, until we reached the spot. We found ourselves about half-way up the precipice, which continued almost perpendicular above us ; and within a few yards of us, on each side, it was one unbroken slope from the bottom to the top. In this snug little nook were we most appropriately fixed, as we thought, for a warm summer's night, out of the reach entirely of musquitoes, and all other earthly obstacles, as we supposed, to the approaching gratification, for which the toils and fatigues of the preceding day and night, had so admirably prepared us. We spread one of our robes, and having ranged ourselves side by side upon it, and drawn the other one over us, we commenced, without further delay, upon the pleasurable forgetfulness of toils and dangers which

---

* The greater part of the world can never, I am sure, justly appreciate the meaning and application of the above sentence, unless they have an opportunity to encounter a swarm of these tormenting insects, on the banks of the Missouri or Mississippi river.

had agitated us for the past day and night. We had got just about to th..t stage of our enjoyment which is almost resistless, and nearly bidding defiance to every worldly obstrusive obstacle, when the pattering of rain on our buffalo robes opened our eyes to the dismal scene that was getting up about us ! *My* head was out, and on the watch ; but the other two skulls were flat upon the ground, and there chained by the unyielding links of iron slumber. The blackest of all clouds that ever swept hill tops of grass, of clay, or towering rock, was hanging about us—its lightning's glare was incessantly flashing us to blindness; and the giddy elevation on which we were perched, seemed to tremble with the roar and jar of distant, and the instant bolts and cracks of present thunder ! The rain poured and fell in torrents (its not enough) ; it seemed *floating* around and above us in waves succeeding waves, which burst upon the sides of the immense avalanche of clay that was above, and *slid* in *sheets*, upon us ! Heavens ! what a scene was here. The river beneath us and in distance, with windings infinite, whitening into silver, and trees, to deathlike paleness, at the lightning's flash ! All about us was drenched in rain and mud. At this juncture, poor Ba'tiste was making an effort to raise his head and shoulders—he was in agony ! he had slept himself, and *slipt* himself partly from the robe, and his elbows were fastened in the mud.

" 'Oh sacré, 'tis too bad by Gar ! we can get some *slips* nevare.'

" 'Ugh ! (replied Yankee Bogard) we shall get ' slips' enough directly, by darn, for we are all afloat, and shall go into the the river by and by, in the twinkling of a goat's eye, if we don't look out.'

" We were nearly afloat, sure enough, and our condition growing more and more dreary every moment, and our only alternative was, to fold up our nether robe and sit upon it ; hanging the other one over our heads, which formed a roof, and shielded the rain from us. To give compactness to the *trio*, and bring us into such shape as would enable the robe to protect us all, we were obliged to put our backs and occiputs together, and keep our heads from nodding. In this way we were enabled to divide equally the robe that we sat upon, as well as receive mutual benefit from the one that was above us. We thus managed to protect ourselves in the most important points, leaving our feet and legs (from necessity) to the mercy of mud.

" Thus we were re-encamped ' A pretty mess' (said I), we look like the ' three graces ;'—'de tree grace, by Gar !' said Ba'tiste. ' Grace ! (whispered Bogard) yes, it's all *grace* here ; and I believe we'll all be buried in *grace* in less than an hour.'

" 'Monsr. Cataline ! excusez my back, si vous plait. Bogard ! comment, comment ?—bonne nuit, Messieurs. Oh ! mon Dieu, mon Dieu ! Je vous rends grace—je vous prie pour for me sauver ce nuit—delivrez nous ! delivrez nous ! Je vous adore, Saint Esprit—la Vierge Marie—oh je vous rends grace ! pour for de m'avoir conservé from de dam Riccree et de diable muskeet. Eh bien ! eh bien !'

"In this miserable and despairing mood poor Ba'tiste dropped off gradually into a most tremendous sleep, whilst Bogard and I were holding on to our corners of the robe—recounting over the dangers and excitements of the day and night past, as well as other scenes of our adventurous lives, whilst we laid (or rather sat) looking at the lightning, with our eyes shut. Ba'tiste snored louder and louder, until sleep had got her strongest grip upon him ; and his specific gravity became so great, that he pitched forward, pulling our corners of the robe nearly off from our heads, reducing us to the necessity of drawing upon them till we brought the back of his head in contact with ours, again, and his body in an erect posture, when he suddenly exclaimed.

"' Bon jour, Monsr. Bogard : bon jour, Monsr. Cataline ; n'est ce pas morning, pretty near ?'

"' No, its about midnight.'

"' Quel temps ?'

" Why it rains as hard as ever.

"' Oh diable, I wish I was *tó hell*.'

"' You may be there yet before morning, by darn.'

"'Pardón ! pardón, Monsr Bogard—I shall not go to night, not *to* night, I was joke—mais ! dis is not joke, sùppose—oh vengeance ! I am slip down considerable—mais I shall not go to hell quite—I am slip off de seat ! '

"' What ! you are sitting in the mud ? '

"' Oui, Bogard, in de muds ! mais, I am content, my *head* is not in de mud. You see Bogard, I avait been sleep, et I raisee my head pretty suddain, and keepee my e back e straight, et I am slip off of de seat. Now, Monsr. Bogard you shall keepee you head straight and moove ————————leet, at de bottom ?——— - ———————remercie, Bogard, remercie,———eh bien, ————————ah well——————————————ha-ha-h——a —by Gar, Bogard, I have a de good joke. Monsr. Cataline will paintez my likeness as I am now look—he will paint us all—I am tink he will make putty coot view ? ha-ha-ha-a———we should see very putty landeescape aboutee de legs, ha ? Ha——ha——h———a——a.'

"Oh, Ba'tiste, for Heaven's sake stop your laughing and go to sleep ; we'll talk and laugh about this all day to-morrow.

"' Pardón, Monsr. Cataline, (excusez) have you got some slips ?'

" No, Ba'tiste, I have not been asleep. Bogard has been entertaining me these two hours whilst you was asleep, with a description of a buffalo hunt, which took place at the mouth of Yellow Stone, about a year ago. It must have been altogether a most splendid and thrilling scene, and I have been paying the strictest attention to it, for I intend to write it down and send it to New York for the cits to read."

"' I like'e dat much, Monsr. Cataline, and I shall take much plaisir pour vous donner to give déscript of someting, provide you will write him down, ha ?'

" Well Ba'tiste, go on, I am endeavouring to learn everything that's curious and entertaining, belonging to this country.

" ' Well Monsr. Cataline, I shall tell you someting very much entertain. mais, but, you will nevare tell somebody how we have been fix to night ? ha ? '

" No, Ba'tiste, most assuredly I shall never mention it nor make painting of it.

" ' Well, je commence,—diable Bogard ! you shall keep your back straight you must sit up, ou il n'est pas possibe for to keep de robe ovare all. Je commence, Mons. Cataline, to describe some *Dog Feast*, which I attend among de dam Pieds noirs. I shall describe some grande, magnifique ceremonay, and you will write him down ? '

" Yes, I'll put it on paper.

" ' Pardón, pardón, I am get most to slip, I shall tell him to-morrow, pérhaps I shall- ———eh bien ;—but you will nevare tell how we look, ha ! Monsr. Cataline ? '

" No Ba'tiste, I'll never mention it.

" ' Eh bien———bon nuit.'

" In this condition we sat, and in this manner we nodded away the night, as far as I recollect of it, catching the broken bits of sleep, (that were even painful to us when we got them), until the morning's rays at length gave us a view of the scene that was around us ! ! Oh, all ye brick-makers, ye plasterers, and soft-soap manufacturers ! put all your imaginations in a ferment together, and see if ye can invent a scene like this ! Here *was* a ' fix' to be sure. The sun arose in splendour and in full, upon this everlasting and boundless scene of ' *saft soap*' and grease, which admitted us not to move. The whole hill was constituted entirely of tough clay, and on each side and above us there was no possibility of escape ; and one single step over the brink of the place where we had ascended, would inevitably have launched us into the river below, the distance of an hundred feet ! Here, looking like hogs just risen from a mud puddle, or a buffalo bull in his wallow, we sat, (*and had to sit,*) admiring the wide-spread and beautiful landscape that lay steeping and smoking before us, and our little boat, that looked like a nutshell beneath us, hanging at the shore ; telling stories and filling up the while with nonsensical garrulity, until the sun's warming rays had licked up the mud, and its dried surface, about eleven o'clock, gave us foothold, when we cautiously, but safely descended to the bottom ; and then, at the last jump, which brought his feet to *terra firma*, Ba'tiste exclaimed, ' Well, we have cheatee de dam muskeet, ha ! ' "

And this, reader, is not ' *the story*,' but one of the little incidents which stood exactly in the way, and could not well be got over without a slight notice, being absolutely necessary, as a key, or kind of glossary, for the proper understanding of the tale that is to be told. There is *blood* and *butchery* in the story that is now to be related ; and it should be read by every one who would form a correct notion of the force of Indian superstitions.

Three mighty warriors, proud and valiant, licked the dust, and all in consequence of one of the portraits I painted ; and as my brush was the prime mover of all these misfortunes, and my life was sought to heal the wound, I must be supposed to be knowing to and familiar with the whole circumstances, which were as—(I was going to say, as follow) but my want of time and your want of patience, compel me to break off here, and I promise to go right on with *the story of the Dog* in my next Letter, and I advise the reader not to neglect or overlook it.

LETTER—No. 55.

RED PIPE STONE QUARRY, CÔTEAU DES PRAIRIES.

WELL, to proceed with the *Story of the Dog*, which I promised; (after which I shall record the tale of *Wi-jun-jon*, (the pigeon's egg head), which was also told by me during the last night, before we retired to rest.

" I think I said that my little canoe had brought us down the Missouri, about eight hundred miles below the mouth of Yellow Stone, when we landed at Laidlaw's Trading-house, which is twelve hundred miles above civilization and the city of St. Louis. If I did *not* say it, it is no matter, for it was even so; and ' Ba'tiste and Bogard who had paddled, and I who had steered,' threw our little bark out upon the bank, and taking our paddles in our hands, and our '*plunder*' upon our backs, crossed the plain to the American Fur Company's Fort, in charge of Mr. Laidlaw, who gave us a hearty welcome; and placed us in an instant at his table, which happened at that moment to be stationed in the middle of the floor, distributing to its surrounding guests the simple blessings which belong to that fair and silent land of buffalo-tongues and beavers' tails! A bottle of good Madeira wine sprung (à l'instant) upon the corner of the table, before us, and *swore, point blank*, to the welcome that was expressed in every feature of our host. After the usual salutations, the news, and a glass of wine, Mr. Laidlaw began thus:—
' Well, my friend, you have got along well, so far; and I am glad to see you. You have seen a great many fine Indians since you left here, and have, no doubt, procured many interesting and valuable *portraits*; but there has been a deal of trouble about the ' *pictures*,' in this neighbourhood, since you went away. Of course, you have heard nothing of it at the Yellow Stone; but amongst us, I assure you, there has not a day passed since you left, without some fuss or excitement about the portraits. The ' Dog' is not yet dead, though he has been shot at several times, and had his left arm broken. The ' Little *Bear's*' friends have overtaken the brother of the Dog, that fine fellow whom you painted, and killed him! They are now sensible that they have sacrificed one of the best men in the nation, for one of the greatest rascals; and they are more desperately bent on revenge than ever. They have made frequent enquiries for you, knowing that you had gone up the river; alleging that you had been the cause of these deaths, and that if the Dog could not be found, they should look to you for a settlement of that unfortunate affair!

" ' That unlucky business, taken altogether, has been the greatest piece of *medicine* (mystery), and created the greatest excitement amongst the Sioux, of anything that has happened since I came into the country. My dear Sir, you must not continue your voyage down the river, in your unprotected condition. A large party of the ' Little Bear's' band, are now encamped on the river below, and for you to stop there (which you might be obliged to do), would be to endanger your life.' " * * * Reader, sit still, and let me change ends with my story, (which is done in one moment,) and then, from a relation of the circumstances which elicited the friendly advice and caution of Mr. Laidlaw just mentioned, you will be better enabled to understand the nature of the bloody affair which I am undertaking to relate.

" About four months previous to the moment I am now speaking of, I had passed up the Missouri river by this place, on the steam-boat Yellow Stone, on which I ascended the Missouri to the mouth of Yellow Stone river. While going up, this boat, having on board the United States Indian agent, Major Sanford—Messrs. Pierre, Chouteau, McKenzie of the American Fur Company, and myself, as passengers, stopped at this trading-post, and remained several weeks ; where were assembled six hundred families of Sioux Indians, their tents being pitched in close order on an extensive prairie on the bank of the river.

" ' This trading-post, in charge of Mr. Laidlaw, is the concentrating place, and principal trading depot, for this powerful tribe, who number, when all taken together, something like forty or fifty thousand. On this occasion, five or six thousand had assembled to see the steam-boat and meet the Indian agent, which, and whom they knew were to arrive about this time. During the few weeks that we remained there, I was busily engaged painting my portraits, for here were assembled the principal chiefs and *medicine-men* of the nation. To these people, the operations of my brush were entirely new and unaccountable, and excited amongst them the greatest curiosity imaginable. Every thing else (even the steam-boat) was abandoned for the pleasure of crowding into my painting-room, and witnessing the result of each fellow's success, as he came out from under the operation of my brush.

" They had been at first much afraid of the consequences that might flow from so strange and unaccountable an operation ; but having been made to understand my views, they began to look upon it as a great *honour*, and afforded me the opportunities that I desired ; exhibiting the utmost degree of vanity for their appearance, both as to features and dress. The consequence was, that my room was filled with the chiefs who sat around, arranged according to the rank or grade which they held in the estimation of their tribe ; and in this order it became necessary for me to paint them, to the exclusion of those who never signalized themselves, and were without any distinguishing character in society.

" The first man on the list, was *Ha-wan-ghee-ta* (one horn), head chief of the nation, of whom I have heretofore spoken ; and after him the subordinate chiefs, or chiefs of bands, according to the estimation in which they were held by the chief and the tribe. My models were thus *placed* before me, whether ugly or beautiful, all the same, and I saw at once there was to be trouble somewhere, as I could not paint them all. The medicine-men or high priests, who are esteemed by many the oracles of the nation, and the most important men in it—becoming jealous, commenced their harangues, outside of the lodge, telling them that they were all fools—that those who were painted would soon die in consequence; and that these pictures, which had life to a considerable degree in them, would live in the hands of white men after they were dead, and make them sleepless and endless trouble.

"Those whom I had painted, though evidently somewhat alarmed, were unwilling to acknowledge it, and those whom I had not painted, unwilling to be outdone in courage, allowed me the privilege; braving and defying the danger that they were evidently more or less in dread of. Feuds began to arise too, among some of the chiefs of the different bands, who (not unlike some instances amongst the chiefs and warriors of our own country), had looked upon their rival chiefs with unsleeping jealousy, until it had grown into disrespect and enmity. An instance of this kind presented itself at this critical juncture, in this assembly of inflammable spirits, which changed in a moment, its features, from the free and jocular garrulity of an Indian levee, to the frightful yells and agitated treads and starts of an Indian battle! I had in progress at this time a portrait of *Mah-to-tchee-ga* (little bear); of the *Onc-pa-pu band*, a noble fine fellow, who was sitting before me as I was painting (PLATE 273). I was painting almost a profile view of his face, throwing a part of it into shadow, and had it nearly finished, when an Indian by the name of *Shon-ka* (the dog), chief of the *Caz-a-zshee-ta* band (PLATE 275); an ill-natured and surly man—despised by the chiefs of every other band, entered the wigwam in a sullen mood, and seated himself on the floor in front of my sitter, where he could have a full view of the picture in its operation. After sitting a while with his arms folded, and his lips stiffly arched with contempt; he sneeringly spoke thus:—

'*Mah-to-tchee-ga* is but *half a man.*'   •   •   •   •   •

•   •   "Dead silence ensued for a moment, and nought was in motion save the eyes of the chiefs, who were seated around the room, and darting their glances about upon each other in listless anxiety to hear the sequel that was to follow! During this interval, the eyes of Mah-to-tchee-ga had not moved—his lips became slightly curved, and he pleasantly asked, in low and steady accent, 'Who says that?' '*Shon-ka* says it,' was the reply; 'and *Shon-ka* can prove it.' At this the eyes of Mah-to-tchee-ga, which had not yet moved, began steadily to turn, and slow, as if upon pivots, and when they were rolled out of their sockets till they had fixed upon the object of their contempt; his dark and jutting brows were shoving down in trembling contention, with the blazing rays that were actually *burning* with contempt, the object that was before them. '*Why* does Shon-ka say it?'

"'Ask *We-chash-a-wa-kon* (the painter), he can tell you; he knows you are but *half a man*—he has painted but one half of your face, and knows the other half is good for nothing!'

" ' Let the *painter* say it, and I will believe it ; but when the Dog says it let him *prove* it.'

" ' *Shon-ka* said it, and *Shon-ka* can prove it ; if *Mah-to-tchee-ga* be a man, and wants to be honoured by the white men, let him not be ashamed ; but let him do as *Shon-ka* has done, give the white man a horse, and then let him see the *whole of your face* without being ashamed.'

" ' When *Mah-to-tchee-ga* kills a white man and *steals* his horses, he may be ashamed to look at a white man until he brings him a horse ! When *Mah-to-tchee-ga* waylays and murders an honourable and a brave Sioux, because he is a coward and not brave enough to meet him in fair combat, *then* he may be ashamed to look at a white man till he has given him a horse ! *Mah-to-tchee-ga* can look at any one ; and he is now looking at an *old woman* and a *coward* !'

"This repartee, which had lasted for a few minutes, to the amusement and excitement of the chiefs, being ended thus :—The Dog rose suddenly from the ground, and wrapping himself in his robe, left the wigwam, considerably agitated, having the laugh of all the chiefs upon him.

"The Little Bear had followed him with his piercing eyes until he left the door, and then pleasantly and unmoved, resumed his position, where he sat a few minutes longer, until the portrait was completed. He then rose, and in the most graceful and gentlemanly manner, presented to me a very beautiful shirt of buckskin, richly garnished with quills of the porcupine, fringed with scalp-locks (honourable memorials) from his enemies' heads, and painted, with all his battles emblazoned on it. He then left my wigwam, and a few steps brought him to the door of his own, where the Dog intercepted him, and asked, ' What meant *Mah-to-tchee-ga* by the last words that he spoke to *Shon-ka?*' ' *Mah-to-tchee-ga* said it, and *Shon-ka* is not a fool—that is enough.' At this the Dog walked violently to his own lodge ; and the Little Bear retreated into his, both knowing from looks and gestures what was about to be the consequence of their altercation.

" The Little Bear instantly charged his gun, and then (as their custom is) threw himself upon his face, in humble supplication to the Great Spirit for his aid and protection. His wife, in the meantime, seeing him agitated, and fearing some evil consequences, without knowing anything of the preliminaries, secretly withdrew the bullet from his gun, and told him not of it.

" The Dog's voice, at this moment, was heard, and recognized at the door of Mah-to-tchee-ga's lodge,—' If Mah-to-tchee-ga be a *whole* man, let him come out and prove it ; it is *Shon-ka* that calls him !'

" His wife screamed ; but it was too late. The gun was in his hand, and he sprang out of the door—both drew and simultaneously fired ! The Dog fled uninjured ; but the Little Bear lay weltering in his blood (strange to say !) with all that side of his face entirely shot away, which had been left out of the picture ; and, according to the prediction of the Dog, ' *good for nothing* ;' carrying away one half of the jaws, and the flesh from the nostrils and corner of the mouth, to the ear, including one eye, and leaving the jugular vein entirely exposed. Here was a 'coup;' and any one accustomed to the thrilling excitement that such scenes produce in an Indian village, can form *some* idea of the frightful agitation amidst several thousand Indians, who were divided into jealous bands or clans, under ambitious and rival chiefs! In one minute, a thousand guns and bows were seized! A thousand thrilling yells were raised; and many were the fierce and darting warriors who sallied round the Dog for his protection—he fled amidst a shower of bullets and arrows; but his braves were about him! The blood of the *Onc-pa-pas* was roused, and the indignant braves of that gallant band rushed forth from all quarters, and, swift upon their heels, were hot for vengeance! On the plain, and in full view of us, for some time, the whizzing arrows flew, and so did bullets, until the Dog and his brave followers were lost in distance on the prairie! In this rencontre, the Dog had his left arm broken; but succeeded, at length, in making his escape.

" On the next day after this affair took place, the Little Bear died of his wound, and was buried amidst the most pitiful and heart-rending cries of his- distracted wife, whose grief was inconsolable at the thought of having been herself the immediate and innocent cause of his death, by depriving him of his supposed protection.

" This marvellous and fatal transaction was soon talked through the village, and the eyes of all this superstitious multitude were fixed upon me as the cause of the calamity—my paintings and brushes were instantly packed, and all hands, both Traders and Travellers, assumed at once a posture of defence.

" I evaded, no doubt, in a great measure, the concentration of their immediate censure upon me, by expressions of great condolence, and by distributing liberal presents to the wife and relations of the deceased; and by uniting also with Mr. Laidlaw and the other gentlemen, in giving him honourable burial, where we placed over his grave a handsome Sioux lodge, and hung a white flag to wave over it.

" On this occasion, many were the tears that were shed for the brave and honourable Mah-to-tchee-ga, and all the warriors of his band swore sleepless vengeance on the Dog, until his life should answer for the loss of their chief and leader.

" On the day that he was buried, I started for the mouth of Yellow Stone, and while I was gone, the spirit of vengeance had pervaded nearly all the Sioux country in search of the Dog, who had evaded pursuit. His brother, however (PLATE 274), a noble and honourable fellow, esteemed by all ·who knew him, fell in their way in an unlucky hour, when their thirst for vengeance was irresistible, and they slew him. Repentance deep, and grief were the result of so rash an act, when they beheld a brave and worthy man fall for so worthless a character; and as they became exasperated, the spirit of revenge grew more desperate than ever, and they swore they never would lay down their arms or embrace their wives and children until vengeance full and complete, should light upon the head that deserved it. This brings us again to the first part of my story, and in this state were things in that part of the country, when I was descending the river, four months afterwards, and landed my canoe as I before stated, at Laidlaw's trading-house.

" The excitement had been kept up all summer amongst these people, and their superstitions bloated to the full brim, from circumstances so well calculated to feed and increase them. Many of them looked to me at once as the author of all these disasters, considering I knew that one half of the man's face was *good for nothing*, or that I would not have left it out of the picture, and that I must therefore have foreknown the evils that were to flow from the omission ; they consequently resolved that I was a dangerous man, and should suffer for my temerity in case the Dog could not be found. Councils had been held, and in all the solemnity of Indian *medicine* and *mystery*, I had been doomed to die ! At one of these, a young warrior of the *Onc-pa-pa* band, arose and said, ' The blood of two chiefs has just sunk into the ground, and an hundred bows are bent which are ready to shed more ! on whom shall we bend them ? I am a friend to the white men, but here is one whose *medicine* is too great—he is a great *medicine-man* ! his *medicine* is too great ! he was the death of Mah-to-tchee-ga ! he made only one side of his face ! he would not make the other—the side that he made was alive: the other was dead, and Shonka shot it off ! How is this ? Who is to die.'

" After him, *Tah-zee-kee-da-cha* (torn belly), of the *Yankton* band, arose and said—' Father, this medicine-man has done much harm ! You told our chiefs and warriors, that they must be painted—you said he was a good man, and we believed you !—you thought so, my father, but you see what he has done !—he looks at our chiefs and our women and then makes them alive ! ! In this way he has taken our chiefs away, and he can trouble their spirits when they are dead !—they will be unhappy. If he can make them alive by looking at them, he can do us much harm !—you tell us that they are not alive—we see their eyes move !—their eyes follow us wherever we go, that is enough ! I have no more to say !' After him, rose a young man of the Onc-pa-pa band ' Father! you know that I am the brother of *Mah-to-tchee-ga* !—you know that I loved him—both sides of his face were good, and the medicine-man knew it also ! Why was half of his face left out ? He never was ashamed, but always looked white man in the face ! Why was that side of his face shot off ? Your friend is not our friend, and has forfeited his life—we want you to tell us where he is—we want to see him !'

" Then rose Toh-ki-e-to (a *medicine-man*) of the Yankton band, and principal orator of the nation.) ' My friend, these are young men that speak—I am not afraid ! your white medicine-man painted my picture, and it was good—I am glad of it—I am very glad to see that I shall live after

I am dead!—I am old and not afraid!—some of our young men are foolish
I know that this man *put many of our buffaloes in his book*! for I was
with him, and we have had no buffaloes since to eat, it is true—but I am
not afraid!! *his medicine* is great and I wish him well—we are friends!'

"In this wise was the subject discussed by these superstitious people during my absence, and such were the reasons given by my friend Mr. Laidlaw,
for his friendly advice; wherein he cautioned me against exposing my life in
their hands, advising me to take some other route than that which I was
pursuing down the river, where I would find encamped at the mouth of
Cabri river, eighty miles below, several hundred Indians belonging to the
Little Bear's band, and I might possibly fall a victim to their unsatiated
revenge. I resumed my downward voyage in a few days, however, with my
little canoe, which 'Ba'tiste and Bogard paddled and I steered,' and passed
their encampment in peace, by taking the opposite shore. The usual friendly
invitation however, was given (which is customary on that river), by skipping
several rifle bullets across the river, a rod or two ahead of us. To those
invitations we paid no attention, and (not suspecting who we were), they
allowed us to pursue our course in peace and security. Thus rested
the affair of the Dog and its consequences, until I conversed with Major
Bean, the agent for these people, who arrived in St. Louis some weeks after
I did, bringing later intelligence from them, assuring me that '*the Dog
had at length been overtaken and killed,* near the Black-hills, and that the
affair might now for ever be considered as settled.'"

Thus happened, and thus terminated the affair of "the Dog," wherein
have fallen three distinguished warriors; and wherein *might* have fallen one
"*great medicine-man*!" and all in consequence of the operations of my
brush. The portraits of the three first named will long hang in my Gallery
for the world to gaze upon; and the head of the latter (whose hair yet remains on it), may probably be seen (for a time yet) occasionally stalking
about in the midst of this Collection of Nature's dignitaries.

The circumstances above detailed, are as correctly given as I could furnish them! and they have doubtless given birth to one of the most wonderful traditions, which will be told and sung amongst the Sioux Indians from
age to age; furnishing one of the rarest instances, perhaps, on record, of the
extent to which these people may be carried by the force of their superstitions.

After I had related this curious and unfortunate affair, I was called upon
to proceed at once with the

STORY OF WI-JUN-JON (THE PIGEON'S EGG HEAD);

and I recited it as I first told it to poor Ba'tiste, on a former occasion,
which was as follows:—

"Well, Ba'tiste, I promised last night, as you were going to sleep, that
I would tell you a story this morning—did I not?

"'Oui, Monsieur, oui—de 'Pigeon's Head.'

" No, Ba'tiste, the ' Pigeon's Egg Head.'

" ' Well den, Monsieur Cataline, de ' Pigeon Egg's Head.'

" No, Ba'tiste, you have it wrong yet. The Pigeon's Egg Head.

" ' Sacré—well, ' Pee—jonse—ec—head.'

" Right, Ba'tiste. Now you shall hear the ' Story of the Pigeon's Egg Head.'

" The Indian name of this man (being its literal translation into the Assinneboin language) was Wi-jun-jon.

" ' Wat! comment! by Gar (pardón); not Wi-jun-jon, le frere de ma douce Wee-ne-on-ka, fils du chef Assinneboin? But excusez; go on, s'il vous plait.'

" Wi-jun-jon (the Pigeon's Egg Head) was a brave and a warrior of the Assinneboins—young—proud—handsome—valiant, and graceful. He had fought many a battle, and won many a laurel. The numerous scalps from his enemies' heads adorned his dress, and his claims were fair and just for the highest honours that his country could bestow upon him; for his father was chief of the nation.

" Le meme! de same—mon frere—mon ami! Bien, I am composé; go on, Monsieur.'

" Well, this young Assinneboin, the ' Pigeon's Egg Head,' was selected by Major Sanford, the Indian Agent, to represent his tribe in a delegation which visited Washington city under his charge in the winter of 1832. With this gentleman, the Assinneboin, together with representatives from several others of those North Western tribes, descended the Missouri river, several thousand miles, on their way to Washington.

" While descending the river in a Mackinaw boat, from the mouth of Yellow Stone, Wi-jun-jon and another of his tribe who was with him, at the first approach to the civilized settlements, commenced a register of the white men's houses (or cabins), by cutting a notch for each on the side of a pipe-stem, in order to be able to shew when they got home, how many white men's houses they saw on their journey. At first the cabins were scarce; but continually as they advanced down the river, more and more rapidly increased in numbers; and they soon found their pipe-stem filled with marks, and they determined to put the rest of them on the handle of a war-club, which they soon got marked all over likewise; and at length, while the boat was moored at the shore for the purpose of cooking the dinner of the party, Wi-jun-jon and his companion stepped into the bushes, and cut a long stick, from which they peeled the bark; and when the boat was again underweigh, they sat down, and with much labour, copied the notches on to it from the pipe-stem and club; and also kept adding a notch for every house they passed. This stick was soon filled; and in a day or two several others; when, at last, they seemed much at a loss to know what to do with their troublesome records, until they came in sight of St. Louis, which is a town of 15,000 inhabitants; upon which, after consulting a little, they pitched their sticks overboard into the river!

" I was in St. Louis at the time of their arrival, and painted their portraits while they rested in that place. *Wi-jun-jon* was the first, who reluctantly yielded to the solicitations of the Indian agent and myself, and appeared as sullen as death in my painting-room—with eyes fixed like those of a statue, upon me, though his pride had plumed and tinted him in all the freshness and brilliancy of an Indian's toilet. In his nature's uncowering pride he stood a perfect model ; but superstition had hung a lingering curve upon his lip, and pride had stiffened it into contempt. He had been urged into a measure, against which his fears had pleaded ; yet he stood unmoved and unflinching amid the struggles of mysteries that were hovering about him, foreboding ills of every kind, and misfortunes that were to happen to him in consequence of this operation.

" He was dressed in his native costume, which was classic and exceedingly beautiful (PLATE 271) ; his leggings and shirt were of the mountain-goat skin, richly garnished with quills of the porcupine, and fringed with locks of scalps, taken from his enemies' heads. Over these floated his long hair in plaits, that fell nearly to the ground ; his head was decked with the war-eagle's plumes—his robe was of the skin of the young buffalo bull, richly garnished and emblazoned with the battles of his life ; his quiver and bow were slung, and his shield, of the skin of the bull's neck.

" I painted him in this beautiful dress, and so also the others who were with him ; and after I had done, Major Sanford went on to Washington with them, where they spent the winter.

" *Wi-jun-jon* was the foremost on all occasions—the first to enter the levee—the first to shake the President's hand, and make his speech to him— the last to extend the hand to them, but the first to catch the smiles and admiration of the gentler sex. He travelled the giddy muze, and beheld amid the buzzing din of civil life, their tricks of art, their handiworks, and their finery ; he visited their principal cities—he saw their forts, their ships, their great guns, steamboats, balloons, &c. &c. ; and in the spring returned to St. Louis, where I joined him and his companions on their way back to their own country.

"Through the politeness of Mr. Chouteau, of the American Fur Company, I was admitted (the only passenger except Major Sanford and his Indians) to a passage in their steamboat, on her first trip to the Yellow Stone; and when I had embarked, and the boat was about to depart, *Wi-jun-jon* made his appearance on deck, in a full suit of regimentals ! He had in Washington exchanged his beautifully garnished and classic costume, for a full dress 'en militaire' (see PLATE 272). It was, perhaps, presented to him by the President. It was broadcloth, of the finest blue, trimmed with lace of gold; on his shoulders were mounted two immense epaulettes; his neck was strangled with a shining black stock, and his feet were pinioned in a pair of water proof boots, with high heels, which made him ' step like a yoked hog.'

271   272

" ' Ha-ha-hagh (pardón, Monsieur Cataline, for I am almost laugh)—well, he was a fine genteman, ha ?'

" On his head was a high-crowned beaver hat, with a broad silver lace band, surmounted by a huge red feather, some two feet high ; his coat collar stiff with lace, came higher up than his ears, and over it flowed, down towards his haunches—his long Indian locks, stuck up in rolls and plaits, with red paint.

" ' Ha-ha-hagh-agh-ah.'

" Hold your tongue, Ba'tiste.

" ' Well, go on—go on.'

" ' A large silver medal was suspended from his neck by a blue ribbon— and across his right shoulder passed a wide belt, supporting by his side a broad sword.

" ' Diable !'

" On his hands he had drawn a pair of white kid gloves, and in them held, a blue umbrella in one, and a large fan in the other. In this fashion was poor Wi-jun-jon metamorphosed, on his return from Washington ; and, in this plight was he strutting and whistling Yankee Doodle, about the deck of the steamer that was wending its way up the mighty Missouri, and taking him to his native land again ; where he was soon to light his pipe, and cheer the wigwam fire-side, with tales of novelty and wonder.

" Well, Ba'tiste, I travelled with this new-fangled gentleman until he reached his home, two thousand miles above St. Louis, and I could never look upon him for a moment without excessive laughter, at the ridiculous figure he cut—the strides, the angles, the stiffness of this travelling beau ! Oh Ba'tiste, if you could have seen him, you would have split your sides with laughter ; he was—' puss in boots,' precisely !

" ' By gar, he is good compare ! Ha-ha, Monsieur : (pardón) I am laugh : I am see him wen he is arrive in Yellow Stone ; you know I was dere. I am laugh much wen he is got off de boat, and all de Assinneboins was dere to look. Oh diable ! I am laugh almost to die, I am split !—suppose he was pretty stiff, ha ?—' cob on spindle,' ha ? Oh, by gar, he is coot pour laugh—pour rire ?'

" After Wi-jun-jon had got home, and passed the usual salutations among his friends, he commenced the simple narration of scenes he had passed through, and of things he had beheld among the whites ; which appeared to them so much like fiction, that it was impossible to believe them, and they set him down as an impostor. ' He has been, (they said,) among the whites, who are great liars, and all he has learned is to come home and tell lies.' He sunk rapidly into disgrace in his tribe ; his high claims to political emi- nence all vanished ; he was reputed worthless—the greatest liar of his nation ; the chiefs shunned him and passed him by as one of the tribe who was lost ; yet the ears of the gossipping portion of the tribe were open, and the camp-fire circle and the wigwam fireside, gave silent audience to the whispered narratives of the ' travelled Indian.'   *   *   *   *   *

"The next day after he had arrived among his friends, the superfluous part of his coat, (which was a laced frock), was converted into a pair of leggings for his wife; and his hat-band of silver lace furnished her a magnificent pair of garters. The remainder of the coat, curtailed of its original length, was seen buttoned upon the shoulders of his brother, over and above a pair of leggings of buckskin; and *Wi-jun-jon* was parading about among his gaping friends, with a bow and quiver slung over his shoulders, which, *sans coat*, exhibited a fine linen shirt with studs and sleeve buttons. His broadsword kept its place, but about noon, his boots gave way to a pair of garnished moccasins; and in such plight he gossipped away the day among his friends, while his heart spoke so freely and so effectually from the bung-hole of a little keg of whiskey, which he had brought the whole way, (as one of the choicest presents made him at Washington), that his tongue became silent.

"One of his little fair enamoratas, or ' catch crumbs,' such as live in the halo of all great men, fixed her eyes and her affections upon his beautiful silk braces, and the next day, while the keg was yet dealing out its kindnesses, he was seen paying visits to the lodges of his old acquaintance, swaggering about, with his keg under his arm, whistling Yankee Doodle, and Washington's Grand March; his white shirt, or that part of it that had been *flapping* in the wind, had been shockingly tithed—his pantaloons of blue, laced with gold, were razed into a pair of comfortable leggings —his bow and quiver were slung, and his broad-sword which trailed on the ground, had sought the centre of gravity, and taken a position between his and dragging behind him, served as a rudder to steer him over the ' earth's troubled surface.'

"' Ha-hah-hagh————ah————o————oo——k, eh bien.'

"Two days' revel of this kind, had drawn from his keg all its charms; and in the mellowness of his heart, all his finery had vanished, and all of its appendages, except his umbrella, to which his heart's strongest affections still clung, and with it, and under it, in rude dress of buckskin, he was afterwards to be seen, in all sorts of weather, acting the fop and the beau as well as he could, with his limited means. In this plight, and in this dress, with his umbrella always in his hand, (as the only remaining evidence of his *quondam* greatness,) he began in his sober moments, to entertain and instruct his people, by honest and simple narratives of things and scenes he had beheld during his tour to the East; but which (unfortunately for him), were to them too marvellous and improbable to be believed. He told the gaping multitude, that were constantly gathering about him, of the distance he had travelled— of the astonishing number of houses he had seen—of the towns and cities, with all their wealth and splendour—of travelling on steamboats, in stages, and on railroads. He described our forts, and seventy-four gun ships, which he had visited—their big guns—our great bridges—our great council-house at Washington, and its doings—the curious and wonderful machines in the patent office, (which he pronounced the *greatest medicine place* he had seen); he described the great war parade, which he saw in the city of New York—the ascent of the balloon from Castle Garden—the numbers of the white people, the beauty of the white squaws; their red cheeks, and many thousands of other things, all of which were so much beyond their comprehension, that they ' could not be true,' and ' he must be the very greatest liar in the whole world.'*

" But he was beginning to acquire a reputation of a different kind. He was denominated a *medicine-man*, and one too of the most extraordinary character; for they deemed him far above the ordinary sort of human beings, whose mind could *invent* and *conjure* up for their amusement, such an ingenious *fabrication* of novelty and wonder. He steadily and unostentatiously persisted, however, in this way of entertaining his friends and his people, though he knew his standing was affected by it. He had an exhaustless theme to descant upon through the remainder of his life; and he seemed satisfied to lecture all his life, for the pleasure which it gave him.

" So great was his *medicine*, however, that they began, chiefs and all, to look upon him as a most extraordinary being, and the customary honours and forms began to be applied to him, and the respect shewn him, that belongs to all men in the Indian country, who are distinguished for their *medicine* or *mysteries*. In short, when all became familiar with the astonishing representations that he made, and with the wonderful alacrity with which ' he *created* them,' he was denominated the very greatest of *medicine*; and not only that, but the ' *lying medicine*.' That he should be the greatest of *medicine*, and that for *lying*, *merely*, rendered him a prodigy in mysteries that commanded not only respect, but at length, (when he was more maturely heard and listened to) admiration, awe, and at last dread and terror; which altogether must needs conspire to rid the world of a monster, whose more than human talents must be cut down, to less than human measurement.

" ' Wat! Monsieur Cataline, dey av not try to kill him ?'

" Yes, Ba'tiste, in this way the poor fellow had lived, and been for three years past continually relating the scenes he had beheld, in his tour to the ' *Far East*;' until his medicine became so alarmingly great, that they were unwilling he should live; they were disposed to kill him for a wizard. One of the young men of the tribe took the duty upon himself, and after much perplexity, hit upon the following plan, *to-wit*:—he had fully resolved, in conjunction with others who were in the conspiracy, that the medicine of Wi-jun-jon was too great for the ordinary mode, and that he was so great a liar that a rifle bullet would not kill him; while the young man was in this

* Most unfortunately for this poor fellow, the other one of his tribe, who travelled with him, and could have borne testimony to the truth of his statements, died of the quinsey on his way home.

distressing dilemma, which lasted for some weeks, he had a dream one night, which solved all difficulties ; and in consequence of which, he loitered about the store in the Fort, at the mouth of the Yellow Stone, until he could procure, *by stealth*, (according to the injunction of his dream,) the handle of an iron pot, which he supposed to possess the requisite virtue, and taking it into the woods, he there spent a whole day in straightening and filing it, to fit it into the barrel of his gun ; after which, he made his appearance again in the Fort, with his gun under his robe, charged with the pot handle, and getting behind poor Wi-jun-jon, whilst he was talking with the Trader, placed the muzzle behind his head and blew out his brains !

" ' Sacré vengeance ! oh, mon Dieu ! let me cry—I shall cry always, for evare—Oh he is not true, I hope ? no, Monsieur, no !'

" Yes, Ba'tiste, it is a fact : thus ended the days and the greatness, and all the pride and hopes of Wɪ-ᴊᴜɴ-ᴊoɴ, the ' *Pigeon's Egg Head*,'—a warrior and a brave of the valiant Assinneboins, who travelled eight thousand miles to see the President, and all the great cities of the civilized world ; and who, for telling the *truth*, and *nothing but the truth*, was, after he got home, disgraced and killed for a wizard.

" ' Oh, Monsieur Cataline—I am distress—I am sick—I was hope he is not true—oh I am mortify. Wi-jun-jon was coot Ingin—he was my bruddare---eh bien---eh bien.'

" Now, my friend Ba'tiste, I see you are distressed, and I regret exceedingly that it must be so ; he was your friend and relative, and I myself feel sad at the poor fellow's unhappy and luckless fate ; for he was a handsome, an honest, and a noble Indian."

" ' C'est vrais. Monsieur, c'est vrai.'

" This man's death, Ba'tiste, has been a loss to himself, to his friends, and to the world ; but you and I may profit by it, nevertheless, if we bear it in mind——

" ' Oui ! yes, Monsr. mais, suppose, 'tis bad wind dat blows nary way, ha?'

" Yes, Ba'tiste, we may profit by his misfortune, if we choose. We may call it a ' caution ;' for instance, when I come to write your book, as you have proposed, the fate of this poor fellow, who was relating no more than what he actually saw, will *caution* you against the *imprudence of telling all that you actually know*, and narrating all that you have *seen*, lest like him you sink into disgrace for telling the truth. You know, Ba'tiste, that there are many things to be seen in the kind of life that you and I have been living for some years past, which it would be more prudent for us to suppress than to tell.

" ' Oui, Monsieur. Well, súppose, perhaps I am discourage about de book. Mais, we shall see, ha ?' "

Thus ended the last night's gossip, and in the cool of this morning, we bid adieu to the quiet and stillness of this wild place, of which I have resolved to give a little further account before we take leave of it.

From the Fall of St. Anthony, my delightful companion (Mr. Wood, whom I have before mentioned) and myself, with our Indian guide, whose name was O-kup-pee, tracing the beautiful shores of the St. Peters river, about eighty miles ; crossing it at a place called " *Traverse des Sioux*," and recrossing it at another point about thirty miles above the mouth of " *Terre Bleue*," from whence we steered in a direction a little North of West for the " Côteau des Prairies," leaving the St. Peters river, and crossing one of the most beautiful prairie countries in the world, for the distance of one hundred and twenty or thirty miles, which brought us to the base of the Côteau, where we were joined by our kind and esteemed companion Monsieur La Fromboise, as I have before related. This tract of country as well as that along the St. Peters river, is mostly covered with the richest soil, and furnishes an abundance of good water, which flows from a thousand living springs. For many miles we had the Côteau in view in the distance before us, which looked like a blue cloud settling down in the horizon ; and we were scarcely sensible of the fact, when we had arrived at its base, from the graceful and almost imperceptible swells with which it commences its elevation above the country around it. Over these swells or terraces, gently rising one above the other, we travelled for the distance of forty or fifty miles, when we at length reached the summit ; and from the base of this mound, to its top, a distance of forty or fifty miles, there was not a tree or bush to be seen in any direction, and the ground everywhere was covered with a green turf of grass, about five or six inches high; and we were assured by our Indian guide, that it descended to the West, towards the Missouri, with a similar inclination, and for an equal distance, divested of every thing save the grass that grows, and the animals that walk upon it.

On the very top of this mound or ridge, we found the far-famed quarry or fountain of the Red Pipe, which is truly an anomaly in nature (PLATE 270). The principal and most striking feature of this place, is a perpendicular wall of close-grained, compact quartz, of twenty-five and thirty feet in elevation, running nearly North and South with its face to the West, exhibiting a front of nearly two miles in length, when it disappears at both ends by running under the prairie, which becomes there a little more elevated, and probably covers it for many miles, both to the North and the South. The depression of the brow of the ridge at this place has been caused by the wash of a little stream, produced by several springs on the top, a little back from the wall ; which has gradually carried away the super-incumbent earth, and having bared the wall for the distance of two miles, is now left to glide for some distance over a perfectly level surface of quartz rock ; and then to leap from the top of the wall into a deep basin below, and from thence seek its course to the Missouri, forming the extreme source of a noted and powerful tributary, called the " Big Sioux."

This beautiful wall is horizontal, and stratified in several distinct layers of light grey, and rose or flesh-coloured quartz ; and for most of the

D D

way, both on the front of the wall, and for acres of its horizontal surface, highly polished or glazed, as if by ignition.

At the base of this wall there is a level prairie, of half a mile in width, running parallel to it; in any and all parts of which, the Indians pro. cure the red stone for their pipes, by digging through the soil and several slaty layers of the red stone, to the depth of four or five feet.* From the very numerous marks of ancient and modern diggings or excavations, it would appear that this place has been for many centuries resorted to for the red stone; and from the great number of graves and remains of ancient fortifications in its vicinity, it would seem, as well as from their actual traditions, that the Indian tribes have long held this place in high superstitious estimation.; and also that it has been the resort of different tribes, who have made their regular pilgrimages here to renew their pipes.

The red pipe stone, I consider, will take its place amongst minerals, as an interesting subject of itself; and the " Côteau des Prairies" will become hereafter an important theme for geologists; not only from the fact that this is the only known locality of that mineral, but from other phenomena relating to it. The single fact of such a table of quartz, in horizontal strata, resting on this elevated plateau, is of itself (in my opinion) a very interesting subject for investigation; and one which calls upon the scientific world for a correct theory with regard to the time when, and the manner in which, this formation was produced. That it is of a secondary character, and of a sedimentary deposit, seems evident; and that it has withstood the force of the diluvial current, while the great valley of the Missouri, from this very wall of rocks to the Rocky Mountains, has been excavated, and its debris carried to the ocean, there is also not a shadow of doubt; which opinion I confidently advance on the authority of the following remarkable facts:

At the base of the wall, and within a few rods of it, and on the very ground where the Indians dig for the red stone, rests a group of five stupendous boulders of gneiss, leaning against each other; the smallest of which is twelve or fifteen feet, and the largest twenty-five feet in diameter, altogether weighing, unquestionably, several hundred tons. These blocks are composed chiefly of felspar and mica, of an exceedingly coarse grain (the felspar often occurring in crystals of an inch in diameter). The surface of these boulders is in every part covered with a grey moss, which gives them an extremely ancient and venerable appearance, and their sides and angles are rounded by attrition, to the shape and character of most other erratic stones, which are found throughout the country. It is under these blocks that the two holes, or ovens are seen, in which, according to the Indian superstition,

---

* From the very many excavations recently and anciently made, I could discover that these layers varied very much, in their thickness in different parts; and that in some places they were overlaid with four or five feet of rock, similar to, and in fact a part of, the lower stratum of the wall.

the two old women, the guardian spirits of the place, reside ; of whom I have before spoken.

That these five immense blocks, of precisely the same character, and differing materially from all other specimens of boulders which I have seen in the great vallies of the Mississippi and Missouri, should have been hurled some hundreds of miles from their native bed, and lodged in so singular a group on this elevated ridge, is truly matter of surprise for the scientific world, as well as for the poor Indian, whose superstitious veneration of them is such, that not a spear of grass is broken or bent by his feet, within three or four rods of them, where he stops, and in humble supplication, by throwing plugs of tobacco to them, solicits permission to dig and carry away the red stone for his pipes. The surface of these boulders are in every part entire and unscratched by anything ; wearing the moss everywhere unbroken, except where I applied the hammer, to obtain some small specimens, which I shall bring away with me.

The fact alone, that these blocks differ in character from all other specimens which I have seen in my travels, amongst the thousands of boulders which are strewed over the great valley of the Missouri and Mississippi, from the Yellow Stone almost to the Gulf of Mexico, raises in my mind an unanswerable question, as regards the location of their native bed, and the means by which they have reached their isolated position ; like five brothers, leaning against and supporting each other, without the existence of another boulder within many miles of them. There are thousands and tens of thousands of boulders scattered over the prairies, at the base of the Côteau, on either side ; and so throughout the valley of the St. Peters and Mississippi, which are also subjects of very great interest and importance to science, inasmuch as they present to the world, a vast variety of characters; and each one, though strayed away from its original position, bears incontestible proof of the character of its native bed. The tract of country lying between the St. Peters river and the Côteau, over which we passed, presents innumerable specimens of this kind ; and near the base of the Côteau they are strewed over the prairie in countless numbers, presenting almost an incredible variety of rich, and beautiful colours ; and undoubtedly traceable, (if they can be traced), to separate and distinct beds.

Amongst these beautiful groups, it was sometimes a very easy matter to sit on my horse and count within my sight, some twenty or thirty different varieties, of quartz and granite, in rounded boulders, of every hue and colour, from snow white to intense red, and yellow, and blue, and almost to a jet black ; each one well characterized and evidently from a distinct quarry. With the beautiful hues and almost endless characters of these blocks, I became completely surprised and charmed ; and I resolved to procure specimens of every variety, which I did with success, by dismounting from my horse, and breaking small bits from them with my hammer ; until I had something like an hundred different varieties, containing all the tints and colours of a painter's palette. These, I at length threw away, as I had on several former occasions, other minerals and fossils, which I had collected and lugged along from day to day, and sometimes from week to week.

Whether these varieties of quartz and granite can all be traced to their native beds, or whether they all have origins at this time exposed above the earth's surface, are equally matters of much doubt in my mind. I believe that the geologist may take the different varieties, which he may gather at the base of the Côteau in one hour, and travel the Continent of North America all over without being enabled to put them all in place; coming at last to the unavoidable conclusion, that numerous chains or beds of primitive rocks have reared their heads on this Continent, the summits of which have been swept away by the force of diluvial currents, and their fragments jostled together and strewed about, like foreigners in a strange land, over the great vallies of the Mississippi and Missouri, where they will ever remain, and be gazed upon by the traveller, as the only remaining evidence of their native beds, which have again submerged or been covered with diluvial deposits.

There seems not to be, either on the Côteau or in the great vallies on either side, so far as I have travelled, any slaty or other formation exposed above the surface on which grooves or scratches can be seen, to establish the direction of the diluvial currents in those regions ; yet I think the fact is pretty clearly established by the general shapes of the vallies, and the courses of the mountain ridges which wall them in on their sides.

The Côteau des Prairies is the dividing ridge between the St. Peters and Missouri rivers ; its southern termination or slope is about in the latitude of the Fall of St. Anthony, and it stands equi-distant between the two rivers ; its general course bearing two or three degrees West of North for the distance of two or three hundred miles, when it gradually slopes again to the North, throwing out from its base the head-waters and tributaries of the St. Peters, on the East. The Red River, and other streams, which empty into Hudson's Bay, on the North ; La Riviere Jaque and several other tributaries to the Missouri, on the West ; and the Red Cedar, the Ioway and the Des Moines, on the South.

This wonderful feature, which is several hundred miles in length, and varying from fifty to a hundred in width, is, perhaps, the noblest mound of its kind in the world ; it gradually and gracefully rises on each side, by swell after swell, without tree, or bush or rock (save what are to be seen in the vicinity of the Pipe Stone Quarry), and everywhere covered with green grass affording the traveller, from its highest elevations, the most unbounded and sublime views of —— nothing at all —— save the blue and boundless ocean of prairies that lie beneath and all around him, vanishing into azure in the distance without a speck or spot to break their softness.

The direction of this ridge, I consider, pretty clearly establishes the course of the diluvial current in this region, and the erratic stones which are distributed along its base, I attribute to an origin several hundred miles North West from the Côteau. I have not myself traced the Côteau to its highest points, nor to its Northern extremity; but it has been a subject, on which I have closely questioned a number of traders, who have traversed every mile of it with their carts, and from thence to Lake Winnepeg on the North, who uniformly tell me, that there is no range of primitive rocks to be crossed in travelling the whole distance, which is one connected and continuous prairie.

The top and sides of the Côteau are everywhere strewed over the surface with granitic sand and pebbles, which, together with the fact of the five boulders resting at the Pipe Stone Quarry, shew clearly that every part of the ridge has been subject to the action of these currents, which could not have run counter to it, without having disfigured or deranged its beautiful symmetry.

The glazed or polished surface of the quartz rocks at the Pipe Stone Quarry, I consider a very interesting subject, and one which will excite hereafter a variety of theories, as to the manner in which it has been produced, and the causes which have led to such singular results. The quartz is of a close grain, and exceedingly hard, eliciting the most brilliant spark from steel; and in most places, where exposed to the sun and the air, has a high polish on its surface, entirely beyond any results which could have been produced by diluvial action, being perfectly glazed as if by ignition. I was not sufficiently particular in my examinations to ascertain whether any parts of the surface of these rocks under the ground, and not exposed to the action of the air, were thus affected, which would afford an important argument in forming a correct theory with regard to it; and it may also be a fact of similar importance, that this polish does not extend over the whole wall or area; but is distributed over it in parts and sections, often disappearing suddenly, and reappearing again, even where the character and exposure of the rock is the same and unbroken. In general, the parts and points most projecting and exposed, bear the highest polish, which would naturally be the case whether it was produced by ignition, or by the action of the air and sun. It would seem almost an impossibility, that the air passing these projections for a series of centuries, could have produced so high a polish on so hard a substance; and it seems equally unaccountable, that this effect could have been produced in the other way, in the total absence of all igneous matter.

I have broken off specimens and brought them home, which certainly bear as high a polish and lustre on the surface, as a piece of melted glass; and then as these rocks have undoubtedly been formed where they now lie, it must be admitted, that this strange effect on their surface has been produced either by the action of the air and sun, or by igneous influence; and if by the latter course, there is no other conclusion we can come to, than that these results are volcanic; that this wall has once formed the side of a crater, and that the Pipe Stone, laying in horizontal strata, is formed of the lava which has issued from it. I am strongly inclined to believe, however, that the former supposition is the correct one; and that the Pipe Stone, which differs from all known specimens of lava, is a new variety of *steatite*, and will be found to be a subject of great interest and one worthy of a careful analysis.*

With such notes and such memorandums on this shorn land, whose quiet and silence are only broken by the winds and the thunders of Heaven, I close my note-book, and we this morning saddle our horses; and after wending our way to the "Thunders' Nest" and the "Stone-man Medicine," we shall descend into the valley of the St. Peters, and from that to the regions of civilization; from whence, if I can get there, you will hear of me again. Adieu.

* In Silliman's American Journal of Science, Vol. xxxvii., p. 394, will be seen the following analysis of this mineral, made by Dr. Jackson of Boston, one of our best mineralogists and chemists; to whom I sent some specimens for the purpose, and who pronounced it, *"a new mineral compound, not steatite, is harder than gypsum, and softer than carbonate of lime."*

Chemical Analysis of the Red Pipe Stone, brought by George Catlin, from the Côteau des Prairies, in 1836:

Water	8.4
Silica . . . , . :	48.2
Alumina	28.2
Magnesia . , . . .	6.0
Carbonate of lime . .	2.6
Peroxide of iron . . .	5.0
Oxide of manganese .	0.6
	——
	99.0
	——
Loss (probably magnesia)	1.0
	——
	100.0

NOTE.—All the varieties of this beautiful mineral, may at all times be seen in the INDIAN MUSEUM; and by the curious, specimens may be obtained for any further experiments.

276

Catlin

277

LETTER.—No. 56.

Iᴛ will be seen by this, that I am again wending my way towards home. Our neat little " dug out," by the aid of our paddles, has at length brought my travelling companion and myself in safety to this place, where we found the river, the shores, and the plains contiguous, alive and vivid with plumes, with spears, and war-clubs of the yelling red men.

We had heard that the whole nation of Sacs and Foxes were to meet Governor Dodge here in treaty at this time, and nerve was given liberally to our paddles, which had brought us from Traverse de Sioux, on the St. Peters river ; and we reached here luckily in time to see the parades and forms of a savage community, transferring the rights and immunities of their natural soil, to the insatiable grasp of pale faced voracity.

After having glutted our curiosity at the fountain of the Red Pipe, our horses brought us to the base of the Côteau, and then over the extended plain that lies between that and the Traverse de Sioux, on the St. Peters with about five days' travel.

In this distance we passed some of the loveliest prairie country in the world, and I made a number of sketches—" *Laque du Cygne,* Swan Lake," (ᴘʟᴀᴛᴇ 276), was a peculiar and lovely scene, extending for many miles, and filled with innumerable small islands covered with a profusion of rich forest trees. Pʟᴀᴛᴇ 277, exhibits the Indian mode of taking muskrats, which dwell in immense numbers in these northern prairies, and build their burrows in shoal water, of the stalks of the wild rice. They are built up something of the size and form of haycocks, having a dry chamber in the top, where the animal sleeps above water, passing in and out through a hole beneath the water's surface. The skins of these animals are sought by the Traders, for their fur, and they constitute the staple of all these regions, being caught in immense numbers by the Indians, and vended to the Fur Traders. The mode of taking them is seen in the drawing ; the women, children and dogs attend to the little encampments, while the men wade to their houses or burrows, and one strikes on the backs of them, as the other takes the inhabitants in a rapid manner with a spear, while they are escaping from them.

PLATE 278, is a party of Sioux, in bark canoes (purchased of the Chippeways), gathering the wild rice, which grows in immense fields around the
shores of the rivers and lakes of these northern regions, and used by the
Indians as an useful article of food. The mode of gathering it is curious,
and as seen in the drawing—one woman paddles the canoe, whilst another,
with a stick in each hand, bends the rice over the canoe with one, and strikes
it with the other, which shells it into the canoe, which is constantly moving
along until it is filled.

PLATE 279, is a representation of one of the many lovely prairie scenes we
passed on the banks of the St. Peters river, near the Traverse de Sioux.

Whilst traversing this beautiful region of country, we passed the bands of
Sioux, who had made us so much trouble on our way to the Red Pipe, but
met with no further molestation.

At the Traverse de Sioux, our horses were left, and we committed our
bodies and little travelling conveniences to the narrow compass of a modest
canoe, that must most evidently have been dug out from the *wrong side
of the log*—that required *us* and everything in it, to be exactly in the bottom—and then, to look straight forward, and speak from the *middle* of our
mouths, or it was "*t'other side up*" in an instant. In this way embarked,
with our paddles used as balance poles and propellers (after drilling a while
in shoal water till we could "get the hang of it"), we started off, upon
the bosom of the St. Peters, for the Fall of St. Anthony. *   *

*   *   *   * ' Sans accident we arrived, at ten o'clock
at night of the second day—and sans steamer (which we were in hopes
to meet), we were obliged to trust to our little tremulous craft to carry
us through the windings of the mighty Mississippi and Lake Pepin, to
Prairie du Chien, a distance of 400 miles, which I had travelled last
summer in the same manner.

"Oh the drudgery and toil of paddling our little canoe from this to Prairie
Éu Chien, we never can do it, Catlin."

"Ah well, never mind, my dear fellow—we *must* 'go it'—there is no other
way. But think of the pleasure of such a trip, ha? Our guns and our fish-
ing-tackle will we have in good order, and be masters of our own boat—we
can shove it into every nook and crevice; explore the caves in the rocks;
ascend '*Mount Strombolo,*' and linger along the pebbly shores of Lake Pepin, to our hearts' content." "Well, I am perfectly agreed; that's fine, by
Jupiter, that's what I shall relish exactly; we will have our own fun, and a
truce to the labour and time; let's haste and be off." So we catered for our
voyage, shook hands with our friends, and were again balancing our skittish
bark upon the green waters of the Mississippi. We encamped (as I had
done the summer before), along its lonely banks, whose only music is the
echoing war-song that rises from the glimmering camp-fire of the retiring
savage, or the cries of the famishing wolf that sits and bitterly weeps out in
tremulous tones, his impatience for the crumbs that are to fall to his lot.

278

279

Oh! but we enjoyed those moments, (did we not, Wood? I would ask you, in any part of the world, where circumstances shall throw this in your way) those nights of our voyage, which ended days of peril and fatigue ; when our larder was full, when our coffee was good, our mats spread, and our musquito bars over us, which admitted the cool and freshness of night, but screened the dew. and bade defiance to the buzzing thousands of sharp-billed, winged torturers that were kicking and thumping for admission. I speak now of *fair weather*, not of the nights of lightning and of rain ! We'll pass them over. We had all kinds though, and as we loitered ten days on our way, we examined and experimented on many things for the benefit of mankind. We drew into our larder (in addition to bass and wild fowls), clams, snails, frogs, and rattlesnakes ; the latter of which, when properly dressed and broiled, we found to be the most delicious food of the land.

We were stranded upon the Eastern shore of Lake Pepin, where head-winds held us three days ; and, like solitary Malays or Zealand penguins, we stalked along and about its pebbly shores till we were tired, before we could, with security, lay our little trough upon its troubled surface. When liberated from its wind-bound shores, we busily plied our paddles, and nimbly sped our way, until we were landed at the fort of " Mount Strombolo," (as the soldiers call it), but properly denominated, in French, *La Montaigne que tromps a l'eau.* We ascended it without much trouble ; and enjoyed from its top, one of the most magnificent panoramic views that the Western world can furnish ; and I would recommend to the tourist who has time to stop for an hour or two, to go to its summit, and enjoy with rapture, the splendour of the scene that lies near and in distance about him. This mountain, or rather pyramid, is an anomaly in the country, rising as it does, about seven hundred feet from the water, and washed at its base, all around, by the river ; which divides and runs on each side of it. It is composed chiefly of rock, and all its strata correspond exactly with those of the projecting promontories on either side of the river. We at length arrived safe at Prairie du Chien ; which was also *sans* steamer. We were moored again, thirty miles below, at the beautiful banks and bluffs of Cassville ; which, too, was *sans steamer*—we dipped our paddles again ——— ——— ——— and

We are now six hundred miles below the Fall of St. Anthony, where steamers daily pass ; and we feel, of course, at home. I spoke of the *Treaty*. We were just in time, and beheld its conclusion. It was signed yesterday; and this day, of course, is one of revel and amusements—shows of war-parades and dances. The whole of the Sacs and Foxes are gathered here, and their appearance is very thrilling, and at the same time pleasing. These people have sold so much of their land lately, that they have the luxuries of life to a considerable degree, and may be considered rich ; consequently they look elated and happy, carrying themselves much above the humbled manner of most of the semi-civilized tribes, whose heads are hanging and drooping in poverty and despair.

In a former epistle, I mentioned the interview which I had with Kee-o-kuk, and the leading men and women of his tribe, when I painted a number of their portraits and amusements as follow :

Kee-o-kuk (the running fox, PLATE 280), is the present chief of the tribe, a dignified and proud man, with a good share of talent, and vanity enough to force into action all the wit and judgment he possesses, in order to command the attention and respect of the world. At the close of the " Black Hawk War " in 1833, which had been waged with disastrous effects along ⁓ rronuer, oy a Sac chief of that name ; *Kee-o-kuk* was acknowledged chief of the Sacs and Foxes by General Scott, who held a Treaty with them at Rock Island. His appointment as chief, was in consequence of the friendly position he had taken during the war, holding two-thirds of the warriors neutral, which was no doubt the cause of the sudden and successful termination of the war, and the means of saving much bloodshed. Black Hawk and his two sons, as well as his principal advisers and warriors, were brought into St. Louis in chains, and *Kee-o-kuk* appointed chief with the assent of the tribe. In his portrait I have represented him in the costume, precisely, in which he was dressed when he stood for it, with his shield on his arm, and his staff (insignia of office) in his left hand. There is no Indian chief on the frontier better known at this time, or more highly appreciated for his eloquence, as a public speaker, than Kee-o-kuk ; as he has repeatedly visited Washington and others of our Atlantic towns, and made his speeches before thousands, when he has been contending for his people's rights, in their stipulations with the United States Government, for the sale of their lands.

As so much is known of this man, amongst the citizens of the United States, there is scarcely need of my saying much more of him to them ; but for those who know less of him, I shall say more anon. PLATE 281, is a portrait of the wife of *Kee-o-kuk*, and PLATE 282, of his favourite son, whom he intends to be his successor. These portraits are both painted, also, in the costumes precisely in which they were dressed. This woman was the favourite one, (I think) of seven, whom he had living, (*apparently* quite comfortably and peaceably,) in his wigwam, where General Street and I visited him in his village on the Des Moines river. And, although· she was the oldest of the " lot," she seemed to be the favourite one on this occasion—the only one that could be painted ; on account, I believe, of her being the mother of his favourite son. Her dress, which was of civilized stuffs, was fashioned and ornamented by herself, and was truly a most splendid affair ; the upper part of it being almost literally covered with silver broaches.

The Sacs and Foxes, who were once two separate tribes, but with a language very similar, have, at some period not very remote, united into one, and are now an inseparable people, and go by the familiar appellation of the amalgam name of " Sacs and Foxes."

These people, as will be seen in their portraits, shave and ornament their heads, like the Osages and Pawnees, of whom I have spoken heretofore ;

G. Catlin

281

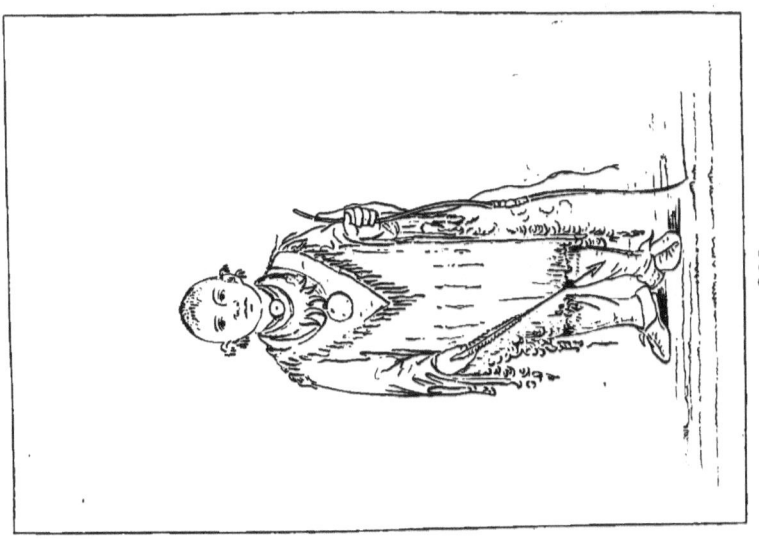

282

283   284

G. Catlin.

285   286

and are amongst the number of tribes who have relinquished their immense tracts of lands, and recently retired West of the Mississippi river. Their numbers at present are not more than five or six thousand, yet they are a warlike and powerful tribe.

Muk-a-tah-mish-o-kah-kaik (the black hawk, PLATE 283) is the man to whom I have above alluded, as the leader of the "Black Hawk war," who was defeated by General Atkinson, and held a prisoner of war, and sen: through Washington and other Eastern cities, with a number of others, to be gazed at.

This man, whose name has carried a sort of terror through the country where it has been sounded, has been distinguished as a speaker or councellor rather than as a warrior; and I believe it has been pretty generally admitted, that "*Nah-pope*" and the "Prophet" were, in fact, the instigators of the war; and either of them with much higher claims for the name of warrior than Black Hawk ever had.

When I painted this chief, he was dressed in a plain suit of buckskin, with strings of wampum in his ears and on his neck, and held in his hand, his medicine-bag, which was the skin of a black hawk, from which he had taken his name, and the tail of which made him a fan, which he was almost constantly using.

·PLATE 284, is the eldest son of Black Hawk, *Nah-se-us-kuk* (the whirling thunder), a very handsome young warrior, and one of the finest-looking Indians I ever saw. There is a strong party in the tribe that is anxious to put this young man up; and I think it more than likely, that *Kee-o-kuk* as chief may fall ere long by his hand, or by some of the tribe, who are anxious to reinstate the family of Black Hawk.

PLATE 285, *Wah-pe-kee-suck* (the white cloud), called "the Prophet," is a very distinguished man, and one of the principal and leading men of the Black Hawk party, and studying favour with the whites, as will be seen by the manner in which he was allowing his hair to grow out.

PLATE 286, *Wee-sheet* (the sturgeon's head), this man held a spear in his hand when he was being painted, with which he assured me he killed four white men during the war; though I have some doubts of the fact.

Ah-mou-a (the whale, PLATE 287, and his wife, PLATE 288), are also fair specimens of this tribe. Her name is Wa-quo-the-qua (the buck's wife, or female deer), and she was wrapped in a mackinaw blanket, whilst he was curiously dressed, and held his war-club in his hand.

Pash-ee-pa-ho (the little stabbing chief, PLATE 289), a very old man, holding his shield, staff and pipe in his hands; has long been the head civil chief of this tribe; but, as is generally the case in very old age, he has resigned the office to those who are younger and better qualified to do the duties of it.

Besides the above-mentioned personages, I painted also the following portraits, which are now in my Collection.

I-o-way (the Ioway), one of Black Hawk's principal warriors; his body curiously ornamented with his " war-paint ;" *Pam-a-ho* (the swimmer), one of Black Hawk's warriors; *No-kuk-qua* (the bear's fat); *Pash-ee-pa-ho* (the little stabbing chief, the younger), one of Black Hawk's braves; *Wah-pa-ko-las-kuk* (the bear's track); *Wa-saw-me-saw* (the roaring thunder), youngest son of Black Hawk; painted while prisoner of war.

PLATE 290, *Kee-o-kuk*, on horseback. After I had painted the portrait of this vain man at full length, and which I have already introduced, he had the vanity to say to me, that he made a fine appearance on horseback, and that he wished me to paint him thus. So I prepared my canvass in the door of the hospital which I occupied, in the dragoon cantonment; and he flourished about for a considerable part of the day in front of me, until the picture was completed. The horse that he rode was the best animal on the frontier ; a fine blooded horse, for which he gave the price of 300 dollars, a thing that he was quite able to, who had the distribution of 50,000 dollars annuities, annually, amongst his people. He made a great display on this day, and hundreds of the dragoons and officers were about him, and looking on during the operation. His horse was beautifully caparisoned, and his scalps were carried attached to the bridle-bits.*

---

* About two years after the above was written, and the portrait painted, and whilst I was giving Lectures on the Customs of the Indians, in the Stuyvesant Institute in New York, Kee-o-kuk and his wife and son, with twenty more of the chiefs and warriors of his tribe, visited the City of New York on their way to Washington City, and were present one evening at my Lecture, amidst an audience of 1500 persons. During the Lecture, I placed a succession of portraits on my easel before the audience, and they were successively recognized by the Indians as they were shewn; and at last I placed this portrait of Kee-o-kuk before them, when they all sprung up and hailed it with a piercing yell. After the noise had subsided, Kee-o-kuk arose, and addressed the audience in these words :—" My friends, I hope you will pardon my men for making so much noise, as they were very much excited by seeing me on my favourite war-horse, which they all recognized in a moment."

I had the satisfaction then of saying to the audience, that this was very gratifying to me, inasmuch as many persons had questioned the correctness of the picture of the horse; and some had said in my Exhibition Room, " that it was an imposition—that no Indian on the frontier rode so good a horse." This was explained to Kee-o-kuk by the interpreter, when he arose again quite indignant at the thought that any one should doubt its correctness, and assured the audience, " that his men, a number of whom never had heard that the picture was painted, knew the horse the moment it was presented; and further, he wished to know why Kee-o-kuk could not ride as good a horse as any white man?" He here received a round of applause, and the interpreter, Mr. Le Clair, rose and stated to the audience, that he recognized the horse the moment it was shewn, and that it was a faithful portrait of the horse that he sold to Kee-o-kuk for 300 dollars, and that it was the finest horse on the frontier, belonging either to red or white man.

In a few minutes afterwards I was exhibiting several of my paintings of buffalo-hunts, and describing the modes of slaying them with bows and arrows, when I made the assertion which I had often been in the habit of making, that there were many instances where the arrow was thrown entirely through the buffalo's body; and that I had several times witnessed this astonishing feat. I saw evidently by the motions of my audience, that

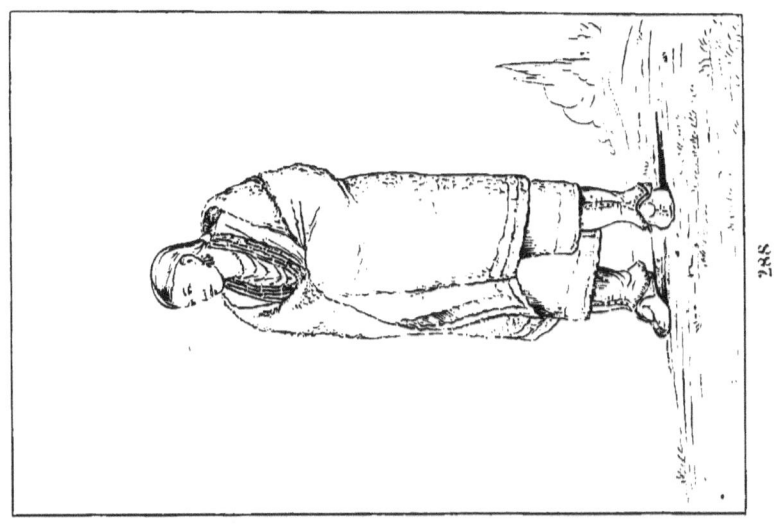

288

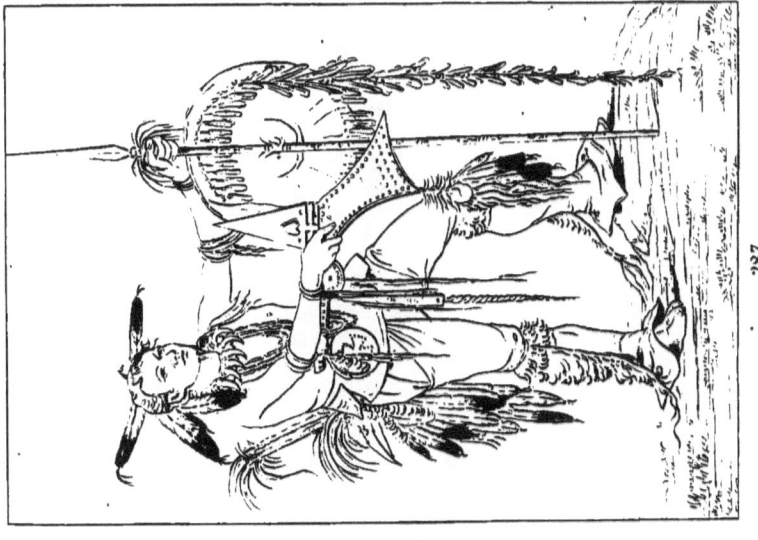

287

G. Catlin.

The dances and other amusements amongst this tribe are exceedingly spirited and pleasing; and I have made sketches of a number of them, which I briefly introduce here, and leave them for further comments at a future time, provided I ever get leisure and space to enable me to do it.

The *slave-dance* (PLATE 291), is a picturesque scene, and the custom in which it is founded a very curious one. This tribe has a society which they call the "*slaves*," composed of a number of the young men of the best families in the tribe, who volunteer to be slaves for the term of two years, and subject to perform any menial service that the chief may order, no matter how humiliating or how degrading it may be; by which, after serving their two years, they are exempt for the rest of their lives, on war-parties or other excursions, or wherever they may be—from all labour or degrading occupations, such as cooking, making fires, &c. &c.

These young men elect one from their numbers to be their master, and all agree to obey his command whatever it may be, and which is given to him by one of the chiefs of the tribe. On a certain day or season of the year, they have to themselves a great feast, and preparatory to it the above-mentioned dance.

Smoking horses (PLATE 292), is another of the peculiar and very curious customs of this tribe. When General Street and I, arrived at Kee-o-kuks village, we were just in time to see this amusing scene, on the prairie a little back of his village. The Foxes, who were making up a war-party to go against the Sioux, and had not suitable horses enough by twenty, had sent word to the Sacs, the day before (according to an ancient custom), that they were coming on that day, at a certain hour, to "smoke" that number of horses, and they must not fail to have them ready. On that day, and at the hour, the twenty young men who were beggars for horses, were on the spot, and seated themselves on the ground in a circle, where they went to smoking. The villagers flocked around them in a dense crowd, and soon after appeared on the prairie, at half a mile distance, an equal number of young men of the Sac tribe, who had agreed, each to give a horse, and who were then galloping them about at full speed; and, gradually, as they went around in a circuit, coming in nearer to the centre, until they were at last close around the ring of young fellows seated on the ground. Whilst dashing about thus, each one, with a heavy whip in his hand, as he came within reach of the group on the ground, selected the one to whom he decided to present his horse, and as he passed him, gave him the most tremendous cut with his

many doubted the correctness of my assertion; and I appealed to *Kee-o-kuk*, who rose up when the thing was explained to him, and said, that it had repeatedly happened amongst his tribe; and he believed that one of his young men by his side had done it. The young man instantly stepped up on the bench, and took a bow from under his robe, with which he told the audience he had driven his arrow quite through a buffalo's body. And, there being forty of the Sioux from the Upper Missouri also present, the same question was put to them, when the chief arose, and addressing himself to the audience, said that it was a thing very often done by the hunters in his tribe.

lash, over his naked shoulders ; and as he darted around again he plied the whip as before, and again and again, with a violent " crack !" until the blood could be seen trickling down over his naked shoulders, upon which he instantly dismounted, and placed the bridle and whip in his hands, saying, " here, you are a beggar—I present you a horse, but you will carry my mark on your back." In this manner, they were all in a little time "*whipped up*," and each had a good horse to ride home, and into battle. His necessity was such, that he could afford to take the stripes and the scars as the price of the horse, and the giver could afford to make the present for the satisfaction of putting his mark upon the other, and of boasting of his liberality, which he has always a right to do, when going into the dance, or on other important occasions.

The *Begging Dance* (PLATE 293), is a frequent amusement, and one that has been practiced with some considerable success at this time, whilst there have been so many distinguished and liberal visitors here. It is got up by a number of desperate and long-winded fellows, who will dance and yell their visitors into liberality ; or, if necessary, laugh them into it, by their strange antics, singing a song of importunity, and extending their hands for presents, which they allege are to gladden the hearts of the poor, and ensure a blessing to the giver.

The Sacs and Foxes, like all other Indians, are fond of living along the banks of rivers and streams ; and like all others, are expert swimmers and skilful canoemen.

Their canoes, like those of the Sioux and many other tribes, are dug out from a log, and generally made extremely light : and they dart them through the coves and along the shores of the rivers, with astonishing quickness. I was often amused at their freaks in their canoes, whilst travelling ; and I was induced to make a sketch of one which I frequently witnessed, that of sailing with the aid of their blankets, which the men carry ; and when the wind is fair, stand in the bow of the canoe and hold by two corners, with the other two under the foot or tied to the leg (PLATE 294) ; while the women sit in the other end of the canoe, and steer it with their paddles.

The *Discovery Dance* (PLATE 295), has been given here, amongst various others, and pleased the bystanders very much ; it was exceedingly droll and picturesque, and acted out with a great deal of pantomimic effect—without music, or any other noise than the patting of their feet, which all came simultaneously on the ground, in perfect time, whilst they were dancing forward two or four at a time, in a skulking posture, overlooking the country, and professing to announce the approach of animals or enemies which they have discovered, by giving the signals back to the leader of the dance.

Dance to the Berdashe (PLATE 296), is a very funny and amusing scene, which happens once a year or oftener, as they choose, when a feast is given to the " *Berdashe*," as he is called in French, (or *I-coo-coo-a*, in their own language), who is a man dressed in woman's clothes, as he is known to

294

295

G. Catlin.

296

to be all his life, and for extraordinary privileges which he is known to possess, he is driven to the most servile and degrading duties, which he is not allowed to escape; and he being the only one of the tribe submitting to this disgraceful degradation, is looked upon as *medicine* and sacred, and a feast is given to him annually; and initiatory to it, a dance by those few young men of the tribe who can, as in the sketch, dance forward and publicly make their boast (without the denial of the Berdashe), that Ahg-whi-ee-choos-cum-me, hi-anh-dwax-cumme-ke on-daig-nun-e how ixt. Che-ne-a'hkt, ah-pex-ian, I-coo-coo-a, wi-an-gurotst, whow-itcht-ne-axt-ar-rah, ne-axt-gun-he, h'dow-k's dow-on-daig-o-ewhicht, nun-go-was-see.

Such, and such only, are allowed to enter the dance and partake of the feast, and as there are but a precious few in the tribe who have legitimately gained this singular privilege, or willing to make a public confession of it, it will be seen that the society consists of quite a limited number of " odd fellows."

· This is one of the most unaccountable and disgusting customs, that I have ever met in the Indian country, and so far as I have been able to learn, belongs only to the Sioux and Sacs and Foxes—perhaps it is practiced by other tribes. but I did not meet with it; and for further account of it I am constrained to refer the reader to the country where it is practiced, and where I should wish that it might be extinguished before it be more fully recorded.

Dance to the *Medicine of the Brave* (PLATE 297.) This is a custom well worth recording, for the beautiful moral which is contained in it. In this plate is represented a party of Sac warriors who have returned victorious from battle, with scalps they have taken from their enemies, but having lost one of their party, they appear and dance in front of his wigwam, fifteen days in succession, about an hour on each day, when the widow hangs his *medicine-bag* on a green bush which she erects before her door, under which she sits and cries, whilst the warriors dance and brandish the scalps they have taken, and at the same time recount the deeds of bravery of their deceased comrade in arms, whilst they are throwing presents to the widow to heal her grief and afford her the means of a living.

The Sacs and Foxes are already drawing an annuity of 27,000 dollars, for thirty years to come, in cash; and by the present Treaty just concluded, that amount will be enlarged to 37,000 dollars per annum. This Treaty with the Sacs and Foxes, held at Rock Island, was for the purchase of a tract of land of 256,000 acres, lying on the Ioway river, West of the Mississippi, a reserve which was made in the tract of land conveyed to the Government by Treaty after the Sac war, and known as the " Black Hawk purchase." The Treaty has been completed by Governor Dodge, by stipulating on the part of Government to pay them seventy-five cents per acre for the reserve, (amounting to 192,000 dollars), in the manner and form following :—

Thirty thousand dollars to be paid in specie in June next, at the Treaty-ground; and ten thousand dollars annually, for ten years to come, at the same place, and in the same manner ; and the remaining sixty-two thousand, in the payment of their debts, and some little donations to widows and half-breed children. The American Fur Company was their principal creditor, whose account for goods advanced on credit, they admitted, to the amount of nearly fifty thousand dollars. It was stipulated by an article in the Treaty that one half of these demands should be paid in cash as soon as the Treaty should be ratified—and that five thousand dollars should be appropriated annually, for their liquidation, until they were paid off.

It was proposed by Kee-o-kuk in his speech (and it is a fact worthy of being known, for such has been the proposition in every Indian Treaty that I ever attended), that the first preparatory stipulation on the part of Government, should be to pay the requisite sum of money to satisfy all their creditors, who were then present, and whose accounts were handed in, acknowledged and admitted.

The price paid for this tract of land is a liberal one, comparatively speaking, for the usual price heretofore paid for Indian lands, has been one and a half or three quarter cents, (instead of seventy-five cents) per acre, for land which Government has since sold out for ten shillings.

Even one dollar per acre would not have been too much to have paid for this tract, for every acre of it can be sold in one year, for ten shillings per acre, to actual settlers, so desirable and so fertile is the tract of country purchased. These very people sold to Government a great part of the rich states of Illinois and Missouri, at the low rates above-mentioned ; and this small tract being the last that they can ever part with, without throwing themselves back upon their natural enemies, it was no more than right that Government should deal with them, as they have done, liberally.

As an evidence of the immediate value of that tract of land to Government, and, as a striking instance of the overwhelming torrent of emigration, to the " Far West," I will relate the following occurrence which took place at the close of the Treaty :—After the Treaty was signed and witnessed, Governor Dodge addressed a few very judicious and admonitory sentences to the chiefs and braves, which he finished by requesting them to move their families, and all their property from this tract, within one month, which time he would allow them, to make room for the whites.

Considerable excitement was created among the chiefs and braves, by this suggestion, and a hearty laugh ensued, the cause of which was soon after explained by one of them in the following manner :—

" My father, we have to laugh—we require no time to move—we have all left the lands already, and sold our wigwams to Chemokemons (white men)—some for one hundred, and some for two hundred dollars, before we came to this Treaty. There are already four hundred Chemokemons on the land, and several hundred more on their way moving in ; and three days before we came away, one Chemokemon sold his wigwam to another Chemokemon for two thousand dollars, to build a great town."

297

In this wise is this fair land filling up, one hundred miles or more West of the Mississippi—not with barbarians, but with people from the East, enlightened and intelligent—with industry and perseverance that will soon rear from the soil all the luxuries, and add to the surface, all the taste and comforts of Eastern refinement.

The Treaty itself, in all its forms, was a scene of interest, and *Kee-o-kuk* was the principal speaker on the occasion, being recognized as the head chief of the tribe. He is a very subtle and dignified man, and well fitted to wield the destinies of his nation. The poor dethroned monarch, old Black Hawk, was present, and looked an object of pity. With an old frock coat and brown hat on, and a cane in his hand, he stood the whole time outside of the group, and in dumb and dismal silence, with his sons by the side of him, and also his *quondam* aide-de-camp, Nahpope, and the prophet. They were not allowed to speak, nor even to sign the Treaty. *Nah-pope* rose, however, and commenced a very earnest speech on the subject of *temperance*! but Governor Dodge ordered him to sit down, (as being out of order), which probably saved him from a much more *peremptory command* from *Kee-o-kuk*, who was rising at that moment, with looks on his face that the Devil himself might have shrunk from. This Letter I must end here, observing, before I say adieu, that I have been catering for the public during this summer at a *difficult* (and almost *cruel*) rate; and if, in my over-exertions to grasp at material for their future entertainment, the cold hand of winter should be prematurely laid upon me and my works in this Northern region, the world, I am sure, will be disposed to pity, rather than censure me for my delay.

LETTER—No. 57.

Since the date of my last Letter, I have been a wanderer as usual, and am now at least 2000 miles from the place where it was dated. At this place are held 250 of the Seminolees and Euchees, prisoners of war, who are to be kept here awhile longer, and transferred to the country assigned them, 700 miles West of the Mississippi, and 1400 from this. The famous *Os-ce-o-la* is amongst the prisoners; and also *Mick-e-no-pah*, the head chief of the tribe, and *Cloud, King Phillip*, and several others of the distinguished men of the nation, who have celebrated themselves in the war that is now waging with the United States' Government.

There is scarcely any need of my undertaking in an epistle of this kind, to give a full account of this tribe, of their early history—of their former or present location—or of their present condition, and the disastrous war they are now waging with the United States' Government, who have held an invading army in their country for four or five years, endeavouring to dispossess them and compel them to remove to the West, in compliance with Treaty stipulations. These are subjects generally understood already (being matters of history), and I leave them to the hands of those who will do them more complete justice than I could think of doing at this time, with the little space that I could allow them; in the confident hope that justice may be meted out to them, at least by the historian, if it should not be by their great Guardian, who takes it upon herself, as with all the tribes, affectionately to *call* them her " *red children.*"

For those who know nothing of the Seminolees, it may be proper for me here just to remark, that they are a tribe of three or four thousand; occupying the peninsula of Florida—and speaking the language of the Creeks, of whom I have heretofore spoken, and who were once a part of the same tribe.

The word Seminolee is a Creek word, signifying runaways; a name which was given to a part of the Creek nation, who emigrated in a body to a country farther South, where they have lived to the present day; and continually extended their dominions by overrunning the once numerous tribe that occupied the Southern extremity of the Florida Cape, called the Euchees; whom they have at last nearly annihilated, and taken the mere

298

remnant of them in, as a part of their tribe. With this tribe the Government have been engaged in deadly and disastrous warfare for four or five years; endeavouring to remove them from their lands, in compliance with a Treaty stipulation, which the Government claims to have been justly made, and which the Seminolees aver, was not. Many millions of money, and some hundreds of lives of officers and men have already been expended in the attempt to dislodge them; and much more will doubtless be yet spent before they can be removed from their almost impenetrable swamps and hiding-places, to which they can, for years to come, retreat; and from which they will be enabled, and no doubt disposed, in their exasperated state, to make continual sallies upon the unsuspecting and defenceless inhabitants of the country; carrying their relentless feelings to be reeked in cruel vengeance on the unoffending and innocent.*

The prisoners who are held here, to the number of 250, men, women and children, have been captured during the recent part of this warfare, and amongst them the distinguished personages whom I named a few moments since; ot these, the most conspicuous at this time is Os-ce-o-la (PLATE 298), commonly called Powell, as he is generally supposed to be a half-breed, the son of a white man (by that name), and a Creek woman.

I have painted him precisely in the costume, in which he stood for his picture, even to a string and a trinket. He wore three ostrich feathers in his head, and a turban made of a vari-coloured cotton shawl—and his dress was chiefly of calicos, with a handsome bead sash or belt around his waist, and his rifle in his hand.

This young man is, no doubt, an extraordinary character, as he has been for some years reputed, and doubtless looked upon by the Seminolees as the master spirit and leader of the tribe, although he is not a chief. From his boyhood, he had led an energetic and desperate sort of life, which had secured for him a conspicuous position in society; and when the desperate circumstances of war were agitating his country, he at once took a conspicuous and decided part; and in some way whether he deserved it or not, acquired an influence and a name that soon sounded to the remotest

---

* The above Letter was written in the winter of 1838, and by the Secretary at War's Report, a year and a half ago, it is seen that 36,000,000 of dollars had been already expended in the Seminolee war, as well as the lives of 12 or 1400 officers and men, and defenceless inhabitants, who have fallen victims to the violence of the enraged savages and diseases of the climate. And at the present date, August, 1841, I see by the American papers, that the war is being prosecuted at this time with its wonted vigour; and that the best troops in our country, and the lives of our most valued officers are yet jeopardised in the deadly swamps of Florida, with little more certainty of a speedy termination of the war, than there appeared five years ago.

The world will pardon me for saying no more of this inglorious war, for it will be seen that I am too near the end of my book, to afford it the requisite space; and as an American citizen, I would pray, amongst thousands of others, that all books yet to be made, might have as good an excuse for leaving it out.

parts of the United States, and amongst the Indian tribes, to the Rocky Mountains.

This gallant fellow, who was, undoubtedly, *captured* a few months since, with several of his chiefs and warriors, was at first brought in, to Fort Mellon in Florida, and afterwards sent to this place for safe-keeping, where he is grieving with a broken spirit, and ready to die, cursing white man, no doubt, to the end of his breath.

The surgeon of the post, Dr. Weedon, who has charge of him, and has been with him ever since he was taken prisoner, has told me from day to day, that he will not live many weeks; and I have my doubts whether he will, from the rapid decline I have observed in his face and his flesh since I arrived here.

During the time that I have been here, I have occupied a large room in the officers' quarters, by the politeness of Captain Morrison, who has command of the post, and charge of the prisoners; and on every evening, after painting all day at their portraits, I have had Os-ce-o-la, Mick-e-no-pa, Cloud, Co-a-had-jo, King Phillip, and others in my room, until a late hour at night, where they have taken great pains to give me an account of the war, and the mode in which they were captured, of which they complain bitterly.

I am fully convinced from all that I have seen, and learned from the lips of Osceola, and from the chiefs who are around him, that he is a most extraordinary man, and one entitled to a better fate.

In stature he is about at mediocrity, with an elastic and graceful movement; in his face he is good looking, with rather an effeminate smile; but of so peculiar a character, that the world may be ransacked over without finding another just like it. In his manners, and all his movements in company, he is polite and gentlemanly, though all his conversation is entirely in his own tongue; and his general appearance and actions, those of a full-blooded and wild Indian.

In PLATE 299, is a portrait of *Ye-how-lo-gee* (the cloud), generally known by the familiar name of "*Cloud.*" This is one of the chiefs, and a very good-natured, jolly man, growing fat in his imprisonment, where he gets enough to eat, and an occasional drink of whiskey from the officers, with whom he is a great favourite.

Ee-mat-la ("King Philip," PLATE 300) is also a very aged chief, who has been a man of great notoriety and distinction in his time, but has now got too old for further warlike enterprize.*

Co-ee-ha-jo (PLATE 301), is another chief who has been a long time distinguished in the tribe, having signalized himself very much by his feats in the present war.

---

* This veteran old warrior died a few weeks after I painted his portrait, whilst on his way, with the rest of the prisoners, to the Arkansas.

299   300

301   302

La-shee (tne licker, PLATE 302), commonly called " Creek Billy," is a distinguished brave of the tribe, and a very handsome fellow.

PLATE 303, is the portrait of a Seminolee boy, about nine years of age ;* and PLATE 304, a Seminolee woman.

Mick-e-no-pah (PLATE 305), is the head chief of the tribe, and a very lusty and dignified man. He took great pleasure in being present every day in my room, whilst I was painting the others ; but positively refused to be painted, until he found that a bottle of whiskey, and another of wine, which I kept on my mantelpiece, by permission of my kind friend Captain Morrison, were only to deal out their occasional kindnesses to those who sat for their portraits ; when he at length agreed to be painted, "if I could make a fair likeness of his *legs*," which he had very tastefully dressed in a handsome pair of red. leggings, and upon which I at once began, (as he sat cross-legged), by painting *them* on the lower part of the canvass, leaving room for his body and head above ; all of which, through the irresistible influence of a few kindnesses from my bottle of wine, I soon had fastened to the canvass, where they will firmly stand I trust, for some hundreds of years.

Since I finished my portrait of Os-ce-o-la, and since writing the first part of this Letter, he has been extremely sick, and lies so yet, with an alarming attack of the quinsey or putrid sore throat, which will probably end his career in a few days. Two or three times the surgeon has sent for the officers of the Garrison and myself, to come and see him "*dying*"—we were with him the night before last till the middle of the night, every moment expecting his death ; but he has improved during the last twenty-four hours, and there is some slight prospect of his recovery.† The steamer starts

---

* This remarkably fine boy, by the name of *Os-ce-o-la Nick-a-no-chee*, has recently been brought from America to London, by Dr. Welch, an Englishman, who has been for several years residing in Florida. The boy it seems, was captured by the United States troops, at the age of six years : but how my friend the Doctor got possession of him, and leave to bring him away I never have heard. He is acting a very praiseworthy part however, by the paternal fondness he evinces for the child, and fairly proves, by the very great pains he is taking with his education. The doctor has published recently, a very neat volume, containing the boy's history ; and also a much fuller account of Os-ce-o-la, and incidents of the Florida war, to which I would refer the reader.

† From accounts which I at Fort Moultrie a few days after I returned home, it seems, that this ill-fated warrior died, a prisoner, the next morning after I left him. And the following very interesting account of his last moments, was furnished me by Dr. Weedon, the surgeon who was by him, with the officers of the garrison, at Os-ce-o-la's request.

" About half an hour before he died, he seemed to be sensible that he was dying ; and although he could not speak, he signified by signs that he wished me to send for the chiefs and for the officers of the post, whom I called in. He made signs to his wives (of whom he had two, and also two fine little children by his side,) to go and bring his full dress, which he wore in time of war ; which having been brought in, he rose up in his bed, which was on the floor, and put on his shirt, his leggings and moccasins—girded on his war-belt— his bullet-pouch and powder-horn, and laid his knife by the side of him on the floor. He then called for his red paint, and his looking-glass, which was held before him, when he

to-morrow morning for New York, and I must use the opportunity; so I shall from necessity, leave the subject of Os-ce-o-la and the Seminolees for future consideration. Adieu.

deliberately painted one half of his face, his neck and his throat—his wrists—the backs of his hands, and the handle of his knife, red with vermilion; a custom practiced when the irrevocable oath of war and destruction is taken. His knife he then placed in its sheath, under his belt; and he carefully arranged his turban on his head, and his three ostrich plumes that he was in the habit of wearing in it. Being thus prepared in full dress, he laid down a few minutes to recover strength sufficient, when he rose up us before, and with most benignant and pleasing smiles, extended his hand to me and to all of the officers and chiefs that were around him; and shook hands with us all in dead silence; and also with his wives and his little children; he made a signal for them to lower him down upon his bed, which was done, and he then slowly drew from his war-belt, his scalping-knife, which he firmly grasped in his right hand, laying it across the other, on his breast, and in a moment smiled away his last breath, without a struggle or a groan."

304

303

305

G. Catlin.

LETTER—No. 58.

HAVING finished my travels in the " Far West" for awhile, and being detained a little time, sans occupation, in my nineteenth or twentieth transit of what, in common parlance is denominated the Frontier; I have seated myself down to give some further account of it, and of the doings and habits of people, both red and white, who live upon it.

The Frontier may properly be denominated the fleeting and unsettled line extending from the Gulf of Mexico to the Lake of the Woods, a distance of three thousand miles; which indefinitely separates civilized from Indian population—a moving barrier, where the unrestrained and natural propensities of two people are concentrated, in an atmosphere of lawless iniquity, that offends Heaven, and holds in mutual ignorance of each other, the honourable and virtuous portions of two people, which seem destined never to meet.

From what has been said in the foregoing epistles, the reader will agree that I have pretty closely adhered to my promise made in the commencement of them; that I should confine my remarks chiefly to people I have visited, and customs that I have *seen*, rather than by taking up his time with matter that might be gleaned from books. He will also agree, that I have principally devoted my pages, as I promised, to an account of the condition and customs of those Indians whom I have found entirely beyond the Frontier, acting and living as Nature taught them to live and act, without the examples, and consequently without the taints of civilized encroachments.

He will, I flatter myself, also yield me some credit for devoting the time and space I have occupied in my first appeal to the world, entirely to the condition and actions of the *living*, rather than fatiguing him with *theories* of the living or the dead. I have theories enough of my own, and have as closely examined the condition and customs of these people on the Frontier, as of those living beyond it—and also their past and present, and prospective history; but the reader will have learned, that my chief object in these Letters, has been not only to describe what I have *seen*, but of *those* things, such as I deemed the most novel and least understood ; which has of course confined my remarks heretofore, mostly to the character and condition of those tribes living entirely in a state of nature.

And as I have now a little leisure, and no particular tribes before me to speak of, the reader will allow me to glance my eye over the whole Indian country for awhile, both along the Frontier and beyond it; taking a hasty and brief survey of them, and their prospects in the aggregate; and by not *seeing* quite as distinctly as I have been in the habit of doing heretofore, taking pains to tell a little more emphatically what I *think*, and what I have *thought* of those things that I have seen, and yet have told but in part.

I have seen a vast many of these wild people in my travels, it will be admitted by all. And I have had toils and difficulties, and dangers to encounter in paying them my visits; yet I have had my pleasures as I went along, in shaking their friendly hands, that never had felt the contaminating touch of *money*, or the withering embrace of pockets; I have shared the comforts of their hospitable wigwams, and always have been preserved unharmed in their country. And if I have spoken, or am to speak of them, with a seeming bias, the reader will know what allowance to make for me, who am standing as the champion of a people, who have treated me kindly, of whom I feel bound to speak well; and who have no means of speaking for themselves.

Of the dead, to speak kindly, and to their character to render justice, is always a praiseworthy act; but it is yet far more charitable to extend the hand of liberality, or to hold the scale of justice, to the *living* who are able to feel the benefit of it. Justice to the dead is generally a charity, inasmuch as it is a kindness to living friends; but to the poor Indian dead, if it is meted out at all, which is seldom the case, it is thrown to the grave with him, where he has generally gone without friends left behind him to inherit the little fame that is reluctantly allowed him while living, and much less likely to be awarded to him when dead. Of the thousands and millions, therefore, of these poor fellows who are dead, and whom we have thrown into their graves, there is nothing that I could now say, that would do them any good, or that would not answer the world as well at a future time as at the present; while there is a debt that we are owing to those of them who are yet living, which I think justly demands our attention, and all our sympathies at this moment.

The peculiar condition in which we are obliged to contemplate these most unfortunate people at this time—hastening to destruction and extinction, as they evidently are, lays an uncompromising claim upon the sympathies of the civilized world, and gives a deep interest and value to such records as are truly made—setting up, and perpetuating from the life, their true native character and customs.

If the great family of North American Indians were all dying by a scourge or epidemic of the country, it would be natural, and a virtue, to weep for them; but merely to sympathize with them (and but partially to do that) when they are dying at our hands, and rendering their glebe to our possession, would be to subvert the simplest law of Nature, and turn civilized man, with all his boasted virtues, back to worse than savage barbarism.

Justice to a nation who are dying, need never be expected from the hands of their destroyers; and where injustice and injury are visited upon the weak and defenceless, from ten thousand hands—from Governments—monopolies and individuals—the offence is lost in the inseverable iniquity in which all join, and for which nobody is answerable, unless it be for their respective amounts, at a final day of retribution.

Long and cruel experience has well proved that it is impossible for enlightened Governments or money-making individuals to deal with these credulous and unsophisticated people, without the sin of injustice; but the humble biographer or historian, who goes amongst them from a different motive, *may* come out of their country with his hands and his conscience clean, and himself an anomaly, a white man dealing with Indians, and meting out justice to them; which I hope it may be my good province to do with my pen and my brush, with which, at least, I will have the singular and valuable satisfaction of having done them no harm.

With this view, and a desire to render justice to my readers also, I have much yet to say of the general 'appearance and character of the Indians—of their condition and treatment; and far more, I fear, than I can allot to the little space I have designed for the completion of these epistles.

Of the *general appearance* of the North American Indians, much might be yet said, that would be new and instructive. In *stature*, as I have already said, there are some of the tribes that are considerably above the ordinary height of man, and others that are evidently below it; allowing their average to be about equal to that of their fellow-men in the civilized world. In girth they are less, and lighter in their limbs, and almost entirely free from corpulency or useless flesh. Their bones are lighter, their skulls are thinner, and their muscles less hard than those of their civilized neighbours, excepting in the legs and feet, where they are brought into more continual action by their violent exercise on foot and on horseback, which swells the muscles and gives them great strength in those limbs, which is often quite as conspicuous as the extraordinary development of muscles in the shoulders and arms of our labouring men.

Although the Indians are generally narrow in the shoulders, and less powerful with the arms, yet it does not always happen by any means, that they are so effeminate as they look, and so widely inferior in brachial strength, as the spectator is apt to believe, from the smooth and rounded appearance of their limbs. The contrast between one of our labouring men when he denudes his limbs, and the figure of a naked Indian is to be sure very striking, and entirely too much so, for the actual difference in the power of the two persons. There are several reasons for this which account for so disproportionate a contrast, and should be named.

The labouring man, who is using his limbs the greater part of his life in lifting heavy weights, &c. sweats them with the weight of clothes which he has on him, which softens the integuments and the flesh, leaving the muscles to stand out in more conspicuous relief when they are exposed ; whilst the Indian, who exercises his limbs for the most of his life, denuded and exposed to the air, gets over his muscles a thicker and more compact layer of integuments which hide them from the view, leaving the casual spectator, who sees them only at rest, to suppose them too decidedly inferior to those which are found amongst people of his own colour. Of muscular strength in the legs, I have met many of the most extraordinary instances in the Indian country, that ever I have seen .in my life ; and I have watched and studied such for hours together, with utter surprise and admiration, in the violent exertions of their dances, where they leap and jump with every nerve strung, and every muscle swelled, till their legs will often look like a bundle of ropes, rather than a mass of human flesh. And from all that I have seen, I am inclined to say, that whatever differences there may be between the North American Indians and their civilized neighbours in the above respects, they are decidedly the results of different habits of life and modes of education rather than of any difference in constitution. And I would also venture the assertion, that he who would see the Indian in a condition to judge of his muscles, must see him in motion ; and he who would get a perfect study for an Hercules or an Atlas, should take a stone-mason for the upper part of his figure, and a Camanchee or a Blackfoot Indian from the waist downwards to the feet.

There is a general and striking character in the facial outline of the North American Indians, which is bold and free, and would seem at once to stamp them as distinct from natives of other parts of the world. Their noses are generally prominent and aquiline—and the whole face, if divested of paint and of copper-colour, would seem to approach to the bold and European character. Many travellers have thought that their eyes were smaller than those of Europeans ; and there is good cause for one to believe so, if he judges from first impressions, without taking pains to inquire into the truth and causes of things. I have been struck, as most travellers, no doubt have, with the want of expansion and apparent smallness of the Indians' eyes, which I have found upon examination, to be principally the effect of continual exposure to the rays of the sun and the wind, without the shields that are used by the civilized world ; and also when in-doors, and free from those causes, subjected generally to one more distressing, and calculated to produce similar results, the smoke that almost continually hangs about their wigwams, which necessarily contracts the lids of the eyes, forbidding that full flame and expansion of the eye, that the cool and clear shades of our civilized domicils are calculated to promote.

The teeth of the Indians are generally regular and sound, and wonderfully preserved to old age, owing, no doubt, to the fact that they live without the spices of life—without saccharine and without salt, which are equally destructive to teeth, in civilized communities. Their teeth, though sound, are not white, having a yellowish cast ; but for the same reason that a negro's teeth are "like ivory," they look white—set as they are in bronze, as any one with a *tolerable* set of teeth can easily test, by painting his face the colour of an Indian, and grinning for a moment in his looking-glass.

Beards they generally have not—esteeming them great vulgarities, and using every possible means to eradicate them whenever they are so unfortunate as to be annoyed with them. Different writers have been very much at variance on this subject ever since the first accounts given of these people; and there seems still an unsatisfied curiosity on the subject, which I would be glad to say that I could put entirely at rest.

From the best information that I could obtain amongst forty-eight tribes that I have visited, I feel authorized to say, that, amongst the wild tribes, where they have made no efforts to imitate white men, at least, the proportion of eighteen out of twenty, by nature are entirely without the appearance of a beard; and of the very few who have them by nature, nineteen out of twenty eradicate it by plucking it out several times in succession, precisely at the age of puberty, when its growth is successfully arrested; and occasionally one may be seen, who has omitted to destroy it at that time, and subjects his chin to the repeated pains of its extractions, which he is performing with a pair of clamshells or other tweezers, nearly every day of his life—and occasionally again, but still more rarely, one is found, who from carelessness or inclination has omitted both of these, and is allowing it to grow to the length of an inch or two on his chin, in which case it is generally very soft, and exceedingly sparse. Wherever there is a cross of the blood with the European or African, which is frequently the case along the Frontier, a proportionate beard is the result; and it is allowed to grow, or is plucked out with much toil, and with great pain.

There has been much speculation, and great variety of opinions, as to the results of the intercourse between the European and African population with the Indians on the borders; and I would not undertake to decide so difficult a question, though I cannot help but express my opinion, which is made up from the vast many instances that I have seen, that generally speaking, these half-breed specimens are in both instances a decided deterioration from the two stocks, from which they have sprung; which I grant may be the consequence that generally flows from illicit intercourse, and from the inferior rank in which they are held by both, (which is mostly confined to the lowest and most degraded portions of society), rather than from any constitutional objection, necessarily growing out of the amalgamation.

The finest built and most powerful men that I have ever yet seen, have been some of the last-mentioned, the negro and the North American Indian mixed, of equal blood. These instances are rare to be sure, yet are occasionally to be found amongst the Seminolees and Cherokees, and also amongst the Camanchees, even, and the Caddoes; and I account for it in this way: From the slave-holding States to the heart of the country of a wild tribe of Indians, through almost boundless and impassable wilds and swamps, for hundreds of miles, it requires a negro of extraordinary leg and courage and perseverance, to travel; absconding from his master's fields, to throw himself into a tribe of wild and hostile Indians, for the enjoyment of his liberty; of which there are occasional instances, and when they succeed, they are admired by the savage; and as they come with a good share of the tricks and arts of civilization, they are at once looked upon by the tribe, as extraordinary and important personages; and generally marry the daughters of chiefs, thus uniting theirs with the best blood in the nation, which produce these remarkably fine and powerful men that I have spoken of above.

Although the Indians of North America, where dissipation and disease have not got amongst them, undoubtedly are a longer lived and healthier race, and capable of enduring far more bodily privation and pain, than civilized people can; yet I do not believe that the differences are constitutional, or anything more than the results of different circumstances, and a different education. As an evidence in support of this assertion, I will allude to the hundreds of men whom I have seen, and travelled with, who have been for several years together in the Rocky Mountains, in the employment of the Fur Companies; where they have lived exactly upon the Indian system, continually exposed to the open air, and the weather, and, to all the disappointments and privations peculiar to that mode of life; and I am bound to say, that I never saw a more hardy and healthy race of men in my life, whilst they remain in the country; nor any who fall to pieces quicker when they get back to confined and dissipated life, which they easily fall into, when they return to their own country.

The Indian women who are obliged to lead lives of severe toil and drudgery, become exceedingly healthy and robust, giving easy birth and strong constitutions to their children; which, in a measure, may account for the simplicity and fewness of their diseases, which in infancy and childhood are very seldom known to destroy life.

If there were anything like an equal proportion of deaths amongst the Indian children, that is found in the civilized portions of the world, the Indian country would long since have been depopulated, on account of the decided disproportion of children they produce. It is a very rare occurrence for an Indian woman to be "*blessed*" with more than four or five children during her life; and generally speaking, they seem contented with two or three; when in civilized communities it is no uncommon thing for a woman to be the mother of ten or twelve, and sometimes to bear two or even three at a time; of which I never recollect to have met an instance during all my extensive travels in the Indian country, though it is possible that I might occasionally have passed them.

For so striking a dissimilarity as there evidently is between these people, and those living according to the more artificial modes of life, in a subject, seemingly alike natural to both, the reader will perhaps expect me to furnish some rational and decisive causes. Several very plausible reasons have been advanced for such a deficiency on the part of the Indians, by authors who have written on the subject, but whose opinions I should be very slow to adopt; inasmuch as they have been based upon the Indian's inferiority, (as the same authors have taken great pains to prove in most other respects,) to their pale-faced neighbours.

I know of but one decided cause for this difference, which I would venture to advance, and which I confidently believe to be the principal obstacle to a more rapid increase of their families; which is the very great length of time that the women submit to lactation, generally carrying their children at the breast to the age of two, and sometimes three, and even four years!

The astonishing ease and success with which the Indian women pass through the most painful and most trying of all human difficulties, which fall exclusively to the lot of the gentler sex; is quite equal, I have found from continued enquiry, to the representations that have often been made to the world by other travellers, who have gone before me. Many people have thought this a wise provision of Nature, in framing the constitutions of these people, to suit the exigencies of their exposed lives, where they are beyond the pale of skilful surgeons, and the nice little comforts that visit the sick beds in the enlightened world; but I never have been willing to give to Nature quite so much credit, for stepping aside of her own rule, which I believe to be about half way between—from which I am inclined to think that the refinements of art, and its spices, have led the civilized world into the pains and perils of one unnatural extreme; whilst the extraordinary fatigue and exposure, and habits of Indian life, have greatly released them from natural pains, on the other. With this view of the case, I fully believe that Nature has dealt everywhere impartially; and that, if from their child-hood, our mothers had, like the Indian women, carried loads like beasts of burthen—and those over the longest journeys, and highest mountains—had swam the broadest rivers—and galloped about for months and even years of their lives, *astride* of their horse's backs; we should have taxed them as lightly in stepping into the world, as an Indian pappoose does its mother, who ties her horse under the shade of a tree for half an hour, and before night, overtakes her travelling companions with her infant in her arms, which has often been the case.

As to the probable origin of the North American Indians, which is one of the first questions that suggests itself to the enquiring mind, and will be perhaps, the last to be settled; I shall have little to say in this place, for the reason that so abstruse a subject, and one so barren of positive proof, would require in its discussion too much circumstantial evidence for my allowed limits; which I am sure the world will agree will be filled up much more consistently with the avowed spirit of this work, by treating of that which admits of an abundance of proof—their actual existence, their customs—and misfortunes ; and the suggestions of modes for the amelioration of their condition.

For a professed philanthropist, I should deem it cruel and hypocritical to waste time and space in the discussion of a subject, ever so interesting, (though unimportant), when the present condition and prospects of these people are calling so loudly upon the world for justice, and for mercy ; and when their evanescent existence and customs are turning, as it were, on a wheel before us, but soon to be lost ; whilst the mystery of their origin can as well be fathomed at a future day as now, and recorded with their exit.

Very many people look upon the savages of this vast country, as an " *Anomaly in Nature* ;" and their existence and origin, and locality, things that needs must be at once accounted for.

Now, if the world will allow me, (and perhaps they may think me singular for saying it), I would say, that these things are, in my opinion, natural and simple ; and, like all other works of Nature, destined to remain a mystery to mortal man ; and if man be anywhere entitled to the name of an anomaly, it is he who has departed the farthest from the simple walks and actions of his nature.

It seems natural to enquire at once who these people are, and from whence they came ; but this question is natural, only because we are out of nature. To an Indian, such a question would seem absurd—he would stand aghast and astounded at the *anomaly* before *him*—himself upon his own ground, " where the Great Spirit made him"—hunting in his own forests ; if an exotic, with a " pale face," and from across the ocean, should stand before him, to ask him where he came from, and how he got there !

I would invite this querist, this votary of science, to sit upon a log with his red acquaintance, and answer the following questions :—

" You white man, where you come from ?"

" From England, across the water."

" How white man come to see England ? how you face come to get white, ha ?"

I never yet have been made to see the *necessity* of showing how these people *came here*, or that they *came here* at all ; which might easily have been done, by the way of Behring's Straits from the North of Asia. I should much rather dispense with such a *necessity*, than undertake the other necessities that must follow the establishment of this ; those of showing how the savages paddled or drifted in their canoes from this Continent, after they had got here, or from the Asiatic Coast, and landed on all the South Sea Islands, which we find to be inhabited nearly to the South Pole. For myself, I am quite satisfied with the fact, which is a thing certain, and to be relied on, that this Continent was found peopled in every part, by savages ; and so, nearly every Island in the South Seas, at the distance of several thousand miles from either Continent ; and I am quite willing to surrender the mystery to abler pens than my own—to theorists who may have the time, and the means to prove to the world, how those rude people wandered there in their bark canoes, without water for their subsistence, or compasses to guide them on their way.

The North American Indians, and all the inhabitants of the South Sea Islands, speaking some two or three hundred different languages, entirely dissimilar, may have all sprung from one stock ; and the Almighty, after creating man, for some reason that is unfathomable to human wisdom, might have left the whole vast universe, with its severed continents, and its thousand distant isles everywhere teeming with necessaries and luxuries, spread out for man's use ; and there to vegetate and rot, for hundreds and even thousands of centuries, until ultimate, *abstract* accident should throw him amongst these infinite mysteries of creation ; the least and most insignificant of which have been created and placed by design. Human reason is weak, and human ignorance is palpable, when man attempts to approach these unsearchable mysteries ; and I consider human discretion well applied, when it beckons him back to things that he can comprehend ; where his reason, and all his mental energies can be employed for the advancement and benefit of his species. With this conviction, I feel disposed to retreat to the ground that I have before occupied—to the Indians, *as* they are, and *where* they are ; recording amongst them living evidences whilst they live, for the use of abler theorists than myself—who may labour to establish their origin, which may be as well (and perhaps better) done, a century hence, than at the present day.

The reader is apprised, that I have nearly filled the limits allotted to these epistles ; and I assure him that a vast deal which I have seen must remain untold—whilst from the same necessity, I must tell him much less than I think, and beg to be pardoned if I withhold, till some future occasion, many of my reasons for, *thinking.*

I believe, with many others, that the North American Indians are a mixed people—that they have Jewish blood in their veins, though I would not assert, as some have undertaken to prove, " *that they are Jews,*" or that they are "*the ten lost tribes of Israel.*" From the character and conformation of their heads, I am compelled to look upon them as an amalgam race, but still savages ; and from many of their customs, which seem to me, to be peculiarly Jewish, as well as from the character of their heads, I am forced to believe that some part of those ancient tribes, who have been dispersed by Christians in so many ways, and in so many different eras, have found their way to this country, where they have entered amongst the native stock, and have lived and intermarried with the Indians, until their identity has been swallowed up and lost in the greater numbers of their new acquaintance, save the bold and decided character which they have bequeathed to the Indian races ; and such of their customs as the Indians were pleased to adopt, and which they have preserved to the present day.

I am induced to believe thus from the very many customs which I have witnessed amongst them, that appear to be decidedly Jewish ; and many of them so peculiarly so, that it would seem almost impossible, or at all events, exceedingly improbable, that two people in a state of nature should have hit upon them, and practiced them exactly alike.

The world need not expect me to *decide* so interesting and difficult a question ; but I am sure they will be disposed to hear simply my opinion, which I give in this place, quite briefly, and with the utmost respectful deference to those who think differently. I claim no merit whatever, for advancing such an opinion, which is not new, having been in several works advanced to the world by far abler pens than my own, with volumes of evidence, to the catalogue of which, I feel quite sure I shall be able to add some new proofs in the proper place. If I could establish the fact by positive proof, I should claim a great deal of applause from the world, and should, no doubt, obtain it ; but, like everything relating to the origin and early history of these unchronicled people, I believe this question is one that will never be settled, but will remain open for the opinions of the world, which will be variously given, and that upon circumstantial evidence alone.

I am compelled to believe that the Continent of America, and each of the other Continents, have had their aboriginal stocks, peculiar in colour and in character—and that each of these native stocks has undergone repeated mutations (at periods, of which history has kept no records), by erratic colonies from abroad, that have been engrafted upon them—mingling with them, and materially affecting their original character. By this process, I believe that the North American Indians, even where we find them in their wildest condition, are several degrees removed from their original character ; and that one of their principal alloys has been a part of those dispersed people, who have mingled their blood and their customs with them. and even in their new disguise, seem destined to be followed up with oppression and endless persecution.

The first and most striking fact amongst the North American Indians that refers us to the Jews, is that of their worshipping in all parts, the Great Spirit, or Jehovah, as the Hebrews were ordered to do by Divine precept, instead of a plurality of gods, as ancient pagans and heathens did—and their idols of their own formation. The North American Indians, are nowhere *idolaters*—they appeal at once to the Great Spirit, and know of no mediator, either personal or symbolical.

The Indian tribes are everywhere divided into bands, with chiefs, symbols, badges, &c., and many of their modes of worship I have found exceedingly like those of the Mosaic institution. The Jews had their *sanctum sanctorums*, and so may it be said the Indians have, in their council or medicine-houses, which are always held as sacred places. As the Jews had, they have their high-priests and their prophets. Amongst the Indians as amongst the ancient Hebrews, the women are not allowed to worship with the men—and in all cases also, they eat separately. The Indians everywhere, like the Jews, believe that they are the favourite people of the Great Spirit, and they are certainly, like those ancient people, *persecuted*, as every man's hand seems raised against them—and they, like the Jews, destined to be dispersed over the world, and seemingly scourged by the Almighty, and despised of man.

In their marriages, the Indians, as did the ancient Jews, uniformly buy their wives by giving presents—and in many tribes, very closely resemble them in other forms and ceremonies of their marriages.

In their preparations for war, and in peace-making, they are strikingly similar. In their treatment of the sick, burial of the dead and mourning, they are also similar.

In their bathing and ablutions, at all seasons of the year, as a part of their religious observances—having separate places for men and women to perform these immersions—they resemble again. And the custom amongst the women, of absenting themselves during the lunar influences, is exactly consonant to the Mosaic law. This custom of *separation* is an uniform one amongst the different tribes, as far as I have seen them in their primitive state, and be it Jewish, natural or conventional, it is an indispensable form with these wild people, who are setting to the civilized world, this and many other examples of decency and propriety, only to be laughed at by their wiser neighbours, who, rather than award to the red man any merit for them, have taken exceeding pains to call them but the results of ignorance and superstition.

So, in nearly every family of a tribe, will be found a small lodge, large enough to contain one person, which is erected at a little distance from the family lodge, and occupied by the wife or the daughter, to whose possession circumstances allot it; where she dwells alone until she is prepared to move back, and in the meantime the touch of her hand or her finger to the chief's lodge, or his gun, or other article of his household, consigns it to destruction at once ; and in case of non-conformity to this indispensable form, a woman's life may, in some tribes, be answerable for misfortunes that happen to individuals or the tribe, in the interim.

After this season of separation, *purification* in running water, and *anointing*, precisely in accordance with the Jewish command, is requisite before she can enter the family lodge. Such is one of the extraordinary observances amongst these people in their wild state ; but along the Frontier, where white people have laughed at them for their forms, they have departed from this, as from nearly everything else that is native and original about them.

In their *feasts, fastings* and *sacrificing*, they are exceedingly like those ancient people. Many of them have a feast closely resembling the annual feast of the Jewish passover ; and amongst others, an occasion much like the Israelitish feast of the tabernacles, which lasted eight days, (when history tells us they carried bundles of *willow boughs*, and fasted several days and nights) making sacrifices of the first fruits and best of everything, closely resembling the sin-offering and peace-offering of the Hebrews.*

These, and many others of their customs would seem to be decidedly Jewish ; yet it is for the world to decide how many of them, or whether all of them, might be natural to all people, and, therefore, as well practiced by these people in a state of nature, as to have been borrowed from a foreign nation.

Amongst the list of their customs however, we meet a number which had their origin it would seem, in the Jewish Ceremonial code, and which are so very *peculiar* in their forms, that it would seem quite improbable, and almost impossible, that two different people should ever have hit upon them alike, without some knowledge of each other. These I consider, go farther than anything else as evidence, and carry, in my mind, conclusive proof that these people are tinctured with Jewish blood ; even though the Jewish sabbath has been lost, and circumcision probably rejected ; and dog's flesh, which was an abomination to the Jews, continued to be eaten at their feasts by all the tribes of Indians ; not because the Jews have been prevailed upon to use it, but, because they have survived only, as their blood was mixed with that of the Indians, and the Indians have imposed on that mixed blood the same rules and regulations that governed the members of the tribes in general.

Many writers are of opinion, that the natives of America are all from one stock, and their languages from one root—that that stock is exotic, and that that language was introduced with it. And the reason assigned for this theory is, that amongst the various tribes, there is a reigning similarity in looks —and in their languages a striking resemblance to each other.

Now, if all the world were to argue in this way, I should reason just in the other ; and pronounce this, though evidence to a certain degree, to be very far from conclusive, inasmuch as it is far easier and more natural for distinct tribes, or languages, grouped and used together, to *assimilate* than to *dissimilate ;* as the pebbles on a sea-shore, that are washed about and jostled together, lose their angles, and incline at last to one rounded and uniform shape. So that if there had been, *ab origine,* a variety of different stocks in America, with different complexions, with different characters and customs, and of different statures, and speaking entirely different tongues ; where they have been for a series of centuries living neighbours to each other, moving about and intermarrying ; I think we might reasonably look for quite as great a similarity in their personal appearance and languages, as we now find : when, on the other hand, if we are to suppose that they were all from one foreign stock, with but one language, it is a difficult thing to conceive how

* See the four days' religious ceremonies of the Mandans, and use of the willow boughs, and sacrifices of fingers, &c. in Vol. I. pp. 159. 170; and also the custom of war-chiefs wearing horns on their head-dresses, like the Israelitish chiefs of great renown, Vol. I. p. 104.

or in what space of time, or for what purpose, they could have formed so many tongues, and so widely different, as those that are now spoken on the Continent.

It is evident I think, that if an island or continent had been peopled with black, white and red ; a succession of revolving centuries of intercourse amongst these different colours would have had a tendency to bring them to one standard complexion, when no computable space of time, nor any conceivable circumstances could restore them again ; re-producing all, or either of the distinct colours, from the compound.

That *customs* should be found similar, or many of them exactly the same, on the most opposite parts of the Continent, is still less surprising ; for these will travel more rapidly, being more easily taught at Treaties and festivals between hostile bands, or disseminated by individuals travelling through neighbouring tribes, whilst languages and blood require more time for their ad-. mixture.

That the languages of the North American Indians, should be found to be so numerous at this day, and so very many of them radically different, is a subject of great surprise, and unaccountable, whether these people are derived from one individual stock, or from one hundred, or one thousand.

Though languages like colour and like customs, are calculated to assimilate, under the circumstances above named ; yet it is evident that, (if derived from a variety of sources), they have been unaccountably kept more distinct than the others ; and if from one root, have still more unaccountably dissimilated and divided into at least one hundred and fifty, two-thirds of which, I venture to say, are entirely and radically distinct ; whilst amongst the people who speak them, there is a reigning similarity in looks, in features and in customs, which would go very far to pronounce them one family, by nature or by convention.

I do not believe, with some very learned and distinguished writers, that the languages of the North American Indians can be traced to one root or to three or four, or any number of distinct idioms ; nor do I believe all, or any one of them, will ever be fairly traced to a foreign origin.

If the looks and customs of the Jews, are decidedly found and identified with these people—and also those of the Japanese, and Calmuc Tartars, I think we have but little, if any need of looking for the Hebrew language, or either of the others, for the reasons that I have already given ; for the feeble colonies of these, or any other foreign people that might have fallen by accident upon the shores of this great Continent, or who might have approached it by Behring's Straits, have been too feeble to give a language to fifteen or twenty millions of people, or in fact to any portion of them ; being in all probability, in great part cut to pieces and destroyed by a natural foe ; leaving enough perhaps, who had intermarried, to innoculate their blood and their customs ; which have run, like a drop in a bucket, and slightly tinctured the character of tribes who have sternly resisted their languages, which would naturally, under such circumstances, have made but very little impression.

Such I consider the condition of the Jews in North America; and perhaps the Scandanavians, and the followers of Madoc, who by some means, and some period that I cannot name, have thrown themselves upon the shores of this country, and amongst the ranks of the savages; where, from destructive wars with their new neighbours, they have been overpowered, and perhaps, with the exception of those who had intermarried, they have been destroyed, yet leaving amongst the savages decided marks of their character; and many of their peculiar customs, which had pleased, and been adopted by the savages, while they had sternly resisted others: and decidedly shut out and discarded their language, and of course obliterated everything of their history.

That there should often be found contiguous to each other, several tribes speaking dialects of the same language, is a matter of no surprise at all; and wherever such is the case, there is resemblance enough also, in looks and customs, to show that they are parts of the same tribes, which have comparatively recently severed and wandered apart, as their traditions will generally show; and such resemblances are often found and traced, nearly across the Continent, and have been accounted for in some of my former Letters. Several very learned gentlemen, whose opinions I would treat with the greatest respect, have supposed that all the native languages of America were traceable to three or four roots; a position which I will venture to say will be an exceedingly difficult one for them to maintain, whilst remaining at home and consulting books, in the way that too many theories are supported; and one infinitely more difficult to prove if they travel amongst the different tribes, and collect their own information as they travel.*
I am quite certain that I have found in a number of instances, tribes who have long lived neighbours to each other, and who, from continued intercourse, had learned mutually, many words of each others language, and adopted them for common use or mottoes, as often, or oftener than we introduce the French or Latin phrases in our conversation; from which the casual visitor

* For the satisfaction of the reader, I have introduced in the Appendix to this Volume, Letter B, a brief vocabulary of the languages of several adjoining tribes in the North West, from which, by turning to it, they can easily draw their own inferences. These words have all been written down by myself, from the Indian's mouths, as they have been correctly translated to me; and I think it will at once be decided, that there is very little affinity or resemblance, if any, between them. I have therein given a sample of the Blackfoot language, yet, of that immense tribe who all class under the name of Blackfoot, there are the Cotonnés and the Grosventres des Prairies—whose languages are entirely distinct from this—and also from each other—and in the same region, and neighbours to them, are also the Chayennes—the Knisteneaux, the Crows, the Shoshonees, and Pawnees; all of whose languages are as distinct, and as widely different, as those that I have given. These facts, I think, without my going further, will fully show the entire dissimilarity between these languages, and support me to a certain extent, at all events, in the opinion I have advanced above.

to one of these tribes, might naturally suppose there was a similarity in their languages; when a closer examiner would find that the idioms and structure of the several languages were entirely distinct.

I believe that in this way, the world who take but a superficial glance at them, are, and will be, led into continual error on this interesting subject ; one that invites, and well deserves from those learned gentlemen, a fair investigation by them, *on the spot ;* rather than so limited and feeble an examination as *I* have been able to make of it, or that *they, can* make, in their parlours, at so great a distance from them, and through such channels as they are obliged to look to for their information.

Amongst the tribes that I have visited, I consider that thirty, out of the forty-eight, are distinct and radically different in their languages, and eighteen are dialects of some three or four. It is a very simple thing for the off-hand theorists of the scientific world, who do not go near these people, to arrange and classify them ; and a very clever thing to *simplify* the subject. and bring it, like everything else, under three or four heads, and to solve, and resolve it, by as many simple rules.

I do not pretend to be able to give to this subject, or to that of the probable origin of these people, the close investigation that these interesting subjects require and deserve ; yet I have travelled and observed enough amongst them, and collected enough, to enable me to form decided opinions of my own ; and in my conviction, have acquired confidence enough to tell them, and at the same time to recommend to the Government or institutions of my own country, to employ men of science, such as I have mentioned, and protect them in their *visits to* these tribes, where " the truth, and the whole truth" may be got ; and the languages of all the tribes that are yet in existence, (many of which are just now gasping them out in their last breath,) may be snatched and preserved from oblivion ; as well as their *looks* and their *customs,* to the preservation of which *my* labours have been principally devoted.

I undertake to say to such gentlemen, who are enthusiastic and qualified, that here is one of the most interesting subjects that they could spend the energies of their valuable lives upon, and one the most sure to secure for them that immortality for which it is natural and fair for all men to look.

From what has been said in the foregoing Letters, it will have been seen that there are three divisions under which the North American Indians may be justly considered; those who are dead—those who are dying, and those who are yet living and flourishing in their primitive condition. Of the *dead,* I have little to say at present, and I can render them no service—of the *living,* there is much to be said, and I shall regret that the prescribed limits of these epistles, will forbid me saying all that I desire to say of them and their condition.

The present condition of these once numerous people, contrasted with what it was, and what it is soon to be, is a subject of curious interest, as well as some importance, to the civilized world—a subject well entitled to the attention, and very justly commanding the sympathies of, enlightened communities. There are abundant proofs recorded in the history of this country, and to which I need not at this time more particularly refer, to shew that this very numerous and respectable part of the human family, which occupied the different parts of North America, at the time of its first settlement by the Anglo-Americans, contained more than fourteen millions, who have been reduced since that time, and undoubtedly in consequence of that settlement, to something less than two millions !

This is a startling fact, and one which carries with it, if it be the truth, other facts and their results, which are equally startling, and such as every inquiring mind should look into. The first deduction that the mind draws from such premises, is the rapid declension of these people, which must at that rate be going on at this day; and sooner or later, lead to the most melancholy result of their final extinction.

Of this sad termination of their existence, there need not be a doubt in the minds of any man who will read the history of their former destruction; contemplating them swept already from two-thirds of the Continent; and who will then travel as I have done, over the vast extent of Frontier, and witness the modes by which the poor fellows are falling, whilst contending for their rights, with acquisitive white men. Such a reader, and such a traveller, I venture to say, if he has not the heart of a brute, will shed tears for them; and be ready to admit that their character and customs, are at *this time*, a subject of interest and importance, and rendered peculiarly so from the facts that they are dying *at the hands* of their Christian neighbours; and, from all past experience, that there will probably be no effectual plan instituted, that will save the remainder of them from a similar fate. As they stand at this day, there may be four or five hundred thousand in their primitive state; and a million and a half, that may be said to be semi-civilized, contending with the sophistry of white men, amongst whom they are timidly and unsuccessfully endeavouring to hold up their heads, and aping their modes; whilst they are swallowing their poisons, and yielding their lands and their lives, to the superior tact and cunning of their merciless cajolers.

In such parts of their community, their customs are uninteresting; being but poor and ridiculous imitations of those that are *bad enough*, those practiced by their first teachers—but in their primitive state, their modes of life and character, before they are changed, are subjects of curious interest, and all that I have aimed to preserve. Their personal appearance, their dress, and many of their modes of life, I have already described.

For their Government, which is purely such as has been dictated to them by Nature and necessity alone, they are indebted to no foreign, native or civilized nation. For their religion, which is simply Theism, they are indebted to the Great Spirit, and not to the Christian world. For their modes of war, they owe nothing to enlightened nations—using only those weapons and those modes which are prompted by nature, and within the means of their rude manufactures.

If, therefore, we do not find in their systems of polity and jurisprudence, the efficacy and justice that are dispensed in civilized institutions—if we do not find in their religion the light and the grace that flow from Christian faith—if in wars they are less honourable, and wage them upon a system of "*murderous stratagem,*" it is the duty of the enlightened world, who administer justice in a better way—who worship in a more acceptable form—and who war on a more *honourable* scale, to make great allowance for their ignorance, and yield to their credit, the fact, that if their systems are less wise, they are often more free from injustice—from hypocrisy and from carnage.

Their Governments, if they have any (for I am almost disposed to question the propriety of applying the term), are generally alike ; each tribe having at its head, a chief (and most generally a war and civil chief), whom it would seem, alternately hold the ascendency, as the circumstances of peace or war may demand their respective services. These chiefs, whose titles are generally hereditary, hold their offices only as long as their ages will enable them to perform the duties of them by taking the lead in war-parties, &c., after which they devolve upon the next incumbent, who is the eldest son of the chief, provided he is decided by the other chiefs to be as worthy of it as any other young man in the tribe—in default of which, a chief is elected from amongst the sub-chiefs ; so that the office is *hereditary on condition,* and *elective* in *emergency.*

The chief has no controul over the life or limbs, or liberty of his subjects, nor other power whatever, excepting that of *influence* which he gains by his virtues, and his exploits in war, and which induces his warriors and braves to follow him, as he leads them to battle—or to listen to him when he speaks and advises in council. In fact, he is no more than a *leader,* whom every young warrior may follow, or turn about and go back from, as he pleases, if he is willing to meet the disgrace that awaits him, who deserts his chief in the hour of danger.

It may be a difficult question to decide, whether their Government savours most of a democracy or an aristocracy ; it is in some respects purely democratic—and in others aristocratic. The influence of names and families is strictly kept up, and their qualities and relative distinctions preserved in heraldric family Arms ; yet entirely severed, and free from influences of wealth, which is seldom amassed by any persons in Indian communities ; and most sure to slip from the hands of chiefs, or others high in office, who are looked upon to be liberal and charitable ; and oftentimes, for the sake of popularity, render themselves the poorest, and most meanly dressed and equipped of any in the tribe.

These people have no written laws, nor others, save the penalties affixed to certain crimes, by long-standing custom, or by the decisions of the chiefs in council, who form a sort of Court and Congress too, for the investigation of crimes, and transaction of the public business. For the sessions of these dignitaries, each tribe has, in the middle of their village, a Government or council-house, where the chiefs often try and convict, for capital offences— leaving the punishment to be inflicted by the nearest of kin, to whom all eyes of the nation are turned, and who has no means of evading it without suffering disgrace in his tribe. For this purpose, the custom, which is the common law of the land, allows him to use any means whatever, that he may deem necessary to bring the thing effectually about ; and he is allowed to *waylay* and shoot down the criminal—so that punishment is *certain* and *cruel,* and as effective from the hands of a feeble, as from those of a stout man, and entirely beyond the hope that often arises from the " glorious un- certainty of the law."

As I have in a former place said, cruelty is one of the leading traits of the Indian's character ; and a little familiarity with their modes of life and govern- ment will soon convince the reader, that *certainty* and *cruelty* in punish- ments are requisite (where individuals undertake to inflict the penalties of the laws), in order to secure the lives and property of individuals in society.

In the treatment of their prisoners also, in many tribes, they are in the habit of inflicting the most appalling tortures, for which the enlightened world are apt to condemn them as cruel and unfeeling in the extreme ; with- out stopping to learn that in every one of these instances, these cruelties are practiced by way of retaliation, by individuals or families of the tribe, whose relatives have been previously dealt with in a similar way by their enemies, and whose *manes* they deem it their duty to appease by this horrid and cruel mode of retaliation.

And in justice to the savage, the reader should yet know, that amongst these tribes that torture their prisoners, these cruelties are practiced but upon the few whose lives are required to atone for those who have been similarly dealt with by their enemies, and that the *remainder are adopted into the tribe,* by marrying the widows whose husbands have fallen in battle, in which capacity they are received and respected like others of the tribe, and enjoy equal rights and immunities. And before we condemn them too far, we should yet pause and enquire whether in the enlightened world we are not guilty of equal cruelties—whether in the ravages and carnage of war, and treatment of prisoners, we practice any virtue superior to this ; and whether the annals of history which are familiar to all, do not furnish abundant proof of equal cruelty to prisoners of war, as well as in many instances, to the members of our own respective communities. It is a re- markable fact and one well recorded in history, as it deserves to be, to the honour of the savage, that no instance has been known of violence to their captive females, a virtue yet to be learned in civilized warfare.

If their punishments are certain and cruel, they have the merit of being

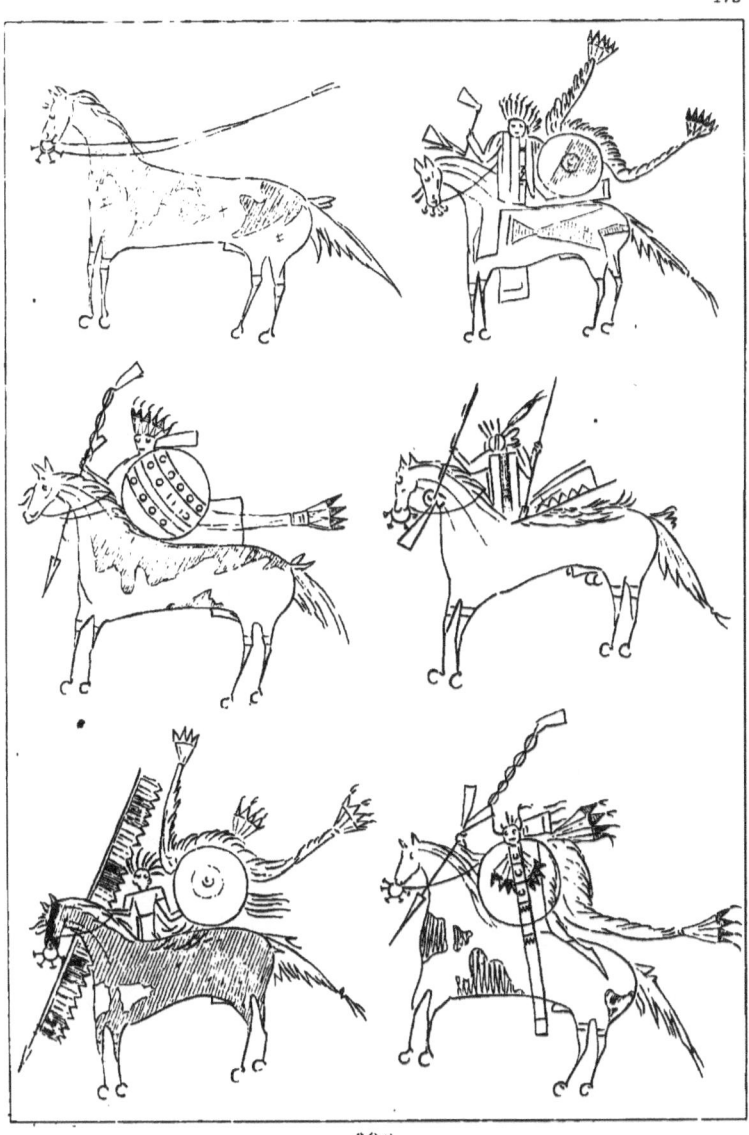

308

G. Catlin

few, and those confined chiefly to their enemies. It is natural to be cruel to enemies ; and in this, I do not see that the improvements of the enlightened and Christian world have yet elevated them so very much above the savage. To their friends, there are no people on earth that are more kind ; and cruelties and punishments (except for capital offences) are amongst themselves, entirely dispensed with. No man in their communities is subject to any restraints upon his liberty, or to any corporal or degrading punishment ; each one valuing his limbs, and his liberty to use them as his inviolable right, which no power in the tribe can deprive him of ; whilst each one holds the chief as amenable to him as the most humble individual in the tribe.

On an occasion when I had interrogated a Sioux chief, on the Upper Missouri, about their Government—their punishments and tortures of prisoners, for which I had freely condemned them for the cruelty of the practice, he took occasion when I had got through, to ask *me* some questions relative to modes in the *civilized world*, which, with his comments upon them, were nearly as follow ; and struck me, as I think they must every one, with great force.

" Among white people, nobody ever take your wife—take your children —take your mother, cut off nose—cut eyes out—burn to death ?" No ! "Then *you* no cut off nose—*you* no cut out eyes—*you* no burn to death— very good."

He also told me he had often heard that white people hung their criminals by the neck and choked them to death like dogs, and those their own people ; to which I answered, " yes." He then told me he had learned that they shut each other up in prisons, where they keep them a great part of their lives *because they can't pay money !* I replied in the affirmative to this, which occasioned great surprise and excessive laughter, even amongst the women. He told me that he had been to our Fort, at Council Bluffs, where we had a great many warriors and braves, and he saw three of them taken out on the prairies and tied to a post and whipped almost to death, and he had been told that they submit to all this to get a little money, " yes." He said he had been told, that when all the white people were born, their white *medicine-men* had to stand by and look on—that in the Indian country the women would not allow that—they would be ashamed— that he had been along the Frontier, and a good deal amongst the white people, and he had seen them whip their little children—a thing that is very cruel—he had heard also, from several white *medicine-men*, that the Great Spirit of the white people was the child of a white woman, and that he was at last put to death by the white people ! This seemed to be a thing that he had not been able to comprehend, and he concluded by saying, " the Indians' Great Spirit got no mother—the Indians no kill him, he never die." He put me a chapter of other questions, as to the trespasses of the white people on their lands—their continual corruption of the morals of their women —and digging open the Indians' graves to get their bones, &c. To all of which I was compelled to reply in the affirmative, and quite glad to close my note-book, and quietly to escape from the throng that had collected around me, and saying (though to myself and silently), that these and an hundred other vices belong to the civilized world, and are practiced upon (but certainly, in no instance, reciprocated by) the " cruel and relentless savage."

Of their modes of war, of which, a great deal has been written by other travellers—I could say much, but in the present place, must be brief. All wars, offensive or defensive, are decided on by the chiefs and doctors in council, where majority decides all questions. After their resolve, the chief conducts and leads—his pipe with the reddened stem is sent through the tribe by his *runners*, and every man who consents to go to war, draws the smoke once through its stem ; he is then a *volunteer*, like all of their soldiers in war, and bound by no compulsive power, except that of pride, and dread of the disgrace of turning back. After the soldiers are enlisted, the war-dance is performed in presence of the whole tribe ; when each warrior in warrior's dress, with weapons in hand, dances up separately, and striking the reddened post, thereby takes the solemn oath not to desert his party.

The chief leads in full dress to make himself as conspicuous a mark as possible for his enemy ; whilst his men are chiefly denuded, and their limbs and faces covered with red earth or vermilion, and oftentimes with charcoal and grease, so as completely to disguise them, even from the knowledge of many of their intimate friends.

At the close of hostilities, the two parties are often brought together by a flag of truce, where they sit in Treaty, and solemnize by smoking through the calumet or pipe of peace, as I have before described; and after that, their warriors and braves step forward, with the pipe of peace in the left hand, and the war-club in the right, and dance around in a circle—going through many curious and exceedingly picturesque evolutions in the "*pipe of peace dance.*"

To each other I have found these people kind and honourable, and endowed with every feeling of parental, of filial, and conjugal affection, that is met in more enlightened communities. I have found them moral and religious : and I am bound to give them great credit for their zeal, which is often exhibited in their modes of worship, however insufficient they may seem to us, or may be in the estimation of the Great Spirit.

I have heard it said by some very good men, and some who have even been preaching the Christian religion amongst them, that they have no religion—that all their zeal in their worship of the Great Spirit was but the foolish excess of ignorant superstition—that their humble devotions and supplications to the Sun and the Moon, where many of them suppose that the Great Spirit resides, were but the absurd rantings of idolatry. To such opinions as these I never yet gave answer, nor drew other instant inferences from them, than, that from the bottom of my heart, I pitied the persons who gave them.

I fearlessly assert to the world, (and I defy contradiction;) that the North American Indian is everywhere, in his native state, a highly moral and religious being, endowed by his Maker, with an intuitive knowledge of some great Author of his being, and the Universe; in dread of whose displeasure he constantly lives, with the apprehension before him, of a future state, where he expects to be rewarded or punished according to the merits he has gained or forfeited in this world.

I have made this a subject of unceasing enquiry during all my travels, and from every individual Indian with whom I have conversed on the subject, from the highest to the lowest and most pitiably ignorant, I have received evidence enough, as well as from their numerous and humble modes of worship, to convince the mind, and elicit the confessions of, any man whose gods are not beaver and muskrats' skins—or whose ambition is not to be deemed an apostle, or himself, their only redeemer.

Morality and virtue, I venture to say, the civilized world need not undertake to teach them; and to support me in this, I refer the reader to the interesting narrative of the Rev. Mr. Parker, amongst the tribes through and beyond the Rocky Mountains; to the narratives of Captain Bonneville, through the same regions; and also to the reports of the Reverend Messrs. Spalding and Lee, who have crossed the Mountains, and planted their little colony amongst them. And I am also allowed to refer to the account given by the Rev. Mr. Beaver, of the tribes in the vicinity of the Columbia and the Pacific Coast.

Of their extraordinary modes and sincerity of worship, I speak with equal confidence; and although I am compelled to pity them for their ignorance, I am bound to say that I never saw any other people of any colour, who spend *so much of their lives* in humbling themselves before, and worshipping the Great Spirit, as some of these tribes do, nor any whom I would not as soon suspect of insincerity and hypocrisy.

Self-denial, which is comparatively a word of no meaning in the enlightened world; and self-torture and almost self-immolation, are continual modes of appealing to the Great Spirit for his countenance and forgiveness; and these, not in studied figures of rhetoric, resounding in halls and synagogues, to fill and astonish the ears of the multitude; but humbly cried forth from starved stomachs and parched throats, from some lone and favourite haunts, where the poor penitents crawl and lay with their faces in the dirt from day to day, and day to day, sobbing forth their humble confessions of their sins, and their earnest implorations for divine forgiveness and mercy.

I have seen man thus prostrating himself before his Maker, and worshipping as Nature taught him; and I have seen mercenary white man with his bottle and its associate vices, *unteaching* them; and after that, good and benevolent and pious men, devotedly wearing out their valuable lives, all but in vain, endeavouring to break down confirmed habits of cultivated vices and dissipation, and to engraft upon them the blessings of Christianity and civilization. I have visited most of the stations, and am acquainted with many of the excellent missionaries, who, with their families falling by the diseases of the country about them, are zealously labouring to benefit these benighted people; but I have, with thousands and millions of others, to deplore the ill success with which their painful and faithful labours have generally been attended.

This failure I attribute not to the want of capacity on the part of the savage, nor for lack of zeal and Christian endeavours of those who have been sent, and to whom the eyes of the sympathizing part of the world have been anxiously turned, in hopes of a more encouraging account. The misfortune has been, in my opinion, that these efforts have mostly been made in the wrong place—along the Frontier, where (though they have stood most in need of Christian advice and example) they have been the least ready to hear it or to benefit from its introduction; where whiskey has been sold for twenty, or thirty, or fifty years, and every sort of fraud and abuse that could be engendered and visited upon them, and amongst their families, by ingenious, *money-making* white man ; rearing up under a burning sense of injustice, the most deadly and thwarting prejudices, which, and which alone, in my opinion, have stood in the way of the introduction of Christianity—of agriculture, and everything which virtuous society has attempted to teach them; which they meet and suspect, and reject as some new trick or enterprize of white man, which is to redound to his advantage rather than for their own benefit.

The pious missionary finds himself here, I would venture to say, in an indescribable vicinity of mixed vices and stupid ignorance, that disgust and discourage him ; and just at the moment when his new theory, which has been at first received as a mystery to them, is about to be successfully revealed and explained, the whiskey bottle is handed again from the bushes ; and the poor Indian (whose perplexed mind is just ready to catch the brilliant illumination of Christianity), grasps it, and, like too many people in the enlightened world, quiets his excited feelings with its soothing draught, embracing most affectionately the friend that brings him the most sudden relief ; and is contented to fall back, and linger—and die in the moral darkness that is about him.

And notwithstanding the great waste of missionary labours, on many portions of our vast Frontier, there have been some instances in which their efforts have been crowned with signal success, (even with the counteracting obstacles that have stood in their way), of which instances I have made some mention in former epistles.

I have always been, and still am, an advocate for missionary efforts amongst these people, but I never have had much faith in the success of any unless they could be made amongst the tribes in their primitive state ; where, if the strong arm of the Government could be extended out to protect them, I believe that with the example of good and pious men, teaching them at the same time, agriculture and the useful arts, much could be done with these interesting and talented people, for the successful improvement of their moral and physical condition.

I have ever thought, and still think, that the Indian's mind is a beautiful blank, on which anything might be written, if the right mode were taken to do it.

Could the enlightened and virtuous society of the East, have been brought in contact with him as his first neighbours, and his eyes been first opened to improvements and habits worthy of his imitation ; and could religion have been taught him without the interference of the counteracting vices by which he is surrounded, the best efforts of the world would not have been thrown away upon him, nor posterity been left to say, in future ages, when he and his race shall have been swept from the face of the earth, that he was destined by Heaven to be unconverted and uncivilized.

The Indian's calamity is surely far this side of his origin—his misfortune has been in his education. Ever since our first acquaintance with these people on the Atlantic shores, have we regularly advanced upon them ; and far a-head of good and moral society have their first teachers travelled (and are yet travelling), with vices and iniquities so horrible as to blind their eyes for ever to the light and loveliness of virtue, when she is presented to them.

It is in the bewildering maze of this moving atmosphere that he, in his native simplicity, finds himself lost amidst the ingenuity and sophistry of his new acquaintance. He stands amazed at the arts and improvements of civilized life—his proud spirit which before was founded on his ignorance, droops, and he sinks down discouraged, into melancholy and despair ; and at that moment grasps the bottle (which is ever ready), to soothe his anguished feelings to the grave. It is in this deplorable condition that the civilized world, in their approach, have ever found him ; and here in his inevitable misery, that the charity of the world has been lavished upon him, and religion has exhausted its best efforts almost in vain.

Notwithstanding this destructive ordeal, through which all the border tribes have had to pass, and of whom I have spoken but in general terms, there are striking and noble exceptions on the Frontiers, of individuals, and in some instances, of the remaining remnants of tribes, who have followed the advice and example of their Christian teachers ; who have entirely discarded their habits of dissipation, and successfully outlived the dismal wreck of their tribe—having embraced, and are now preaching, the Christian religion ; and proving by the brightest example, that they are well worthy of the sincere and well-applied friendship of the enlightened world, rather than their enmity and persecution.

By nature they are decent and modest, unassuming and inoffensive—and all history (which I could quote to the end of a volume), proves them to have been found friendly and hospitable, on the first approach of white people to their villages on all parts of the American Continent—and from what I have seen, (which I offer as proof, rather than what I have read), I am willing and proud to add, for the ages who are only to read of these people, my testimony to that which was given by the immortal Columbus, who wrote back to his Royal Master and Mistress, from his first position on the new Continent, " I swear to your Majesties, that there is not a better people in the world than these ; more affectionate, affable, or mild. They love their neighbours as themselves, and they always speak smilingly."

They are ingenious and talented, as many of their curious manufactures will prove, which are seen by thousands in my Collection.

In the *mechanic arts* they have advanced but little, probably because they have had but little use for them, and have had no teachers to bring them out. In the *fine arts*, they are perhaps still more rude, and their productions are very few. Their materials and implements that they work with, are exceedingly rare and simple ; and their principal efforts at pictorial effects, are found on their buffalo robes ; of which I have given some account in former Letters, and of which I shall herein furnish some additional information.

I have been unable to find anything like a *system* of hieroglyphic writing amongst them ; yet, their *picture writings* on the rocks, and on their robes, approach somewhat towards it. Of the former, I have seen a vast many in the course of my travels ; and I have satisfied myself that they are generally the *totems* (symbolic names) merely, of Indians who have visited those places, and from a similar feeling of vanity that everywhere belongs to man much alike, have been in the habit of recording their names or symbols, such as birds, beasts, or reptiles ; by which each family, and each individual, is generally known, as white men are in the habit of recording their names at watering places, &c.

Many of these have recently been ascribed to the North-men, who probably discovered this country at an early period, and have been extinguished by the savage tribes. I might have subscribed to such a theory, had I not at the Red Pipe Stone Quarry, where there are a vast number of these inscriptions cut in the solid rock, and at other places also, seen the Indian at work, recording his totem amongst those of more ancient dates ; which convinced me that they had been progressively made, at different ages, and without any system that could be called hieroglyphic writing.

The paintings on their robes are in many cases exceedingly curious, and generally represent the exploits of their military lives, which they are proud of recording in this way and exhibiting on their backs as they walk.

In PLATES 306 and 307, are *fac-similes* of the paintings on a Crow robe, which hangs in my Collection, amongst many others from various tribes ; exhibiting the different tastes, and state of the fine arts, in the different tribes. All the groups on these two plates, are taken from one robe ; and on the original, are quite picturesque, from the great variety of vivid colours which they have there given to them. The reader will recollect the robe of *Mah-to-toh-pa*, which I described in the First Volume of this work. And he will find here, something very similar, the battles of a distinguished war-chief's life ; all pourtrayed by his own hand, and displayed on his back as he walks, where all can read, and all of course are challenged to deny.*

In PLATE 308, are *fac-simile* outlines from about one-half of a group on a Pawnee robe, also hanging in the exhibition ; representing a procession of doctors or medicine-men, when one of them, the foremost one, is giving freedom to his favourite horse. This is a very curious custom, which I found amongst many of the tribes, and is done by his announcing to all of his fraternity, that on a certain day, he is going to give liberty to his faithful horse that has longest served him, and he expects them all to be present ; at the time and place appointed, they all appear on horseback, most fantastically painted, and dressed, as well as armed and equipped ; when the owner of the horse leads the procession, and drives before him his emancipated horse, which is curiously painted and branded ; which he holds in check with a long laso. When they have arrived at the proper spot on the prairie, the ceremony takes place, of turning it loose, and giving it, it would seem, as a sort of sacrifice to the Great Spirit. This animal after this, takes his range amongst the bands of wild horses ; and if caught by the laso, as is often the case, is discharged, under the superstitious belief that it belongs to the Great Spirit, and not with impunity to be appropriated by them.

Besides this curious custom, there are very many instances where these magicians, (the avails of whose practice enable them to do it, in order to enthral the ignorant and superstitious minds of their people, as well as, perhaps, to quiet their own apprehensions,) sacrifice to the Great or Evil Spirit, their horses and dogs, by killing them instead of turning them loose. These sacrifices are generally made *immediately* to their *medicine-bags*, or to their *family-medicine*, which every family seems to have attached to their household, in addition to that which appropriately belongs to individuals. And in making these sacrifices, and all gifts to the Great Spirit, there is one thing yet to be told—that whatever gift is made, whether a horse, a dog, or other article, it is sure to be the *best* of its kind, that the giver possesses, otherwise he subjects himself to disgrace in his tribe, and to the ill-will of the power he is endeavouring to conciliate.†

In PLATE 309, there is a *fac-simile* copy of the paintings on another Pawnee robe, the property and the designs of a distinguished doctor or medicine-man. In the centre he has represented himself in full dress on his favourite

* The reader will bear it in mind, that these drawings, as well as all those of the kind that have heretofore been given, and those that are to follow, have been correctly traced with a *Camera*, from the robes and other works of the Indians belonging to my Indian Museum.

† Lewis and Clarke, in their Tour across the Rocky Mountains, have given an account of a Mandan chief, who had sacrificed seventeen horses to his *medicine-bag*—to conciliate the good will of the Great Spirit. And I have met many instances, where, while boasting to me of their exploits and their liberality, they have claimed to have given several of their horses to the Great Spirit, and as many to white men !

horse; and, at the top and bottom, it would seem, he has endeavoured to set up his claims to the reputation of a warrior, with the heads of seven victims which he professes to have slain in battle. On the sides there are numerous figures, very curiously denoting his profession, where he is vomiting and purging his patients, with herbs ; where also he has represented his *medicine* or totem, the Bear. And also the rising of the sun, and the different phases of the moon, which these magicians look to with great dependence for the operation of their charms and mysteries in effecting the cure of their patients.

In PLATE 310, is a further exemplification of symbolic representations, as well as of the state of the arts of drawing and design amongst these rude people. This curious chart is a *fac-simile* copy of an Indian song, which was drawn on a piece of birch bark, about twice the size of the plate, and used by the Chippeways preparatory to a *medicine-hunt*, as they term it. For the bear, the moose, the beaver, and nearly every animal they hunt for, they have certain seasons to commence, and previous to which, they " make medicine" for several days, to conciliate the bear (or other) Spirit, to ensure a successful season. For this purpose, these doctors, who are the only persons, generally, who are initiated into these profound secrets, sing forth, with the beat of the drum, the songs which are written in characters on these charts, in which all dance and join in the chorus ; although they are generally as ignorant of the translation and meaning of the song, as a mere passing traveller ; and which they have no means of learning, except by extraordinary claims upon the tribe, for their services as warriors and hunters ; and then by an extraordinary fee to be given to the mystery-men, who alone can reveal them, and that under the most profound injunctions of secrecy. I was not initiated far enough in this tribe, to explain the mysteries that are hidden on this little chart, though I heard it sung over, and listened, (I am sure) at least one hour, before they had sung it all.

Of these kinds of *symbolic writings*, and totems, such as are given in PLATE 311, recorded on rocks and trees in the country, a volume might be filled ; and from the knowledge which I have been able to obtain of them, I doubt whether I should be able to give with them all, much additional information, to that which I have briefly given in these few simple instances. Their *picture writing*, which is found on their robes, their wigwams, and different parts of their dress, is also voluminous and various ; and can be best studied by the curious, on the numerous articles in the Museum, where they have the additional interest of having been traced by the Indian's own hand.

In PLATE 312, is also a *fac-simile* of a Mandan robe, with a representation of the sun, most wonderfully painted upon it. This curious robe, which was a present from an esteemed friend of mine amongst those unfortunate people, is now in my Collection ; where it may speak for itself, after this brief introduction.

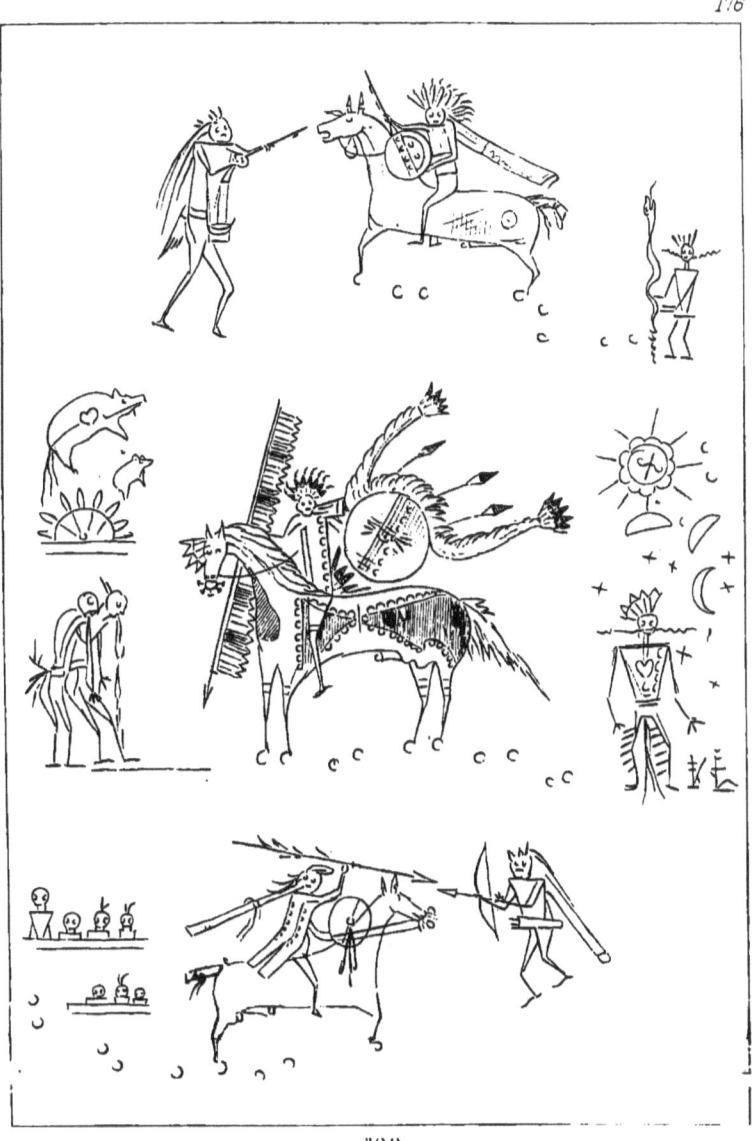

C. Catlin

G. Catlin

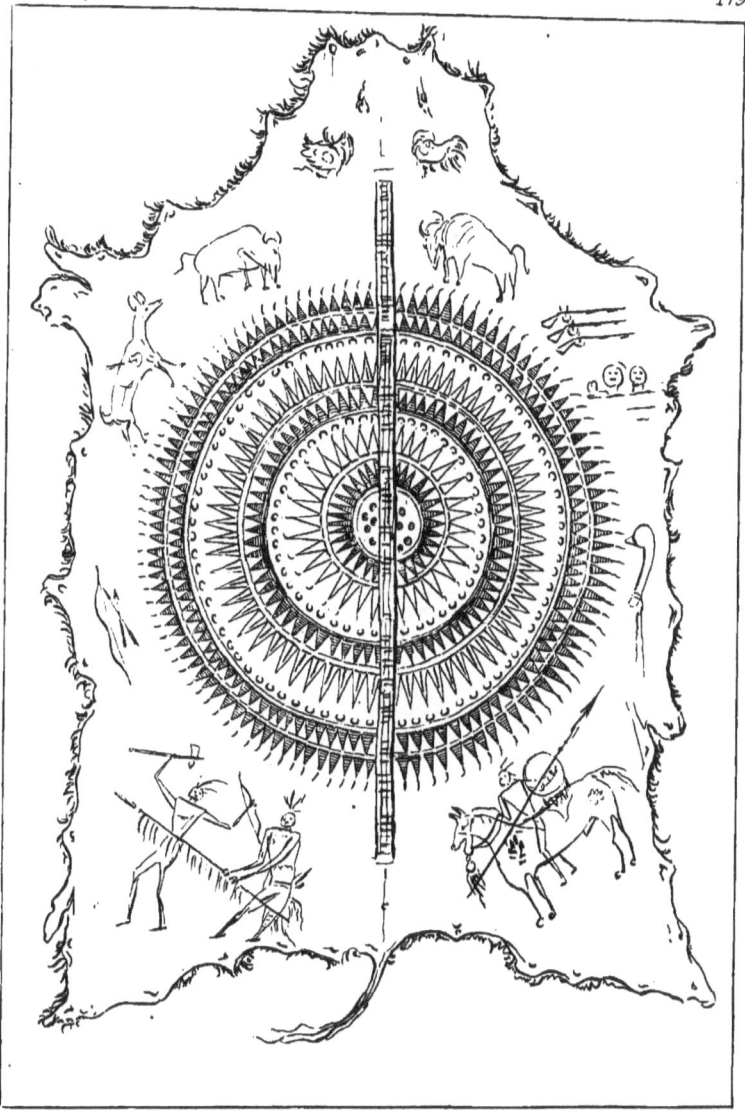

C. Cathn.

From these brief hints, which I have too hastily thrown together, it will be seen that these people are ingenious, and have much in their modes as well as in their manners, to enlist the attention of the merely curious, even if they should not be drawn nearer to them by feelings of sympathy and pity for their existing and approaching misfortunes.

But he who can travel amongst them, or even sit down in his parlour, with his map of North America before him, with Halkett's Notes on the History of the North American Indians (and several other very able works that have been written on their character and history), and fairly and truly contemplate the system of universal abuse, that is hurrying such a people to utter destruction, will find enough to enlist all his sympathies, and lead him to cultivate a more general and intimate acquaintance with their true character.

He who will sit and contemplate that vast Frontier, where, by the past policy of the Government, one hundred and twenty thousand of these poor people, (who had just got initiated into the mysteries and modes of civilized life, surrounded by examples of industry and agriculture which they were beginning to adopt), have been removed several hundred miles to the West, to meet a second siege of the whiskey-sellers and traders in the wilderness, to whose enormous exactions their semi-civilized habits and appetites have subjected them, will assuredly pity them. Where they have to quit their acquired luxuries, or pay ten times their accustomed prices for them—and to scuffle for a few years upon the plains, with the wild tribes, and with white men also, for the flesh and the skins of the last of the buffaloes ; where their carnage, but not their *appetites*, must stop in a few years, and with the ghastliness of hunger and despair, they will find themselves gazing at each other upon the vacant waste, which will afford them nothing but the empty air, and the desperate resolve to flee to the woods and fastnesses of the Rocky Mountains; whilst more lucky white man will return to his comfortable home, with no misfortune, save that of *deep remorse* and a *guilty conscience*. Such a reader will find enough to claim his pity and engage his whole soul's indignation, at the wholesale and retail system of injustice, which has been, from the very first landing of our forefathers, (and is equally at the present day, being) visited upon these poor, and naturally unoffending, untrespassing people.

In alluding to the cruel policy of removing the different tribes to their new country, West of the Mississippi, I would not do it without the highest respect to the motives of the Government—and to the feelings and opinions of those worthy Divines, whose advice and whose services were instrumental in bringing it about ; and who, no doubt were of opinion that they were effecting a plan that would redound to the Indian's benefit. Such was once my own opinion—but when I go, as I have done, through every one of those tribes removed, who had learned at home to use the ploughshare, and also contracted a passion, and a taste for civilized manufactures ; and after that, removed twelve and fourteen hundred mil

their wants are to be supplied by the traders, at eight or ten times the prices they have been in the habit of paying; where whiskey can easily be sold to them in a boundless and lawless forest, without the restraints that can be successfully put upon the sellers of it in their civilized neighbourhoods; and where also they are allured from the use of their ploughs, by the herds of buffaloes and other wild animals on the plains; I am compelled to state, as my irresistible conviction, that I believe the system one well calculated to benefit the interests of the voracious land-speculators and Indian Traders; the first of whom are ready to grasp at their lands, as soon as they are vacated—and the others, at the *annuities* of one hundred and twenty thousand extravagant customers. I believe the system is calculated to aid these, and perhaps to facilitate the growth and the wealth of the civilized border; but I believe, like everything else that tends to white man's aggrandizement, and the increase of his wealth, it will have as rapid a tendency to the poverty and destruction of the poor *red men*; who, unfortunately, *almost* seem *doomed*, never in any way to be associated in interest with their pale-faced neighbours.

The system of trade, and the small-pox, have been the great and wholesale destroyers of these poor people, from the Atlantic Coast to where they are now found. And no one but God, knows where the voracity of the one is to stop, short of the acquisition of everything that is desirable to money-making man in the Indian's country; or when the mortal destruction of the other is to be arrested, whilst there is untried flesh for it to act upon, either within or beyond the Rocky Mountains.

From the first settlements on the Atlantic Coast, to where it is now carried on at the base of the Rocky Mountains, there has been but one system of trade and money-making, by hundreds and thousands of white men, who are desperately bent upon making their fortunes in this trade, with the unsophisticated children of the forest; and generally they have succeeded in the achievement of their object.

The Governments of the United States, and Great Britain, have always held out every encouragement to the Fur Traders, whose traffic has uniformly been looked upon as beneficial, and a source of wealth to nations; though surely, they never could have considered such intercourse as advantageous to the savage.

Besides the many thousands who are daily and hourly selling whiskey and rum, and useless gewgaws, to the Indians on the United States, the Canada, the Texian and Mexican borders, there are, of hardy adventurers, in the Rocky Mountains and beyond, or near them, and out of all limits of laws, one thousand armed men in the annual employ of the United States' Fur Companies—an equal number in the employment of the British Factories, and twice that number in the Russian and Mexican possessions; all of whom pervade the countries of the wildest tribes they can reach, with guns and gunpowder in their hands, and other instruments of death, unthought of by the simple savage, calculated to terrify and coerce him to favourable terms in his trade : and in all instances they assume the right, (and prove it, if necessary, by the superiority of their weapons,) of hunting and trapping the streams and lakes of their countries.

These traders, in addition to the terror, and sometimes death, that they carry into these remote realms, at the muzzles of their guns, as well as by whiskey and the small-pox, are continually arming tribe after tribe with fire-arms; who are able thereby, to bring their unsuspecting enemies into unequal combats, where they are slain by thousands, and who have no way to heal the awful wound but by arming themselves in turn ; and in a similar manner reeking their vengeance upon *their* defenceless enemies on the West. In this wholesale way, and by whiskey and disease, tribe after tribe sink their heads and lose their better, proudest half, before the next and succeeding waves of civilization flow on, to see or learn anything definite of them.

Without entering at this time, into any detailed history of this immense system, or denunciation of any of the men or their motives, who are engaged in it, I would barely observe, that, from the very nature of their traffic, where their goods are to be carried several thousands of miles, on the most rapid and dangerous streams, over mountains and other almost discouraging obstacles ; and that at the continual hazard to their lives, from accidents and diseases of the countries, the poor Indians are obliged to pay such enormous prices for their goods, that the balance of trade is so decidedly against them, as soon to lead them to poverty ; and, unfortunately for them, they mostly contract a taste for whiskey and rum, which are not only ruinous in their prices, but in their effects destructive to life—destroying the Indians, much more rapidly than an equal indulgence will destroy the civilized constitution.

In the Indian communities, where there is no law of the land or custom denominating it a vice to drink whiskey, and to get drunk; and where the poor Indian meets whiskey tendered to him by white men, whom he considers wiser than himself, and to whom he naturally looks for example ; he thinks it no harm to drink to excess, and will lie drunk as long as he can raise the means to pay for it. And after his first means, in his wild state, are exhausted, he becomes a beggar for whiskey, and begs until he disgusts, when the honest pioneer becomes his neighbour ; and then, and not before, gets the name of the " poor, degraded, naked, and drunken Indian," to whom the epithets are well and truly applied.

On this great system of carrying the Fur Trade into the Rocky Mountains and other parts of the wilderness country, where whiskey is sold at the rate of twenty and thirty dollars per gallon, and most other articles of trade at a similar rate ; I know of no better comment, nor any more excusable, than the quotation of a few passages from a very popular work, which is being read with great avidity, from the pen of a gentleman whose name gives currency to any book, and whose fine taste, pleasure to all who read. The work I refer to "The Rocky Mountains, or Adventures in the Far West, by W. Irving," is a very interesting one; and its incidents, no doubt, are given with great candour, by the excellent officer, Captain Bonneville, who spent five years in the region of the Rocky Mountains, on a furlough; endeavouring, in competition with others, to add to his fortune, by pushing the Fur Trade to some of the wildest tribes in those remote regions.

"The worthy Captain (says the Author) started into the country with " 110 men; whose very appearance and equipment exhibited a piebald mix- " ture—half-civilized and half-savage, &c." And he also preludes his work by saying, that it was revised by himself from Captain Bonneville's own notes, which can, no doubt, be relied on.

This medley group, it seems, traversed the country to the Rocky Moun- tains, where, amongst the Nez Percés and Flatheads, he says, " They were " friendly in their dispositions, and honest to the most scrupulous degree " in their intercourse with the white men. And of the same people, the Captain " continues—Simply to call these people religious, would convey but a faint " idea of the deep hue of piety and devotion which pervades the whole of " their conduct. Their honesty is immaculate; and their purity of purpose, " and their observance of the rites of their religion, are most uniform and re- " markable. They are, certainly, more like a nation of saints than a horde " of savages."

Afterwards, of the " Root-Diggers," in the vicinity of the Great Salt Lake, who are a band of the Snake tribe, (and of whom he speaks thus :— " In fact, they are a simple, timid, inoffensive race, and scarce provided " with any weapons, except for the chase"); he says that, " one morning, " one of his trappers, of a violent and savage character, discovering that his " traps had been carried off in the night, took a horrid oath that he would " kill the first Indian he should meet, innocent or guilty. As he was returning " with his comrades to camp, he beheld two unfortunate Root-Diggers seated " on the river bank fishing—advancing upon them, he levelled his rifle, shot " one upon the spot, and flung his bleeding body into the stream."

A short time afterwards, when his party of trappers " were about to cross " Ogden's river, a great number of Shoshokies or Root-Diggers were posted " on the opposite bank, when they *imagined* they were there with hostile in- " tent; they advanced upon them, levelled their rifles, and killed twenty- " five of them on the spot. The rest fled to a short distance, then halted " and turned about, howling and whining like wolves, and uttering most " piteous wailings. The trappers chased them in every direction; the poor " wretches made no defence, but fled with terror; neither does it appear from " the accounts of the boasted victors, that a weapon had been wielded, or " a weapon launched by the Indians throughout the affair."

After this affair, this " piebald" band of trappers wandered off to Mon- terey, on the coast of California, and on their return on horseback through an immense tract of the Root-Diggers' country, he gives the further fol- lowing accounts of their transactions :—

" In the course of their journey through the country of the poor Root-
" Diggers, there seems to have been an emulation between them, which could
" inflict the greatest outrages upon the natives. The trappers still considered
" them in the light of dangerous foes ; and the Mexicans, very probably,
" charged them with the sin of horse-stealing ; we have no other mode of
" accounting for the infamous barbarities, of which, according to their own
" story, they were guilty—hunting the poor Indians like wild beasts, and
" killing them without mercy—chasing their unfortunate victims at full
" speed ; noosing them around the neck with their lasos, and then dragging
" them to death."

It is due to Captain Bonneville, that the world should know that these
cruel (not " *savage*") atrocities were committed by his men, when they were
on a Tour to explore the shores of the Great Salt Lake, and many hundreds
of miles from him, and beyond his controul ; and that in his work, both the
Captain and the writer of the book have expressed in a proper way, their
abhorrence of such fiendish transactions.

A part of the same " piebald mixture" of trappers, who were encamped
in the Riccaree country, and trapping the beavers out of their streams,
when, finding that the Riccarees had stolen a number of their horses one
night, in the morning made prisoners of two of the Riccarees, who loitered
into their camp, and probably without knowledge of the offence committed,
when they were bound hand and foot as hostages, until every one of the
horses should be returned.

" The mountaineers declared, that unless the horses were relinquished, the
" prisoners should be burned to death. To give force to their threat, a pyre
" of logs and faggots was heaped up and kindled into a blaze. The Riccarees
" released one horse, and then another ; but finding that nothing but the
" relinquishment of all their spoils would purchase the lives of their cap-
" tives, they abandoned them to their fate, moving off with many parting
" words and howlings, when the prisoners were dragged to the blazing pyre,
" and burnt to death in sight of their retreating comrades.

" Such are the savage cruelties that white men learn to practice, who
" mingle in savage life ; and such are the acts that lead to terrible recrimi-
" nation on the part of the Indians. Should we hear of any atrocities com-
" mitted by the Riccarees upon captive white men ; let this signal and recent
" provocation be born in mind. Individual cases of the kind dwell in the
" recollections of whole tribes—and it is a point of honour and conscience
" to revenge them."*

* During the summer of this transaction I was on the Upper Missouri river, and had
to pass the Riccaree village in my bark canoe, with only two men, which the reader will
say justly accounts for the advice of Mr. M'Kenzie, to pass the Riccaree village in the
night, which I did, as I have before described, by which means it is possible I preserved
my life, as they had just killed the last Fur Trader in their village, and as I have learned
since, were " *dancing his scalp*" when I came by them.

To quote the author further ———— "The facts disclosed in the present
" work, clearly manifest the policy of establishing military posts, and a
" mounted force to protect our Traders in their journeys across the great
" Western wilds ; and of pushing the outposts into the heart of the singular
" wilderness we have laid open, so as to maintain some degree of sway over
" the country, and to put an end to the kind of ' black mail,' levied on all
" occasions, by the savage ' chivalry of the mountains ' "!

The appalling cruelties in the above quotations require no comment;
and I hope the author, as well as the Captain, who have my warmest approbation for having so frankly revealed them, will pardon me for having
quoted them in this place, as one striking proof of the justice that may be
reasonably expected, in *prospect ;* and that may fairly be laid to the *past*
proceedings of these great systems of trading with, and civilizing the savages;
which have been carried on from the beginning of our settlements on the
Atlantic Coast, to the present day—making first acquaintance with them,
and first impressions of the glorious effects of civilization—and of the
sum total of which, this instance is but a mere point; but with the singular merit which redounds to the honour of Captain Bonneville, that he
has frankly told the whole truth; which, if as fully revealed of *all other
transactions in these regions*, I am enabled to say, would shake every breast
with ague-chills of abhorrence of *civilized* barbarities. From the above
facts, as well as from others enumerated in the foregoing epistles, the dis-
cerning reader will easily see how prejudices are raised in the minds of the
savage, and why so many murders of white people are heard of on the Frontier, which are uniformly attributed to the wanton cruelty and rapacity of the
savage—which we denominate " Indian murders," and " ruthless barbarities,"
before we can condescend to go to the poor savage, and ask him for a
reason, which there is no doubt he could generally furnish us.

From these, and hundreds of others that might be named, and equally
barbarous, it can easily be seen, that white men may well feel a dread at
every step they take in Indian realms, after atrocities like these, that call so
loudly and so justly for revenge, in a country where there are no laws to
punish; but where the cruel savage takes vengeance in his own way—and
white men fall, in the Indian's estimation, not as *murdered*, but *executed*,
under the common law of their land.

Of the hundreds and thousands of such *murders*, as they are denominated
by white men, who are the only ones to tell of them in the civilized world;
it should also be kept in mind by the reader, who passes his sentence on
them, that they are all committed on Indian ground—that the Indian hunts
not, nor traps anywhere on white man's soil, nor asks him for his lands—or
molests the sacred graves where they have deposited the bones of their
fathers, their wives and their little children.

I have said that the principal means of the destruction of these people,
were the system of trade, and the introduction of small-pox, the in-

fallible plague that is consequent, sooner or later, upon the introduction of trade and whiskey-selling to every tribe. I would venture the assertion, from books that I have searched, and from other evidence, that of the numerous tribes which have already disappeared, and of those that have been traded with, quite to the Rocky Mountains, each one has had this exotic disease in their turn—and in a few months have lost one half or more of their numbers; and that from living evidences, and distinct traditions, this appalling disease has several times, before our days, run like a wave through the Western tribes, over the Rocky Mountains, and to the Pacific Ocean—thinning the ranks of the poor Indians to an extent which no knowledge, save that of the overlooking eye of the Almighty, can justly comprehend.*

I have travelled faithfully and far, and have closely scanned, with a hope of fairly pourtraying the condition and customs of these unfortunate people; and if in taking leave of my readers, which I must soon do, they should censure me for any oversight, or any indiscretion or error, I will take to myself these consoling reflections, that they will acquit me of intention to render more or less than justice to any one; and also, that if in my zeal to render a service and benefit to the Indian, I should have fallen short of it, I will, at least, be acquitted of having done him an *injury*. And in endeavouring to render them that justice, it belongs to me yet to say that the introduction of the fatal causes of their destruction above-named, has been a subject of close investigation with me during my travels; and I have watched on every part of the Frontier their destructive influences, which result in the overthrow of the savage tribes, which, one succeeding another, are continually becoming extinct under their baneful influences. And before I would expatiate upon any system for their successful improvement and preservation, I would protrude my opinion to the world, which I regret to do, that so long as the past and present system of trade and whiskey-selling is tolerated amongst them, there is little hope for their improvement, nor any chance for more than a temporary existence. I have closely studied the Indian character in its native state, and also in its secondary form along our Frontiers; civilized, as it is often (but incorrectly) called. I have seen it in every phase, and although there are many noble instances to the contrary, and with many of whom I am personally acquainted; yet the greater part

* The Reverend Mr. Parker in his Tour across the Rocky Mountains says, that amongst the Indians below the Falls of the Columbia at least seven-eighths, if not nine-tenths, as Dr. M'Laughlin believes, have been swept away by disease between the years 1829, and the time that he visited that place in 1836. "So many and so sudden were the deaths which occurred, that the shores were strewed with the unburied dead, whole and large villages were depopulated, and some entire tribes have disappeared." This mortality he says "extended not only from the Cascades to the Pacific, but from very far North to the coast of California." These facts, with hundreds of others, shew how rapidly the Indian population is destroyed, long before we become acquainted with them.

of those who have lingered along the Frontiers, and been kicked about like dogs, by white men, and beaten into a sort of a civilization, are very far from being what I would be glad to see them, and proud to call them, civilized by the aids and examples of good and moral people. Of the Indians in their general capacity of civilized, along our extensive Frontier, and those tribes that I found in their primitive and disabused state, I have drawn a Table, which I offer as an estimate of their comparative character, which I trust will be found to be near the truth, generally, though like all general rules or estimates, with its exceptions. (Vide Appendix C.)

Such are the results to which the present system of civilization brings that small part of these poor unfortunate people, who outlive the first calamities of their country; and in this degraded and pitiable condition, the most of them end their days in poverty and wretchedness, without the power of rising above it. Standing on the soil which they have occupied from their childhood, and inherited from their fathers; with the dread of " pale faces," and the deadly prejudices that have been reared in their breasts against them, for the destructive influences which they have introduced into their country, which have thrown the greater part of their friends and connexions into the grave, and are now promising the remainder of them no better prospect than the dreary one of living a few years longer, and then to sink into the ground themselves; surrendering their lands and their fair hunting grounds to the enjoyment of their enemies, and their bones to be dug up and strewed about the fields, or to be labelled in our Museums.

For the Christian and philanthropist, in any part of the world, there is enough, I am sure, in the character, condition, and history of these unfortunate people, to engage his sympathies—for the Nation, there is an unrequited account of sin and injustice that sooner or later will call for *national retribution*—and for the American citizens, who live, every where proud of their growing wealth and their luxuries, over the bones of these poor fellows, who have surrendered their hunting-grounds and their lives, to the enjoyment of their cruel dispossessors, there is a lingering terror yet, I fear, for the reflecting minds, whose mortal bodies must soon take their humble places with their red, but injured brethren, under the same glebe; to appear and stand, at last, with guilt's shivering conviction, amidst the myriad ranks of accusing spirits, that are to rise in their own fields, at the final day of resurrection!

APPENDIX—A.

EXTINCTION OF THE MANDANS.

From the accounts brought to New York in the fall of 1838, by Messrs. M'Kenzie, Mitchell, and others, from the Upper Missouri, and with whom I conversed on the subject, it seems that in the summer of that year the small-pox was accidentally introduced amongst the Mandans, by the Fur Traders; and that in the course of two months they all perished, except some thirty or forty, who were taken as slaves by the Riccarees; an enemy living two hundred miles below them, and who moved up and took possession of their village soon after their calamity, taking up their residence in it, it being a better built village than their own; and from the lips of one of the Traders who had more recently arrived from there, I had the following account of the remaining few, in whose destruction was the final termination of this interesting and once numerous tribe.

The Riccarees, he said, had taken possession of the village after the disease had subsided, and after living some months in it, were attacked by a large party of their enemies, the Sioux, and whilst fighting desperately in resistance, in which the Mandan prisoners had taken an active part, the latter had concerted a plan for their own destruction, which was effected by their simultaneously running through the piquets on to the prairie, calling out to the Sioux (both men and women) to kill them, "that they were Riccaree dogs, that their friends were all dead, and they did not wish to live,"—that they here wielded their weapons as desperately as they could, to excite the fury of their enemy, and that they were thus cut to pieces and destroyed.

The accounts given by two or three white men, who were amongst the Mandans during the ravages of this frightful disease, are most appalling and actually too heart-rending and disgusting to be recorded. The disease was introduced into the country by the Fur Company's steamer from St. Louis; which had two of their crew sick with the disease when it approached the Upper Missouri, and imprudently stopped to trade at the Mandan village, which was on the bank of the river, where the chiefs and others were allowed to come on board, by which means the disease got ashore.

I am constrained to believe, that the gentlemen in charge of the steamer did not believe it to be the small-pox; for if they had known it to be such, I cannot conceive of such imprudence, as regarded their own interests in the country, as well as the fate of these poor people, by allowing their boat to advance into the country under such circumstances.

It seems that the Mandans were surrounded by several war-parties of their more powerful enemies the Sioux, at that unlucky time, and they could not therefore disperse upon the plains, by which many of them could have been saved; and they were necessarily inclosed within the piquets of their village, where the disease in a few days became so very malignant that death ensued in a few hours after its attacks; and so slight were their hopes when they were attacked, that nearly half of them destroyed themselves with their knives, with their guns, and by dashing their brains out by leaping head-foremost from a thirty foot ledge of rocks in front of their village. The first symptom of the disease was a rapid swelling of the body, and so very virulent had it become, that very many died in two or three hours after their attack, and that in many cases without the appearance of the disease upon the skin. Utter dismay seemed to possess all classes and all ages, and they gave themselves up in despair, as entirely lost. There was but one continual crying and howling and praying to the Great Spirit for his protection during the nights and days; and there being but few living, and those in too appalling despair, nobody thought of burying the dead, whose bodies, whole families together, were left in horrid and loathsome piles in their own wigwams, with a few buffalo robes, &c. thrown over them, there to decay, and be devoured by their own dogs. That such a proportion of their community as that above-mentioned, should have perished in so short a time, seems yet to the reader, an unaccountable thing; but in addition to the causes just mentioned, it must be borne in mind that this frightful disease is everywhere far more fatal amongst the native than in civilized population, which may be owing to some extraordinary constitutional susceptibility; or, I think, more probably, to the exposed lives they live, leading more directly to fatal consequences. In this, as in most of their diseases, they ignorantly and imprudently plunge into the coldest water, whilst in the highest state of fever, and often die before they have the power to get out.

Some have attributed the unexampled fatality of this disease amongst the Indians to the fact of their living entirely on animal food ; but so important a subject for investigation I must leave for sounder judgments than mine to decide. They are a people whose constitutions and habits of life enable them most certainly to meet most of its ills with less dread, and with decidedly greater success, than they are met in civilized communities ; and I would not dare to decide that their simple meat diet was the cause of their fatal exposure to one frightful disease, when I am decidedly of opinion that it has been the cause of their exemption and protection from another, almost equally destructive, and, like the former, of civilized introduction.

During the season of the ravages of the Asiatic cholera which swept over the greater part of the western country, and the Indian frontier, I was a traveller through those regions, and was able to witness its effects ; and I learned from what I saw, as well as from what I have heard in other parts since that time, that it travelled to and over the frontiers, carrying dismay and death amongst the tribes on the borders in many cases, so far as they had adopted the civilized modes of life, with its dissipations, using vegetable food and salt ; but wherever it came to the tribes living exclusively on meat, and that without the use of salt, its progress was suddenly stopped. I mention this as a subject which I looked upon as important to science, and therefore one on which I made many careful enquiries ; and so far as I have learned along that part of the frontier over which I have since passed, I have to my satisfaction ascertained that such became the utmost limits of this fatal disease in its travel to the West, unless where it might have followed some of the routes of the Fur Traders, who, of course, have introduced the modes of civilized life.

From the Trader who was present at the destruction of the Mandans I had many most wonderful incidents of this dreadful scene, but I dread to recite them. Amongst them, however, there is one that I must briefly describe, relative to the death of that noble *gentleman* of whom I have already said so much, and to whom I became so much attached, *Mah-to-toh-pa*, or "the Four Bears." This fine fellow sat in his wigwam and watched every one of his family die about him, his wives and his little children, after he had recovered from the disease himself; when he walked out, around the village, and wept over the final destruction of his tribe ; his braves and warriors, whose sinewy arms alone he could depend on for a continuance of their existence, all laid low ; when he came back to his lodge, where he covered his whole family in a pile, with a number of robes, and wrapping another around himself, went out upon a hill at a little distance, where he laid several days, despite all the solicitations of the Traders, resolved to *starve* himself to death. He remained there till the sixth day, when he had just strength enough to creep back to the village, when he entered the horrid gloom of his own wigwam, and laying his body along-side of the group of his family, drew his robe over him and died on the ninth day of his fatal abstinence.

So have perished the friendly and hospitable Mandans, from the best accounts I could get ; and although it may be *possible* that some few individuals may yet be remaining, I think it is not probable ; and one thing is certain, even if such be the case, that, as a nation, the Mandans are extinct, having no longer an existence.

There is yet a melancholy part of the tale to be told, relating to the ravages of this frightful disease in that country on the same occasion, as it spread to other contiguous tribes, to the Minatarees, the Knisteneaux, the Blackfeet, the Chayennes and Crows; amongst whom 25,000 perished in the course of four or five months, which most appalling facts I got from Major Pilcher, now Superintendent of Indian affairs at St. Louis, from Mr. M'Kenzie, and others.

It may be naturally asked here, by the reader, whether the Government of the United States have taken any measures to prevent the ravages of this fatal disease amongst these exposed tribes ; to which I answer, that repeated efforts have been made, and so far generally, as the tribes have ever had the disease, (or, at all events, within the recollections of those who are now living in the tribes,) the Government agents have succeeded in introducing vaccination as a protection ; but amongst those tribes in their wild state, and where they have not suffered with the disease, very little success has been met with in the attempt to protect them, on account of their superstitions, which have generally resisted all attempts to introduce vaccination. Whilst I was on the Upper Missouri, several surgeons were sent into the country with the Indian agents, where I several times saw the attempts made without success. They have perfect confidence in the skill of their own physicians, until the disease has made one slaughter in their tribe, and then, having seen white men amongst them protected by it, they are disposed to receive it, before

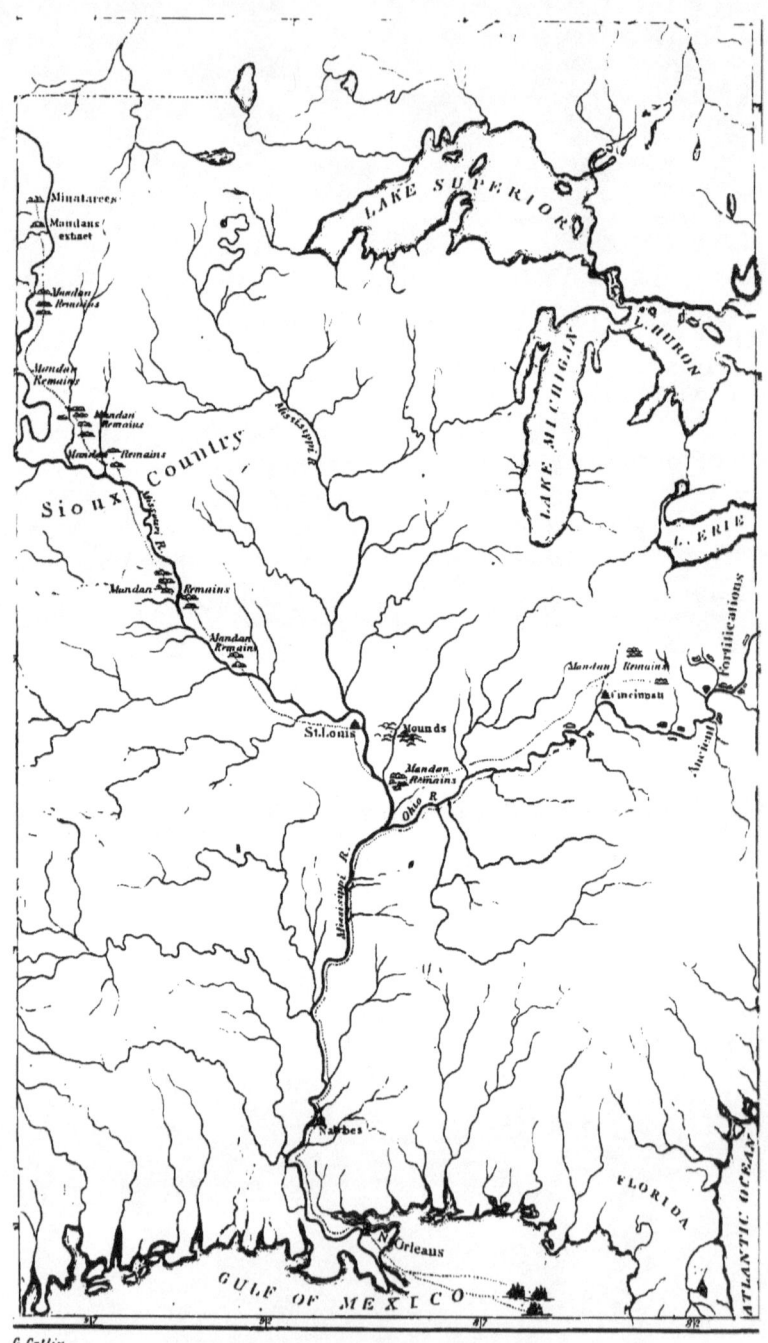

G. Catlin

A CHART SHEWING THE MOVES OF THE MANDANS & THE PLACE OF THEIR EXTINCTION.

which they cannot believe that so minute a puncture in the arm is going to protect them from so fatal a disease ; and as they see white men so earnestly urging it, they decide that it must be some new mode or trick of pale faces, by which they are to gain some new advantage over them, and they stubbornly and successfully resist it.

THE WELSH COLONY,

Which I barely spoke of in page 206, of Vol. I. which sailed under the direction of Prince Madoc, or Madawc, from North Wales, in the early part of the fourteenth century in ten ships, according to numerous and accredited authors, and never returned to their own country, have been supposed to have landed somewhere on the coast of North or South America ; and from the best authorities, (which I will suppose everybody has read, rather than quote them at this time,) I believe it has been pretty clearly proved that they landed either on the coast of Florida, or about the mouth of the Mississippi, and according to the history and poetry of their country, settled somewhere in the interior of North America, where they are yet remaining, intermixed with some of the savage tribes.

In my Letter just referred to, I barely suggested, that the Mandans, whom I found with so many peculiarities in looks and customs, which I have already described, might possibly be the remains of this lost colony, amalgamated with a tribe, or part of a tribe, of the natives, which would account for the unusual appearances of this tribe of Indians, and also for the changed character and customs of the Welsh Colonists. provided these be the remains of them.

Since those notes were written, as will have been seen by my subsequent Letters, and particularly in page 9 of this Volume, I have descended the Missouri river from the Mandan village to St. Louis, a distance of 1800 miles, and have taken pains to examine its shores ; and from the repeated remains of the ancient locations of the Mandans, which I met with on the banks of that river, I am fully convinced that I have traced them down nearly to the mouth of the Ohio river ; and from exactly similar appearances, which I recollect to have seen several years since in several places in the interior of the state of Ohio, I am fully convinced that they have formerly occupied that part of the country, and have, from some cause or other, been put in motion, and continued to make their repeated moves until they arrived at the place of their residence at the time of their extinction, on the Upper Missouri.

In the annexed chart of the Missouri and Ohio rivers, will be seen laid down the different positions of the ancient marks of their towns which I have examined ; and also, nearly, (though not exactly) the positions of the very numerous civilized fortifications which are now remaining on the Ohio and Muskingum rivers, in the vicinity of which I believe the Mandans once lived.

These ancient fortifications, which are very numerous in that vicinity, some of which enclose a great many acres, and being built on the banks of the rivers, with walls in some places twenty or thirty feet in height, with covered ways to the water, evince a knowledge of the science of fortifications, apparently not a century behind that of the present day, were evidently never built by any nation of savages in America, and present to us incontestable proof of the former existence of a people very far advanced in the arts of civilization, who have, from some cause or other, disappeared, and left these imperishable proofs of their former existence.

Now I am inclined to believe that the ten ships of Madoc, or a part of them at least, entered the Mississippi river at the Balize, and made their way up the Mississippi, or that they landed somewhere on the Florida coast, and that their brave and persevering colonists made their way through the interior, to a position on the Ohio river, where they cultivated their fields, and established in one of the finest countries on earth, a flourishing colony ; but were at length set upon by the savages, whom, perhaps, they provoked to warfare, being trespassers on their hunting-grounds, and by whom, in overpowering hordes, they were besieged, until it was necessary to erect these fortifications for their defence, into which they were at last driven by a confederacy of tribes, and there held till their ammunition and provisions gave out, and they in the end have all perished, except, perhaps, that portion of them who might have formed alliance by marriage with the Indians, and their offspring, who would have been half-breeds, and of course attached to the Indians' side ; whose lives have been spared in the general massacre ; and at length, being despised, as all half-breeds of enemies are, have gathered themselves into a band, and severing from their parent tribe, have moved off, and increased in numbers and strength, as they have advanced up the Missouri river to the place where they have been known for many years past by the name of the *Mandans*, a corruption or abbreviation, perhaps, of "*Madawgwys*," the name applied by the Welsh to the followers of Madawc.

If this be a startling theory for the world, they will be the more sure to read the following brief reasons which I bring in support of my opinion; and if they do not support me, they will at least be worth knowing, and may, at the same time, be the means of eliciting further and more successful enquiry.

As I have said, in page 9 of this Volume, and in other places, the marks of the Mandan villages are known by the excavations of two feet or more in depth, and thirty or forty feet in diameter, of a circular form, made in the ground for the foundations of their wigwams, which leave a decided remain for centuries, and one that is easily detected the moment that it is met with. After leaving the Mandan village, I found the marks of their former residence about sixty miles below where they were then living, and from which they removed (from their own account) about sixty or eighty years since ; and from the appearance of the number of their lodges, I should think, that at that recent date there must have been three times the number that were living when I was amongst them. Near the mouth of the big Shienne river, 200 miles below their last location, I found still more ancient remains, and in as many as six or seven other places between that and the mouth of the Ohio, as I have designated on the chart, and each one, as I visited them, appearing more and more ancient, convincing me that these people, wherever they might have come from, have gradually made their moves up the banks of the Missouri, to the place where I visited them.

For the most part of this distance they have been in the heart of the great Sioux country, and being looked upon by the Sioux as trespassers, have been continually warred upon by this numerous tribe, who have endeavoured to extinguish them, as they have been endeavouring to do ever since our first acquaintance with them ; but who, being always fortified by a strong piquet, or stockade, have successfully withstood the assaults of their enemies, and preserved the remnant of their tribe. Through this sort of gauntlet they have run, in passing through the countries of these warlike and hostile tribes.

It may be objected to this, perhaps, that the Riccarees and Minatarees build their wigwams in the same way : but this proves nothing, for the Minatarees are Crows, from the north-west ; and by their own showing, fled to the Mandans for protection, and forming their villages by the side of them, built their wigwams in the same manner.

The Riccarees have been a very small tribe, far inferior to the Mandans ; and by the traditions of the Mandans, as well as from the evidence of the first explorers, Lewis and Clarke, and others, have lived, until quite lately, on terms of intimacy with the Mandans, whose villages they have successively occupied as the Mandans have moved and vacated them, as they now are doing, since disease has swept the whole of the Mandans away.

Whether my derivation of the word *Mandan* from *Madawgwys* be correct or not, I will pass it over to the world at present merely as *presumptive* proof, for want of better, which, perhaps, this enquiry may elicit ; and, at the same time, I offer the Welsh word *Mandon*, (the woodroof, a species of madder used as a red dye,) as the name that might possibly have been applied by their Welsh neighbours to these people, on account of their very ingenious mode of giving the beautiful red and other dyes to the porcupine quills with which they garnish their dresses.

In their own language they called themselves *See-pohs-ka-nu-mah-ka-kee*, (the people of the pheasants,) which was probably the name of the primitive stock, before they were mixed with any other people ; and to have got such a name, it is natural to suppose that they must have come from a country where *pheasants* existed, which cannot be found short of reaching the timbered country at the base of the Rocky Mountains, some six or eight hundred miles West of the Mandans, or the forests of Indiana and Ohio, some hundreds of miles to the South and East of where they last lived.

The above facts, together with the other one which they repeatedly related to me, and which I have before alluded to, that they had often been to the bill of the *Red Pipe Stone*, and that they once lived near it, carry conclusive evidence, I think, that they have formerly occupied a country much farther to the South ; and that they have repeatedly changed their locations, until they reached the spot of their last residence, where they have met with their final misfortune. And as evidence in support of my opinion that they came from the banks of the Ohio, and have brought with them some of the customs of the civilized people who erected those ancient fortifications, I am able to say, that the numerous specimens of pottery which have been taken from the graves and tumuli about those ancient works, (many of which may be seen now, in the Cincinnati Museum, and some of which, my own donations, and which have so much surprised the enquiring world,) were to be seen in great numbers in the use of the Mandans ; and scarcely a day in the summer, when the visitor to their village would not see the women at work with their hands and fingers, moulding them from black clay, into vases, cups, pitchers, and pots, and baking them in their little kilns in the sides of the hill, or under the bank of the river.

In addition to this art, which I am sure belongs to no other tribe on the Continent, these people have also, as a secret with themselves, the extraordinary art of manufacturing a very beautiful and lasting kind of blue glass beads, which they wear on their necks in great quantities, and decidedly value above all others that are brought amongst them by the Fur Traders.

This secret is not only one that the Traders did not introduce amongst them, but one that they cannot learn from them; and at the same time, beyond a doubt, an art that has been introduced amongst them by some civilized people, as it is as yet unknown to other Indian tribes in that vicinity, or elsewhere. Of this interesting fact, Lewis and Clarke have given an account thirty-three years ago, at a time when no Traders, or other white people, had been amongst the Mandans, to have taught them so curious an art.

The Mandan canoes which are altogether different from those of all other tribes, are exactly the Welsh *coracle*, made of *raw-hides*, the skins of buffaloes, stretched underneath a frame made of willow or other boughs, and shaped nearly round, like a tub; which the woman carries on her head from her wigwam to the water's edge, and having stepped into it, stands in front, and propels it by dipping her paddle *forward*, and *drawing it to her*, instead of paddling by the side. In referring to PLATE 240, letter c, page 138, the reader will see several drawings of these seemingly awkward crafts, which, nevertheless, the Mandan women will *pull* through the water at a rapid rate.

How far these extraordinary facts may go in the estimation of the reader, with numerous others which I have mentioned in Volume I., whilst speaking of the Mandans, of their various complexions, colours of hair, and blue and grey eyes, towards establishing my opinion as a sound theory, I cannot say; but this much I can safely aver, that at the moment that I first saw these people, I was so struck with the peculiarity of their appearance, that I was under the instant conviction that they were an amalgam of a native, with some civilized race; and from what I have seen of them, and of the remains on the Missouri and Ohio rivers, I feel fully convinced that these people have emigrated from the latter stream; and that they have, in the manner that I have already stated, with many of their customs, been preserved from the *almost total* destruction of the bold colonists of Madawc, who, I believe, settled upon and occupied for a century or so, the rich and fertile banks of the Ohio. In adducing the proof for the support of this theory, if I have failed to complete it, I have the satisfaction that I have not taken up much of the reader's time, and I can therefore claim his attention a few moments longer, whilst I refer him to a brief vocabulary of the Mandan language in the following pages, where he may compare it with that of the Welsh; and better, perhaps, than I can, decide whether there is any affinity existing between the two; and if he finds it, it will bring me a friendly aid in support of the position I have taken.

From the comparison, that I have been able to make, I think I am authorized to say, that in the following list of words, which form a part of that vocabulary, there is a striking similarity, and quite sufficient to excite surprise in the minds of the attentive reader, if it could be proved that those resemblances were but the results of accident between two foreign and distinct idioms.

English.	Mandan.	Welsh.	Pronounced.
I	Me	Mi	Me
You	Ne	Chwi	Chwe
He	E	A	A'
She	Ea	E	A
It	Ount	Hwynt	Hooynt
We	Noo	Ni	Ne
		Hwna *mas.*	Hoona
They	Eonah	Hona *fem.*	Hona
Those ones		Yrhai Hyna	
No, or, there is not	Megosh	Nagoes	Nagosh
No		{ Nage { Nag { Na	
Head	Pan	Pen	Pan
The Great Spirit	Maho peneta	Mawr penaethir*	Maoor pannether
		Yaprid mawr†	Uspryd maoor

* To act as a great chief—head or principal—sovereign or supreme.

† The Great Spirit.

APPENDIX—B.

The following brief Vocabularies of several different Indian languages, which have been carefully written by the Author from the lips of the Indians as they have pronounced them, and which he has endeavoured to convey with the simplest use of the English alphabet, have been repeatedly referred to in the text, as a conclusive proof of the radical difference that actually exists amongst a vast many of the languages spoken by the North American Indians. And the Author here repeats, as he has said in page 236, that of the forty-eight languages which he has visited, he pronounces thirty of them as radically different as these are, whilst the remaining eighteen may be said to be dialects from four or five distinct roots.

ENGLISH.	MANDAN.	BLACKFOOT.	RICCAREE.	SIOUX.	TUSKARORA.
I	Me	Nistoa	Nem to	Mi a	Ee
You	Ne	Cristoa	Kag hon	Nia	Kets
He	E	Amo	Wite	Dai	Rawonroo
She	Ea	.....	Sapaiah	Hai chay	Unroo
It	Ount	.....	Tihai	Dai Chay	Hay
We	Noo	Ne stoa pinnan	Apa	On kia	Dinwuh
They	Eoneh	Maex	Arrish	Ni a pe	Ka ka wen roo
Great Spirit	Mah ho peneta	Cristecoom	Te wa rooh teh	Wakon shecha	Ya wunni yoh
Evil Spirit	Mahho penakheka	Cristecoom sah	Ka ke wa rooh teh	Wakon tonka	Katickuhmrihu
Medicine (*Mystery*)	Hopeneche	Nahtoya	Wa rooh teh	Wa kon	Yunnu-kwet
Mystery-man	New mohk hopeneche	Nah tose	So niah wa rooh teh	We chasha wakon	Yunnu kwat haw
Sacrifice	Wa pa shee	Ogh tum	....	We ob pa	Yunnu wonus
Drum	Bereck hah	....	....	Chon obo a ha	Ye nuf hens
Rattle	Eeh na de	Cristeque ahtose	Sha-koons	Waga moo	Wuntits u runtha
Sun	Menahka	Cogue ahtose	We-tah	Wee	Hiday
Moon	Esto menahka	Ca cha tose	Sa ca	On wee	Autsunyehaw
Stars	H'ta ka	Shotts	Tas sou	Wc chash pe	Ojisnok
Rain	H'ka hoosh	Cane	Tch hnh	Ma how jea	Wara
Snow	Cop caze	Caquey	Eo nahght	Wah	Wun
Night	Estogr	Cristoque	Sha coma	On ha pee	Autsunye
Day	Humpah	Staymaisee	Te ka tistat	On pah	Yor huh uh
Dark	Ham pah eriskah	Cristequemats	Sha koona	Ee obk pa zee	Yor weta s yuh
Light	Edayhmah	Secosy	Tah tash	O jm jee	Yoohooks
Heavy	T'kash	Mahis cosy	Kak s taeh	Te kay	Wau wis na
Not heavy	Ho heah			Ka po jel la	Wau ri yoa

ENGLISH.	MANDAN.	BLACKFOOT.	RICCAREE.	SIOUX.	TUSKARORA.
Yes	K'hoo	Ah	Nee coo la	How	Unhuh
No	Megosh	Sah	Ka ka	Ea	Gwuss
Good	Shusu	Ahghsee	Toh noe	Wash tay	Wa grast
Bad	K'he cusb	Pah kaps	Kah	Shee chu	Wa shuh
Very bad	Keks-cusha [hush	Eehcoon pah kaps	Koo nah hee	Shee chu lahgcha	Array wa shuh
How do you do?	Tash kah thak mah kah	How ne tucka?	Chee na se uun?	How che cho wa?	Dati yoot hay its?
Very well	Mah shuse	Neet ahkse	Ah teesh te	Tran wou an	Array as gu nuh
I am sick	Me au guna bush	Fatse no stum	Na too te rate	Ma koo je	Ee wuk nu wax
Are you tired?	E da e tenche?	Cho hetta ke tesistico?	Kah ka nee now a?	Won ne too ka?	Was na ru huh?
I am not tired	Wah ee wah ta hiah	Nemnh tesistico	.....	Won ne tooka shee ne	Grons a runk ra rahouk
Look there	Etta haunt tah	Fssummissa	Hey nah ho too tayrick	Wi a ka	Tsotkathoo
Come here	Roo-hoo tah	Pohka a pote	Shee sha	Ta hu na dah pe	Kajee
Hot	Dsa shosh	Ea cristochis	Tow war ist	Mush ta	Yoo nau ri bun
Cold	Shinee hush	Stuya	Teep se	Sinnee	Aut hooh
Long	Hash kah	Innuya	Tac chess	Honska	Ee wats
Short	Sonnnh ka	Suh kee	Nee hootch	Pe tah cha	Di wats a
War eagle	Mah sish	Pehta	Nix war roo	Wa me day wah kee	Akwieh
Buffalo	Ptemday	Eneuh	Wa tush	Pe tay	Hohats
Elk	Omepah	Ponokah	Wah	Opon	Joowaroowa
Deer	Muh mena coo	Ouacasee	A noo nach	Teh cha	Avgray
Beaver	Warralupa	Kekstakee	Chee tooghs	Chapa	Jonockuh
Porcupine	Pahhee	.....	Pan ha e	.....	Onhatau
Horse	Ompah meneda	Ponokah ueta	Ha wah rooh te	Shon ka wakon	Tyanootsruhuh
Robe	Mah he toh	Aihahwa	Sa booche	Shee na	Otskiyatsra
Moccasins	Hormpah	Itseekist	Hooche	Hong pa	On ok qua
Shirt	Emn shotah	Assokas	Kraitch	O ken dee	.....
Leggings	Iloh shee	Ahtsaiks	Kah hooche	Ilons ka	Oristreh
Bow	Warah e noo pah	Netsinnam	Nache	Eta zee pah	Awraw
Quiver	Fehkticka	.....	Niah kratch	O ju ah	Yonnts ronurhoost pah
Arrow	Mahha	Olpsis	Neeche	Wonhee	Kanah
Shield	Wah kee	.....	.....	Woh ha chon k	Yununay nabquaw
Lance	Moena etorook shoka	Sapa pistats	Na se wa roo	Wow oo ke za	.....
Woman	Ote	Moeese	Acaee	Wah kee on	Onassahunwa
Wigwam	Neba	Ahkeea	Sa pat	Wee on	Kuu nuh wuh
Wife	Moorse	Netoskenmnn	Tah ban	We noh cha	.....
Child	Sookhomaha	Polka	Pe rn	Chin cha	Yetyatshoyuh
Girl	Sook meha	Ahkeoquein	Soo nahtch	Wee chin cha	.....

ENGLISH.	MANDAN.	BLACKFOOT.	RICCAREE.	SIOUX.	TUSCARORA.
Bag	Sook numohk	Sah komape	Wee nahtch	Okee chin cha	Kunjookwher
Head	Pan	Otokan	Pahgh	Pah	Otabra
Arms	Arda	Otchist	Armi	Eas ta	Orunjha
Legs	Doka	Ahcatches	Ahgha	Hoo	Orusay
Eyes	Estume	Uwopapec	Chee ree coo	Uatah	Ookaray
Nose	Paboo	Ohcrisis	....	Pah soo	Oojyasu
Mouth	Ea	Mah oi	....	Poo tay	Ooshsrunwa
Face	Estah	Oestocris	....	Ea tay	Ooknhsa
Ears	Nakoha	Ohtokiss	Tickokite	Noh ghee	Ookahnay
Hand	Onka	Ohkitchis	Teho nnne	Non pay	Ohahna
Fingers	On ka hah	Ahocatchis	Pa rick	....	Oosookway
Foot	Shee	Otokan	Abgh	See	Oosa
Hair	Pah hee	Ahkeosehts	Pa hi	Pay kee	Auwaynah
Canoe	Menauka	Neyu tobta	Lah kee hoon	Wahta	Oohuwa
River	Passah ah	....	Sa hon nee	Wah ta pah	Kinah
Paddle	Mamuk pah sho	Mummea	Natoh-catogh	Kee chah bo ka	Okawetsreh
Fish	Poh	Absain	....	Oh hoog	Runjiub
Vermilion	Wah sah	Ahsainahkee	Pa hate	....	Yout kojun ya
Painter	Wah ka pooska	Nah heeoh kee	....	Eo cha'zoo kah ga	Ah ah
Whiskey	Men e pah da	Ahquayneman	Te sou nun	Me ne wah kn	Wis ky
Pipe	E hudka	Pistacan	Laps	Tchon de oopa	Yet jy arhoot hah
Tobacco	Mannah aha	Nahma	Lapscon	Tchondee	Jarhooh
Gun	Eroopah	Ohks kos moi nema	Tnan kee	Mon za wakon	Au naw
A man runs	Numohk p''chush	Oyeet	Sa riah ka tar ree	We chasha ee onka	....
He eats	E roosh toosh	Neetsata	Te wu wa	U tab pee	Yusyboory
I think	Wah push e dah hush	Neetaabpea	Nanto te wiska	Ea me doo ke cha	Kery
I am old	Wah k'hee hush	Mahto mahtrim	Nanto oo nahose	We ma chain cha	Auk'hoor
She is young	Es sook me bom mehan	Otokan	Tesoonock	Ha chee nah tum pee	Akatsah
Scalp	Poa dope khee	Soopascat	Sen isu po	Wecha sha pa	....
Scalp dance	Pon dope thee nah pish	Enenh quisix sinnum	Pah te ra ka rohk	Wah kee ta no wah	Onahray na yun kwah
War dance	Keeruck sah nah pish	Mastos	....	....	Ne yunk wah
White buffalo	Woka da	Keahyu	Toh n lmh tah ka	Ta his ka	Owaryakuh
Raven	Ka ka	Saw kee owa kasee	To kah ka	Koong hee	....
Bear	Mahto	Ah eene	Koo nooghk	Matto	Jotakry yukuh
Antelope	Ko ka	Aiipace	Annoo notche	Tah to ka no	Ojiruk
Spirits, or Ghosts	Mounoh he ka		....	Wa noogh hgee	Oonowak
Wolf	Harratta		Steerich	....	Tskwarinuh

ENGLISH.	MANDAN.	BLACKFOOT.	RICCAREE.	SIOUX.	TUSKARORA.
Dog	Monse waroota	A meeteh	Hahtch	Shon ka	Jir
A brave	Numohk harica	Mahtsee	Too ne roose	O eet e ka	.....
A great chief	Numohk k'ahese k'tich	Abeccoa nin nah	Nay shon tee rekoo	We chasha on ta pe ka	Yego wa nuh
Old woman	Rokah kah kaee ha	Kee pe tah kee	Sooht snhat	Wa kon kana	Kaskwary
Fire	Waroday	Steea	Te ki seht	Pah ta	Yoneks
Council fire	Kaberookah Warsday	Nahto steea	Ki eeht te warooht	Pah ta wah ke	......
Council house	Kaberookah kohar	Nahto yeweis	Warooht ta ko	Ta pe wah ka	Yunt kunis ah thab
Good-bye	......	How	....	How ke che wa	Tyowits nah na
One	Mah han nah	Jeh	Asco	On je	Unji
Two	Nompah	Nah tohk	Pit co	Non pa	Nekty
Three	Namsry	No oks kum	Tow wit	Hi ami ni	Au suh
Four	Tobpa	Ne sooyim	Tchee tiah	Tau pah	Hun tak
Five	Kakhoo	Ne see tsee	Tchee hoo	Za pe tah	Wisk
Six	Kemah	Nah oo	Tcha pis	Shab pai	Ooyak
Seven	Koo pah	E kitch ekum	To tcha pis	Shab co	Jarnak
Eight	Ta tuck a	Nah ne suyim	To tcha pis won	Shab en do hen	Nakruh
Nine	Mah pa	Psex o	Nah e ne won	Nen pe che once	Ni ruh
Ten	Perug	Kay pee [chee	Nah en	Oka che min en	Wutsnh
Eleven	Auga mahnanah	Kay pee nay tchee kopo-	Ko tchee te won	Oka on je	Unjita kahar
Twelve	Auga nompah	Kay pee nah kopochee	Pit co nah en	Oka noopa	Nekty takahar
Thirteen	Auga namsry	Kay pee nay ohk kopochee	Tow wit nah en	Oka hiamini	Au su takahar
Fourteen	Auga tohpn	Kay pee nay nay kopochee	Tchee tiah nah en	Oka tau pah	Untak takahar
Fifteen	Ag kak hoo	Kay pee nee ne ichee kopochee	Tchee hoo nahen	Oka zn petah	Wisk takahar
Sixteen	Ag kemah	Kay pee nay nay kopochee	Tch a pis nahen	Oka shab pai	Ooyok takahar
Seventeen	Ag koopah	Kay pee ok kee chie kopochee	To tcha pis nahen	Oka shahko	Jarnak takahar
Eighteen	Agr tah tucks	Kay pee nay nay kopochee	To tcha pis won nahen	Oka shab en do hen	Nakruh takahar
Nineteen	Aga mahpa	Kay pee psex sdicktopochee	Nah e ne won nahen	Oka nen pe chi on ka	Niruh takahar
Twenty	Nompah perug	Kay pee psex stickopochee	Weetah	Oka chiminen non pa	Na wots huh
Thirty	Namsry amperug	Natchip pee	Sah wee	Oka chiminen hiamini	Au suh tiwotshuh
Forty	Toh pa samperug	Ne hippe	Nahen tcbee tiah	Oka chiminen taupah	Huntak tiwotshuh
Fifty	Kah hoo samperug	Ne sippe	Naben tcbee boo	Oka chiminen za petah	Wisk tiwotshuh
Sixty	Kesmah amperug	Ne see chippe	Naben tchee pis	Oka chiminen shab pai	Ooyak tiwotshuh
Seventy	Koopah amperug	Nah chippe	Naben to tcha pis	Oka chiminen shahco	Jannak tiwotshuh
Eighty	Ta tuck samperug	O kitch chippe	Nah en tcha pis won	Oka chiminen nha ken do hen	Nakruh tiwotshuh
Ninety	Mah pa amperug	Nahne sippe	Nah en nah e ne won	Oka chiminen nen pe cher once	Niruh tiwotshuh
One hundred	Ee sooo mah hannah	Psex sippe	Shob tan	O pounkrni	Kau yanary
One thousand	Ee sooo perug	Kay pee pee pee	Shob tuo tera boo	Kaut o poun krai	Wusu-kau yanstry

APPENDIX—C.

CHARACTER.—(Page 256.)

Original.	Secondary.	Original.	Secondary
Handsome	Ugly	Warlike	Peaceable
Mild	Austere	Proud	Humble
Modest	Diffident	Honest	Honest
Virtuous	Libidinous	Honourable	Honourable
Temperate	Dissipated	Ignorant	Conceited
Free	Enslaved	Vain	Humble
Active	Crippled	Eloquent	Eloquent
Affable	Reserved	Independent	Dependent
Social	Taciturn	Grateful	Grateful
Hospitable	Hospitable	Happy	Miserable
Charitable	Charitable	Healthy	Sickly
Religious	Religious	Long-lived	Short-lived
Worshipful	Worshipful	Red	Pale-red
Credulous	Suspicious	Sober	Drunken
Superstitious	Superstitious	Wild	Wild
Bold	Timid	Increasing	Decreasing
Straight	Crooked	Faithful	Faithful
Graceful	Graceless	Stout-hearted	Broken-hearted
Cleanly	Filthy	Indolent	Indolen
Brave	Brave	Full-blood	Mixed-blood
Revengeful	Revengeful	Living	Dying
Jealous	Jealous	Rich	Poor
Cruel	Cruel	Landholders	Beggars

FINIS.